Multiplicity

Also by Rita Carter

Exploring Consciousness
Mapping the Mind

Multiplicity

The New Science of Personality, Identity, and the Self

Rita Carter

Little, Brown and Company

NEW YORK   BOSTON   LONDON

Little, Brown and Company
Hachette Book Group USA
237 Park Avenue, New York, NY 10017
Visit our Web site at www.HachetteBookGroupUSA.com

First United States Edition: March 2008
First published in Great Britain by Little, Brown, January 2008

ISBN 978-0-316-11538-4
LCCN 2008921699

10 9 8 7 6 5 4 3 2

RRD-IN

Printed in the United States of America

For RH, with thanks from all of us

Contents

Contents

Contents

Preface

This book was germinated during a spot of light relief after a heavy dinner. The meal had been a tricky one. It was a formal do that marked the end of a three-day medical conference, and I was stuck up at the far end of the table next to an eminent ear, nose and throat specialist who had earlier delivered a mind-numbingly technical lecture in an unrelieved monotone. Our conversation (blocked sinuses) had stalled and I was itching to go. Before I had a chance, however, the master of ceremonies announced an after-dinner entertainment.

A nondescript man in a crumpled tuxedo walked into the room and did a few magic tricks. Then he asked us all to stand up. "Now close your eyes," he said, "and put your hand out in front of you. Make it into a fist and imagine it is clutching a bunch of gas-filled balloons." Pause. "Think of the balloons pulling upward," he continued, "pulling their strings tight, tugging and struggling to fly away." Pause. "Up, they are pulling, up and up and up, dragging your hand toward the sky." Pause. "How hard they pull. Feel your hand is being pulled up and your arm is being stretched . . ."

Around this point I opened my eyes to see what was happening. I noticed my own arm had risen a few inches and so had most others. But here and there among the diners I saw people whose arms were pointing straight up to the ceiling. Some of them were reaching so high they were standing on tiptoe, their bodies taut and straining, fists clenched, heads thrown back, looking for all the world as though they were about to be borne aloft. To my surprise I saw that the ENT specialist at my side was among them.

One by one the more obviously entranced audience members were brought forward to entertain us. A prim-looking woman did an excellent imitation of Mick Jagger, a knee man relived his sixth birthday party, and a distinguished liver consultant seemed wholly persuaded that he had come out by mistake in his pajamas. Each one performed like a seasoned comic, including the ENT doctor, who became a Martian invader who happened to have landed on a nudist beach. "Blogdrachnop!" he spluttered, twitching his eyebrows like twin antennae. "Channy tom der kump? Glup!"

Apart from how funny it was (you had to be there), the thing that really riveted me about this spectacle was the utter transformation of the performers. It seemed for all the world as though the banal patter of the hypnotist had released in each of them a previously hidden personality. In some cases, the difference was so marked that it was almost impossible to believe the two were generated by the same brain.

You have probably seen enough vaudeville hypnotism to know that this happens. But have you ever wondered how? Could it be that we all have an uninhibited entertainer within us, capable of acting out any role that is suggested? If so, where are they lurking when not on show? Do we have to be hypnotized to release them, or might we switch from one to another in other circumstances too? And what about the roles they played? Was the six-year-old birthday boy just a public performance, or did the man's feelings match the goggle-eyed excitement displayed on his face? Was the gyrating Mick Jagger impersonator looking out at the world through her own eyes or with the jaded perception of an aged rock star?

These questions took root in my mind and I knew they would nag away at me until I found some answers. I thought I knew where to start looking. In my 1998 book *Mapping the Mind* I examined some of the brain mechanisms—the laying down of personal memories, for example—that produce our sense of identity. Then in my subsequent book *Consciousness*, I looked at the weird effects that can occur if these mechanisms cease to work in the normal way. One of them is the breakdown of our usual sense of oneness. Instead of having a single consistent identity, a person behaves and may feel as though he or she is one personality now, and then another and perhaps yet another—each with a separate name, personality and set of personal memories.

Preface

The mental state that produces entirely separate personalities, or alters, is a seriously dysfunctional condition, and it seems at first to be too bizarre to have anything to do with normal people. But watching those utterly sane and sensible medical folk going through their party paces at the behest of the hypnotist, I realized they looked very much like people switching from one alter ego to another. Could the brain-state produced in them by hypnosis be in some way similar to the condition that causes the dramatic mental shape-shifting seen in people with identity disorders?

Then I started thinking about other personality transformations I had seen—switches occurring in everyday situations rather than in response to hypnotism. There was the boss I once endured who ran his department with cold, impersonal efficiency but turned into a lurching, sentimental moron after his end-of-day dose of alcohol. The so-together female colleague who fell into inarticulate giggles whenever a man paid her a compliment. The girlfriend who always ran any show—except in her own home, where she turned into a doormat for her vile husband. The devoted family man who turned out to have a twice-a-week gay cruising habit. The shy-as-a-mouse academic who when asked to deliver a quick talk on her area of expertise ended up hogging the microphone for two hours.

And then, of course, there is me: a finicky perfectionist half the time and a reckless ignorer of detail the other half. A party pooper one week, queen of the night the next. Careful plate-watcher on Wednesday, fridge-emptying seagull come Sunday. Could inconsistencies of character such as these also be seen as a form of mental multiplicity?

With this question in mind I took a fresh look at what recent brain research has revealed about human memory and our sense of personal identity. I found that if one thinks of each person as a group rather than as a single, unchanging personality, many familiar but previously puzzling things made much more sense. In particular, certain features of our memory system generally treated as unrelated phenomena clicked together like pieces of a jigsaw. The way that we can remember some things at some times and not at others, for instance, is entirely understandable if you think of each person as a vessel in which different personalities—each carrying their own "bag" of memories—come and go. So is the way our behavior alters in response to different situations and different people. And it removes the mystery of why so many of us display entirely contradictory character traits: introverted and extroverted, generous and mean, ambitious and lazy . . .

Then I started to talk to people about their own experience. Were they aware of major shifts of perspective, emotion and attitudes within themselves? Did they ever look back on things they had done and wonder what on earth they had been thinking? Had they observed sudden changes of behavior and demeanor in others? Had they ever met a friend and found they were talking to a stranger?

As I got better at framing my questions, the stories tumbled out. Almost everyone I asked recounted some example of what could be interpreted as personality switching, either in themselves or in others. Those stories form the backbone of this book, and I am grateful to all those friends, acquaintances and strangers who shared them with me. Combined with the scientific evidence that is emerging about the way our brains create a sense of identity, they have persuaded me that personalities, or selves, do not come one to a person, but are created by that person in as many forms and as great or small a number as is required. Multiplicity of mind is not some strange aberration but the natural state of human being. Furthermore, our ability to shift and change has evolved because it is potentially useful—and today, more than ever, we need to *make* use of it. I hope this book will help you to do that.

One division that is commonly seen in an individual is between a personality that likes to get a good grasp of a subject before trying to apply it and one that prefers to try a thing in practice first and then go back to see how and why it works. This book is designed to work for both types, because it is itself divided into a first part that is mainly explanatory and a second part that is practical. You can either read it in the conventional way, from start to finish, or begin with Part II and come back to the first part later.

In Part I the first chapter starts by charting the curious history of multiplicity, from its roots in superstition through the discovery of hypnosis to modern-day brain-imaging. Chapter Two describes the shifting inner landscape of mind on which our personalities are built. It explains why conventional personality tests fail to capture the full complexity of human beings, and why the search for an essential or authentic self is doomed to failure.

Chapter Three explains the mechanism by which personalities are created in our brains, and how and why some live a separate existence from their neighbors. Chapter Four explains why multiplicity is becoming more visible, its potential benefits and likely problems. Finally, Chapter Five introduces the main types of personality: anxious parents, frightened children, stereotypes, rebels and shadows.

Part II is practical. It shows you how to identify and get to know the members of your own inner family and to see how their different skills, knowledge and ways of looking at the world can be used to the advantage of you all. For those who read this part first I have provided back references to various explanatory passages in Part I in order to prevent repetition.

It includes a new tool, the Personality Wheel, which I have designed to give you a graphic representation of your various personalities and to show at a glance how they interact and contrast with one another. Finally, there are a number of exercises that will help to get your personalities communicating with one another, and encourage them to work together as a team. My hope is that if you discover how to tease apart the different people you are, you will be in a better position to get your act together in a world where increasingly people feel they are falling apart.

Multiplicity

PART I

CHAPTER 1

A Brief History of Our Selves

The idea of there being two or more selves in a single body sounds crazy. Look carefully, though, and you will see that the evidence for human plurality is all around us and always has been. We glimpse it wherever people talk to ancestors, get divine wisdom from spirit guides, receive messages from personified gods, consult oracles, get "taken over" by the souls of the dead or tune in to an "inner helper." It is on view when we act out a part, take on roles, live up to expectations and reinvent ourselves. More commonly, but less obviously, it shows in day-to-day shifts of feeling and behavior. When someone says "I don't know what got into me," or "I just wasn't myself," they are implicitly acknowledging the existence of a self other than the one who is speaking.

Most of our greatest philosophers, psychologists and therapists have recognized the essential multiplicity of the human mind. In ancient Greece, Plato saw the psyche as a three-part affair consisting of a charioteer (the rational self) and two horses (one the spirit and one the "appetite"). In the fourth century St. Augustine wrote of his "old pagan self" popping up at night to torment him. Shakespeare's characters endlessly morph from one identity to another. Serious cases have been made to attach the label of Multiple Personality Disorder to Hamlet, Othello, Macbeth and several others.

In the twentieth century, Freud's enduring id, ego and superego model introduced the idea of a horizontal split between the conscious and unconscious mind, and Jung's theory of archetypes held that there are

3

separate powerful entities within the unconscious. The influential "object-relations" school of psychiatry taught that external "objects" could be internalized and become personalities of a sort, and Transactional Analysis, developed in the 1950s by Eric Berne, was based on the concept of three inner beings: child, adult and parent.

The idea that each of us is made up of often conflicting multiple personalities was stated most clearly, perhaps, by the Italian psychologist Roberto Assagioli, who founded a form of therapy called Psychosynthesis. "We are not unified," he wrote. "We often feel we are because we do not have many bodies and many limbs, and because one hand doesn't usually hit the other. But, metaphorically, that is exactly what does happen within us. Several subpersonalities are continually scuffling: impulses, desires, principles, aspirations are engaged in an unceasing struggle."

Twenty years later American psychologist John "Jack" Watkins and his wife Helen pioneered Ego-State Therapy, which envisages our personalities as a family of self and uses hypnotic techniques to bring them out. Around the same time California psychologists Hal and Sidra Stone started to develop a therapeutic system called Voice Dialogue, between inner personalities.*

In parallel with this, neuroscientific investigation strongly suggests that there is no essential self to be found in the human brain. The more we learn about the workings of that amazing organ, the more we see that each of us is just a bundle of learned and/or biologically programmed responses that click in as and when the situation demands. As Robert Ornstein, professor of human biology at Stanford University, put it: "The mind contains a changeable conglomeration of 'small minds' . . . fixed reactions, talents, flexible thinking . . . and these different entities are wheeled into consciousness and then usually discarded, returned to their place, after use."[1] Since he wrote that, imaging technology has made it possible to watch this kaleidoscopic brain activity on a computer screen.

---

*Ego-state Therapy, Pychosynthesis and Voice Dialogue are all still going strong, and details of how to track down therapists trained in these disciplines can be found at the back of this book.

Brain scans of extreme multiple personalities have even shown the neurons associated with one personality turn off, like an electric light, and another lot turn on, as a person changes in demeanor and behavior and in what he or she can remember. Even in the dry prose of scientific reporting the researchers speak of different selves within a single brain.[2]

Despite all this, personality shifting is still seen as something weird and spooky—a manifestation of spiritual possession rather than a natural physiological phenomenon. Even the language of possession persists. Describing the process of composing, for example, songwriter David Gray says: "You start off by tinkering around with a few sounds and having a really good time. But when you get deeper into it and your demands get greater and more ambitious, something rears its ugly head. You become possessed."[3]

Yet multiplicity has a long history of scientific investigation, albeit much of it entangled with superstition.

Priests, possession and Mesmer's plural pianist

In the latter part of the eighteenth century cases of possession were generally dealt with by exorcism. One of the most celebrated exorcists of the day was a Catholic priest called Father Johann Gassner, who practiced in Switzerland. His technique involved swinging a metal crucifix in front of his subjects while chanting ritual incantations.

While Father Gassner became famous for his victories over demons, another flamboyant character, an Austrian physician called Franz Anton Mesmer, was struggling toward a natural (rather than supernatural) explanation for the healing powers of person-to-person interaction. At that time there was much interest (as there is today) in mysterious forces and fluids and energies. And (again, as today) it was often difficult to distinguish between superstitious nonsense and the cutting edge of scientific discovery.

Mesmer believed he had discovered animal gravitation (later animal magnetism)—a mysterious life-giving substance or energy that flowed through countless channels in the body and could be influenced by magnets. Illness, according to Mesmer's theory, was caused by blockages of the flow, and these could be released by crises—acute attacks of whatever the ailment might be. A person with asthma, for example, might be cured in the course of a severe asthma attack, while someone with epilepsy might be cured during a seizure.

Mesmer believed the magnetic flow joined everyone together in an invisible force field, and that physicians could therefore help restore their patients' health by using the harmonizing influence of their own magnetic flow. One way to bring this about was for the physician to make passes—sweeps of the arm over the patient's body—to induce a healing crisis and rebalance the patient's energy.

Animal magnetism was widely regarded as a scientific breakthrough, and Mesmer's treatment was reputed to have remarkable effects. Wrong though it turned out to be, the theory behind it was at least rational, given the biological knowledge of the time. And it chimed happily with the mood of enlightenment that was sweeping Europe.

Meanwhile, for the same social climatic reasons, Father Gassner and his theatrical exorcisms were coming under critical scrutiny. In 1775 Mesmer was asked to observe Gassner at work and give his opinion to the Munich Academy of Sciences. Mesmer noted the rhythmic swinging of Gassner's crucifix, and presumably saw some parallel with his own passes. He concluded that Gassner's often dramatic healing effects on the possessed were brought about by the priest's powerful animal magnetism and his deployment of the metal crucifix. Although Mesmer observed that he thought Father Gassner was entirely sincere in his beliefs, his report more or less finished off the priest's career.

Mesmer's own practice, by contrast, flourished. His theory became increasingly sophisticated, and over the years he invented elaborate paraphernalia to aid healing sessions. One of his techniques, for example, was to seat patients around a vat of dilute sulfuric acid and then get them to hold hands while the healing force—facilitated, somehow, by the acid—passed through them. The setup was similar to a séance—more similar, in fact, than Mesmer knew, because with hindsight it is clear that, as with spiritual mediums, most of his success was due to the power of trance, suggestion and belief.

6

A Brief History of Our Selves

A couple of years after bringing Johann Gassner's career to an end, Mesmer met someone who unwittingly triggered a crisis in his own life. Maria-Theresa von Paradies was an eighteen-year-old pianist, singer and composer who had been born into elevated social circles in Europe and became a favorite of the Austro-Hungarian empress. Maria-Theresa had been blind since infancy, but despite the attentions of Europe's leading eye specialists, no cause or cure for her condition had been found.

In Mesmer's care, Maria-Theresa regained her sight. However, with the cure came a disaster: she completely lost her ability to compose and play music. Not only was this a tragic loss of talent; for her parents it meant a disastrous loss of money, because Maria-Theresa received a generous artistic scholarship from the empress. Much to the girl's distress, her parents took her away from Mesmer, upon which her blindness promptly returned.

Mesmer's reputation never fully recovered after this episode, and although he made a number of high-profile comebacks, by the time of his death in 1815 he had been practically forgotten by the outside world.

Mesmerism did not die with its inventor, though. It continued to flourish in different guises, and eventually, stripped of its cosmic fluid, it laid the foundations of modern hypnosis. Although Mesmer himself did not realize it, his passes and trance-inducing healing sessions were a means of accessing and manipulating brain-states that were not usually conscious. By hypnotizing Maria-Theresa he had turned on a personality that could see, but turned off the pianist. In at least one crucial way the two states were different personalities.

The term "hypnosis" comes from the Greek *hypnos*, meaning sleep. It was coined by a Scottish physician, James Braid, in the 1840s. He chose it because he thought at first that mesmerized subjects were asleep. Later, though, when more familiar with the state, he concluded it came about from extreme narrowing of attention and tried to rename it as "monoideism." This, as we will see, is a pretty accurate description of what happens, but by the time Braid came up with it, the technique was being used under the name of hypnosis by hundreds of physicians, as well as a growing number of entertainers and quacks. It was too late to change, and to this day we are stuck with the rather misleading notion of hypnosis as a form of slumber.

Pierre Janet and the vanishing furniture

Hypnotic techniques were refined throughout the nineteenth century, and various verbal inductions ("Look into my eyes," etc.) came to be used in addition to the sort of rhythmic movements that Mesmer had stumbled upon. Most practitioners, though, had no real idea of what was happening in the hypnotic state. Braid was on the right track when he proposed that hypnosis altered attention. But it was a French physician—Pierre Janet—who realized that in some circumstances it could effectively switch off one personality and switch on another.

Janet theorized that the human brain can generate many different ways of seeing and responding to the world—mind-states that he called "existences." Only one existence is generally conscious at any time, and a person might therefore be entirely unaware of the existences within himself or herself who are not currently conscious. In a hypnotic trance, however, a person can be easily induced to switch attention from one to another, and in doing so, bring the second existence into consciousness and put the other out of it.

Janet's theory emerged from hundreds of experiments in which hypnotized subjects underwent extraordinary transformations. Entranced volunteers would be told by him, for example, that when they opened their eyes, they would not see any furniture in the room. Subjects would then come around, be asked if they saw any furniture, and dutifully reply that they did not. If asked to walk around the room, however, they would carefully skirt around the table and chairs. When Janet asked why they had taken such an indirect route they would offer some weak explanation or simply say that they did not know. Asked specifically if they did it to avoid the furniture, the subjects would hotly deny such an absurdity.

Janet also discovered that it is not necessary to take a person through a hypnotic ritual in order to access a secondary existence. He developed what he called the method of distraction, which involved first engrossing his subject in some fascinating task, or getting him to engage in an intense conversation with a third party and then whispering a command or question in a voice so quiet that the subject would not consciously notice it. The second self, however, clearly received the subliminal message, because the subject's body would signal a reply with unconscious movements, such as raising an arm. Janet found that he could even place a pencil in the person's hand and he would write a response, all the while continuing his task or conversation as though entirely oblivious to what his hand was doing.

Janet used the French word *disaggregation* to describe the separation of existences. His explanation was that the human mind consisted of many elements and systems, each of which can combine with others to form complex states. Some of them draw others to them—including certain memories—and so become centers for distinct personalities. These successive existences may interact with external reality and develop further by absorbing and retaining new impressions. They might even develop higher psychological functions such as desires and ambitions, and—crucially—a sense of self, so that when they became conscious they feel (as well as behave) like an autonomous person.[4]

This description of what we would now call multiple personalities cannot be bettered today. The main difference between Janet's ideas and those held by many contemporary psychologists is that Janet recognized multiplicity as a normal, albeit often hidden, state of mind, whereas today it is generally assumed to exist only in people who are ill. The nearest translation, in modern English psychology, of *disaggregation* is "dissociation"—defined as the separation of mental processes, thoughts, sensations and emotions that are normally experienced as a whole. And this term is usually used—wrongly, I shall argue—to mean a psychiatric disorder.

Severe dissociation can certainly be disturbing and destructive, but as we will see later, it is not in itself abnormal. Rather, it is a manifestation of the extraordinary flexibility of the human psyche and is often perfectly healthy or even beneficial. Far from being pathological, the separate existences it helps to create and maintain can help us cope with the complexity of modern life and exploit the opportunities it offers.

Multiple Personality Disorder—the first wave

Although Mesmer did not, apparently, interpret what he was seeing in Maria-Theresa as the switching from one personality, or existence, to another, a pupil of his, the German physician Eberhardt Gmelin, was soon to do so in another patient. In 1791 Gmelin reported the case of a young German woman who regularly transformed into a French aristocrat: "[She] suddenly 'exchanged' her own personality for the manners and ways of a French-born lady, imitating her and speaking French perfectly and speaking German as would a Frenchwoman." These "French" states repeated themselves. In her French personality, the subject had complete memory for all that she had said and done during her previous French states. As a German, she knew nothing of her French personality. With a motion of his hand, Gmelin was easily able to make her shift from one personality to another.[5]

With that Gmelin kicked off what in recent decades has become the highly contentious history of multiple personality disorder (MPD). Throughout the nineteenth and into the twentieth century there was a steady trickle of reports of dual or multiple consciousnesses. Some of the more sensational ones became known beyond the medical profession; their stories were published in popular magazines or written up by the patients themselves—for example: *The Three Faces of Eve* and *Sybil*.

There was Mary Reynolds, who alternated between being "buoyant, witty, fond of company and a lover of nature" and "melancholy, shy and given to solitary religious devotions," and Felida X, whose three different personalities each had their own illnesses. One of them even had her own pregnancy, unknown, at first, to the others.

Then there was the most famous of all, the pseudonymous Christine Beauchamp, whose numerous different personalities would, according to her therapist, "come and go in kaleidoscopic succession, many changes often being made in the course of twenty-four hours."[6]

In 1906, Harvard Medical School hosted an international conference on MPD, but this, it turned out, marked the high point of the first surge of interest in the condition. Over the next thirty years interest died away, perhaps because MPD was eclipsed by the new fashions of hysteria and neurosis. In 1943 one eminent psychiatrist declared that MPD was extinct.

The announcement, however, turned out to be premature. A second wave of MPD was to erupt in the late seventies, and would turn out to be far more controversial than the first. In the meantime, though, the idea of multiplicity went seriously out of fashion.

Ego-states and hidden observers

Therapeutic hypnosis fell out of favor, too, but a few academics and practitioners continued to research and apply it. One of these was Professor Ernest Hilgard, a psychologist at Stanford University. By 1975 Hilgard had already pioneered the use of hypnosis in pain relief, and as part of his teaching, he routinely demonstrated to his psychology students how to induce hypnotic dissociation. One such session led to the discovery of a phenomenon he called the Hidden Observer.

Hilgard did a conventional hypnotic induction on one of his students, lulling him by suggestion into a state of relaxation and compliance. He then told him that, on feeling a touch on his shoulder, he would become unable to hear anything. Another touch would bring his hearing back to normal. Sure enough, after the first touch, the student ceased to respond to questions or remarks and he didn't jump when two blocks of wood were banged together right next to his ear. Hilgard explained to the other students that the subject was, effectively, deaf. Yet his ears are fine, objected one of them. The sounds must be getting into this brain, so at some level he *must* be hearing.

Hilgard decided to test this idea. He spoke quietly to the hypnotized student, observing that there are many systems at work in the brain—those governing digestion and blood pressure, for instance—which respond to the environment but of which we have no conscious knowledge. Perhaps, he suggested, there was such a system at work in the student now, processing sounds but not offering them to his conscious

11

mind. Then he asked: If there is a part of you which is hearing and understanding these words, please would it raise a finger?

When, after a few seconds, the subject's index finger lifted, it came as a surprise to everyone—including, it seemed later, the subject himself. Hilgard restored the student's normal hearing by touching him again on the shoulder. The lecturer then asked his subject to describe what he had been aware of from the time of his induction into hypnosis.

The student had little to report: he hadn't been able to hear anything from the time of the induction until now, he said, and the session had thus been rather boring. To keep himself occupied he had been working on a mathematical problem. Then, he said, he felt his finger lift. He had no idea why. Fascinated by this turn of events, Hilgard put the subject back in a trance and suggested to him that there were two parts within him, one of which had heard everything that went on in the prior session, while the other part was deaf. Hilgard said that he would touch the student's arm in a particular way, and that would be the signal for the hearing part to talk to him. A second touch would signal the return of the part that had been deaf.

At the prearranged signal the student duly described things he had heard in the previous session. The instructor's voice, the students' remarks, the banging of the blocks—it had all been perfectly clear. "This part of me responded," he said, "so it's all clear now." At the second touch, however, he told the same story as before: he had not heard a sound.

Hilgard discovered that such a Hidden Observer could be created under hypnosis in almost anyone. He subsequently used the phenomenon to enable people who were unable to tolerate anesthesia to undergo surgery. Before the operations he would hypnotize them and tell them they would not feel the knife, but that a Hidden Observer would feel it for them. After the operation they duly said they had felt nothing. But when Hilgard put them back into hypnosis and addressed the Hidden Observer directly, it spoke freely of the excruciating pain that it had suffered.

Around the same time Jack Watkins—one of the few therapists who had continued to work on MPD through the middle part of the century—discovered that under hypnosis alters could be brought out in people who had displayed no obvious signs of them in their normal waking state. In the early 1970s Watkins met his wife Helen, another hypnotherapist, who was then working with disturbed college students. Helen, too, noticed that under hypnosis her clients would quite often reveal different personalities. She found that these covert ego-states, as they called them, were often responsible in one way or another for the students' problems and that the best way to deal with them was to treat them as separate entities. As Helen describes them: "Ego-states may be large and include all the various behaviors and experiences activated in one's occupation. They may be small, like the behaviors and feelings elicited in school at the age of six. They may represent current modes of behavior and experiences or, as with hypnotic regression, include many memories, postures, feelings, etc., that were apparently learned at an earlier age."

The Watkinses recognized that ego-states were similar in content to Hilgard's hidden observers and also to the alters found in their MPD patients. In one study, wrote Helen: "when Hilgard's 'hidden observers' were activated in normal college students as hypnotic subjects, further inquiry into their nature and content elicited organized ego-states. We . . . consider that hidden observers and ego-states are the same class of phenomena. They represent cognitive structural systems that are covert, but are organized segments of personality, often similar in content to true, overt multiple personalities."[7]

The Watkinses, however, noted a clear distinction between the ego-states found in normal people and the alters in their MPD patients. Ego-states did not "take over" their hosts entirely because, as the Watkinses put it, the boundaries between them were permeable. Instead of being entirely cut off from each other, they shared memories and acknowledged each other's existence.

Modern MPD—a manufactured madness?

In the late 1970s and 80s, MPD made an explosive comeback. By then known more widely as dissociative identity disorder (DID), the term which replaced multiple personality disorder in the U.S. *Diagnostic and Statistical Manual* (which lists psychiatric conditions and their symptoms).*

Between 1985 and 1995 some forty thousand cases are estimated to have been diagnosed—twice as many as in the entire preceding century. Some therapists claimed the disorder affected at least one percent of the population.[8] The apparent discovery of thousands—maybe millions—of MPD/DID cases was fantastically controversial because the condition was by then closely associated with cruelty in childhood and particularly with sexual abuse. The implication of such an epidemic was that child abuse was far more pervasive than anyone had dreamed. Either that or an awful lot of people were lying, deluded or both. The atmosphere surrounding the issue became so heated that more or less everyone concerned was forced to take a stand in one of two opposing camps.

Skeptics claimed (and many still do) that MPD/DID is a bogus condition created by a collusion (usually unwitting) between unhappy patients and overzealous therapists. The patients—encouraged by a climate in which self-revelation and victimhood is a matter of pride rather than shame—look for a framework in which to express some vague psychic discontent. Therapists see in such people the exciting possibility of a (relatively) rare and strange condition and, often without realizing what they are doing, encourage them to act out being various other personalities. They then induce these manufactured entities to fabricate stories of childhood abuse that are presented as recovered memories.

The opposing theory is that children who are repeatedly abused learn to go away in their heads when the situation becomes intolerable. Their brains continue to respond to what is happening, but the experience is

---

*The name change in the U.S. coincided with a slight change in the diagnostic criteria, but it is thought to have been made mainly to allay criticism from skeptics who thought "MPD" gave the condition too much credence. "DID" suggests identity confusion, rather than any genuine separation, so patients were henceforth treated for the delusion of multiplicity rather than for the condition itself. The other major psychiatric handbook, however, *The International Classification of Diseases*, which is widely used outside the U.S., still refers to MPD. In this book I will usually use the term Multiple Personality Disorder (MPD) rather than DID.

not integrated with the personal memories that contribute to the child's major identity. Instead it is stored in the brain as a separate little package of bad feelings and horrible memories. These remain unconscious until another traumatic episode triggers them into life. Each time the nasty memories are revived they collect more experiences, so repeated "outings" gradually turn the package of trauma-related responses into a complex entity with a distinct personality. It might give itself a name and develop its own opinions and ambitions. Such personalities usually remain rather two-dimensional and childlike because while they are unconscious they are not (usually) privy to what is happening, and thus tend not to learn much beyond their small, traumatic world.

So which is right? The answer, I think, is that it is not an either/or situation. There is certainly persuasive evidence to show that memories of childhood abuse recovered from apparently traumatized alters can be false.[9] But the reality or otherwise of the events that are recounted by a personality have no bearing on whether the personality itself is real. Remembering things wrongly or lying about past events does not mean a personality doesn't exist—it just means it has got things wrong or is lying!

As for the charge that personality switching is just acting, the problem is that there is no sharp division between being a character and acting it. Of course, it is possible to affect a role—deliberately acting and speaking in a way that is quite at odds with your inner thoughts and feelings. Equally, though, if you are totally immersed in a part, your thoughts, perceptions and feelings *become* those of that character. In this state your behavior is an honest reflection of your inner self, and as I'll explain in a moment, it therefore seems reasonable to describe it as the adoption of a different identity rather than an act.

Until recently there was no objective way of knowing whether a change in someone's behavior corresponded with an alteration in their subjective identity. The only way to assess whether those with MPD were acting was to look at their behavior and guess. But that is no longer the case. Brain-imaging technology has made it possible to see inside a person's head and observe the neural machinations that produce sensations, thoughts and feelings. The generation of their inner life can be displayed on a screen for all to see.

Brain imaging shows what is going on in a person's mind by signaling which parts of the brain are active. When one part flares up, a person feels angry, and another creates fear. Hunger is produced by one lot of neurons, lust by another. A true statement is marked by a pattern of activity different from that marking a lie. You can even see, by looking at a scan of a person's brain, whether he is looking at a face or a cat or a house.[10]

When the inner workings of MPD patients' brains are displayed, what we see is a pattern that suggests very strongly that alters are not just acts. As one set of behaviors disappears and another takes its place the neuronal patterns in their brain change in tandem with the altered demeanor. The brain scans even suggest that different memories are available to each personality.

One study, for example, involved eleven women, each of whom seemed to have two distinct states of being. In one state they claimed to recall some kind of childhood trauma, while in the other they denied any such memory. The women's brains were monitored while they listened to tape recordings of someone reading out some of their own previously related recollections. One of the recordings described the traumatic memory. When the women were in their nontraumatized personality, the parts of their brains that would be expected to respond to a personal anecdote remained quiet. In other words, they registered the information as though it was something that had happened to someone else. When they switched to the other personality, however, the trauma story stirred a flurry of activity in the brain areas associated with a sense of self. Instead of just registering what they were hearing, they *identified* with it, remembering the story rather than just recognizing it. Just as the women's behavior suggested, their two personalities had different autobiographies.[11]

Another imaging study was done on a forty-seven-year-old woman who could switch from one personality to another more or less on cue. During the transition from one to the other the part of the brain that processes memories momentarily closed down, as though it was shutting off one bag of memories while switching to another.[12] A third study of personality switchers found that their brain-wave coherence—a measure of which neurons are firing in synchrony—was completely different in each of their personalities. This suggests that the subjects were thinking and feeling quite differently in each state.[13] No such changes were seen in actors trying to mimic the condition, nor in the subjects themselves when they were asked to act out a change of identity. Taken together these studies suggest that alters do not just behave differently—their brains think, feel and recollect things differently too.

Most people now being diagnosed with MPD have a number of alters, rather than just one, which are combined in what is conventionally called a system. There are endless variations: some make angry, aggressive alters to protect the children, or friends to alleviate loneliness, or torturers who mimic abusers. Some people have only child alters, but others go on making new personalities, which may be any age. Most MPD systems contain at least one member of the opposite sex. Some include animals.

Usually at least one member in a system is in some way disruptive, and the behavior of alters—promiscuity, self-harm, addiction, aggression, phobias—is often what first brings people with MPD to the attention of a therapist. However, the crucial thing about the disorder, which distinguishes it from normal multiplicity, is not the nature and behavior of the alters but the fact that they do not share a common memory. Although some personalities may share information there is always a communication gap in an MPD system. The normal household, as multiple systems are sometimes called, is open-plan, while in people with MPD, at least some of the personalities live in watertight compartments.

One reason for the spectacular rise in MPD diagnoses in the 1980s and 90s is that the Watkinses' careful distinction between alters and ego-states was often ignored: "Too many practitioners today are hypnotically activating covert ego-states and announcing that they have discovered another multiple personality," lamented Helen Watkins in 1993. For every true case of MPD that was diagnosed there were probably many whose normal multiplicity was uncovered by hypnosis and mislabeled.

This book is not for or about people with MPD—it is about the normal multiplicity common to us all. But understanding a little about that extreme form of multiplicity may help us to understand our own selves, because although the behavior of people with this condition seems bizarre, they are probably not as different from the rest of us as we like to believe.

The strangeness of MPD arises from a mistaken assumption: that we start with a single, whole personality. MPD is thus assumed to be the result of this single personality being smashed. As I hope to show you, though, personalities do not come ready-plumbed in every baby, one to each body. An infant comes equipped with many built-in drives and individual genetic leanings but its personalities still have to be constructed from the building blocks of experience. You might think of a newborn's mind as a building site with a unique form—dips and hillocks, obstacles and pitfalls, soft spots and rocky areas. These influence and constrain what is erected on it, but they do not dictate it.

So what is a personality, anyway?

Before we go further, it is probably a good idea to clarify what I mean when I refer to personality. We don't usually stop to ask what someone is talking about when she uses the word because it seems obvious. Yet there is no single accepted definition of it in psychology, and dictionaries are not particularly helpful. Mine gives several definitions. The main one is "the sum of a person's mental and behavioral characteristics by which they are recognized as being unique," while another is "the distinctive character of a person that makes them attractive."[14] Obviously these are quite different things. Your dictionary may say something else again.

If we were to accept the definition of personality as "the sum" of a person's characteristics, it would, of course, rule out the possibility of them having more than one. But it would also make the word meaningless—just another term for a person. And a moment's thought will show that we don't really think of personality that way. If we did, phrases such as "that remark was out of character" and "she was a different woman after her illness" would be incomprehensible.

So I am using personality to mean something which I think is closer to the way the word is actually used. A short definition might be: *a coherent and characteristic way of seeing, thinking, feeling, and behaving.*

The crucial word is "characteristic." By my definition a personality has a certain style or pattern to it—something that binds the thoughts, feelings and acts into a distinctive set consistent enough to allow us to say about any part of it, "Oh! that's typical of Linda!" or "That sounds like me!"

A personality might, for example, have a whole bunch of ideas and behaviors that could be thought of as personal ambition. It might be determined to be the best at its job, the winner of every competition, the most competent sportsperson, the top salesman. It might like to travel fast, in straight lines, get angry with people who get in its way, forget to take time off, and try to bully its children to be more like itself. The personality may not do all these things (God forbid!), but it *could*, because they are not in conflict with one another. Another personality might believe that personal success is really not important at all. It might drift happily along in a nondemanding job, meander along country lanes rather than drive ferociously along expressways and allow its children to do exactly what they like. Although it is unlikely, both these personalities could exist in the same person. However, there would have to be some separation between them simply because the brain-states that generate rampant ambition and those that produce worry-free relaxation are too different from each other to occur at the same time. For the person to function normally, without perpetual inner conflict, her two personalities would have to take turns at being onstage. When one was active, the other would have to be unconscious.

Either/or brain-states operate at every level of cognition, from complex thoughts and behaviors to simple visual perceptions. If two experiences are entirely at odds with one another, the brain has to choose to be conscious of one or other, and the best it can do by way of entertaining both is to switch rapidly between them. The simplest example of this is a thing called the Necker cube (below).

19

The box is drawn in such a way that the front panel could either be to your left and angled down, or to your right and up—both interpretations are equally "correct." Even when you know that, though, your brain will allow you to see only one at a time . . . it just can't "do" both patterns simultaneously. You probably know of other visual illusions that work in much the same way: the shapes that switch between being twin profiles and a vase, or the drawing that looks like a pretty girl when it is seen one way and an old hag the other.

This inability to see things in two ways simultaneously occurs throughout the brain, including areas concerned with thoughts and emotions. When we are listening intently to one conversation, the areas of brain concerned with attending to and processing information from that source effectively turn down the volume of any other noise in the room. That is why people in conversation often fail to notice background music that would seem quite loud if heard alone, or ignore the call to dinner when they are concentrating on a TV program. Similarly, with emotions the fear-generating areas of the brain are inhibited when the parts that create serenity are active, and the sadness part is quietened when the parts that create pleasure are triggered.

The seesaw effect is not absolutely cut-and-dried, of course; at times we are all aware of mixed emotions and conflicting thoughts. But when our conflicting beliefs, desires or urges become conscious simultaneously, we have to make a conscious decision to act on one or the other. We have to decide between "I want to smoke" and "I don't want to die of cancer," "I want to stay up and party" and "I want a decent night's sleep." At least at the level of behavior we cannot "be" more than one personality at a time. We have to switch from one to another.

Some people (though very few) go through life without ever confronting the lifestyle equivalent of a Necker cube. The situations they encounter offer them no choice of response—there is only one way to interpret them, one way to react, one way to be. Or they may meet situations that offer options and simply fail to see them. These people do not harbor other existences, they really are what they feel themselves to be—single and whole personalities.

Most of us, though, do not find life to be like this. We often encounter situations that can be seen and responded to in myriad different ways. For most of us the options presented to us are increasing—life is getting more, not less, complicated. Hence we switch from one way of seeing things to another, one way of being to another. And as we do it, we accumulate an inner family of selves—Janet's existences—which take turns to be the self of the moment.

Rest assured, though, we are not talking Jekyll and Hyde. Although our personalities are by definition distinguishable from one another, in most of us they are more like conjoined twins than entirely separate individuals. Just being subjected to the same sensory stimuli blurs the dividing line between them. Their coexistence in the same body means they necessarily share so much that it may be difficult to spot exactly where one starts and another ends.

For this reason personality switches may easily be overlooked. The only giveaway may be a slight change of voice, the use of a slightly different vocabulary, or perhaps a subtle alteration in the way a person stands or laughs. For example, the wife of a Church of England vicar once told me: "When Gerry is with our friends he is a full six feet tall. But when he puts on his dog collar he shrinks half an inch. The vicar in him feels embarrassed about looking down on people, so he somehow becomes compressed. He laughed at me when I pointed it out and said it's nonsense—but one day I'm going to find a way of measuring him and I know I'll be right!"

Like Gerry, it is tempting to scoff at the suggestion that we shift from personality to personality. From inside it just doesn't feel like that—most of us have a strong and enduring sense of being a single more or less unchanging entity: the "I" I am now is the same "I" I will be tomorrow. If you look carefully at human behavior, however, you find this sense of certainly is misplaced. The next chapter examines the shifting and sometimes blurred landscape of our personalities, and shows how our fond notion of inner stability, consistency and unity has been shown, time and again, to be a myth.

CHAPTER 2

The Landscape of Mind

One of the flight paths taken by aircraft heading from London to North America carries you first up the spine of Britain, then in a northwesterly arc over the Highlands and islands of Scotland. On a clear day you can look down and see the landscape spread out beneath you like a full-color three-dimensional atlas.

During the first part of the journey England spreads out like a gently undulating quilt, all of a piece until it is punctuated by velvety hills marking the beginning of the Highlands. These soon give way to mountains and plunging valleys bordering broad seaways as the coastal lochs carve their way into the mainland. Then you are looking down on islands, scattered like pieces of a massive jigsaw puzzle. Some of them are connected to the mainland by causeways, and you may just make out a ferry moving between others. On the larger islands you can see spreading settlements, industrial chimneys and public buildings. On the smaller ones, scattered roofs tell of a lonelier existence.

If you were to liken your inner landscape to one of those views, which would it be? Do you feel your personality to be all of a piece, a consistent, clearly bounded and densely woven fabric of thoughts and emotions? Or are you aware of a more complex geography: a central hub, perhaps, but also outlying areas that others rarely see, and far-flung places whose existence is just a rumor, even to you?

Surprisingly little work has been done concerning the way that we visualize our inner landscape, particularly the extent to which we think of ourselves as separate personalities. You have only to listen to people speaking to realize that on one level we know they are there: "That's the schoolteacher in him coming out" we might say of someone who, uncharacteristically, launches into a lecture. Or "I was a real slut that night!" But because we do not yet have a well-developed model of healthy multiplicity we tend not to see it even when it stares us in the face.

The English therapist John Rowan, one of a very few psychologists who recognize multiplicity as normal, reckons that most people have four to nine subpersonalities, as he calls them. "More than nine and I begin to suspect that some of them are simply aspects of others, and should be grouped with them," he says. "Fewer than four and I begin to wonder if sufficient attention has been paid to the less visible ones."[1]

Other researchers have looked at the self-aspects or self-schemas that people hold. These are not quite the same as personalities, but they are similar. Most of these studies have been done on students.* These suggest that we vary enormously in the degree to which we feel ourselves to be one or many. In one study the volunteers ranged in their reported number of "selves" from one to twenty, with an average of seven.[2]

Our inner landscape is constantly changing. Various personalities form, change, fade away, re-form, merge, shrink and grow. In young people the landscape changes rapidly, like clouds blown about on a windy day, but over the years a more settled pattern emerges. Typically, in my observation, it might consist of one, or perhaps two, of what I will call major personalities, plus a handful of minor characters and any number of fragmentary micros.

Majors, minors and micros

A major is a fully fleshed out character with thoughts, desires, intentions, emotions, ambitions and beliefs. Minors are less complex (though often very strong) personalities that come out in particular situations. Micros

*Students are the guinea pigs of social psychology, being numerous, cheap, easy to capture and often normal.

are the building blocks of personalities—individual responses, thoughts, ideas, habits. Micros may be as tiny as a physical or vocal tic or a repeated intrusive thought, emotion or desire that stands out in contrast to a person's normal behavior.

Compatible micros tend to get attached to one another to form minors, which in turn coalesce into majors. Most people retain a smattering of free-floating micros such as the odd verbal tic or some mild and inexplicable phobia.

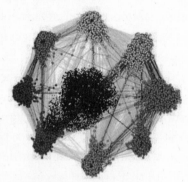

Major–Minor

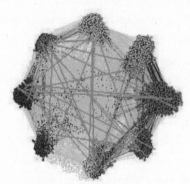

Multiple Minor

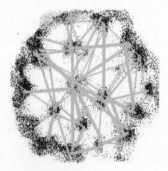

Multiple Minor

Single Major

Inner landscapes

Some people have one major and several minors (top left) while others have varying numbers of minors (top right and bottom left). A few have just one almost wholly integrated major (bottom right).

The Landscape of Mind

Personalities cohere as a result of experiences connecting up in the brain, forming a web that holds our memories (this process is explained in detail in Chapter Three). If everything that happened to us was bound tightly together we would develop just one densely integrated web. But few of us end up like this because another process, dissociation, ensures that dissimilar experiences are only loosely connected or perhaps not connected at all. Hence the things that happen to us get bound together in clusters, each one of which incorporates a personality.

In some people the clusters are so closely associated that they merge into one and the person exhibits a single major personality. In others there may be one large cluster (a major) and several minors. Some people just have minors—lots of different personalities that are more or less all equally active.

A major is built up from a dense web of experiences that have bound together over a very long period. It may include bits of the person's parents that were absorbed as children, characteristics borrowed from siblings, ideas from the dominant culture and behavior designed to find favor with friends and colleagues. People may take in an entire way of looking at things from someone else—a perpetual sense of anxiety from their mother, perhaps, or a friend's quirky sense of humor, or a set of beliefs adopted from the dominant religious dogma. Majors may include a very wide range of characteristics but they cannot contain *conflicting* characteristics. One might be, say, hardworking and extrovert, or hardworking and introvert, but not extrovert *and* introvert.

Minors tend to be more idiosyncratic than majors, because by definition they have not fitted together with enough others to merge into a major. A minor may consist of just a small clutch of responses—enough to deal with a fairly specific type of event. It may, for example, consist just of a compulsion to argue with certain people, or a habit like binge-eating or smoking in certain situations.

You may need to know people quite well before you get to see their minors. You may think you know someone very well, then share an unfamiliar situation—a vacation with a work pal, say—and suddenly get a glimpse of a personality you never knew existed. If you only ever see

25

someone in a particular type of situation—when they are in charge, perhaps, or when they are with their partner—you may be familiar with *only* one of their minors, and be surprised to discover that other people, who know them in quite different contexts, seem to know a completely different person.

Minors may be quite complex or extremely narrow in their focus, and although they may not do much, they may be very distinctive. Some exist to do just one thing—domestic chores or driving or looking for things to buy. While they are active, much of the world around them is neglected. "I must have been dreaming," mutters our major personality when it returns to remove the laundry from the dishwasher or apologize for cutting a friend in the street.

Major personalities are more often in evidence than minors—indeed, it is the greater range of experience they accumulate by being onstage most of the time that makes them major. Because a person's major is the one that other people usually see, it tends to be regarded, both by itself and by others, as the person's real self.

The big "I am"—developing the sense of self

With a very few exceptions (which we will come to later) people normally feel as though they are just one. The conviction persists even in those who have quite dramatic personality switches. The recognition that there is more than one self in a single body might be quite obvious to an outside observer, but the subjective illusion of singularity is so strong that each personality invariably claims ignorance of any other.

Hence when we are in our extrovert personality we accept invitations to future parties without a qualm, thinking we are always in the mood for a get-together even if history recounts that we often have to drag ourselves to such events and hate them when we arrive. When we tell the boss to get lost we see ourselves as decisive, strong and brave. We forget that we also contain a frightened, insecure person who needs the money. During periods of elation it seems ridiculous to think that we have it in us to be depressed.

26

Just occasionally, however, our comfortable conviction of unshifting singularity is undermined. It happens when two or more of our personalities become active at the same time. If we don't understand what is going on, the feeling may be deeply unsettling, and the active personalities will launch into battle, scuffling to take control of the person's behavior. Usually this results in a dominant personality shouting down a less strident one, even if the quieter one is talking more sense. And when several personalities come out together, their clamor is interpreted as doubt, indecision and confusion.

Most of the time, though, the illusion of singularity remains undisturbed. It is created by a powerful trick of the brain, which ensures (in most of us) that only one personality is fully conscious at any time—rather as only one view of the Necker cube is experienced in any one moment. It is socially useful, for reasons we'll see in Chapter Five, that people believe themselves to be singular, so the illusion is heavily supported by social convention.

The sense of singularity is part of a larger sense of self—a whole bag of cognitive tricks that kick in throughout childhood. The crucial development is the ability of a child to see itself from the outside—an "object" that can be seen (and judged) by others and that continues through time. She realizes, for example, that she continues to exist even while she is asleep, and that the "me" of the moment—hungry, say—is connected with the person that was not hungry at all three hours ago and the person who will not be hungry in half an hour, after tea. Hence the me of the moment—the hungry me of now, the angry me of yesterday, the sleepy me of later—get strung together in a single, continuous thread.

For many years, however, this thread of self is a fragile creation and any small shift in emotion or attention can break it. Hence when five-year-old Mandy puts on Mom's high heels and strides down the hallway being a supermodel, there is little or no connection in her head with the tomboy Mandy who fought her brother for possession of the rocking horse the day before; or the studious Mandy who spent all morning trying to learn her alphabet.

The children in the child

Children may also fail to recognize their personalities as themselves, seeing them instead as external, autonomous entities, commonly referred to as imaginary companions (ICs). Skippy—the creation of my friend Pat's daughter, Amy—is a fairly typical IC. He arrived suddenly, when Amy was four, complete with a firm set of dietary foibles. Every mealtime for more than a year Pat was coerced into laying a place at the table for Skippy, and woe betide her if she served up something he didn't like. Once when I was there, Pat slithered a token portion of strawberry ice cream on to Skippy's plate. "Don't give Skippy pink ice cream!" screamed Amy. "He'll sick it up all over the table!"

Children who create imaginary companions were once assumed to be lonely or socially incompetent. Their invisible playmates were regarded by adults (if they knew about them) as sad substitutes for "proper" social interaction that were dumped as soon as the child got real friends. This theory no longer stands up, not least because nowadays it is more common for children to report having imaginary companions than not. In the 1930s, about one in nine children admitted to an IC, but by the 1990s it was one in three. Now it is more than two-thirds, and the ICs do not necessarily disappear with age or increasing social engagement. Research by Dr. Marjorie Taylor, a psychologist at the University of Oregon, and her colleagues found that having an imaginary companion is at least as common among school-age children as it is among preschoolers.

Imaginary companions described by the children came in a fantastic variety of guises, including invisible boys and girls, a squirrel, a panther, a dog, a seven-inch-tall elephant and a hundred-year-old G.I. Joe doll. Some children reported having multiple and serial imaginary companions. The number of imaginary companions described by children ranged from one to thirteen different entities.[3]

Not all imaginary companions are friendly—they can be quite uncontrollable and even aggressive. One of their functions may be to act as a vehicle for experimental personalities—minors the child wants to try out at a safe distance before adopting internally. Having placed them in the IC the child can observe how this or that response goes down in the outside world. Does Skippy get into trouble for not accepting pink ice cream? Is a naughty IC able to get away with it? The child can try out all sorts of social behaviors vicariously, safe in the knowledge that, should the IC do anything disastrous, the child itself is safe from the consequences.

Traditionally ICs are thought of as a thing of childhood—if adults admitted to one, they would probably be viewed with some suspicion. Writers and actors, however, have a special license to create external minors for others' amusement, and the degree to which the characters appear to break free from their creators is often regarded—probably correctly—as a measure of the artist's talent. Marjorie Taylor's team interviewed fifty fiction writers, ranging from an award-winning novelist to scribblers who had never been published, and found that forty-six had invented characters who had subsequently taken over the job of composing their life stories. Some of them also resisted their creators' attempts to control the narrative. Some fictional folk wandered around in the writers' houses or otherwise inhabited their everyday world. The writers who had published their work had more frequent and detailed reports of these personalities seeming to break free of their creator's control, suggesting that the faculty of projecting personalities into the external world really is a measure of creative expertise.[4]

One common way that children reveal a sense of being multiple is by speaking of "we" instead of "I" or referring to themselves in the third person. Adults are usually very quick to correct these errors (as they see them), and the effect of this is to encourage children toward the adult illusion of singularity.

J is one of a very small number of adults who does not have a sense of being alone in his body. It may be that he has hung on to a sense of multiplicity most of us have discarded.

"When I was a kid I thought everyone experienced lots of different people," he says. "Then I started to have rows with my mother because she thought I was playing around with her when I told her things like 'I can't do that because Jay wouldn't like it' or 'Chrissy is crying again.'

29

Eventually my parents packed me off to a therapist and I cottoned on pretty quickly that if I didn't want to get some freaky psychiatric label I should start talking as though I was a single."

As J discovered, forcing children to use the word "I" makes it much more difficult for them to sustain their multiple selves: "When you talk like a singlet you tend to think of yourself as one. I can see how, if you are pressed into acting like an integrated person, you could start to think you really are alone in your skin. But the guys in my family [household] never went away, even when I tried to shut them out, and as soon as I was away from home I let them talk freely again."

Ariel and several other children were working at the art table, making a collage out of buttons glued to construction paper. I was absentmindedly gluing buttons to the paper, while Ariel seemed to have a pattern to her work. On her paper were red and green buttons, red on the right, green on the left. Each hand seemed to be working independently. Suddenly she let out a howl, tore up her paper and ran to her "hideout." I followed her so I could find out what went wrong.

"I get so mad at him!" (When she said "him," I assumed it was her "imaginary" friend Sam.)

"I can see that. Sam made you very angry."

"I didn't want any green buttons on my side. I just like red," she said, stamping her foot. And then: "But I want green! Only green! And *she* never lets me do it."

I looked at Anise and Jennifer, who are with me when we work with children. I could not believe what I was hearing. "Well, maybe you can make two pictures, one with red and the other with green," I suggested, "and you could help each other out."

She/they sniffled, and nodded. "Okay."

– incident in a classroom, reported by a teacher's assistant

Most of us succumb much more easily to the insistence that we are singular. Up to the age of about twelve, children's personalities seem to rub along fairly happily together, but as they grow up, people come under increasing pressure to settle for being one personality or another. "What are you going to be when you grow up?" they are asked. "Which subjects do you want to study?," "Are you mathematical or artistic?" These questions do not necessarily come from adults. The child's own developing personalities want answers to these things, too, so the pressure comes from inside as much as out.

During adolescence, after several years of relatively smooth operating, the brain undergoes a major rewiring exercise. Many of the changes take place in the frontal lobes, which are responsible for maintaining our conscious sense of self, as well as for rational thought, emotional control and the behavioral constraints we think of as our conscience. They also play an important part in the formation of our notion of what we are like.[5] One effect of this seems to be that personalities that had until then been operating more or less independently start to compete for dominance, and what had been a murmur of different but coexisting viewpoints erupts into a shouting match. This, for example, is how one fairly typical teenager describes herself:

I'm responsible, even studious every now and then, but on the other hand I'm a goof-off too, because if you're too studious, you won't be popular. I don't usually do that well at school. I'm a pretty cheerful person, especially with my friends, where I can even get rowdy. At home I'm more likely to be anxious around my parents. They expect me to get all As . . . I worry about how I probably should get better grades. But I'd be mortified in the eyes of my friends. So I'm usually pretty stressed-out at home, or sarcastic, since my parents are always on my case. But I really don't understand how I can switch so fast. I mean, how can I be cheerful one minute, anxious the next, and then be sarcastic? Which one is the real me?[6]

Construction work continues in the frontal lobes of the brain right up to the age of thirty or so. Well before this work is complete, though, most people, if asked, will offer a fairly coherent description of themselves. Instead of the confusion and contradictions admitted by the teenager, the young adult gives a clear and tidy account of strengths and weaknesses, attitudes and beliefs. The message is clear: this person knows who he is and where he is going.

Close observation of adult behavior, however, shows that we are not nearly as consistent or well defined as we like to think. Rather we change constantly to suit whatever situation we happen to be in. When a situation calls for us to please or impress, for example, most people obligingly slip into an appropriate personality. The changes are not just outward— mere behavioral concessions to necessity. We change inwardly too.

In an experiment carried out by psychologist Kenneth Gergen, students were given what they were told were self-descriptions of people they would be partnering in a project. Half of them were given biographies that spoke of failure, low self-esteem and self-loathing. The other half were given self-assessments that described the author as brilliant, confident and attractive. The students were then asked to give a description of themselves in return.

By far the majority of the students responded with tales of themselves mirroring the self-assessment of their putative partners. Those who thought they were being partnered by insecure, incompetent people said that they, too, were far from perfect. Those that thought they were being put with someone brilliant, however, found all sorts of positive qualities to report about themselves and very few bad ones.[7]

This in itself is hardly surprising. What is, though, is that the students were not simply presenting, like a gift, the personalities they thought would go down best. They actually seemed to hop into them, abandoning whatever personality was there before and becoming this personality that matched the situation so obligingly. They sincerely believed that they were giving a neutral and honest description of their real personality.

How situations create personalities

The extent to which people will switch personality to match what is required of them was dramatically demonstrated almost half a century ago in a series of extraordinary experiments. First, the maverick psychologist Stanley Milgram horrified the world by showing that a majority of perfectly ordinary, usually benign citizens could be transformed into apparently sadistic torturers just by placing them in a situation where they felt such behavior was demanded of them by a figure of authority.

Milgram's most famous experiment, which was first published in 1963, involved asking volunteers to give people increasingly severe electric shocks as penalties in a laboratory situation that the volunteers thought was about studying memory and learning. In fact the victims of the shocks were stooges who were just pretending to be in pain, and the study was actually about just how far ordinary people would go in obedience to authority. Milgram was staggered to find that more than 60 percent of his subjects were prepared to subject their fellow citizens to shocks that would make them scream with pain.

A man we will call B, for example, continued to deliver what he thought were electric shocks to another volunteer even after the victim was seen to "resist strongly and emit cries of agony." According to the study report, B related to the experimenter in the laboratory coat in a "submissive and courteous fashion, and did his work with robotic impassivity" even though the "learner" begged him to stop. At the 330-volt level, B was told the learner was no longer physically capable of answering the questions. Annoyed, B is reported to have said: "You better answer and get it over with—we can't stay here all night." This ruthless commander personality then switched to a craven minion as he turned to the white-coated experimenter and asked: "Where do we go from here, Professor?"

The experiment was repeated in other places and with other groups of subjects, including some selected from particular professions. The results were worst (that is, the highest percentage of testers went all the way to 450 volts) with a group of nurses.[8]

Then, in 1968, the psychologist Walter Mischel published a book analyzing the results of hundreds of studies in which people's character profiles were matched against their actual behavior in different situations. For example, schoolchildren and students were rated on personality tests for the trait of "honesty," and then observed in a variety of situations where their honesty was actually put to the test. They were, for example, placed in situations where they could steal money or cheat in an exam, and seem likely to get away with it.

The results showed the character assessments that had been made on the basis of the children's behavior in one situation did practically nothing to predict how they would behave in another. A child who stole money would not be much more likely to cheat in an exam than one who did not.[9]

Next, in 1971, the Stanford Prison Experiment found that in just six days ordinary students could be turned into monsters by being cast—quite arbitrarily—in the role of guard in a simulated prison situation where their prisoners were fellow students. The study's designer, Professor Philip Zimbardo, recalled: "My guards repeatedly stripped their prisoners naked, hooded them, chained them, denied them food or bedding privileges, put them into solitary confinement, and made them clean toilet bowls with their bare hands . . . Over time, these amusements took a sexual turn, such as having the prisoners simulate sodomy on each other."

He concluded: "Human behavior is much more under the control of situational forces than most of us recognize or want to acknowledge."

Milgram agreed: "The social psychology of this century reveals a major lesson," he declared. "It is not so much the kind of person a man is as the kind of situation he finds himself in that determines how he will act."[10]

The conclusions of the Stanford and Milgram studies have since been validated time and again, including in several real-life situations such as the inhumane behavior of U.S. soldiers with regard to their captives at Guantánamo Bay. A meta-analysis of twenty-five thousand social psychology studies carried out by researchers at Princeton University concluded that almost everyone is capable of torture and other evil acts if "cued" by the situation.[11]

Of course, everyone knows that people behave differently in different situations. The conventional view of this, though, is that people are showing different sides of a single self rather than being entirely separate personalities. The distinction may sound rather academic, but it actually signifies a profoundly different view of what we are.

34

The "many-sides" view holds that although people may change on the surface, deep down in each of us there is a solid, singular and unchanging authentic self. A visual metaphor of this model would be a cut gem turning slowly in the light. Its angled surfaces sparkle in turn as the light changes, but in the center there lies an unchanging core.

Multiplicity, on the other hand, recognizes that we consist only of our faces—there is no real self lurking behind them. One self may look back on the embarrassing doings of another and bewail them. In some people one personality may even watch others and bewail their actions as they occur. But the bewailer is no more authentic than the bewailed—it is just that in retrospect we *prefer* to identify with one cluster of characteristics than another.

This is not a popular idea. We badly want to think of others and ourselves as essentially unchanging beings. Useful and beneficial though it might be, our shiftiness makes us uneasy. Hence we embark on an inevitably hopeless and unending quest for our "real" selves.

Searching for the essential self

This search for authenticity is one of several misconceptions that lie behind our enduring enthusiasm for astrology. Type "star signs" into Google and—as I write this—you get more than forty-two million results. By the time you come to read this, there will probably be millions more. Presumably the people who visit these sites think they are getting meaningful information. Can so many be wrong?

Actually, yes. Astrology is almost certainly nonsense. Yet it often seems startlingly accurate, because people unconsciously change their ideas of themselves to match what the stars have decreed they are like. So desperate are we to discover a real me that it seems we will willingly identify with any real me that is on offer.

Professional skeptic James Randi sometimes demonstrates this by walking into a college classroom posing as an astrologer and casting horoscopes for all the students. He then asks the students to read and then rate each one for accuracy. Invariably, the overwhelming majority give the results a high accuracy rating, claiming they reflect their personalities to a T. Randi then gets the students to pass the horoscopes around, at which point they discover that every horoscope is exactly the same. Although the wording seems to refer to definite, individual-sounding characteristics, it is actually so vague that every student can identify with it.

You can do the same experiment for yourself: pluck any astrological "character reading" from a website or magazine, take off the star sign, then offer it to people, saying it has been drawn up for them personally based on their birth date. Even people who are skeptical of astrology will invariably express amazement at how much of it seems to be accurate.

The desire to pin down an essential personality also fuels the expanding industry that offers "scientific" personality testing. Many personality tests are little more use than a zodiac reading. These are the five-minute coffee-break distractions—a selection of patterns to choose from, or a dozen questions to answer, the results of which are obvious. The scientifically sanctioned end of the business, however, is a serious matter. Psychometric testing—which includes personality profiling—is used routinely in almost every branch of industry to help select employees. In the United States alone, one estimate of its worth, in terms of people employed and tests sold, is $400 million a year.[12] It is also used by psychiatrists and psychologists to aid medical diagnosis, and by various other agencies with the power to regulate our lives. The result of a personality test could, in theory, determine whether you are fit to fly a passenger plane, give evidence in court or adopt a child. Given the potential power of personality testing, we might hope it has more to recommend it than astrology. Certainly a few of the personality tests—generally the longest and priciest—are scientific instruments in that they have been tested over many decades and hundreds of thousands of people.

The trouble with personality tests

If there is no such thing as a real you to discover, though, what is it that these tests are revealing? To answer this we need to look quite closely at the tests themselves. Personality tests fall into two groups: those that put people into categories or types, and those that measure personality traits. Many of them effectively combine the two.

The Myers-Briggs Type Indicator (MBTI) is the most widely employed and influential personality test. It is used by psychologists and psychiatrists, employers, educators and sociologists to test more than two million people every year. The MBTI consists of a lengthy and complex questionnaire meant to be given to people by qualified assessors, trained to interpret the results. These take the form of identifying a person as one of sixteen different psychological types.

Most of those who take it think their MBTI result reflects something authentic about them. The U.S. National Research Council, a subgroup of the National Academy of Sciences, investigated the test's impact in advanced training programs for U.S. army officers and found that 84 percent of those who took it thought the MBTI gave a "true" and "valuable" assessment of their character.

Yet the objective reliability of the test—that is, the extent to which it yields the same results each time a person takes it—does not measure up to its popularity. The NRC report cited a review of eleven studies of MBTI test-retest outcomes that showed that as few as 24 percent of respondents—and no more than 61 percent—were put in the same type as before when they took the test a second time.[13] In other words, like Randi's universal star sign, the MBTI types are loose enough for a person to slip on one, then another, and believe both are tailor-made.

The second type of personality test does not attempt to put people into types, but instead describes them by where they lie on various dimensions, each of which defines a particular personality trait. Trait theory is based on the idea that characteristics that matter in daily life have come to have words attached to them, and the more important they are, the more likely they are to be expressed by a single word. So, for example, there is a whole range of behavior generally approved of by other people: kindness, sympathy, considerateness—all of which can be brought together under the umbrella word of "goodness" or "niceness."

Of course, a person could be kind without being considerate, or sympathetic without being kind, but generally speaking if a person rates highly on one of the measures, they will be expected to rate highly on the others. By rating people on the single dimension of "niceness," therefore, you are saying a whole lot of things about them very economically. Over the years psychologists have whittled down the number of dimensions required to give a more or less complete picture of a personality to just five:

Openness to Experience
Conscientiousness
Extroversion
Agreeableness
Neuroticism

"Goodness" or "niceness," you will see, is not among the Big Five. In fact, apart from extroversion, the dimensions are probably not characteristics that anyone would arrive at intuitively. Nevertheless, years of number-crunching has shown that when all the descriptions that fall under their umbrella are taken into account (e.g., when you include under extroversion the degree to which a person is talkative, outgoing, sociable and so on), these five dimensions contain nearly everything that can be said of a personality. By assessing where each testee lies on the five dimensions—where they are between, say, agreeableness and disagreeableness or extroversion and introversion—you are therefore meant to have a complete, if crude, picture of them.

Trait testing is a fuzzier sort of test than the type testing. Rather than saying that people who score high on, say, conscientiousness will indeed be conscientious whenever they are tested, they predict that a person will be conscientious *most of the time*. This gets around the problem that the MBTI Johnnies posed when a person slid from one type to another because it doesn't presume to tell you what your core self is—just what the likelihood is of you being like this or that. Someone might be conscientious, say, 80 percent of the time and careless 20 percent; extrovert on one in four occasions and a shrinking violet on the others.

But what on earth does it mean to say that there is an 80 percent probability that a conscientious person will behave conscientiously? Are personalities prone to off days—failing to hit their targets sometimes, like second-rate pool players? And what if the person displays an entirely different personality 20 percent of the time? If that is not their personality showing, what on earth is it? Someone else's?

Multiplicity, obviously, makes sense of this, just as it makes sense of the slippage in the type testing. A person with a conscientious major personality will display that trait just so long as their major is active. When a minor takes over who does not share that trait, it will temporarily disappear. As our circumstances change, so do our personalities.

Big Five testers seem slowly to be coming around to this idea themselves, although they don't express it in quite that way. They have found that the predictive value of trait testing is hugely improved when people are invited to do the test within a frame of reference. This means that they are instructed to put themselves mentally into a particular role or situation and answer the questions from that perspective only. If a person is doing the test as part of the selection procedure for a job, for example, the candidates are instructed to answer the questions "as though they are in the working environment." In addition, questions such as "do you become irritable if a person is late to meet you?" may be rephrased to ask: "would you issue a reprimand if an employee is late for a meeting without good excuse?"

Tests given with instructions like these are proving to be much more effective at predicting the behavior of people when they are in the same frame of reference as the one they were in when they did the test. For example, when people did a Big Five test in each of several roles—friend, student, employee, lover and child—they rated differently on every one of the dimensions in each role. In the "friend" mode, they were more extroverted; in the student role they were more neurotic and less agreeable; in the employee role they were more conscientious; and in the romantic role they were more open to experience.[14]

In other words: the friend is a different personality from the student, and the student is different from the employee. They don't call it multiplicity (yet), but that is what this new testing implies.

Sharing the stage

While most of us slip-slide sequentially from one train of consciousness to another, a few people remain simultaneously aware of more than one personality. Instead of feeling themselves to be just the one, they are privy to the thoughts and feelings of "back room" personalities running as a parallel stream of consciousness alongside the thoughts and feelings of the one that is in charge of behavior. This unusual state of mind is known as co-consciousness, and although few of us will ever experience it completely, a little of it might help us all.

Alex is one such person. He works as an estate agent, and to his friends he is an entirely regular guy with a fairly conventional view of life. In a way this assessment is absolutely right. Alex *is* conventional. His main concern is to sell more houses than his competitors, make money and establish a materially secure lifestyle.

What his colleagues do not know, however, is that the Alex they recognize is only one of eight quite separate Alexes that his brain is generating at any moment. While Alex-1 is out, these other personalities look on as though from the wings, each one harboring their own thoughts. And when Alex leaves work, he steps into the wings himself and allows another of his household to take control of their body.

Sometimes it is Alexander who emerges, the slightly pompous, tweed-clad ex–public school boy who takes his fishing rods to visit his parents in the country. Sometimes it is A, the lager-drinking couch potato who can tell you the details of every goal scored by his football team in the last three seasons. Occasionally it is Alex the cook, who will spend an entire day preparing a special meal for a few friends. Once in a blue moon it is the Alex that gets blindingly drunk and then drives too fast through city streets.

Alex has never been diagnosed with any sort of psychological disorder. Far from being pathological, his multi-streamed mental life works perfectly well because the various members of the group are in close and constant communication. Their continuous multi-way inner conversation allows them to pool their memories so there are no memory gaps. And they share tasks, by arrangement, to ensure that the front or active personality is the one best able to manage current circumstances. The only problem is Alex the drunk, but the other Alexes are working on him.

Co-consciousness sounds, at first, simply impossible, just as MPD tends to sound impossible to someone who is unfamiliar with it. Certainly it is difficult to imagine what it is like to be aware of being more than one self at the same time. If you think about it, though, you may realize that you too have had glimpses of how it feels. One co-conscious multiple describes it like this:

Imagine being in a theater, in front of the stage. From that viewpoint, you can see all the actors and props up close and firsthand. Now picture standing at the very back of this large theater, what the view from this vantage point might be. You could still see and hear everything; however it would not be as lucid or meaningful as it was in front of the stage.

For the multiple, being in front of the stage is similar to being out and in control of the body, and being in the back is similar to experiencing what is taking place externally, from the inside.

The degree to which co-conscious multiples feel they are simultaneously inside each of their backstage personalities varies. Sometimes they are aware of a household member's thoughts as silent knowledge, and sometimes they manifest as internal voices. Teresa, one of a large co-conscious household, says: "Sometimes I get a whole flash or a shift in perception, where I see/hear/taste/smell/feel a piece of memory really strongly that is also not related to anything near by that I can see. I interpret this as getting information from someone else."

Other members' thoughts (as opposed to sensory perceptions) manifest mainly as voices inside her head. Such voices should not be confused with the voices that plague schizophrenics. Those, for the people who hear them, are usually indistinguishable from the voices of people outside.

"My own thoughts might run something like this: Gee, I really like that dress. But we're really low on cash right now so I won't get it," explains Teresa. "But I also hear other voices in my head. Sometimes they are talking to me, or relevant to the situation at hand. Sometimes, though, they're not—it's like eavesdropping on someone, or catching pieces of a TV show when you're doing something else. Occasionally I even hear discussions between other people, so it's like hearing a conversation. To me, all the voices are fairly distinct, although sometimes they go into what I think of as 'neutral,' which means I can't figure out who they are."

Teresa also experiences the others' emotions, though these, she says, are less easy to distinguish from her own than thoughts.

"Usually they aren't related to anything I see in front of me and have a vaguely . . . untrue feeling to them," she says. "It's hard to explain, but it's like a paler version of a real feeling."

Even if this does not accord at all with your normal waking experience, you might recall something like it occurring in your dreams. The illusion of unity is maintained by activity in the brain's frontal lobes, and during sleep these are effectively turned off, or down. One effect is that our critical faculties—among them the bit that usually says "Hey! Something odd is happening here!"—are not very active. Hence dream narrative is often so bizarre—it gets past the usual reality check. Another effect is that in dreams we may find ourselves to be both an actor and an observer in a situation, seeming to inhabit two characters' minds at the same time. The feeling may just be one of knowing what is in another mind as well as your own. Or it may be more complete than that—a feeling of actually looking out through two pairs of eyes.

In one of my own recent dreams, for instance, I was sitting on a bank fishing, and at the same time I was under the water watching the fish swim up to the bait. Never mind what (if any) psychological significance this may have—the important thing about it for me is that in the dream I experienced two distinct streams of consciousness. My ability to do this, even if only in sleep, persuades me that the sense of multiplicity that some people claim is their normal state is as real to them as the sense of singularity is to the rest of us

Living co-consciously may not be easy, what with the clamor of competing voices and the constant negotiating between personalities. In some ways, though, co-conscious multiples may function better than what they describe as singlets because effectively they are able to draw on the combined talents of several people, rather than just on one. Romy, a member of another co-conscious household, explains:

> Not many of us—individually—are more intelligent than the average person. But what happens is that everyone brings their own skills and abilities to the body for the time that they are out, and so we seem more intellectually able because we bring such a variety of skills with us. I myself am very technically inclined, and the courses I've been doing at the college have been a breeze for me. But if one of the others happens to get out, they can stare blankly at the page, knowing that I (Romy) know this stuff, and being able to access that yes, we have seen it before and it is in Common Knowledge, but they don't have a damn clue what to do with it! And I in turn could not write poetry or draw a portrait to save my soul, but there are some amazing poets and artists who share this body, making it seem like we all have those skills. So it's not a matter of multiples being superior so much as that the combination of skills in any system/household can make it seem like we're able to do and understand a whole lot more.

As this account suggests, it is not enough just to share information, it is also important that the personality best suited to a particular task comes out, on cue, to do it. Some households seem to have more control over this than others. "Our work involves doing a whole range of completely different things," says Jo, the spokesperson for a household that owns and runs an interior decorating shop:

> First thing we have to do each week is check the stock lists on the computer, and that is really painstaking, detailed stuff. Personally I would be hopeless at it, but Immy (another household member) is great at it. Then we have to check on the product displays. That's a job I share with P; we both have a talent for making stuff look pretty, showing it off to best advantage.

43

People who know us well can always tell which of us has done a particular display, though, because we have different styles. I like to spread the goods out so you can see at a glance what's there, but P likes to do it more artistically. He'll take three or four contrasting fabrics and drape them over the back of a chair as though they've just been discarded there. I can feel myself itching to straighten them out; tidy it up and show the patterns more clearly, but if I do that, we can get locked into a tussle, with me arranging them one way, then P sneaking back and rearranging them, and then me doing it again . . . we wasted a lot of time doing that until we came to this arrangement: I do it for a couple of weeks, then P does it.

Student multiples sometimes send different personalities to different classes or to take different exams. "Carly did all my history papers last year," says a member of one household. "We ended up with straight As. But Carly never comes out on social occasions, so people get really puzzled when something to do with history comes up in a conversation and I don't have anything to say about it."

Another way in which co-conscious people have an advantage over others is that if they have a problem personality among them, they are able to conduct a multi-way conversation with it, in which all sides can be heard together.

Part II of this book describes how you can get a conversation going between personalities even if you currently experience them only as a muted burble rather than a clear stream of parallel consciousness. It will also help you to identify your personalities as individuals, with their own interests and quirks. First, though, let's look at the way that personalities are made.

CHAPTER 3

Mechanisms of Mind

Memory, experience and I-memories

We tend to think of memories as a replay of past events—a personal library of documentary film footage which we can select and watch at will. In fact it is not like that, because memories are not events but *experiences*.

To recall a past episode in your life is to reconstitute the mind-state you were in at the time. Part of this is, literally, sensational. That is, it includes the experience of seeing, hearing, tasting and so on. These are the components we tend to think of as events. Along with them, though, you also reconstitute (in part at least) the thoughts, emotions and behavioral responses you were generating at that moment. These are the "I" component of memories—the bits that become the habits of mind which cluster into personalities. Because they are bound together with the sensational part of each experience, when you reconstitute something that you saw or heard, you also reproduce the personality *to whom* it happened. More of this in a moment.*

---

*Of course, you never normally reconstitute a previous brain-state in its entirety. If you did you would have no way of telling the memory apart from the original experience. The only possible exception to this is the intense flashbacks suffered by people with post-traumatic stress disorder. These can be so similar, subjectively, to the original experience that the person is unaware of the present and acts as though he is back in time.

No two people ever have exactly the same experience. You and I may both think we remember Belinda's wedding, but I remember my experience of it and you remember yours and the two may be very different. Even if the facts of the matter are accurately recalled by us both (as far as we can tell) the emotional coloring of our recollections will probably be different because event memories include at least a trace of the mood we were in at the time the memory was laid down. Details will be different, too, because each one of us notices slightly different aspects of an unfolding scene. At Belinda's wedding we may both have noted that Hermione was wearing a particularly flamboyant hat. But your eye may also have been caught by the fall of a rose petal from a table decoration, while mine might have picked up the sound of a glass breaking at the far end of the room. Even if we didn't consciously register these fragmentary experiences, they may have triggered a cascade of other memories in each of us. The rose petal may have reminded you of a funeral and thus may have subtly clouded your mood for a few minutes. The glass breaking might have reminded me of a car accident I was in, and so infected the moment with a tiny trace of fear.

We are able to recall past experiences, complete with their idiosyncratic details, because they are encoded in the flesh, rather as a tune may be etched into the surface of an audio disc. A memory (and the personality incorporated in it) thus has a physical basis—it is there in your brain even when it is out of mind.

This is how it works. Each moment of experience is generated by electrical activity created by rapid on-off firing of individual cells. Firing is a sort of mini-explosion that occurs only in nerve cells, or neurons. If one neuron fires strongly and frequently enough, it has a knock-on effect on its neighbors. Sometimes the effect is inhibitory— it signals them *not* to fire. But at other times it causes a whole bunch of neighboring neurons to start firing in synchronized bursts like a line of chorus girls kicking their legs in sequence to create a wave. These flurries of organized activity are our sensations and thoughts and emotions. Gentle flutterings pass unnoticed, but if a bout of synchronous firing is rapid, energetic and sustained, it becomes conscious. And activity that is particularly energetic or sustained—

whether conscious or not—causes the neurons involved to change physically.

These changes are minute—a matter of subtle rearrangement of individual molecules. Their effect, though, is profound, because it is this that creates memory. The tiny alterations in cells strengthen the links between simultaneously firing neurons in such a way that in the future when one fires, its original "dancing partners" are likely to fire too. The process is known as long-term potentiation (LTP), and is summed up by the T-shirt slogan: "Neurons that fire together, wire together!" So as you can see, the more a particular group of neurons get to dance together, the more the physical changes in them encourage them to do it again.

A memory, then, is a brain *habit*—a pattern of neural firing that the brain produces easily because it has done it before. Some memories are episodic—that is, when they are active they partially reconstitute the experience of a previous episode in our lives. Over time they change, and large parts of them fade away altogether. Sometimes the parts that fade are the "I" components, leaving only the factual bits—so-called semantic memories. The residue of a distant geography lesson, for example, may be some arcane fact about the gross national product of Ecuador. Or the factual elements may be lost, leaving only an emotional or "I-memory"—a sense of paralyzing boredom in the face of anything remotely geographical, perhaps.

These free-floating "I-memories" can be thought of as micro personalities, and those that are similar to one another—the boredom with geography and a similar sense of boredom with, say, math—might join up to make a "bored with schoolwork" minor. Minors, in turn, may coalesce into a major. For example, if you smoke when you drink, the pattern of neuronal firing (micro) that is your smoking habit is activated simultaneously with the neuronal pattern that is your drinking habit (another micro). Let's say you limit your drinking to Friday nights when you don't have to get up to go to work the next day. The micro that is the thought "Thank God it's Friday! Let's relax!" thus occurs at the same time as the drinker/smoker micros. Relaxing, for you, might mean dancing all night. For someone else it might involve slumping in front of the TV. So you will probably develop a Friday night/drinking/smoking/dancing habit while they get a Friday night/drinking/smoking/slumping habit. To which might be added "dressing up" or "dressing sloppily," and so on. Little by little a small nexus of habits may grow into a whole way of seeing, thinking, feeling and behaving, so that what begins just as a cluster of memories becomes in time a full-fledged personality. It may become hugely complex, complete with intentions and ambitions. The Friday night dance, for example, may become an all-consuming way of life with which you and other people come to identify yourself. In other words, the clubbing "you" may become your major personality. Or it may remain a skeletal little minor who comes out for a few hours only and returns to sleep the moment you leave the club.

Given that personalities are made of memories, and no two people ever have the same experience, it is easy to see how different personalities arise in different people. But how can two (or more) distinct personalities coexist in a single brain? After all, you may suppose, they have shared a lifetime of experience.

In fact our various personalities do not share the same experiences. Or at least they do not share the same experiences *equally*. Although they are products of the same brain, they are not generated by the same brain processes.

It is a little like one of those advertising signs made of thousands of lightbulbs: turn on one set and it blazes out "Pepsi-Cola!" Turn on another and it says "Drink Coke!" Some of the lightbulbs may be common to both (the "Co" in "Cola" and "Coke," for example, overlap), but the messages are still quite different.

The switch from one neural pattern (Coke!) to another (Pepsi!) is clean enough in some people to be visible on a brain scan. But you don't need fancy laboratory equipment to be aware of these internal shifts even when they are far more subtle than those detected (so far) by brain-imaging.

State-dependent recall

If you examine your inner life carefully, you will almost certainly find that your memories of some things are clear and intense while others are vague and gappy. Your schooldays may have been reduced to a few snap-shots perhaps, or last year's summer vacation may seem, after only a few weeks back at work, like a distant dream. Vague memories, however, tend to become quite clear if you put yourself back in a state similar to the one you were in when they were laid down. This curious phenome-non is known as state-dependent memory.

A classic experiment demonstrates in neatly quantifiable terms just how potent state-dependent memory can be. Volunteers were asked to learn a string of words one day and then recall them the next. Half of them were given a stiff drink before the learning exercise while the other half did the memorizing sober. Next day both groups were given alcohol before being asked to recall the words. The drink, as you might expect, undermined both groups' ability to recall the list, and neither of them did as well as a third group who were sober both when they learned and when they recalled the list. But what you might not expect is that the group who were drunk on both occasions did better—more than twice as well, in fact—than the group who had learned them while they were sober but tried to remember them when they were drunk.[1]

In other words, it wasn't the fact they were drunk when they learned the words that prevented the volunteers recalling them sober so much as the fact that they were in a different brain-state. If you think of each state as a different personality you can see why—the words were stashed in the bag of memories laid down by the drinker and were not therefore fully available to the sober one.

Other studies have shown that other mind-states, such as moods, are also associated with their own bags of memories. People remember more happy memories when they are happy themselves, and more sad ones when they are sad. Furthermore, when people are in a particular mood they experience the world in a way that matches it. Experiences that chime with the mood—the sight of spring flowers in the sun when you are feeling bright, the glimpse of a person crying when you are sad—capture attention more than things that go against it. Both types of events may be happening, but people will *notice* only the ones that resonate with how they feel.[2] Mood-congruent processing, as this is known, ensures that each mind-state is not "polluted" by experience or perceptions that would dilute its character. So in time, each mood—happy, sad, angry, scared—accumulates its distinct memories as well as its characteristic way of seeing the world. The sunny mood, for example, gets to have a big collection of sunny associations, so it develops an optimistic attitude and sees itself as a happy person. Moods thus become minors. A mood may even be the central kernel around which a person's major grows.

Once you are tuned in to it you can see state-dependent memory and mood-congruent processing at work in all sorts of situations. Sandy, for example, recounted to me the odd transformation she experienced when she looked after her grandchild.

This competent middle-aged woman spent more than a decade caring full-time for her children before building a successful career as a marketing manager. A little while ago her eldest daughter had her first child. It had been a complicated pregnancy and the daughter was exhausted by the time the child arrived, so Sandy took a month off work and moved in with her daughter to help with the new baby.

"It took a lot of persuading to get me to do it," she says. "Not so much because I didn't want to but because I really thought I had forgotten how to look after a baby; the time when I was a new mum seemed like another lifetime—a distant blur of broken nights and milky stains. Yet the moment I held that baby it was as though I had been looking after my own just yesterday."

State-dependent memory is often concealed from us because when we are in one state we rarely need to call on the experience held by another state. On vacation, for example, we may not realize how out of touch we have become with our working personality until we run into a work colleague and find, for a moment, that we can't place them. Sandy found that once the mum in her reemerged, her bag of work memories was almost entirely inaccessible.

"I had a crisis call while I was at my daughter's from the person who was standing in for me at work. She wanted to know in what order to do things during a training session. I had run those training sessions every fortnight for five years, but at that moment, standing with the baby in one hand and the phone in the other, I couldn't remember how I started the sessions or what came next. The knowledge had just gone."

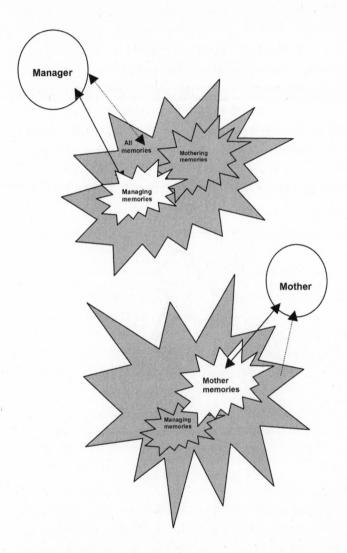

While Sandy is manager (top), her experiences are bound with other "managing memories" in the manager's "bag." She still has access to other memories, but they are not as bright or easy to recall. When she becomes mother (below), her previous "mothering memories" become clear, but her access to others are compromised.

How memories fit together—the brain-wide web

Memory recall fluctuates in all of us, but more so in those of us, like Sandy, who have developed very clearly distinguished personalities. The reason for this is that memories are encoded in the brain in a web or a net. You could think of each element of a memory (the sight of a particular hat, say) as a node, or knot in a fishing net, connected to others by strings. When a memory comes to mind it pulls on all the strings leading out from it, and the memories at the other end get jogged. The jogged memories in turn jog those they are connected to, and so on. The farther away you go from the initial recollection, the weaker the jogging effect. But so long as two memories are part of the same net, there is the possibility that one will bring to mind the other.

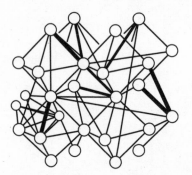

Memories are stored as though in a three-dimensional network: some are connected very strongly and directly and some are not directly connected at all. So long as they are all part of the same network, however, when one is jogged the effect is felt, however faintly, by all the rest.

In order to get linked up with others and thus woven into the network, memories have to share something. This shared material is the "strings" that bind them together. Things that happen at the same time are usually linked automatically by their shared time slot. Hence the memory of Hermione's hat is bound to the memory of Belinda's wedding. And if it happened to be raining at Belinda's wedding, that too will get attached. The nodes in the net are the events and the string that links them is their shared timing.

This little cluster of new experiences slots into the net by joining with other memories that share something with them. The wedding bit of it connects to all the other weddings you have been to. Rainy weddings get doubly attached. And the rain bit links up with, say, memories of rainy vacations.

The links take off far and wide . . . the purple of Hermione's hat may get linked via its color to a skirt you once foolishly bought and never wore. Which in turn may link to a little guilty memory about pretending not to have any change when a charity worker shook a collecting tin at you as you left that same shop on another occasion. The rattling of change may link to some distant recollection of a baby's rattle, and the guilt may remind you that you still have to buy Belinda a wedding present . . . Rain, of course, has countless connections—with rainy picnics, rainy walks, rainy journeys . . .

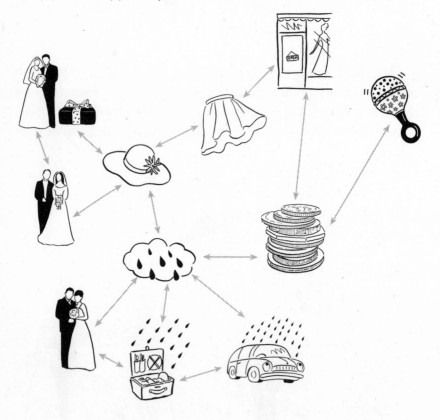

You can see that providing every experience has *some*thing in common with what has gone before—timing, color, location, sound, emotion—you end up with a vast network in which everything is connected to everything else. Hence if one memory is jogged, the others will feel it too, with its immediate neighbors feeling it most.

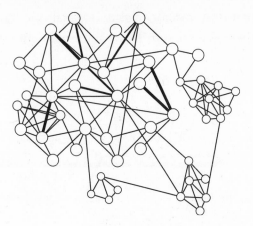

Most of us end up with a memory web that could be represented by the pattern above (though infinitely more complicated!). Although everything is connected to everything else, the memories are clustered or "bagged" together. When a single memory is activated, therefore, it tends to trigger its associated memories, but has very little effect on distantly connected ones.

The interconnectivity of all our experiences normally ensures that when a situation jogs to life one particular set of responses we continue to have access (should we need it) to a wider web of recollections, including autobiographical information such as our name, where we live, what day of the week it is and why we are in a particular place at that particular moment. The neural firing patterns that encode this background may not be active enough to make it conscious, but they are poised to burst into life given a cue. If someone asks you for your address, for example, the firing pattern that incorporates that information will strike up instantly.

Imagine, though, that you had one cluster of memories that had somehow failed to get connected up with the rest of your memory web. Most of the time you would be unconscious of it because there would be no strings running to it from your daily experiences, and thus nothing would usually shake it into life. Conversely, on the rare occasions when it *was* jogged into consciousness, there would be no strings running back to your everyday experience, so your consciousness would be *limited* to that memory—if someone asked you for your address you would not be able to retrieve it. If the memory cluster is a small one, it might not contain *any* autobiographical knowledge. You would not even know who you are.

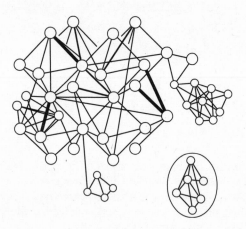

If a small cluster of memories fails to bind into the web (ringed, right), the personality incorporated in them is isolated. When the memories in this isolated cluster are jogged, the personality that is activated no longer has access to the recollections giving them their Major identity.

This, essentially, is what happens in people with the "Who am I?" type of amnesia that features in so many thrillers. Their most recent experiences are not woven into the larger part of their memory web so they are marooned in the here and now without a bridge to the rest of their life. The condition is very similar to that of a person with MPD, except that in the latter case the person is marooned in a detached bit of their *past* life.

In adults, only memories of extreme experiences are likely to be disconnected from the rest. This is because most experiences, even novel or nasty ones, connect with *some*thing that has happened to the person in the past just because he has been around long enough to accumulate lots and lots of experiences. Children, though, have far fewer stowed experiences to link new events with, so much more of what happens to them is—initially, at least—free-floating.

Take, for instance, Tom—just sprung to life, miraculously, with an entirely clean slate for a memory. He has various genetic dispositions, of course, and in real life they would have a great influence on what follows. Just now, though, for the sake of simplicity we are going to ignore these. The important thing is that Tom has no learned responses other than those that are pretty much common to all human beings.

So let's give Tom his first experience. We'll start with a nice one: Tom is given a puppy for Christmas.

This makes Tom very happy, so the puppy experience incorporates "I-memories" that add up "Happy Tom." Next Tom is taken to the seaside and this makes him happy too. So the "I" bits of the two experiences—happiness—overlap.

It is not just any old happiness, though—this is *Tom's* happiness. In fact, as happiness is so far all that Tom has ever been, it *is* him: Happy Tom. Every experience he has had and every memory he can have so far bring out this single personality. Tom's next experiences are happy too: a first flight in a plane and a big bar of chocolate. So now he has a cluster of memories that all produce Happy Tom. The Happy Toms share so many brain-states that they are effectively bound into a single personality.

You can see from this that if Tom's experiences continued in this vein—every one of them giving him unalloyed joy—he would develop just one rather limited personality. He would be what I am calling a "Single Major"—a completely integrated self with no ragged edges or threadbare patches in his memory net.

But let's make Tom's life a little more real. He gets sent to school and hates it. He gets a cold: horrid. He gets attacked by the school bully. Scary. He has to do homework. Boring. And the coalition of these experiences, bound by their common unpleasantness, creates a new entity: Unhappy Tom.

Now we have two quite separate Toms—Happy Tom, with his little bag of memories, and Unhappy Tom, dragging around his rotten baggage. The Tom who is "there" at any moment depends entirely on which situation he finds himself in: seaside, airplanes, chocolate and puppies jog out Happy Tom, and school, illness, bullies and homework bring out Unhappy Tom. The two Toms can't access each other's memories because there are no connections between them, so Unhappy Tom does not even know that Happy Tom exists and vice versa. When the situation changes from one that brings out Happy Tom (playing with his dog, for example) to one that calls up Unhappy Tom (going to school), the switch is clean and sudden. It is as though one actor leaves the stage and another sweeps in from where he has been waiting for his cue in the wings.

As Tom grows up, however, he accumulates more experiences, many of which create links between the previously disjointed memories. The seaside visit and the journey to school might be linked by a trip in the family car. Tom might get bored ("Are we there yet?") or carsick during both trips, and thus the two otherwise different events would both be associated with Unhappy Tom as well as with Happy Tom. The experience of his first flight, though happy, may include a bout of turbulence that frightens him. This would link it to the fright he got when he was beaten up at school. Tom might do his homework on his computer and punctuate the slog with surreptitious spells of video games, which connect back to the Happy Tom.

Already you can see that all Tom's memories are interconnected. Rattle any one of them and Happy Tom and Unhappy Tom will both vibrate. Some of the memories, though, shake up Unhappy Tom more than Happy Tom and vice versa. Cue "school," for example, and the more you shake it, the more Unhappy Tom comes to life. Cue "chocolate" and Happy Tom is the one who becomes most active. Tom does not have multiple personality *disorder* because his personalities retain some connection to each other. When Happy Tom is out, Unhappy Tom is still quietly purring along, unconsciously, ready to perk up and take over if jogged to life by a situation resonating with his particular bag of memories.

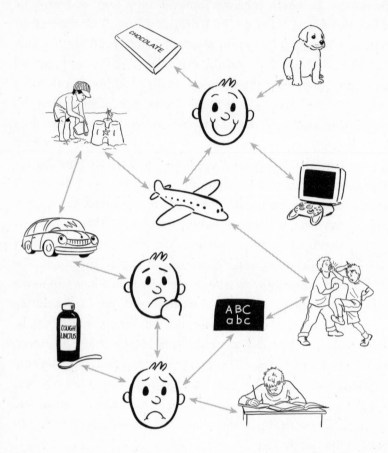

The brain as building site

In real life, Tom's inner landscape would develop in a much more complicated way because his reactions to the things that happened to him would be idiosyncratic right from the start, due to his unique genetic inheritance.

Experiences, as we have seen, are not things that happen to us but our *responses* to those things—the sensations, emotions and thoughts that our brain produces in response to events. Our responses depend largely on our previous experiences, which in turn depend on the ones before that, and so on and so forth. But they also depend to some extent on the way we are *made*. For example, the structure of a person's visual cortex—the density of his or her color-encoding neurons, say—will affect his or her perception of a visual image even *before* the sight is recognized and assessed in terms of what it is and what it means.

Hence an identical external event can produce quite different experiences in two different brains. If Tom happened to have a genetic inheritance that inclined him toward anxiety, for example, his first flight might not have been a mixture of fun and fear but an experience of unmitigated terror. Flying would have connected with school bullies and homework rather than puppies and chocolate, and so his personalities would take a different shape from that of a naturally less nervous person, even if the two of them (somehow) were subjected to identical environmental influences.

Genes influence more than the way people respond to events; they also influence the *range* of responses they have. Some people are naturally emotionally stable, so however diverse the external events that happen around them, their experiences tend to share a similar emotional tone or "color." Magnolia, perhaps. Others have quite dramatically varying responses, plunging from bubbling joy to abject misery. When they are happy, they are conscious *only* of happiness, and when they are sad, they can imagine no other way to be. These same people tend to get utterly caught up in the events of the moment. Their attention is like a narrow beam of light, illuminating target mental events intensely but casting a shadow over everything else.

Dissociation

"Slicing up" the world like this, into a tiny conscious focal point and an unconscious hinterland, is known as dissociation—the English equivalent of Janet's *disaggregation*. Dissociation is used as an umbrella term to cover all sorts of states involving the separation of various mental processes. It is usually discussed in the context of dissociative *disorders*—dysfunctional states (such as amnesia and MPD) which, given the problems they cause, are rightly treated as psychiatric illnesses.

But dissociation itself is not an illness or even abnormal. We all filter out of consciousness many or most of the thoughts, feelings and sensations registered at any moment by our brain. Whenever we put something such as a nagging worry, an unwelcome emotion or the noise of a road drill "out of mind" when we are trying to work, we are dissociating.

Usually we keep out only those experiences that fall roughly into the category of "background interference"—the irritating buzz and hum of city traffic or the meaningless faces of the crowd as we move toward the one familiar one we are seeking. Far from being unhealthy, this sort of everyday dissociation is essential because if our brains did not edit out most of the barrage of information competing for consciousness we would simply be overwhelmed.

Hypnotic induction is a way of producing dissociation on cue. The ease with which a person can be hypnotized generally corresponds to his or her ability to dissociate spontaneously. Indeed, spontaneous dissociation could be seen as unwitting self-hypnosis.

Hypnotizability is often measured on a scale from 0 to 5. Grade 5s, those who are most susceptible, make up about 4 percent of the general population, and the vast majority of people with MPD/DID. A slightly larger proportion of people are Grade 0—they do not respond at all to hypnotic suggestion. Most people are somewhere between the extremes.

A simple way to get a rough idea of people's hypnotizability is to see if they can roll their eyes backward into their head. To perform the eye roll test, tell the subject to:

1 Keep his (or her) head steady and look straight ahead.
2 Without moving your head, look upward with your eyes toward your eyebrows, then higher, toward the top of your head.
3 With your eyes held in this upward gaze, slowly close your eyelids.
4 Open your eyelids and let your eyes return to normal focus.

Hypnotizability corresponds to how much of the iris is visible during the upward gaze. Grade 0s continue to look quite normal, while Grade 5s show barely any iris at all. The eye-roll test was developed by Manhattan psychiatrist Dr. Herbert Spiegel in the 1970s and has been found to be almost as good at predicting hypnotizability as the long and complex testing methods used to determine it in a formal psychiatric setting.

Adaptive dissociation

While in ordinary situations we dissociate background noise in order not to be overwhelmed, in extraordinary situations it is often the experiences that are potentially the most intense that get cut out of consciousness. This is a natural consequence of the way our experiences are associated—anything that has nothing in common with those already stored in the web will inevitably be out on a limb. The effect, in traumatic situations, is that of a ferociously efficient doorkeeper. It bars the way to experiences—present and past—that are likely to be too much for us to cope with. Whenever you hear someone saying "All I could think of . . ." or "All I can remember . . ." as he or she recalls an event, you can be pretty sure you are hearing someone talking of a dissociative experience.

Even severe pain can be cut out of consciousness by dissociation. Hilgard (see page 12) discovered that almost everyone can dissociate pain under hypnosis, but it can also happen when a person is shocked or distracted by more urgent business. Colin, for example, recalls the time his car skidded out of control and hit a tree, bursting the gas tank. "I thought, I must get out in case it explodes," he recalls, "but when I tried to move I found my legs were trapped. It turned out that both of them were broken, but at the time I didn't feel a thing."

Like pain, intense emotion can also be cut out. A rape victim, for example, telling her story after the conviction of her attacker, recalls: "I was dreading giving evidence, but when it came to it I answered the questions as though I was reciting a laundry list. Only it didn't seem to be me in the witness box—it felt as though there was a puppet there, and I was watching from the sidelines."

The woman who spoke to me about this particular ordeal was astonished by her own calmness in court. But she recalled then that she had also been calm during and after the rape itself: "Once I realized there was nothing I could do I just went slack and divorced myself from it all. So in court I was doubly divorced from what I was describing. It was very odd."

Failure to be consciously aware of a potentially excruciating injury or intense emotion is of course abnormal. But abnormal does not necessarily mean *unhealthy*. In situations like the one Colin found himself in, dissociation is both a blessing and a direct aid to survival because it allows a person's conscious mind to concentrate on thinking how best to cope. In Colin's case, for example, it gave him time to wriggle out of his car and crawl off the road before succumbing to pain. And the woman who was raped probably could not have got through the ordeal and come out as emotionally intact as she has had it not been for the merciful numbness that came over her.

You can trace the origin of adaptive dissociation to the "freeze" response you see in scared animals. If an animal feels threatened, the first thing its brain does is to tell its body to run away. If it can't do that, the brain comes up with plan number two: fight. And if it can't do that, or it perceives that the threat is too big to take on, it goes into a third mode: switch-off. Parts of the brain responsible for responding consciously to what is happening close down. In small animals this is particularly obvious—the creature goes limp or becomes paralyzed. A rabbit that is caught petrified in headlights, for example, is displaying the classic signs of adaptive dissociation. If the headlights were the gaze of a predatory fox, the rabbit's utter stillness would increase its chances of being overlooked.

As in the case of rabbits, our own ability to distance ourselves from terrible events may once have saved human lives in a direct way. In the face of a physical threat that was impossible to run from or fight off, our ancestors would have been smart to keep quiet and still, like rabbits caught in headlights, in the hope that the threat would pass by.

Those whose brains pulled the "play dead" trick were thus more likely to live to pass on their genes, including the ones that made them behave like that. A person who jumped to the last-ditch "play dead" tactic too soon, however, would fail to make best use of the less extreme measures: flight and fight. So natural selection would have resulted in the majority of people being somewhere between very dissociative and not dissociative at all—which is, in fact, exactly what seems to be the case.

Defending the self

In today's world a threat is as likely to be to people's pride or mental comfort as to their body, so the defense mechanisms mammals evolved to cope with physical danger have adapted in humans to kick in when a person feels psychologically as well as physically threatened. Hence we may dissociate in situations where we are exposed to ridicule or when we are bereaved or heartbroken, embarrassed or insecure.

Lucy, for example, is pretty hazy about the period immediately before her parents' divorce. "My brother says that our parents used to bellow at each other till the walls shook," she tells me. "But I can only remember hearing them arguing once."

Looking back, Lucy pinpoints that event as the moment when she learned, as she puts it, "to go away in my mind":

> I was flipping through this kiddies' book and there was this picture of a pretty country garden sort of place, with a little grassy path winding away toward a cottage in the distance. On the path, with their backs to you, there was this little girl and a little boy. They were holding hands and walking toward the cottage.
>
> I was looking at this when I heard them start up at each other—my mum's voice sounding like nails on a blackboard, Dad roaring. I felt my stomach flip over. And then this odd thing happened—suddenly, instead of just looking at the picture I was actually *in* it! I *was* the little girl, walking home.

It was such a nice experience that I tore out the picture and kept it. Then at night when I was in bed, I would get it out and practice "becoming" the girl in it. It got easier and easier until eventually I didn't even need the picture. I would just think of that garden and I'd be there.

Lucy's escape into her garden is what most of us would call daydreaming, but technically it is a form of dissociation—she was separating the sound of her parents' voices and her other current sensations, thoughts and emotions from the picture of the children in the garden and the fantasy she wrapped around it. The fearful Lucy in her bedroom was temporarily put to sleep while another Lucy—a little girl in a garden—was created in her stead.

Lucy no longer needs to escape her parents' rows, but she still dissociates. Nowadays she uses the skill she learned as a child to cut out the tedious here and now of a dead-end job: "I'm on the assembly line," she says. "It is all mechanized, so you don't even have to use your hands—just watch a needle on a meter and twiddle buttons to keep it in the right range. The other girls yatter on about their boyfriends and stuff but I prefer to go off on my own. I make up stories and live them out, have conversations with the people I invent, do romantic things, go to places I've only read about. The others often tell me I'm talking to myself, but I don't care."

Lucy is an example of someone whose natural tendency toward dissociation was nurtured by childhood events and thus became habitual. The end result is that she has developed at least one minor personality to do the tedious stuff she can't be bothered with. Meter-minder spends most of its life unconscious, but it registers every flicker of the needle and guides her fingers, becoming daily more expert in its own tiny domain. The other people she works with barely know of its existence, but if the needle ever goes out of range it springs into consciousness in an instant. Anyone watching Lucy at such a time would see her dreamy, vacant expression and relaxed stance replaced by a sharp-eyed, quick-acting, highly focused technician who—in contrast to the other Lucys—is absolutely wedded to its job.

The dissociative spectrum

The best way to view dissociation, then, is as a spectrum. At one end there is the everyday, entirely normal neglect of background distractions. Then there are states such as daydreaming and fantasy. The teenager who doesn't hear the call to dinner because he is concentrating on a computer game, the filmgoer who weeps at a sentimental ending, the child who doesn't hear the teacher because she is lost in a daydream . . . these people are all dissociating. Far from being unhealthy, though, they are in some ways engaging more fully and completely in the world than if a single integrated personality was obliged to be present at all times.

Edging along the spectrum there is adaptive dissociation—an abnormal state such as physical or emotional distancing or numbness that occurs in frightening or otherwise traumatic situations. Similar states can be deliberately induced by various types of ritual and drugs.

NORMAL	ADAPTIVE	DISORDERED
Absorption/daydreaming	Detachment in traumatic situations	Chronic detachment
Trance/OBE		Compartmentalization

Beyond here on the spectrum, dissociation becomes pathological. This is the realm of the dissociative disorders, which include MPD. This book is not about these conditions, but there is a thin and moving line between adaptive dissociation—a healthy and useful trick of the brain that gives us mental flexibility and maintains a degree of separation between our personalities—and the disorders. There is therefore a danger of sliding from one to the other.

Dissociative disorders can be divided into two categories: chronic detachment and compartmentalization. Chronic detachment is a state in which even in normal circumstances a person feels distanced from or has some strange perception of either themselves or the rest of the world. When they are detached from themselves it is known as depersonalization, and when the detachment is from the rest of the world it is called derealization.

Depersonalization is often described by those who have experienced it as feeling like a puppet or a robot. "The first time it happened was when I was walking home after visiting my mother in hospital," reports Cherie. "She was really poorly that day and I think I had finally realized that she was going to die. As I turned into our road I realized I couldn't feel my feet touching the ground. It was as though I faded out somewhere around the knees.

"And I had this odd sensation—I have had it in dreams but never before while I was awake—that I was watching myself from outside. I met some neighbors as I got to my door, and when I spoke to them it seemed as though my voice was coming from somewhere to the side of me."

If Cherie's odd sense of detachment had limited itself to the period around her mother's death it would merely have signaled adaptive dissociation kicking in to protect her from the full impact of her loss. The trouble is that Cherie has gone on feeling distanced from herself, sometimes for days at a time, even though it is now years since her mother's death and her life is objectively secure and pleasant. Dissociation has become a sort of default mode—a habit so deeply ingrained that she is no longer able to snap back into the here and now or reactivate her normal sense of self. She has slipped beyond the crucial point on the dissociative spectrum where detachment ceases to be a survival mechanism and becomes dysfunctional.

"I feel as though I'm living behind a sort of screen, watching the world move by, but not really part of it," she says. "I can't engage with people on the other side—it seems sometimes as though they are mouthing things at me and I can work out what they are, but they don't mean anything. And sometimes I am not sure whether things really happened or not. It is like living in a waking nightmare, except that I can't even feel the fear. If I'm in a situation where I know I ought to feel something, I sort of work out what it should be and then act out feeling it. But inside I feel nothing."

Derealization is different from depersonalization in that people usually feel fairly normal in themselves but perceives the outside world as distant or crushingly close, or in some other way distorted and weird. Geoffrey, for instance, started to experience derealization during his final few months at university, when he was working through the night on a cocktail of caffeine, amphetamines and internally generated adrenaline. It culminated in an alarming experience during one of his final exams:

> I looked up and suddenly felt the ceiling was on top of me. Then the room expanded again, and all the people in it seemed tiny, like little ants toiling away over their desks. I felt enormous, though. I looked down at my hand with the pen in it, and it seemed to swell until I thought it would just take over the room. I must have made a noise or looked funny, because the invigilator [proctor] stood up and started walking toward me. That kind of snapped me out of it. I tried not to look at the other people and just kept writing. When I looked up next the people had gone back to normal size, but the feeling of unreality hung about for several hours.

Like depersonalization, isolated episodes of derealization—especially when they have an obvious cause like Geoffrey's preexam drug regime— do not signify a disorder; it is when derealization becomes *habitual* that there is room for concern.

Compartmentalization is generally regarded as more extreme than detachment, and it also produces different symptoms. This is the term used to describe the complete separation of personalities seen in MPD, and also the kind of amnesia where people "forget" entirely who they are. Hysterical blindness and paralysis—now called conversion disorders— are also a form of compartmentalization. So are the flashback memories seen in post-traumatic stress disorders. What all these states have in common is that particular bags of memories are completely cut off from all the other memories, so when they are triggered, they are experienced in isolation.

Abnormal dissociation—the danger signs

- Deliberately picking up a book or turning on the TV when an unpleasant but necessary task needs doing.
- Constantly imagining a future scenario instead of living the present.
- Suddenly "coming to" and realizing you have not heard what someone has been saying because you have been daydreaming.
- Forgetting important appointments because you have been too absorbed in something else.
- Acting out daydreams (e.g., speaking fantasy dialogue aloud) in public.
- Finding yourself somewhere with no idea how you got there.
- Finding things among your belongings that you don't recognize.
- Seeing yourself as though from the outside.
- Failing to recognize friends and family who should be familiar.
- Feeling that the world around, or people or objects in it, are not real.
- Feeling that your body does not belong to you.
- Hearing voices that give you instructions or comment on your actions.

Extreme dissociation is generally rather disturbing when it happens unbidden—it is the sort of experience that can make people feel they are going mad. Yet it can also be pleasurable or even ecstatic, and a vast recreational drug industry has grown up largely to provide dissociation on demand.

What seems to make the difference between pleasure and discomfort is the intention or assumptions that people have in mind when they dissociate. People who take drugs for reasons other than to get high (morphine, for example, for pain relief) often describe the psychological side effects as unpleasant, even though similar effects (that is, effects on brain function) are described by experienced drug users as euphoric. Similarly, the dreamlike effect of detachment may be pleasant if you are sleeping in on a Sunday morning and can allow yourself to drift along the top edge of a dream. If you have overslept, however, and find yourself unable to pull out of the dream despite being aware of the need to, the half-waking, half-dreaming state may be quite nightmarish.

The very pleasantness of dissociation in some situations is what sets many people off on the road to a dissociative disorder. The younger people are when they learn to dissociate, the more likely they are to develop a dissociative disorder in later life. Some people are naturally more inclined to get hooked on dissociation than others. These are probably the people who are genetically inclined toward it in the first place. Studies of twins who have been brought up apart show that they tend to be more alike in this respect than would be expected if their shared genes had nothing to do with it.[3]

Sliding into disorder

Very little research has been done on normal dissociation but what there is suggests that the vast majority of people are well within the normal part of the spectrum.[4] There is evidence, though, to suggest that there is a general shift, at least in some cultures, toward the end of the spectrum that ends in chronic detachment and compartmentalization.

It is impossible to get firm figures for dissociative disorders because milder cases tend to be categorized—if they come to the attention of doctors at all—simply as anxiety, stress or depression. Severe cases are frequently misdiagnosed as schizophrenia or some type of personality disorder.

However, one estimate—gleaned from several separate surveys—is that some thirty million people in the United States (7 million in the UK) regularly experience symptoms of depersonalization and derealization, and seven million in the United States (1.5 million UK) fulfill the diagnostic criteria for multiple personality disorder.[5] These figures are based on studies of the normal population. In other words, these are not people who are already considered mentally ill.

Dissociative symptoms and disorders are far more prevalent in the general population than previously recognized. According to Marlene Steinberg, associate professor of psychiatry at Massachusetts University Medical Center: "Research has shown that these symptoms are as common as those of depression and anxiety, but the person who is unfamiliar with them may not regard them as significant. If someone doesn't know that 'not feeling like a real person' or feeling 'apart from who I am' is a dissociative symptom that might indicate a problem, why would that person report it?"[6]

Professor Steven Gold, a former president of the International Society for the Study of Dissociation, thinks that depersonalization and derealization are now so common that they can be considered "a normative characteristic of modern life." Gold cites the best-selling novel (written by Chuck Palahniuk) and feature film *Fight Club* as an example of how the frantic, disjointed, dizzying nature of contemporary life promotes what Gold calls "normative" dissociation. *Fight Club* features an "everyman" character and the forceful and charismatic Tyler. At the start of the film the narrator describes in voice-over his experience of the frequent traveling that, as in the case of millions of others, has become a core part of his life: "You wake up at Seatac, SFO, LAX. You wake up at O'Hare, Dallas–Fort Worth. Pacific . . . Mountain . . . Central. Lose an hour, gain an hour. If you wake up at a different time in a different place, could you wake up as a different person?"

Which is, in fact, exactly what happens to the narrator. As we discover at the very end, he and Tyler are two different personalities sharing the same body.

If it was a real-life story, *Fight Club* would feature a clear case of MPD/DID. But as Gold points out, the plot device of multiplicity is not used here as it usually is, to illustrate some extreme of individual human experience. Rather it is meant to show what is happening, in a less dramatic way, to us all. "The central message of both the written and cinematic versions of *Fight Club* is that the structure of contemporary society promotes a dissociative mode of existence," he says. "In this sense dissociation is not an exotic diagnostic entity . . . [it] is a normative characteristic of modern life."[7]

You'd be forgiven for thinking that modern life must be pretty catastrophic if our brains are forced into emergency mode to cope with it. But this is to assume that dissociation is necessarily dysfunctional and/or unpleasant, which, as we've seen, it is not. The totally focused, "in the moment" state known as flow, for example, is associated with heightened performance and intense pleasure.

Perhaps, then, a dissociative mode of existence is simply a demonstration of our staggering ability to remodel our inner landscapes to fit the terrain in which we find ourselves. As Bob Dylan noted nearly half a century ago:

Then you better start swimmin'
Or you'll sink like a stone
For the times they are a-changin'*

---

*Dylan is a self-ascribed multiple; by his own description "a different person every day." *I'm Not There*, the 2007 biopic about his life, features six different actors, each playing a different Dylan. "The thing about Dylan that's so fascinating is that he has completely and utterly changed his identity time and time again," said movie producer Christine Vachon. "This movie is a play on that—I think it's kind of the only way to look at him."

73

CHAPTER 4

Changing Times, Changing Selves

The rise of the pick 'n' mix culture

Last night I caught up with a pile of newspapers and magazines I had put aside over the past couple of weeks to read when I had enough time. There is never enough time, of course, so I skim-read selected bits, threw out the rest, then turned on the TV to catch up with the latest news.

In that single brief dip into contemporary media I came across:

- A TV advertisement for a credit card featuring a vacationer who had lost her money in a foreign country where—we are led to imagine—she was seeking spiritual awakening rather than sun, sea and sand. In quick succession she alternated between shrieking with hysteria about her plight and then smiling serenely as she flipped between being a stressed-out Western tourist and a serenely fatalistic traveler.
- A magazine article about a Korean man who runs a hamburger stand by day and lords it over an elaborate fantasy kingdom in cyberspace by night. In cyberspace his twenty-seven million "subjects" are hunters, sorcerers, wizards, warriors and warlocks. In "earthworld" they are bankers, architects, clerks and shopkeepers.
- An interview with author Jonathan Safran Foer in which he spoke of

his nervousness about public speaking and how, as he puts it, "I just go away . . . dissociate until it's over."

- A review of a TV thriller about a CIA investigation into the disappearance of a "perfect wife and mother" who turns out to be living a second life as a hooker.
- A promotional item illustrating (again!) the "many faces" of the singer Madonna.
- A fashion piece entitled: "Virgin to Vamp in Twenty Seconds."

In addition there were at least a dozen other items touching on issues of identity, memory and personal transformation. These are current preoccupations; it is as though we have only just discovered our ability to shift and change, to be two or more "people" at the same time.

One reason for the burgeoning interest in personal metamorphosis is that until recently most people weren't allowed to do it. Lives were constrained by duty, custom, limited horizons and a culture that feared and suspected change. Suddenly we have found ourselves in a world where flexibility, adaptability and personal reinvention are not just acceptable but positively encouraged. We are also open to a much wider range of voices and influences. Compare, for example, a day in the life of a typical middle-class woman in Britain today with that of her mother at the same age.

Rose is one of the rapidly increasing number of people who works mainly from her own home. This does not mean she gets to relax. On a typical day she is up at six a.m. and by six-thirty she has dealt with a dozen or so overnight e-mails (and forwarded or deleted a dozen others), has checked online for news relevant to the industry in which she works and is flicking through the online editions of two daily newspapers and four trade newsletters. As she reads, the morning TV news show flickers in the corner of the room, and every so often she glances at the ticker-tape update running along the bottom of the screen to check she's not missing anything.

On one particular day Rose noted for me the number of distant interactions she had one way or another with other people. By the time she had dressed, grabbed some toast and gotten back to her computer, she had eighteen e-mails in addition to the overnights and her answering service had taken three calls. Seven hours later, when she packed up work for the day, she had communicated, by phone or e-mail, with eighty-three different people across three continents. She had also absorbed news reports, including thousands of live images, from all over the world. And this was all before her social life had even begun for the day.

Thirty-five years ago Rose's mother, Jeanette, almost certainly spent the day at home too. She was then about the same age as Rose is now, and photographs of her show that if you could cheat time and put them side by side they would look surprisingly similar, in their faded jeans and T-shirts, even if you discount the family resemblance.

Jeanette, however, was in many ways a very different being. She can say with some confidence that she spent that day at home because she spent nearly every day at home during that period. She had lived in the city for a while, then moved back to the small town where she was brought up in order to get help with her young children from her own mother, who had never moved away at all. Back home, she picked up many friendships dating back to her days at school, many of which are still intact today.

Jeanette was (and still is) a chatty and engaged person, but compared to Rose, she had limited social interactions. In the course of a typical day she would probably have talked face-to-face with her husband, her children, a couple of neighbors, her mother, a shopkeeper or tradesman and perhaps a visiting friend. She would have made and received a handful of telephone calls, all of them from people who lived within ten miles of her. Long-distance calls—especially abroad—were reserved for special occasions, rather as telegrams were for her mother. In the entire course of the day she might not have interacted with a single person who had been born in another country.

Until recently the relatively insulated existence lived by Rose's mother was common to most people in the Western world. It was not unusual for people to live in the same place, among the same neighbors, married to the same partner and doing the same job, for their entire adult life. Even those people who lived in cities kept mainly to a village-style community life within the metropolis.

Changing Times, Changing Selves

Such an existence in the developed world today is almost unthinkable. People who would once have followed their parents and possibly their grandparents into predictable family ruts now pursue their individual ambitions as a matter of course, not rebellion. Families are often scattered across the world and absorbed into cultures that they probably would not even have visited a generation ago. Jobs are hardly ever for life, and the notion of marriage for life has in some places become a slightly cultish lifestyle choice alongside an increasingly normal pattern of serial monogamy. If present trends continue, in twenty-five years' time, half the middle-aged people in the UK will be single, compared to less than 30 percent today.[1]

This new way of living presents each of us with a phenomenally wide array of viewpoints and ways of being. Newspapers, magazines, TV and radio carry an almost infinite range of opinions and beliefs. Interviews and documentaries probe the thoughts, feelings and activities of celebrities, and warts 'n' all biographies dissect the private lives of public figures. Reality programs—currently 60 percent of the entire global output of TV[2]—display the most intimate behavior of everyone from members of royal families to vacuous wannabes.

Much reality TV focuses on personal transformation, and change is seen as good *in itself.* The message is that whatever comes along, it must be better simply because it is new. The public platform no longer displays a normal or right way to be, but a help-yourself buffet of lifestyles to pick 'n' mix as you please.

At the same time our patterns of social interaction have changed enormously. For many of us, like Rose, it is an everyday event to talk to and swap opinions with dozens of different citizens of the world, each one of which is likely to come from a different culture, hold different political views and religious beliefs and engage in different family and sexual relationships. Wider but looser friendship networks have evolved thanks to the ease of communication made possible by e-mail, texting and low-cost international transport.

One effect of this is to make friendships seem intimate while actually making them more superficial. Courtesy titles, for instance, have largely been abandoned, so we are instantly on a first-name basis with every otherwise anonymous telephone salesperson. Not so long ago, to start calling people (other than a child) by their first name was an important milestone in the gradual development of a friendship, but now using a forename is more or less meaningless. It might not even be the person's name at all. In the course of a recent conversation with a woman who worked on a technical helpline I asked for her name so that I could call her—specifically—back. "I'm Jane," she said. And then: "Oh no, sorry, I mean Karen." She explained that the workers were not allowed to reveal their real names, but that each was given a name for the day, according to which work station they happened to be sitting at. So today she was Karen, while yesterday, when she was in the booth next door, she had been Jane.

How multiplicity can protect your health

Instant intimacy at first meeting—the sharing of personal information such as your salary or your religious beliefs—is now quite normal, whereas once such things would have been known only to your nearest and dearest. Many bloggers (online diarists) and newspaper columnists go much further and happily share the most intimate details of their lives—or seem to.

Over the last few months I have been reading, fascinated, a regular column written by a journalist with whom I happen to share some friends. Her writing would lead you to believe that she is revealing every tiny detail of her life: each spat with her partner, every bitchy thought about her mother-in-law, every episode of chaotic child-rearing. Nothing seems to be left out. She writes amusingly, and the picture that emerges is of a blessedly privileged woman whose worst miseries can easily be turned into entertainment. Yet I know that she is actually coping with an ongoing health problem in the family that is so severe you would expect it to entirely eclipse the day-to-day tribulations she writes about. She seems to be telling us everything, but the biggest thing of all in her life is never referred to.

It is easy to leap to the conclusion that this woman is putting on a mask when she writes, hiding her sadness and fear behind a false personality. Last time I met this woman, however, I asked her: wasn't it a strain, making out that the small irritations of her life are so central to her when they clearly aren't?

"Oh but they *are*," she replied. "When I write the column those things are my only concerns. That is why I do it, and love doing it. For a while each week I am a woman with nothing more to worry about than my husband using my silk knickers as a baby's bib. I'm not pretending to find it maddening. At the time it really is the biggest thing in my life because the other me, the one with real problems, just isn't there!"

Not so long ago such a response would be seen as evidence of "shallowness" or duplicity, but in this woman's case it just indicated her ability to switch in to a different mode—to *become* the frivolous, not-a-care-in-the-world columnist that her readers have come to expect.

It is tempting simply to bemoan all this and get sentimental about the days of fixed identities, enduring relationships, unchanging habits and constant values. But in doing that we forget that in many ways those days were, for many, cruelly restrictive.

Anyway, to look back to such times is simply pointless. Unless there is some catastrophic social upheaval on a global scale, it is unlikely that the pace of technological change and social expansion will slow down. If we are to swim in a disjointed and ever-changing world we need more than ever to pull on our ability to see things from multiple viewpoints and to adopt different behaviors in different situations. As we hurtle from one encounter to another, the "self" that we project has to be altered, if ever so slightly, for each one.

A trend toward multiplicity, like the shift toward greater dissociation suggested by Steven Gold, can be seen, then, as an adaptive response to a changing environment. The wider the range of experiences we are offered, the greater the number and variety of personalities a person is likely to develop. Far from being unhealthy, this is a natural consequence of the astonishing flexibility of the human brain.

Recognizing the many inner yous may even protect you from illness. A research project conducted by psychologist Patricia Linville, now of Duke University (previously Yale), suggests that the more of what she calls "personality tributaries" or "self-aspects" a person can identify, the better equipped he or she to weather stressful events.

Linville asked a hundred college students to select characteristics such as "outgoing," "lazy" and "affectionate" that they thought described themselves. She found that the more of these qualities that a student selected and the more distinctive the qualities were from one another, the less likely he or she was to suffer backaches, headaches, infections and menstrual cramps when under stress. The more complex students also reported fewer symptoms of depression.

Linville concluded that this was because a stressful event has less impact on a person who is aware of his multiplicity because it affects only one, or some, of the group. As she puts it: "a tennis player who has just lost an important match is likely to feel dejected, and these negative feelings are likely to become associated with this person's 'tennis-player' self-aspect. But it won't spill over and color the individual's other self-aspects if they are both numerous and distinct from one another. You have these uncontaminated areas of your life that act as buffers."[3]

Problem families

Useful though it potentially is, multiplicity does not always make our lives easier. Like any group of people who are bound together, our various personalities may not always work as a team. Sometimes they withhold information from one another, fight for control or refuse to step forward when needed.

Have you, for example, ever *really* wanted something, then thrown it away just as it is within your grasp? Or sabotaged a relationship for no reason you understand? Have you blurted out the thing that you least wanted someone to know, or exploded with anger at the very moment you most needed to stay calm? Can you recall flunking out of an important event you spent weeks preparing for, or turning over in bed and going back to sleep on a morning when it was vital you rose early? Do you ever, in the wee hours of the morning, *groan* with embarrassment at some stupid thing you have done?

Perhaps you never experience any of these things. But if this is true, you are unusual, to say the least. Practically all of us do and feel contrary things from time to time. Afterward we talk of "not being ourselves." We berate ourselves for our stupidity or self-destructiveness, or agonize over what's wrong with our lives. Should we divorce? Resign? Downsize? Change continents? Change sex?

To be in two or more "minds" about what to do is generally considered to be bad because it tends to produce the discomfort of uncertainty and inner conflict. Most of us therefore try to quash all but one of our personalities. Invariably it is the quieter, less assertive minors that are made to shut up, even when they might be speaking better sense than the major who vanquishes them. The problem, in other words, is not that we are multi-minded but that we refuse to acknowledge our multiplicity and so use it to advantage.

Feeling as if we are just one has its uses, as we'll see. Paradoxically, though, a strong conviction of unity can actually create inner conflict. A thought experiment might help to explain why.

The early riser and the alarm-clock saboteur

Imagine you are due to start a new job next morning, so you go to bed determined to get up bright and early. During the night, however, the personality who commanded "bright and early" is ousted by one who couldn't care less about work but really likes the comfort of his bed. When the alarm clock goes off at some unearthly hour this new "you" sensibly says "to hell with it," turns off the alarm, and goes right back to sleep.

Now imagine that during this lie-in, the old you is reinstated. When it wakes up and finds the alarm clock switched off and the new job already in jeopardy, it is of course very annoyed.

If the two personalities were completely separate—as in a person with MPD—the up-with-the-lark personality would just be baffled because it would have no memory of the earlier brief awakening. We are not talking about entirely separate personalities, but the sort that exist in most of us: different in many ways but able to peer into each other's memory bags and thus recall, at least vaguely, what they did and why they did it.

So the lark personality recalls the earlier awakening, the irritation with the alarm and the decision to go back to sleep. Indeed, it recalls it *as though it made that decision itself.* So rather than just be baffled by the earlier act, it is irritated about it. And because it does not realize it was done by a different personality, it is angry with *itself.* The shared memory gives it the illusion that it is responsible for its neighbor's behavior, which it perceives as a fault—a weakness—in itself. So it blames itself. Feels guilty. Thinks itself unreliable, flawed and "neurotic."

Meanwhile, of course, the alarm-clock saboteur has exercised its will and got clean away with it! The early riser takes the rap for both of them, so although it knows the consequences of its actions, the alarm-clock saboteur doesn't care. As this pattern repeats itself over years and decades, the alarm-clock saboteur becomes more and more irresponsible, while the early riser becomes guilt-ridden, undermined, increasingly convinced that it is bad. To others, the individual who comprises these personalities seems inconsistent, moody and unreliable.

Renegades

Minors that have thoughts, emotions and behavior that are directly at odds with a person's major grow so far apart that they cut off from it completely. This is especially likely when a person is under unusual external pressure. In some cases a perfectly normal person can experience the sort of memory blackouts that plague those with MPD.

An old friend of mine, Sara, recently told me about something she did when her daughter (now twelve) was a toddler. Sara has always seemed to me to be an exceptionally conscientious mother (which is probably why she never mentioned this until I spoke to her about this book), and in my experience she is about as steady and reliable as it is possible to be. Both the uncharacteristic nature of the act and her subsequent haziness of memory suggest it was done by a character very different from her major personality:

Changing Times, Changing Selves

Emma was going through that awful tantrummy stage and one day we were in a crowded store when she lay down on the floor and simply squalled. I think it happened because I wouldn't let her have a packet of crisps. Normally I would have tried to reason with her, or I'd have ignored her for a bit, or physically picked her up and taken her out of the shop. But this time I did none of those things. I walked out. Just left her there.

Looking back—which of course I have done endlessly—I honestly don't know what I was thinking when I did it. I remember looking at Emma kicking her legs on the floor and seeing her little face scrunched up with such fury. Then the next thing I remember is being in a shoe shop surrounded by sandals. I must have walked out of the supermarket, crossed the road, walked into the shoe shop and asked the assistant to get me the shoes. It must have taken ten minutes at least.

When I got back to the supermarket Emma was being walked up and down the aisles by a member of staff, looking for me. I made up some story about turning my back for a moment and losing her . . . said I had panicked and run outside to see if she had wandered off. I got away with it—no harm done. But it was a very frightening thing to happen—not for Emma, as it turned out, but for me.

Until she left Emma squalling, Sara didn't know that she—literally—had it in her to do such a thing. The personality that took her off to buy shoes was just not visible to the good mother who was usually so firmly in charge. It was only by looking back on what happened, viewing it as though from outside, that Sara realized she is not quite the wholly integrated person she imagined. In her attempt to be a perfect mother she had locked away the personality in her that—before Emma came along—had indulged a passion for fashionable clothes, fun outings and independence. Just for a moment, in that supermarket, it flared back into life, eclipsing the mother for just as long as it took to get Sara to the shoe shop.

Taking responsibility

One reason, perhaps, why people are reluctant to acknowledge human multiplicity is the fear that to do so would be to undermine the principle of personal responsibility. If everyone started blaming their less acceptable behavior on someone else, there would be chaos, so it is safer to hang on to the illusion of singularity. Indeed, our brains may even have evolved to generate the illusion because, in our socially interdependent species, it aided peaceful coexistence by forcing us to hold ourselves responsible for all our actions.

In fact the notion of personal responsibility is a frail one even without introducing the notion of multiplicity. This is why: responsibility is generally taken to mean *conscious* responsibility. I'm not likely to hold you responsible for treading on my toe if you are pushed onto it by the lurch of a train we are traveling on. And sleepwalkers who commit crimes without apparent conscious intention or knowledge are generally not held to be criminally responsible (providing they can persuade a court or other accuser that they really were asleep!). It is conscious intent that matters—the *decision* to do the act.

When you look closely at decisions, however, you find a funny thing. A decision to do something seems quite obviously to be made *before* the action is started. Indeed, it is difficult to see, at first, how it could possibly be any other way. But this apparent timing—the very thing that makes a decision a decision—turns out to be another illusion.

If you were to look at your brain activity in the second or so before you move your hand to do something—reaching for a cup, say—you would find that the bits of it that produce the action (the part that works out exactly which muscle fibers need to contract in order to carry it out and so on) become active before you decide to make the movement. By the time you think, I'll take a sip of coffee, your body is already prepared to reach for the mug.

In other words, it is not the conscious you—not *any* of them—who dictates the action. It is the dancing neurons in your brain, responding to cues of which the currently conscious personality may be entirely unaware. We know this because of a remarkable series of experiments carried out by the U.S. neuroscientist Benjamin Libet nearly a quarter of a century ago. What he did was to rig up volunteers with brain sensors and then, while monitoring the activity in their cortex, invite them to make a hand movement in their own time while noting very precisely when they decided to do it. Libet then compared three things: the time when the neural activity associated with the movement began; the time when the volunteers said they decided to move; and the time when their hands actually moved.

What he found—to his own surprise—was that the brain activity that would lead to the hand movement started more than a quarter of a second before the volunteers made the decision to move. And the actual movement occurred a fraction of a second after that. The brain, it seemed, was way ahead of the conscious self that thought it was controlling the event.

What feels like a decision, then, is really only the conscious recognition of a decision your brain has already made without any help from a conscious personality. The conscious thought seems to dictate the action because it occurs in the split second between your body being prepared for it and the muscle fibers actually contracting and carrying it out.

Given that we experience this thousands of times a day—we think of an action, then we see it happen—it is not surprising that we learn to feel as though we are controllers, rather than mere observers, of our behavior. The illusion of self-determination is such a good one that to all intents and purposes it really doesn't matter that it is illusory. We *feel* as though we are in control, we talk as though we are in control, and we assume everyone else is in control. The question of whether we really are seems pretty academic—a more current version of how many angels can dance on the head of a pin.

Intruders and gate-crashers

The question of responsibility becomes very difficult to ignore, however, when we consider multiplicity because it acts as the leading edge in what philosopher Daniel Dennett has called creeping exculpation. Increasingly people have denied responsibility for their acts by claiming it wasn't them who did it but—variously—their upbringing, their education, their genes, or their brain. Multiplicity could be seen as an encouragement to go one step further still—to claim they weren't even there at the time! Indeed, this has already happened. There have been several instances of killers claiming the deed was done by an alter, and in one case a person tried to get off on the basis that the personality who committed a crime was below the age of consent, even though the body the personalities inhabited was well past it.

Furthermore, as we discover more about precisely which bits of the brain produce which responses, it is going to get easier and easier to alter behavior and consciousness—in other words, to create and trigger different personalities—through drugs and surgery.

There is nothing new about this, of course. We have known for at least a century that changes to the brain, particularly to the frontal lobes, can produce quite dramatic alterations in a person's behavior. In the early twentieth century some doctors and psychiatrists tried to turn this observation to good use by altering the frontal lobes surgically. The idea was to improve the inner life (and behavior) of the hordes of mentally distressed people who were languishing miserably in asylums or failing to be helped by the only talking therapy then available, psychoanalysis. Tens of thousands of these people were thus given lobotomies—a procedure that involved inserting a small ice pick into the front of the brain and swishing it about to cut various connections.

Contrary to received wisdom, the personality changes wrought by this crude operation were a godsend to a large proportion of those who had them. But it was horrendously crude, based on only the vaguest understanding of frontal lobe function, and it was used too often, on the wrong people for the wrong reasons. The ensuing scandal that resulted from this was one reason why psychosurgery for mood and personality fell out of fashion and has since come to be widely regarded with fear and loathing.

A sophisticated form of lobotomy remains, though, a last-ditch option for the treatment of severe and otherwise intractable mood disorders. Its ability to silence one personality and create or revive another is clear in this account of the aftermath of one such operation.

British doctor Cathy Wield suffered eight years of horrendously severe depression. During that time she was plagued by a self-destructive personality that constantly urged her to self-harm. One week after the surgery a defiant, protective personality suddenly became active and successfully challenged the one that had been active for so long.

Cathy describes the moment her personalities first switched like this: "I was sitting in the TV room with a nurse beside me quite late in the evening. L., the patient who had shared the room with me before the operation, came in. She had returned from home leave and was clearly fed up. She slumped into a chair, saying, 'All I want is to be at home with my husband and children.' I was thinking, I wish she would just be quiet, when all of a sudden a light switched on in my head! It was as if a power cable had been connected and the generator had gone on: this tremendous sensation of light blazing through my innermost being happened in an instant. I was amazed, startled, almost bewildered. I started to cry, realizing that the darkness had gone, the depression was over! Now I was like her—all I wanted was to be at home with my husband and children."

At this point Cathy asked the nurse for permission to leave the room to assimilate things (she was under twenty-four-hour observation because of her habit of cutting herself). "As I left the room," she recalls, "I experienced a very clear internal voice. It did not seem to come from me at all. 'What about the self-harm?' I answered it defiantly: 'I do not want it anymore. I want to be at home with my family.' It left me alone. After three days it left, never to return again."[4]

Apart from its maligned reputation, another reason lobotomies became and remain very rare is because drugs have been developed that can do a similar job without the stomach-turning business of cutting flesh. Whereas the lobotomist's ice pick physically severed the "wires" that carried messages from one part of the brain to another, drugs work by altering the effect of neurotransmitters—chemicals that transmit messages from cell to cell and "instruct" brain areas to spark up or shut down. The effects of a drug, like those of the ice pick, are not entirely predictable, and sometimes they do nothing at all. When they work, though, they can they can produce a new personality as effectively as a lobotomy.

Millions of people have discovered this for themselves through the use of mood-altering drugs such as antidepressants. The drugs not only alter the way people feel but also seem to switch the bag of memories a person holds. If you ask people with depression to recall happy memories they will typically be hard-pressed to find any. Negative recollections, by contrast, come to mind only too easily.[5]

As you might expect, if the drugs are actually creating a switch in personality, the mood and memory changes are accompanied by a change, too, in the way people see the world. "It wasn't just that I felt happier when the antidepressants kicked in," recalls my friend Isobel. "I saw things differently. This really came home to me once when I was falling about with laughter at a film on TV and J [her husband] said: 'You didn't laugh once when we saw this in the cinema.' Only then I remembered that, yes, I had seen it before. And I hadn't found it funny at all. So who was this person clutching her ribs? I liked being her, but she felt like a stranger."

It is easy to understand why a drug-induced personality may seem like an interloper or even an alien. Most of our personalities have developed slowly, growing up within our environment like local flora and fauna. Their characteristics don't just spring up from nowhere—they have been molded, usually quite slowly, by repeated experience. Often we can see (or think we see) why we developed that particular response to that particular situation.

Personalities produced by direct physiological changes in the brain bypass this developmental process. The functional and anatomical changes that usually happen slowly are produced instead in a matter of days or weeks. Older personalities—if they are still active at all—may well feel the new one is not "one of them." So it is perhaps not surprising that our increasing awareness of multiplicity is producing more and more situations in which major personalities are refusing to take the rap for minors who fail to comply with group values.

The gate-crashing quality of some drug-induced personalities makes them an easy target for this sort of rejection, especially if the previous personality (or personalities) never asked to be relieved from duty in the first place.

At the time of this writing, U.S. lawyers are preparing to sue the producers of a type of drug used for Parkinson's disease. The suit is being brought on behalf of dozens of people who claim the medicine turned them into sex-mad and gambling-addicted obsessives. The drugs in question enhance the effect of a neurotransmitter called dopamine, the neurotransmitter depleted in Parkinson's patients. The chemical is responsible for keeping us moving steadily, which is why Parkinson's patients develop a jerky gait and sometimes come to a halt altogether. Dopamine also motivates us in a more general way, and when we are motivated, the direction we go in is to seek things that will give us a pleasurable kick. In some people, it seems, upping the effect of dopamine produces such a strong push for pleasure that they cannot walk away from situations that seem to promise kicks, even when people know these situations to be ultimately bad for them.

One woman litigant claims, for example, that after twenty-nine years of faithful marriage, starting the drug caused her to quit her religion and embark on a torrid extramarital love affair. Another woman became addicted to gambling. It started, she says, on a weekend visit to Las Vegas with her sister when she surprised herself by playing the tables in the casinos until dawn—and then went right back in next day. When she got home she began gambling over the Internet, and soon she had exhausted her credit cards, emptied her retirement accounts and sold jewelry to fuel her habit.

"I won huge amounts of money," she said. "I stood in front of a machine and won $62,000 and $28,000 in single spins." Yet, with one exception, she never walked out of a casino with money, because the gambler in her could never walk away. "You always put it back in," she says, "because no amount of money is enough."[6]

Although this woman's new, apparently drug-created personality clearly had a strong grip by now, her previous major was still active enough to make the occasional attempt to control it. First it put a filter on her computer to block the gambling websites, but the new personality responded by driving her to casinos. Her major then got her voluntarily banned from the casinos in her home state of Illinois, but the new minor started driving to play in Indiana. Now her major (presumably) is seeking compensation for being so rudely usurped.

Acknowledging we are not alone does not itself create responsibility where there was none. Once our personalities realize there are others sharing their mind, however, they can start to get to know one another, explore their strengths and weaknesses, discover what situations bring each of them to life, and allow each its moment in the sun. Majors can learn to give way on occasions to those who are more retiring, imaginative or patient. Fearful, pessimistic and distrustful personalities might learn to come out only when they are really useful. Overconscientious majors can agree to give ne'er-do-wells and shopping queens their rests and indulgences.

The sections of this book that show how to engage inner personalities in conversation with one another should also help these personalities to sort out their various responsibilities. But first let's look at where our personalities come from—the raw material, if you like, from which we construct the people we are.

CHAPTER 5

The People You Are

Every personality within us is unique because no two share an identical personal history. They tend, however, to fall into types: naughty or fearful or playful children, controllers and subordinates, censorious or protective adults, pacifists and troublemakers. As we have seen, the stuff from which they are constructed are experiences that click together, like building bricks, because they share some common (usually emotional) factor. I have already explained how they are linked together into the clusters forming our personalities. This chapter looks at the various ways that our brains select this raw material, and the different types of personalities that result.

Inner parents

Babies are natural mimics, and they are also both literally and metaphorically shortsighted. So the first building blocks of their personalities—the fragmentary responses I am calling micros—inevitably come from the people closest to them. Some of these responses may stick as isolated quirks, but others form the cornerstones of minors that may stick around for a lifetime, or the kernel of what may in time become the child's major.

"My granny had this odd expression that she came out with sometimes," remembers Maureen:

"Oo-er!" she'd go. "Oo-eeer!" I was only ten when she died, but I can remember her making this sound, just these two vowels. I suppose it made a particular impression on me because she only said it when something kind of frightening was happening, something she didn't understand. Even as a child I remember finding it irritating, because it conveyed the sort of childlike fear of the unknown that I thought was silly even then.

I had forgotten all about it until the other day, when I walked into my bedroom and saw my drawers had been tipped out and the things scattered. And what do I say? Not "**** it! I've been burgled!" No, I say—clearly as anything—"Oo-er!" I hadn't heard that sound for forty years and suddenly there it was—coming out of my own mouth!

Although Maureen's "Oo-er" might not seem to mean much, it carried a whole clutch of nervous, superstitious beliefs born of ignorance. This wisp of a personality lay dormant for decades, but given an appropriate trigger it emerged with all the strength and clarity it had when it was part of her grandmother.

Micros derived from our parents and other early caregivers inevitably creep into our repertoire of learned responses. But as children grow up they tend to seek out new ways of being and actively resist copying their parents. Indeed, by the teenage years the influence of a child's parents has been largely eclipsed by that of their peers.[1]

When children reject those bits of themselves which they have absorbed from their parents, though, it doesn't necessarily kill those traits off. Habits of mind that are picked up in the first few years of life often just go underground, like Maureen's "Oo-er." And although some may remain dormant for a person's entire lifetime, others may babble away constantly just beneath the level of consciousness. Such semi-buried minors may be useful sources of comfort, wisdom or creativity—our parents' most valuable legacy to us. But some seem intent on waging guerrilla warfare with the dominant major.

Eleanor, for example, hosts an almost continual skirmish between a part of her mother that she took in as a child and her own major. The first is a clutch of harsh and judgmental ideas with which her mother was inculcated during her constrained Scottish Presbyterian upbringing and which she in turn passed on to her daughter. Eleanor's major, on the other hand, was created largely during the 1970s, when she lived in an urban commune embracing a set of values almost entirely at odds with her mother's. She says:

I think of "me" as liking people who are unconventional and carefree. But when I actually meet people like that, I often find that even as I'm smiling at them and thinking how nice they are, little words or thoughts pop into my head, like "Wastrel!" or "Lazy!" or "Selfish!" For instance, several years ago my son brought home a girlfriend. This girl had a ring in her tummy button and a tattoo below it, disappearing into her jeans. When I saw this girl, a voice piped up in my head, saying, "Common tart!"

It really quite surprised me because I wasn't thinking that. I mean, I didn't THINK I was thinking that! I went over it in my head afterward—kind of replaying it. And I realized that not only were the words my mother's (she was always calling girls "tarts"), but I actually heard them in my mother's voice.

Parentally derived minors often come to the fore when people have children of their own. "My mum wrapped me up in cotton wool when I was little," says Suzanne:

She would keep me back from school if there was any sort of illness going round, and she wouldn't let me go horse-riding because she had once read about a girl who got dragged along the road with her foot caught in a stirrup. Once she stopped me going on a rock-climbing holiday with the school because she thought I'd fall off and break all my precious little bones.

After I left home she turned her worry on the world in general. She used to cut out stories of peculiar accidents from the newspapers—people who got struck by lightning or got their limbs bitten off by crocodiles. She'd show them to people when they came round to the house—it got really embarrassing.

I thought I had escaped all of that. I made a point of not being scared of danger. I took up hang-gliding and waterskiing and even tried drag-car racing, just to prove to myself that I could. But when I had Jamie, everything changed. Of course you expect to be changed by having a baby, but what I never expected was to be changed into my mum. I found myself reading about cot deaths all the time, and rare baby diseases. And when he started toddling, the whole planet seemed to be made of objects put there just to kill him.

One day a couple of years ago, my partner came home and found Jamie squalling with anger and me trying to explain to him that he couldn't go swimming because the pool was probably polluted. John [Suzanne's partner] was usually really tolerant about my obsessions, but for some reason on this occasion he went ballistic. That was when he pointed out that I was turning into my mother.

Another event that often jogs internalized parents into action is when a person's real parent dies. Immediately after the death of his father, neuroscientist Robert Sapolsky found himself spouting the older man's sayings, and taking on his mannerisms. "I found myself arranging the utensils as he had, or humming his favorite Yiddish tune," he recalls. "Soon I had forsaken my own blue flannel shirts and put on his. I developed an interest in his profession, architecture, absentmindedly drawing floor plans of my apartment."

About a month after his bereavement, the father inside Sapolsky "broke through" while he was lecturing to his students. He says:

I thought to tell them about what a spectacular lecturer my father had been, to pass on some of what I had learned from his teaching. I intended a eulogy, but something became confused, and soon, wearing his shirt, I was lecturing for him, offering the frail advice of an octogenarian.

I warned them to expect setbacks amid their ambitious plans, because every commitment would entail turning their backs on many others. I told them that though they wanted to change the world, they should prepare for the inconceivable—someday they would become tired. This was not me speaking, still with a sheltered optimism, but him with his weathered disappointments.[2]

Inner children

Young children, as we have seen, are natural multiples. The illusion of unity doesn't kick in until they learn to see themselves as though from the outside—in other words, to be self-reflective. Until then there is only the I of the here and now, quite unconnected with the I of yesterday or the I that will be around tomorrow. Hence the child generates countless I's—each one a distinct state of mind.

In late infancy children develop the ability to think in symbolic terms. This releases them from the here and now and allows them to imagine things existing in the past and the future. With that, children begin to join their multiple I's together. The toddler realizes that the I that chucked the pretty yellow paint on the pink carpet a minute ago is connected with the I that is now being sent quite unreasonably early to bed. The child may not yet feel a sense of responsibility for the experiment in interior decor, but he does remember it as though it was his own action. And with this, the notion of a continuing single self takes root.

Children get better at weaving together their I's as they get older, but the juvenile network of self is generally much patchier than that of adults. Most of the little I's that children generate just fade away, like wispy clouds in a summer sky. But some are too intensely experienced to disappear. If the experiences in which they are incorporated are also very different from anything the child has previously experienced, these small characters may not merge with others and will remain isolated from the rest of the previous and future I's and frozen in time.

Most of us do not have terrified child minors like those so often seen in MPD, and the existence of child minors certainly does not mean that a person was abused. But many of us have a nervous child or a shy child or a needy, jealous or insecure child. This is because the intense experiences that create unforgettable infant personalities are often highly charged with pain or shame or embarrassment.

When we experience these emotions as adults, the child that first experienced them may be shaken back into life, even if the particular experiences that brought it into being may be lost. Not for nothing do we speak of feeling small when we are humiliated or ashamed.

"Recently I was at a party, feeling like a wallflower," says Hazel:

I didn't know anyone there and no one was taking any notice of me, but I still felt very self-conscious. And suddenly I had this memory of being in the playground at my first school. All the other children were playing with each other and shrieking and laughing and I had no one to play with and I was sort of slinking along what seemed to be a massive redbrick wall and wanting it to kind of—absorb me, I suppose. I was trying to make myself disappear.

Just for a moment, at that party, I was that child. I mean, I really felt that small, and I found myself leaning against the wall of the room wanting it to swallow me up just like I did that day at school. Thankfully a friend came and rescued me and I sort of snapped back to being grown-up.

Another woman I interviewed for this book, Gail, also described the emergence of an angry and hurt child. In her case it appeared when she entered shops:

For years I loathed shopping because I always felt I was being watched with suspicion. I would constantly survey the other customers and wonder if they were store detectives. If I picked something up to take to the till I would hold it aloft in order to make it quite clear that I was not about to slip it into some concealed pocket. If I saw something else that I was interested in on my way to the pay desk, rather than lingering with the unpaid-for item in my hand, I would go and pay for it, then come back to the second thing. If I decided to buy that, too, I would have to make two separate transactions. All the time I was doing this absurd thing, I would feel angry. As though I was suspected of shoplifting and was feeling the fury of the false accusation.

The child responsible for this came to light when Gail saw a book jacket featuring a partly demolished sandcastle:

> Quite suddenly I was transported into a memory of a particular day at the beach. I must have been about two and a half or three. In my mind my mother is sitting in a deckchair, dozing, while I make a sandcastle. There is another little girl playing in much the same way just a few yards away. I see her putting a little flag in the top of her sandcastle. I want it. Badly.
>
> Now I know I can't just take it. I know that you have to have permission for that sort of thing. So I crawl up to my mother and ask her if I may have the little girl's flag. My mother doesn't respond at first, and I realize she has dropped off. So I pluck a bit at her skirt and ask again. And this time she stirs and says, "Mmmmmm . . . yes, dear." Or something like that. Certainly not "No."
>
> So, confident with parental approval, I crawl over to the other child's sandcastle and take the flag off the top. Next thing is that the child's mother is grabbing my hand and removing the flag, and then leaning in toward me and saying something with an ugly expression on her face. It is scary, so I open my mouth and scream.
>
> Somewhere in the midst of this my mother arrives, but instead of comforting me she picks me up and carries me away quite roughly. And then—to my astonishment—she gives me a slap on the leg. I don't remember feeling the slap, but I remember howling louder after it—not with pain but with outrage!

As she recalled this incident Gail realized the emotions she felt when she shopped were identical in quality (though obviously less intense) to those generated in her in that early situation. Her fear of store detectives belonged to the mistakenly accused three-year-old.

Child personalities are not always angry or scared. Qualities such as playfulness, curiosity, wonder, trustfulness, naïveté, creativity and sheer fun are quite often held by child minors because the adult self (or selves) did not incorporate them. This is most likely to occur in a person who is thrust suddenly into a grown-up world and feel obliged to "put away childish things."

Jim's childhood was abruptly ended at fifteen when his father died and he was forced to go out to work to earn money to help support his mother and four siblings. His wife, Ellen, believed that this early introduction to the responsibilities of adulthood prevented Jim from enjoying his own children. "He was a 'good' father, but distant," she says. "He never played games with [our son] or made model airplanes with him, or even took him to football matches. All that was left to me."

As a grandfather, though, Jim is entirely different. Because he does not feel responsible for his grandchildren in the way he did for his own children, they seem to release in him a child invisible for six decades. Unlike children that have merged with adult personalities, though, Jim's juvenile personality is *purely* childlike. "When our two grandchildren are here, Jim gives them a wonderful time," says Ellen. "But it is awful for me because I find myself dealing with *three* children. And however much I warn him not to overdo it physically (he is nearly seventy), he always does. So next day he is back to his dour old self and complaining about a stiff back!"

Roles and stereotypes

Mimicry and ultimately empathy depends on special brain cells called mirror neurons. These are cells that are activated both when we do something and when we see another person doing that same thing. If I see you, say, picking up a cup, my mirror neurons give me a faint cup-picking-up experience myself. I don't have to work out what you, the picker-upper, is experiencing because I have a shadowy but firsthand echo of it. I might not actually move my hand to grasp the handle, as you do, but the neurons that make the grasping muscles contract will prod me to just that. This is why people copy one another's body language so faithfully—you cross your legs and I, seeing it, get prompted by my mirror neurons to do the same even if I am not conscious of it.

At an unconscious level mirror neurons continually simmer away, bringing us in line with the behavior we see going on around us. Riding a commuter train, for example, most people tend to adopt typical commuter behavior, avoiding eye and—if possible—body contact with fellow commuters, moving determinedly through the concourse, rushed, distracted. For the duration of the journey a person becomes just that insular, single-minded commuter—a minor personality that comes out for this single daily activity.

Stereotypical minors like this exist in nearly all of us, created by the demands of a situation or the pressure of others' expectations. Certain jobs encourage their development. A nurse is expected to be efficient, kindly, calm, organized. A doctor is meant to be confident, all-knowing. A mother nurturing, a teenager rebellious, a gang leader aggressive.

Of course the stereotypical commuter, doctor, mother and so on does not get created in every person who travels to work, practices medicine or is a mother. Some people do not adopt these roles at all. The tendency to do so, though, is great because stereotypical behavior is often useful. A doctor who fails to create a professionally detached personality to deal with suffering patients may become emotionally overwhelmed or exhausted by her work. A gang leader who does not behave aggressively will not lead the gang for long.

Over and above the specific demands of day-to-day life, most societies also impose more general expectations. In some cultures, for instance, girls are still meant to be shy and submissive, while men are meant to be assertive. Individuals growing up in such a society almost inevitably develop personalities incorporating these characteristics. Frequently, though, these are minors shed as soon as societal pressure is lifted. Hence people brought up in two (or more) distinctly different cultures often have a different personality in each one. Such differences tend to be amplified in people who speak more than one language.

The Turkish writer and commentator Elif Shafak was brought up in what she describes as "a life of discontinuities," constantly moving from a fairly conservative culture in Turkey to a far more liberal world in England. She subsequently forged a career in Turkey, but then moved to the United States, where she discovered that switching back to writing in English brought out "voices that were already inside me." She sees this happen all the time in her multicultural friends: "In every language a person is different," she says. "It is not just the voice that changes—the whole mindset changes too. I know many girls who find they can't swear in Turkish, for example, because the culture prohibits it so strongly. But when they speak in English they have no inhibitions about it."[3]

Bilinguals have even been shown to have different profiles on standard personality tests, depending on which language they are speaking. Researchers at the University of Texas tested individuals who were bilingual in English and Spanish for various personality traits and found that the subjects answered the questions differently according to the language they took the tests in. In English they came out as more extroverted, agreeable and conscientious. Another study found that Chinese-American bilingual managers seemed more ambitious and egotistical when they were quizzed in English than when questioned in Chinese.[4]

The ease with which stereotypes can be created and subsequently activated by other people's expectations has been demonstrated in several intriguing studies. In one, researchers took a group of both black and white college students who had previously gained similar grades in school. The students were split into two groups, then asked to fill in a form that involved giving verbal answers to some tricky questions. At that time (and still to some extent today), there was a widespread notion that black people are less good at verbal reasoning than whites. Before the test the students in one of the two groups were subtly reminded of this prejudice by being asked to declare their racial origin before being informed, pointedly, that the quiz was a verbal reasoning test. The other group was simply told that they would be filling in an unimportant "research tool" with no hint that there was anything competitive about it. Under these circumstances the black students in the first group performed notably less well than the white students in their group. Those in the second group, however, did just as well as their fellow whites.

What seems to have happened is that in the context of a competitive word test, the forced reminder of their color triggered in the black students a minor personality that dutifully fulfilled what was expected of it. As Julius Caesar is said to have observed: "In the end it is impossible not to be what others think you are."

Similar effects of stereotyping have been found in several other groups. Some of the most telling experiments have involved Asian-American women. These people are subject to two contradictory stereotypes. One is that as Asians, they are good at numbers, but bad at anything involving use of the English language; two is that as women, they are good at verbal tasks but bad at numbers. One study found that when the women were subtly primed to think of themselves primarily as Asians, their performance on a math test improved while their performance on a verbal test became worse. When they were primed to think of themselves as primarily female, the opposite happened: their math performance declined while their language ability improved.

Other studies confirmed that the stereotypical minors triggered in the Asian women didn't just *behave* according to what was expected of them—they also felt more Asian or more female according to the situation. Asked to recall memories primarily about their ethnicity—a visit to the country from which their ancestors came, say, or participation in a ritual or celebration traditional to that country—they proved better at retrieving such memories when they were asked to do it after a math test rather than after a language test. They also rated the memories as happier. The opposite was true of their female identity. Memories of their first date, for example, came more quickly and were remembered more happily after the women did the language test.[5]

Another cunning experiment showed how women will produce a stereotypical weak personality when they were reminded of the perceived shortcomings of their sex. A group of female students were asked to put up with having their hands squeezed for as long as they could as a measure, they were told, of their self-control and tenacity. Half of them were warned, before the hand-grip test, that they would subsequently be taking part in a test of mathematical ability. This acted as a reminder that women are meant to be bad at math; the effect of it was to undermine the women's performance not just in the math test but in the hand-squeezing exercise, too. The women who had been told about the forthcoming test begged to be released significantly sooner than the women who had not had the warning. It seemed that the reminder of one anti-female prejudice (lousy at sums) jogged another (weak-handed and weak-willed) and hence brought out a stereotypically girlie personality in the women.[6]

Opposites, shadows and renegades

One effect of the extraordinary expansion of opportunities and challenges in the last twenty years or so is that more and more people are developing personalities that differ quite dramatically from one another. In some people two or more personalities may be so unalike that they effectively live separate lives, sometimes even under separate names. Each may dress differently, have different friends, interests and habits. One may binge and another starve; one may pursue a hermetic existence and the other a wild social life; one may be heterosexual and another gay. One or more may even appear to be the opposite sex to the others.

Take, for example, Grayson Perry, the English potter who won the prestigious Turner Prize in 2003. Perry collected his award wearing a frilly pink frock and a bow. Claire, the personality that came out for the occasion, coexists perfectly happily with Grayson the man, a devoted husband and father and proud possessor of a Harley-Davidson motorcycle.

Perry does not have MPD—he and Claire are well aware of one another and she only comes out when he wants her to. Indeed, Claire was quite consciously created by Perry's male major during his adolescence. "Claire is to be looked at and treasured because that's what I want," says Grayson. "That is why I dress up: to externalize my need for attention; almost like a child, to be doted upon. So I'm doted on, hopefully, while I'm Claire."[7]

Personalities like Grayson and Claire complement each other, but others may live in perpetual conflict. The most obvious examples are the increasing number of people who alternate between bingeing and being very self-restrictive in their consumption of food, drugs or alcohol. In 2001 some four million Americans were estimated to fulfill the diagnosis of binge-eating disorder.[8] Five years later the number had risen to nearly nine million—more than those with bulimia and anorexia nervosa combined.[9] Bingeing on alcohol and drugs, meanwhile, is rapidly becoming normal behavior among the young. A recent study of American college students found that nearly half of them admitted to bingeing on drugs and/or alcohol.[10]

Addicts and bingers may be held in check very successfully, but they are rarely vanquished altogether. One study on rats' brains (which, like those of students, have much in common with normal adults) showed very clearly how reward-related habits can flicker back to life after they seem to be extinguished.

Neuroscientists at the Massachusetts Institute of Technology used tiny electrodes to record the electrical activity in a part of the rats' brains where habits are known to be encoded. The animals then learned to associate certain sounds with a rewarding piece of chocolate—a classic bit of Pavlovian conditioning. As the rats learned, the researchers noted the electrical patterns in their brains. Then they played the sounds without the chocolate, repeating them until the rats took no notice of them. Later, long after the rats had given up on their chocolate habit, the researchers put the reward back and again played the sounds. Almost instantly the old pattern popped up again. As one of the researchers, Ann Graybiel, noted: "It's like all that time they spent trying to break the habit doesn't count."[11]

Addict personalities may emerge only in very particular situations. Juliana, for instance, has smoked for most of her adult life and was smoking when she met her current lover. Recently she gave up the habit and has successfully overcome it for several months. But when she is with her lover the desire to smoke returns. "It's only with him that it happens," she says. "I think the reason is that our smoking helped bring us together because we were the only two people at work who did it and at some level I think our relationship was to do with being 'the naughty ones' in the office. Now when he is smoking and I'm not, I feel a bit as though I'm aligning myself with the others."

At their simplest, addicts and their opposites, self-deniers, are just opposing drives—one composed of the urge to eat and the other of the desire to be slim; the urge to get pleasurably high and the urge to stay in control. But addicts can turn into complex personalities.

Ego-state therapist Marcia Degun-Mather reports a patient whose destructive eating binges were instigated by a child personality who was terrified of starvation. The patient, Mrs. Z, was aware of some "other" personality besides her major, but it was only under hypnosis that the child articulated what it was about. The personality confessed:

I am not really powerful, but Mrs. Z thinks I am. In fact I am more pathetic than she is. I won't let her have a life. I need her more than she needs me. I want to keep her helpless, it's best. I can fool her and manipulate her. She makes me feel powerful, and I don't want her to know that I am not brave enough to be on my own. I have to teach her a lesson when she tries to get rid of me, but I don't actually help her at all. I feed her things and she stays stuck, and I don't have to move. I am smug but not happy. I pull strings and make her do what she does— like bingeing. I am not her friend. I am just a manipulator and keep her scared.[12]

Encouraging troublesome personalities to explain themselves can be useful, and bringing them to consciousness can help to engage them in dialogue with their neighbors. Such conversations may need to be carried on over a long period however. The co-conscious Alexes I described in Chapter Two, for example, have been working for years on curbing the activities of a renegade personality in their otherwise exemplary household. About twice a year this particular Alex risks his life and the lives of the others, by driving at breakneck speed through the streets of London. There is a particular spot near his home where the road curves around a couple of gentle S-bends and then twists sharply around a blind corner. Alex can take the bends at 85 mph providing he brakes sharply at the oak tree just before the final turn. If he leaves the braking for another twenty yards, the car skids off the road. The night he discovered this fact was one of several he has spent in a police cell.

The officer who scooped Alex out of his wrecked vehicle and arrested him for drunken driving encountered a rude and obstreperous personality, but the officer who brought him a cup of tea next day met one who was polite and apologetic. As the drink wore off, the reckless, criminal Alex slid into the background, leaving one of the responsible members of this co-conscious household to clear up the mess.

"It's like we have this stupid teenage thug living with us," explains the estate agent Alex later. He goes on:

Most of the time he sleeps, but once in a while—if the rest of us are off our guard and there's drink about—he just takes over. Hijacking the car is his favorite thing. It's particularly terrifying because when he's driving the rest of us are in there with him—in the backseat, if you like—but are unable to control our body. It used to happen all the time, but in the last few years we've started to get control of him. After the rest of us have apologized and done whatever has to be done to minimize the damage, we force him out and confront him. We've made a deal: if you want to come out you can—but wait until after we drive home. Then you can put on your CDs and annoy the neighbors if you must, make a mess, do whatever you like, but no driving! It's starting to work—he hasn't got loose for over a year now. But we have to watch him the whole time.

Identikits and celebrities—personalities from pieces

While some personalities construct themselves out of desires or needs denied by the other inhabitants, others are deliberately put together to achieve something existing personalities may feel is missing from them-selves. A major, for example, will pluck little bits of behavior from its images of other people and then try to make them its own. If these bits do not fit easily with the major, however, they may form a separate personality.

So, for instance, we might take a particular way of walking from a film star, a certain tone of voice from a friend, a way of dressing from a peer group. In so doing, the personality who wants these attributes might succeed in changing itself, or it may create a new personality altogether.

Once we would have had to find our personality fragments from people in our own community or by embellishing in our heads the people we heard or read about in stories. But when photos and then movies came along, people started to cast their net wider.

The crazed celebrity culture that has developed in the last two decades has expanded the range and vastly multiplied the number of living icons to ape. We are surrounded by walking, talking, full-color and ever more revelatory images of a huge cast of characters who have become the primary reference point for people searching for a new personality. Why model a self on your mum or dad when you can make yourself into Johnny Depp or Nicole Kidman?

Although the gossip columns and fan magazines peddle endless "intimate" details about these people's lives, they are presented primarily as visual objects and those who seek to become them go first and foremost for the look. Two out of three women admit to spending money on deliberately copying some aspect of a celebrity's appearance—a hairstyle, way of dressing and so on—and many go much further.[13] A TV program called *I Want a Famous Face*, for example, helps people transform themselves into their idols through plastic surgery. In one episode, two twenty-year-old males from Arizona had nose jobs, chin implants and major dentistry designed to make them look like their idol, Brad Pitt. Following the surgery, Mike and Matt were ebullient about these changes. Other episodes of *I Want a Famous Face* allowed contestants to look more like their favorite stars: Kate Winslet, Pamela Anderson, Jennifer Lopez and Elvis Presley.

Copying another person's look is only the beginnging of what can become a profound *internal* transformation triggered by other people's responses to the new image. If people see a Kate Winslet look-alike in front of them, they are inclined to treat that person a little as they would treat the real Kate. As we have seen, other people's reactions to us trigger or create different personalities in us, so if people treat you like a film star, the wannabe film star personality in you will be fleshed out and encouraged to express itself.

Just seeing yourself in the mirror will begin the process. An acquaintance of mine who had a nose job found, when the swelling diminished, that it had lent her something of the look of a young Julie Christie. "I had never felt glamorous before," she told me. "In fact I had always thought of myself as ugly. But once I had seen that likeness I started to think of myself as a beauty, and it altered my behavior in ways that I hadn't expected. I started to wear clothes that drew attention to me rather than disguised me, and that in turn made people look at me, especially men. And I found I looked back instead of scuttling past. I started flirting, I suppose, for the first time in my life. So what started as taking a tiny bit of bone out of my nose ended up completely changing me."

You do not have to go under the knife, of course, to kick off the process that can end in the creation of a new personality. Simply altering your expression or hairstyle can have a profound effect on how you feel. Mimicking the external features of another person—physical features, walk, voice, gestures, expression—is recognized as a quick way to get the sense of being them. It is what actors call "getting into character," though it might be more accurate to say that the character gets into *them*. Those who are particularly good at it are known in the profession as "shape changers." In the film *Aviator,* for example, Leonardo DiCaprio adopted the walk and manner of the film's subject, Howard Hughes, so completely that his director, Martin Scorsese, said the crew would sometimes fail to recognize the actor as he walked on set. "He *was* Howard," said Scorsese. "Each time he came on, it gave us a jolt of surprise."

Similar stories are told of Dame Helen Mirren. When she was making the film in which she played Queen Elizabeth II, she started rehearsals "just being Helen in a wig," according to the film's writer, Peter Morgan. But a few days later "she suddenly became this rather squat, piggy woman with enormous presence. She would walk onto the set and you would find yourself stiffening slightly. You minded your Ps and Qs and started saying things like 'Goodness gracious.'"[14]

Some actors wear their roles externally, but others absorb them to the extent that the adopted character ousts the actors' other personalities, even beyond the duration of the performance. The British actor David Suchet, for example, had a long stage run in *Timon of Athens,* during which he found it increasingly difficult to flip back into his own major when the nightly performance ended. One evening a psychiatrist friend visited him backstage and observed that he seemed still to be acting like

Timon. Suchet dismissed his concern, at which point the psychiatrist shot at him a number of questions such as: ages of your children? phone number? date of birth? To his own consternation, Suchet found he had to work hard to retrieve the answers—the Timon personality he had created was so firmly in charge that his major's memories were temporarily irretrievable.[15]

It is not just actors who deliberately use powers of mimicry to create new personalities for specific purposes. This is how the trainer of a large sales force instructs his representatives to improve their pitch:

I get them to think of someone they really admire—someone they think projects confidence and success, someone they would like to be. It could be an actor, Brad Pitt or Pierce Brosnan, or a corporate head or a world leader—it doesn't matter who so long as it is someone they really admire. Then I tell them to go and get some video clips or a DVD of that person and watch it and watch it, and look for particular gestures, or a characteristic posture, or maybe some tone of voice that is absolutely distinctive. Then I tell them to mimic it. Get in front of a mirror and walk the walk or make the gesture. I tell them to keep right on doing it until if they just caught a glimpse of themselves in the mirror they could—anyone could—for a moment mistake them for the person they are imitating. Eventually it becomes second nature, and by imitation a little bit of that person will get into them, and make them feel better about themselves. Eventually they will forget it was ever NOT a part of them, and when that happens it will be a part of them.

Something as simple as mimicking the way a person speaks may be enough to produce a new minor in yourself. An English friend of mine says:

A few years ago my children started to talk in a way that I associate with Australians. Every sentence ended on an upswing, as though it was a question. At first I was irritated and told them it sounded affected. But my elder daughter said: "And YOU sound like you are giving orders all the time—it's like you're so sure of yourself no one dares answer back."

So when I was with them, or other people who spoke that way, I started mimicking them—deliberately making statements sound like questions. And I found when I did it that I became less domineering, less sure of myself and more open to others' viewpoints. Now if I hear myself getting into some sort of altercation with another person or sense that I am intimidating someone, I deliberately slip into "upswing" and suddenly I find I am hearing more of what the other person is saying. I become a more tolerant person.

Deliberate mimicry can also be used in psychotherapy. Therapists are well aware that some clients tend to dump negative personalities on other people, including the therapists themselves. And good therapists are alert to the converse—the danger of dumping on their clients. But some deliberately mimic the visible expressions of their clients' problems in order better to understand them.

"I first recognized the physical force of empathy as a college student, with the help of my friend Nancy, who was studying to be a physical therapist," says Babette Rothschild, a Los Angeles psychotherapist who has worked extensively with traumatized clients:

As we walked down a street together, she would follow total strangers and subtly mimic their walking style. Copying a stranger's gait, and feeling it in her own body, gave her practice in identifying where one of her patients might be stiff, or in locating the source of a limp. Intrigued by this mysterious way of "knowing" someone, I asked her to teach me to do it, too. What startled me was that not only did "walking in someone else's shoes" change the way I felt in my body, but it often altered my mood as well. When I copied the swaggering gait of a cocky young man, for example, I would momentarily feel more confident—even happier—than before.[16]

Virtual personalities

The personalities we make are strengthened by being acknowledged in the real world, so externalized minors that get to be read about or seen by the public tend to be more robust and enduring than those which are known only to their creators. Plus of course, there is much more incentive to create external minors if there is a chance that they will be seen and get to interact with others.

Until quite recently it was difficult to send your minor out into the world; to publish or act you needed to be exceptionally good, lucky or rich. But today anyone can put creations into the public domain via the Internet. Minors in cyberspace take many forms. Some of the most elaborate are packaged as avatars—cartoon or graphic symbols of their maker. Avatars come to life in online multiuser fantasy games, many of which are played by millions of people.

Some avatars are effectively replications of the creator's own major. "I change my avatar every couple of weeks so that it could represent more truly how I look and dress and what I do these days," says one multiuser game player. "My current avatar is indoors with a pile of book beside it. This represents me at the moment—I'm studying hard for the upcoming exams and I practically don't leave my room, just like my avatar." Others are deliberately designed to go and live a very different life from that lived the rest of the time by their inventor.

As cyberworld becomes more and more realistic and challenging, the avatars that work and play in it inevitably become more complex personalities. In doing so they often diverge quite sharply from the original intentions of their creators. One player describes how he was completely taken by surprise by his avatar's furious reaction to having its virtual homestead trespassed upon in a game that involves, among other things, territorial colonization: "At first I wonder why I (or my avatar) has such a visceral reaction to this perceived intrusion. Then a flush of parental pride washes over me: my avatar, which so far has acted much like me, hanging back from crowds and minding his punctuation in text chats, suddenly is taking on a life of his own. Who will my alter ego turn out to be? I don't know yet."[17]

You do not have to create an avatar, of course, to send a personality out into cyberspace. You can simply wander into a chat room or sign up on a networking or dating site. These intimate but distanced meeting places seem to serve as a rehearsal room for people who want to try out new personalities in relative safety. A massive survey of teenage girls, carried out by a U.S. government department as part of an attempt to assess the risks to children of online communication, found that practically all of them project an online personality that differs substantially from the one they would describe as their own.

"You can be absolutely *anyone* you want to be," explained one girl, "which is why a lot of people do things that they would not normally do. In real life, people everywhere judge you based on your looks, actions, and who knows what else, but online, all that really matters is your attitude and personality."

Not surprisingly, the relative anonymity of Internet communication leads people to be less restrained—the personality exercised online is likely to be more extroverted, flirtatious and provocative. "I am much more bold online than in real life," said one. And another: "I am *very* shy and I say things on the Internet that I normally wouldn't say in public."

Teenagers in particular use the Net explicitly to try out new personalities: "I changed myself to be someone I wasn't because I wanted to get a different reaction from people," said one girl. "It gave me a way to see myself as who I wanted to be. You pretend to be older or you pretend to be a guy or you just pretend to be whoever you wanna be." One of them summed it up: "We've *all* pretended to be older or to have a different name or something. Who doesn't? It's part of the fun about being online. You can be whoever you want to be for a little while."

These, then, are some of the psychological mechanisms that we use to manufacture the personalities who come to be part of our inner—and sometimes extended—families. The next section of this book describes how you can recognize your personalities and get to know who they are, where they come from and what triggers them into action. Like the

Alexes, you may discover characters in you that you do not approve of. You may also discover some that have strengths and virtues you never dreamed you had because the personalities who encompass them have been pushed so far off the stage. You may rediscover people you thought you had left behind decades ago, along with ones who come out only on rare occasions or with certain people. You can't be sure who you will find, but you can be sure that the encounters will be interesting—a little like meeting up with a whole crowd of people you once knew but have since lost touch with. Enjoy the party!

PART II

Introduction

This part of the book is made up of practical exercises supplemented with illustrative case histories. The first section will help you to get an overall view of the landscape of your mind: whether you are composed of many disparate minor personalities or a more integrated cluster— perhaps so integrated that they have become a single major. To make this easier I have devised a tool, the Personality Wheel, which allows you to chart your minors in graphic form, so you can see at a glance their main attributes and how they differ, complement or oppose one another.

For those of you who are reading this section first, do not assume that integrated is necessarily better than multiple. Multiplicity is an adaptive response—the brain's clever way of coping with a complex and rapidly changing world. Today, when practically all of us have to deal with a dizzying rate of cultural change and contradiction, those who have developed a multiple mindscape have an advantage over those who have a one-size-fits-all way of reacting to the world.

Multiplicity can, however, go too far. If your personalities are so separated that they no longer communicate (a state that manifests at its extreme as multiple personality/dissociative identity disorder), you will be unable to cope in the ordinary world, where at least some degree of continuity and consistency are essential.

The second set of exercises is designed to help you recognize your minors and find out who they are and what they are like. The Personality Wheel is one of several techniques that will help with this; others include visualization and forms of what might loosely be called psychodrama.

The final exercises are to help you to work with and on your minors—encouraging them to communicate together, to become active when they are needed and hold back when they are not, to strengthen the ones that are beneficial to you and curb those that threaten to get out of hand.

Before you start, a word of warning. These exercises are not intended for people who have, or have reason to think they have, multiple personality disorder/MPD (or, as it is more commonly known today, dissociative identity disorder/DID). Indeed, this section is unlikely to be helpful to anyone who has been pushed into the "disordered" range of the dissociation spectrum (see page 67). It could even be harmful.

The reason for this is that minors are not the same as the totally compartmentalized personalities, commonly known as alters, that exist in people with MPD/DID. Practically all of us have minors, but few have alters. Unlike the latter, minors are linked together in the memory web (page 52), like conjoined siblings rather than entirely separate beings. Hence they each know, hazily at least, of one another's existence and they are accessible to one another without resort to techniques such as hypnosis, which rely on inducing an abnormal (though not unhealthy) form of dissociation in order to work (see Chapter Three).

The exercises here therefore use ordinary introspection, imagination and observation to make minors more visible to one another and to promote greater understanding and cooperation between them. The idea is not to bring out anything that has hitherto been entirely buried, but to throw more light on minors currently lurking in the shadows.

These exercises should not, therefore, trigger any dramatic switches of personality of the sort seen in dramas and documentaries about people with MPD. Even if they are done by someone who unknowingly harbors an entirely compartmentalized personality, it is very unlikely that such an entity will suddenly leap out of the closet, quaking with terror or demanding revenge for childhood traumas.

That said, triggering alters, should they exist, is always a possibility when people are encouraged to probe their memory in the way that these exercises demand. Before embarking on them, therefore, please take time to answer the questions below. They refer to some of the more common signs of MPD. This is not a diagnostic test, but if you answer yes to any of them you should not continue with the exercises. You may like to turn instead to page 254, where I have listed some sources of information, support and professional help for people with dissociative disorders (including MPD).

- Do you have an entirely blank memory for certain periods or events in your life? For example, do you have no recollection of your teenage years, or do you sometimes find it hard to recall being on vacation, or on a course, even if it was within the last year?
- When you go from one place to another—from home to work, perhaps, or from the street into a store—do you have a hard time recalling where you were immediately before?
- Do people ever accuse you of saying things, just a moment earlier, which you could swear you did not say?
- Do they mention things you have done recently that you can't remember?
- Do you ever find yourself a day behind, or look at the clock and see that hours have passed and you have no idea what you were doing during them?
- Do people you don't recognize regularly come up to you and claim to know you?
- Do you own things you don't remember buying?

Preparation

Most of the exercises depend on your ability to place yourself into another state of mind—to create, if you like, a virtual reality and then put yourself in it and report back. For them to work properly you need to get yourself into a relaxed, neutral frame of mind so that you can roam your memory and exercise your imagination.

Do not attempt to do them, therefore, when you are very caught up in another project, or when you are particularly excited about something or in a particularly intense mood—depression or elation or irritation, say.

Such states lock you into a particular personality and make it difficult to see others. If you are very sad, for example, you will find it very difficult to reconstitute your happier minors (see pages 48–51 on state-dependent memory).

Most of these exercises can be done with a friend or friends or a partner. There are benefits to doing them this way because companions may point out personalities you were not aware of and may be able to help you with identifying situations that bring certain minors out.

There are potential drawbacks to the communal approach, though, which you should bear in mind. One is that even those who are closest to you are unlikely to know all your minors. Other people are the most powerful situations we encounter, and you may find that just being with a particular person makes it impossible for you to access certain personalities. You may even find that you get stuck in a particular minor so long as you are with them. Furthermore, it may be socially or emotionally risky for another person to see all the minors within you, and the minors themselves might not want to be seen by certain people! Ideally, then, you need to do the exercises with *and* without other people, and with different people at different times.

Some personalities like well-defined, clear-cut tasks, while others favor an intuitive, "feely" method of exploration. The exercises here allow for both approaches. The Personality Wheel, for instance, relies primarily on you remembering how you behave in certain roles. If you can also reconstitute your feelings and thoughts in the role—*become* the personality you are considering rather than just observe it—it will be a huge bonus, but the exercise can be done relatively objectively. Other exercises, however, depend on your getting right into the personality you are working with. Some use visualization and will therefore come more easily to those who are able to conjure up vivid images in their mind's eye.

It is likely that some of your personalities are good at some of the exercises and others good at others—but to find and activate the right personality for each exercise requires first that you *do* the exercises, so there is an element of trial and error here. On the other hand, situations bring out the minors best suited to them, so you might find that the image-maker in you naturally comes out when you get to the visualization task and so on. This is great, except that it means that you might find a different minor is doing each exercise, with the result that you get seemingly conflicting results. The image-maker in you, for instance, may have a clearer (and kinder) view of the sensual or artistic minors in the family, whereas the character who does the Personality Wheel may be closer to the one who likes to keep things cut and dried and logical. Recognizing these biases makes it all very complicated, but this is all part and parcel of getting to know your selves.

However you do the exercises, alone or in company, in the order they are presented or in one of your own choosing, keep an ongoing record. This can be a written or visual journal using painting or drawing, or a combination of both. If you are more of a verbal person, then perhaps a pocket tape recorder would be a better tool. Some people supplement their journal or scrapbook with pictures or objects they find that seem to symbolize your personalities. This can be very useful as a "touchstone" to take you into that personality on cue. Keep your Personality Wheel too, because you will almost certainly find that you can add to it as you become more familiar with your selves. You might find it useful to redraw it at regular intervals, to see how you are changing. You may find, for instance, that some of your minors are merging with your major as you get a better working relationship with them, or that troublesome minors are shrinking.

The following general pointers may help you to get the best out of the exercises:

- Find time. It is important not to rush work requiring introspection and self-analysis. You need time to prepare and, afterward, to reflect on what you have done. Setting aside time on weekends or vacation may work well, or you might like to set aside an hour for it at the beginning or end of the day. If necessary, schedule it in your diary to ensure you will not be interrupted.
- Create a peaceful atmosphere. Turn off your computer and cell phone and set the answering machine to pick up your calls silently. At the end of the exercise, do not rush back into your routine; take some time to reflect on what has happened.

- Stay with the process. Do not expect instant revelations. You may need several sessions before you have even named your personalities, let alone explored them. This kind of introspection may not come easily to you, but the more you practice, the better you will get at it. As well as providing specific insights, the exercises should also equip you with a whole new way of seeing people—a sort of lens through which people's behavior, including your own, will in future look quite different. Such a change of perspective is very unlikely to happen overnight.

- Stay open. People are complicated. No two are the same. Indeed, no two *personalities* are the same, let alone any two people. As far as possible I have tried to present questions in checklists, but don't necessarily expect checklist results. You will have to work at this to get anything out of it. Sorry. That's just the way it is.

CHAPTER 6

How Multiple Are You?

Like dissociation (Chapter Three), to which it is closely allied, multiplicity can be seen as a spectrum. At one end lie people whose inner landscape is completely smooth and continuous—every part of it attached to every other part. At the other end there are those whose personal geography is ragged and discontinuous. The following exercise is designed to find out where you lie on it. That is, it will help determine the *degree of separation* between your personalities, not the number you have or what they are like. These you will discover later.

Most of us lie somewhere in the middle of the multiplicity spectrum. We may not manifest entirely different characters with their own names, ages and histories, but our moods fluctuate, our desires alter and our behavior varies. We might refer to our "reckless side" or "obsessive streak" or the "food addict" in us. At work we may make major decisions with ease, then on the way home find ourselves dithering over what to have for dinner. A man may be a devoted husband and father at home, and a faithless womanizer when he is away on business. A woman may be a compliant, exploited daughter and a domineering, bitchy wife.

It is possible to complete this questionnaire on your own, but the result will probably be better if you do it with the help of someone who knows you. Ideally your helper will be someone who has seen you in many different situations over a long period of time, rather than someone who knows you very well in one sphere of your life only.

The reason for this is that if you don't have an external observer to check with, the personality active at the time you complete the questionnaire may discount or neglect the feelings and behavior of your other personalities and answer just for itself. Normal multiplicity does not involve complete ignorance of our other personalities, but it does mean that whichever personality is active at any particular time gives more weight to its own concerns and has better access to its own memories than to its neighbors'.

If you do answer the questions on your own, try to do it as a detached outsider looking back at your own thoughts and behavior over a period rather than as an insider monitoring your current state of mind.

Take your time. Unlike most personality tests, which instruct you to give a quick answer without thinking about it too much, you will get a better result from this if you give careful consideration to each of your answers. Some of the questions also lend themselves to being checked objectively. Before answering question 2, for example, try to find some examples of your handwriting—things written at different times and for different purposes. Compare the handwriting in a shopping list, say, with that in a recipe you once took down or on an application form. Look at the appointments written in your calendar and see how they differ in appearance according to when and under what circumstances you entered them. Before answering the question about nicknames, run through your friends' emails to you and see how they address you. Go and look at your clothes before answering question 14.

Where are you on the spectrum?

Score 0 for "never," 1 for "sometimes," and 2 for "absolutely, all the time."

1 Do you find your mental skills, including memory for facts, vary from time to time for no obvious reason (e.g., not connected with tiredness or drinking)? For example, are you aware that sometimes you can romp through a crossword puzzle while at other times, given a similar puzzle, you cannot get a single clue? ☐

How Multiple Are You?

2 Does your handwriting change noticeably at different times? ☐

3 Do you ever refer to yourself as "we"? ☐

4 Do your personal memories sometimes feel like a film you have seen, rather than something that actually happened to you? ☐

5 Are you called by a number of different names or nicknames, and/or do you think of yourself by different names? ☐

6 Are you ever gripped with enthusiasm for a while by a hobby or pastime (DIY, exercise, gardening) that you find utterly boring at other times? ☐

7 Do you ever find yourself uttering the phrase "What on earth made me do that [or words to that effect]?" ☐

8 Do you talk to yourself? ☐

9 Do you have "binges"—of food, cigarettes or alcohol? ☐

10 Is your behavior chamelion-like—e.g., do you find yourself adopting the accent or intonation of the person you are talking to or putting on a "telephone voice"? ☐

11 Do you swing suddenly from one mood to another for no apparent reason? ☐

12 Do certain circumstances trigger skills or knowledge not usually available to you? For example, in a foreign country do you find yourself speaking the language better than you thought possible? ☐

13 Do your tastes—in food, music, films, literature—differ widely from time to time? ☐

14 When you look in your wardrobe do you see clothes that you cannot imagine wearing and wonder why you bought them? ☐

15 Do vague acquaintances treat you as though they know you far better than you would expect? ☐

16 Do friends and acquaintances refer to events they claim to have shared with you which you cannot recall? ☐

17 Do people you would regard as trustworthy claim you have told them things which you cannot believe you would have said? ☐

18 If you come across something you wrote a while ago—an unposted letter from you to a friend, perhaps, or an old diary or notebook—do you sometimes fail to realize at first that the author is you? ☐

19 Do you find yourself laughing or crying, to your own surprise, for no reason you can think of? ☐

20 Does your level of self-esteem/self-love go up and down regardless of others' expressed opinion of you? ☐

Now add up your total score. ☐

Scoring

Basically, the lower your score, the nearer you are towards the singlet end of the spectrum. Most people score between 10 and 30. A very low score (less than 8) can mean one of two things: either you are exceptionally unified or the personality who completed this questionnaire is unable to see the others and is answering just for itself.

To distinguish between these two, come back to these questions at another time—ideally when you are in a different place, doing a different thing, with different people and at a different time of day. If your score is similar and your answers to each question are more or less the same, it is likely that you really are fairly unitary. If the score is different, it suggests that you have at least one more personality than you might at first think.

A high score (over 30) puts you well up toward the multiple end. There is nothing wrong with this in itself—it can even be advantageous.

But if you are disturbed by any of the things you have scored 1 or 2 on—laughing or crying unpredictably, say, or things that seem like memory glitches (failing to remember events your friends claim to have shared with you)—you may like to recheck yourself on the MPD-marker questions (page 117) and also read the section on dissociative disorders (pages 71–3).

The Personality Wheel

The very nature of multiplicity makes it difficult simply to look inside yourself and see who is there. Whichever personality is doing the looking—the one that is the I of the moment—may have only a hazy view of the others, depending on how dominant it is or how alien the situation is to the others. However, as we saw in Chapter Two, background personalities can be ushered to the fore by inviting them into their own frame of reference, as psychologists call it. For this exercise the frames we are going to employ are roles—sets of behaviors clearly linked to the demands of particular situations.

Personalities grow into their roles like Jell-O taking the shape of a mold. You begin with one personality *behaving* in a way that fits a particular situation and go through a period of playing that part. Sometimes the role is so alien to your existing personalities that you abandon it. A person with a strongly pessimistic major may find it difficult to act like a Pollyanna-style optimist, for instance. Or it might be a role that you need to play for a short time only. In these cases the act might remain just an act and soon be forgotten. But if you repeat a piece of role-playing enough, you end up *learning* the part. As we have seen (Chapter Three), learning involves a physical change to the neural structure of the brain, and once those changes have consolidated, it is difficult to reverse them. In learning a role, then, you effectively create a new personality—one that is semi-detached from the one that originally acted it out. Thereafter, when you slip into that way of behaving, you are no longer acting—you *are* the role.

So although roles and personalities are not, strictly speaking, one and the same, by imagining yourself in a role (i.e., getting into the frame) you can often activate the personality that has come to inhabit it. That essentially is what this exercise is about. It depends on recalling or even activating the minor who plays a particular role by imagining yourself in the situation that usually prompts it to come out.

To start, you need to spend a little time in advance relaxing and trying to attain a fairly neutral state of mind—one allowing you to range freely in thought and memory. If you are unable to activate the minor—get "into it"—don't worry. This exercise can be done from the outside, so to speak, provided you can recall enough details of the behavior the target minor displays when it is active. This is where other people can be useful—reminding you of things you do or have done in the role. You can also jog your own memory by, for example, looking at photographs of you taken when you were in that role. If one of your minors is a character you have dubbed "off-duty," say, it might be helpful to browse through the vacation pictures. If one is "mother," get out the pictures taken of you with the children. Identifying clothes that you wear in the target role may also serve as a useful reminder. You might even put them on to make the effect more powerful. If you are trying to pin down a minor that comes out only when you are with a particular friend or friends, try phoning them and having a chat immediately before you do the exercise. If you have a minor noted for sentimentality, turn on your favorite weepie movie and watch half of it. If you have an angry minor, recall or seek out something that really, really gets you going.

Once you have a clear view of the minor you will be invited to rate it on a trait-type personality test, similar to the Big Five, or OCEAN, model discussed in Chapter Two.

If you have already read Part I you will remember that the Big Five are character dimensions: open-mindedness, conscientiousness, extroversion, agreeableness and neuroticism, each with an implied opposite: close-mindedness, carelessness, introversion, disagreeableness and emotional stability. Psychologists arrived at these dimensions by analyzing all the words that describe personality—some eighteen thousand of them. They found that almost every one of them could be considered to fit somewhere in the spectrum of the five big descriptors. Words such as "chattiness," "outgoing," "fun-loving" and "gregarious," for example, were all indications of extroversion that would place a person toward one end of that dimension, while words like "shyness," "retreating" and "bashful" would locate them at the other end.

If you gather together all the information on a personality, therefore, you can place it somewhere on just these five dimensions and be confident that very little is left out. Economical though the end description may be, you still have to find some way of deciding *where* a personality lies on each dimension and to do that you really need to do a lot of questioning.

To get over this psychologists have come up with what they call mini-markers for each of the dimensions. These are sets of a hundred or even just forty words on which a personality can be rated and which give results very nearly as good as an hours-long assessment session.

I have used a similar—though simplified—system to arrive at a graphic way of describing minors. The spokes on the Personality Wheel represent character dimensions similar to the Big Five and should therefore allow practically all the characteristics of a personality to be mapped onto them. To decide where the personality lies on each dimension I have given a set of mini-markers, each of which requires a simple yes/no answer.

To begin work with the Personality Wheel, you first need to identify some roles you play in life in which you know you have a distinct set of behaviors. Most of us have at least two fairly clearly defined roles in life—for example, mother/worker; son/employee; businessperson/neighbor. It is easy to identify these roles because they have publicly visible markers. The mother role, for example, applies when the person is actually dealing with her children in some way or acting on their behalf. The businessperson role is marked by being at a place of work or traveling to work, and of course by actually working. It might be marked also by wearing particular clothes (a suit rather than a sweater and jeans, perhaps).

The roles adopted by a person need not be stereotypes. Your "worker" may be a very different character from my "worker," and neither might be the stereotype of how a worker should be. Nor does the personality bound into a role necessarily pop up as soon as you step into the situation associated with it. For instance, a woman may have a distinct "mother" personality that usually fills the public mother role. On a weekday, however, she may already have become "worker" or "commuter" by breakfast time. So although she may still carry out actions associated with the public "mother" role (giving children food, getting them ready for school), her personality is out of synch with the external situation. Instead of coming out in response to the events that are happening in the outside world, her role is triggered by the woman's interpretation of the situation; others may see it as a domestic scene, but she sees it as "preparation for work." Hence in imagining yourself "in the frame," you need to ensure that you are stepping into the *right* frame—in this case the "mother" frame rather than the "commuter" frame.

At this stage the idea is not to examine the personalities as individuals. Rather it is to survey the general layout of your inner landscape, especially the extent to which your personalities overlap or are separated. The entire exercise will take at least an hour to complete, but you can split it into parts and do each one at a different time. In some ways this may be better than doing it all in one session. As with the previous questionnaire, you can do it alone, but you will get a better result if you do it as well with another person or even a group of friends. You will need at least three different colored pens or pencils.

The dimensions on which you will be rating each personality are similar to the Big Five (see Chapter Two), but whereas Big Five personality tests are designed to produce a single, coherent character reading, the Personality Wheel detects and amplifies the inconsistencies that reveal our different personalities.

To start, identify the major roles that you regularly play in life. For example, if you have children, you will have a "mother" or "father" personality; if you work outside the home, you will have a "worker"; and if you play an active part in the community, you may have a role as, say, "charity fund-raiser" or "drama club secretary" or "board member." If you are a keen sportsperson or a serious hobbyist, that might be a "mountaineer" or "poker player." You will probably find that you have at least two such roles, although you may have half a dozen or so. For the purposes of this exercise you are probably best to limit it to the main two or three or perhaps four.

You may also be aware of roles without standard labels that are nevertheless clearly delineated in your own mind. You may have noticed, for instance, that you behave and feel in a specific way when you are on vacation, or when you are with one particular set of friends rather than another or with neighbors rather than coworkers. Give names to these roles—such as "townie," "off-duty," "shopper"—and include them in your list.

Try to place the roles in the order that they are most commonly on stage. So if you spend more time being "mother" than, say, being "student" or "painter," think of "mother" as role number one. Next, look at the lists of qualities on page 132. As you will see, each eight-term list comes under a general heading. These include four of the "Big Five" discussed in Chapter Two—openness, conscientiousness, extroversion and agreeableness—plus their opposites: conservativeness, carelessness, introversion and disagreeableness. There is also a dimension which I have called "uptight" and "laid-back," which is similar to neuroticism on the Big Five, with its attendant opposite: stability. The qualities listed under each of these headings are aspects of the more general term. Under extroversion, for example, the characteristics include talkative, assertive and cheerful. An extremely extroverted personality would probably exhibit all of these qualities, but a moderately extroverted personality might just be positive for, say, five of them.

Now concentrate on one of your chosen roles. Think back to when you were last in it and try to remember as much as you can about how you felt and thought and behaved at that time. You will probably find it helpful to recall specific events or incidents and then try to pin down what was in your head at that time. Let's say you have nominated a role you have called "rebel," which is a personality that constantly seems to be breaking the rules or challenging figures of authority. Think back to the last time rebel was actually in action—an altercation with a senior colleague, say, or an incident in which you broke a rule in a demonstrable way. Close your eyes and visualize the scene, then try to remember exactly which words you said or what thoughts went through your mind and how you felt emotionally.

If you can't get inside the role it does not mean that the personality is in some way unreal. Make a note of your difficulty, however, and if possible, repeat this exercise on that personality when you are next aware of its emerging, or when you come across something that jogs your memory of it.

Once you have a clear sense of yourself as the personality that you are charting, look at each eight-term group and check off the qualities you feel to be true of you in that state. Only check off the ones that you certainly feel or display—leave blank any that you are unsure about.

Ideally, in scoring each personality you should ask the opinion of someone who knows you well in that role. Your partner, for example, might know you extremely well in a domestic situation but have absolutely no clue what you are like at work. If you can't or don't want to canvass others' opinion, try to do the scoring for each role *while you are in that role*. And if you can't do that, then try hard to score it objectively.

If you want to do this exercise thoroughly, the way to improve your results is to take each characteristic and put it into the form of a specific question relating to a real event. If you are trying to determine how you should score "dutiful" in the worker role, ask yourself: "Did I finish the report I was working on before I left the office today, or did I put it aside when X came in and suggested I knock off and go for a drink?" Apart from giving you an objective benchmark against which to score, recalling specific situations in which you were in a role will help to make that personality more active.

Don't worry if you do not have any characteristics in an entire eight-term set—it is practically impossible to have a high score in two opposite sets because they are opposing characteristics! And don't be concerned if you have no check marks in a set and none in its opposite either. Minor personalities by definition are not wholly rounded characters, so they are quite likely to score 0 on at least one dimension and its converse.

There may be no reason to expect the "neighbor" to have any place on the conservative/open-minded dimension, say, or for the "painter" to rate on "agreeable/disagreeable." Some minors, indeed, are so narrow that they may score on only one or two dimensions.

When you have completed the scores for Role 1, count up the check marks in each box and record them in the score chart on page 133. Now take a colored pen and turn to the Personality Wheel on page 134. Look at how many check marks you made in, say, the Extrovert box, then find the "spoke" marked "extrovert" on the wheel. Put a mark on the spoke according to how many check marks you have. For example, if you have one check mark, place the mark between the innermost and the circle marked two. If you have three, mark it between circles two and four. If you have no check marks, mark on the innermost circle. Move on to the next section and do the same thing until each spoke has a mark on it. Then join up the dots to make a shape.

You may break the exercise here and come back to repeat it with each of the other roles at another time. Make sure that you use a different colored pen or pencil to mark up the wheel for each personality.

Keep your completed Personality Wheel. The personalities distinguished in it so far are only those associated with your main public roles, so the picture may not be anything like complete. Later, as you learn more about minor personalities, you may discover some in yourself that are not linked to specific roles. By adding these to the wheel, as you find them, you will gradually build up a complete picture of your inner family.

Before completing this exercise you might like to look at the example that follows on page 134.

OPEN-MINDED	EXTROVERT	STABLE	AGREEABLE	CONSCIENTIOUS
Creative	Talkative	Even-tempered	Warm	Organized
Questioning	Bold (socially)	Satisfied/content	Kind	Efficient
Artistic interests	Energetic	Relaxed	Cooperative	Methodical
Emotionally open	Gregarious	Optimistic	Trusting	Dutiful
Adventurous	Assertive	Self-accepting	Friendly	Tenacious
Liberal	Thrill-seeking	Tolerant	Open	Dependable
Romantic	Cheerful	Laid-back	Forgiving	Hardworking
Playful	Enthusiastic	Self-sufficient	Teamworker	Responsible

CONSERVATIVE	INTROVERT	UPTIGHT	DISAGREEABLE	CARELESS
Uncreative	Shy	Moody	Unsympathetic	Disorganized
Dogmatic	Quiet	Jealous	Rude	Sloppy
Cautious	Bashful	Envious	Stubborn	Inefficient
Habit-driven	Withdrawn	Touchy	Critical	Reckless
Routine-bound	Reserved	Anxious	Quarrelsome	Immature
Unromantic	Polite	Angry	Distant	Extravagant
Unquestioning	Timid	Depressed	Distrustful	Rebellious
Conventional	Reclusive	Self-obsessed	Obstructive	Exhibitionist

Score chart

Name

	Role 1	Role 2	Role 3	Role 4
Open-minded				
Conservative				
Extrovert				
Introvert				
Stable				
Uptight				
Agreeable				
Disagreeable				
Conscientious				
Careless				

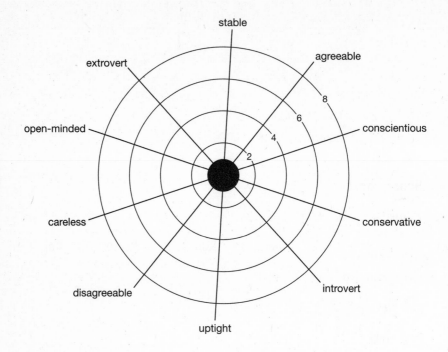

The Personality Wheel

Example

Stephanie is a twenty-eight-year-old nurse-turned-flight attendant. She left nursing because she wanted to travel widely and enjoy a more exciting life than nursing seemed to offer. Most of the time she is very competent at her job, diligent and hardworking. Her work is extremely important to her, and therefore Stephanie selects "flight attendant" as her number-one role.

Stephanie's parents had a rocky marriage to start with, and as a child she often worried that they would split up. However, the marriage got stronger, and by the time Stephanie left college they acted as though they were and always had been a devoted couple. When her mother died two years ago her father was bereft. Stephanie is an only child and now feels obliged to spend more time with her father than she would ordinarily choose. She finds this boring, but works hard to be consistently cheerful and affectionate. Given the time she spends caring for him, Stephanie's second role is "daughter."

The only time Stephanie really lets herself go is when she is on a stopover in a foreign city. Given the chance, and with a like-minded colleague, she will seek out the wildest nightclub in town and dance the night away, fueled by whatever mood-manipulating substances are on offer. A couple of times she has failed to report back for duty, and once she was disciplined for turning up for a flight still drunk. Stephanie privately refers to these occasions as her "away days." She chooses this title for her third role.

Her scorecard therefore might look like this:

OPEN-MINDED	Flight attendant	Daughter	Away day
Creative			
Questioning			▪
Artistic interests			
Emotionally open			▪
Adventurous			▪
Liberal	▪		▪
Romantic			
Playful	▪		▪
Total	2	0	5

CONSERVATIVE	Flight attendant	Daughter	Away day
Uncreative		▪	
Dogmatic			
Cautious		▪	
Habit driven		▪	
Routine bound		▪	
Unromantic		▪	
Unquestioning	▪	▪	
Conventional			
Total	1	6	0

EXTROVERT	Flight attendant	Daughter	Away day
Talkative		■	■
Bold (socially)	■		■
Energetic	■	■	■
Gregarious	■		■
Assertive	■		■
Thrill-seeking			■
Cheerful	■	■	■
Enthusiastic	■	■	■
Total	6	4	8

INTROVERT	Flight attendant	Daughter	Away day
Shy			
Quiet			
Bashful			
Withdrawn			
Reserved			
Polite	■		
Timid			
Reclusive			
Total	1	0	0

STABLE	Flight attendant	Daughter	Away day
Even-tempered	■	■	
Satisfied/Content	■		
Relaxed	■	■	
Optimistic		■	
Self-accepting	■		
Tolerant	■	■	
Laid-back	■	■	
Self-sufficient			■
Total	6	5	1

UPTIGHT	Flight attendant	Daughter	Away day
Moody			
Jealous			
Envious			
Touchy			■
Anxious	■		
Angry			■
Depressed			
Self-obsessed			
Total	1	0	2

How Multiple Are You?

AGREEABLE	Flight attendant	Daughter	Away day
Warm			▦
Kind	▦	▦	▦
Cooperative	▦		
Trusting	▦	▦	
Friendly	▦		▦
Open			▦
Forgiving	▦	▦	▦
Teamworker	▦	▦	
Total	6	4	5

DISAGREEABLE	Flight attendant	Daughter	Away day
Unsympathetic			▦
Rude			
Stubborn			▦
Critical			▦
Quarrelsome			▦
Distant			▦
Distrustful			▦
Obstructive			▦
Total	0	0	7

CONSCIENTIOUS	Flight attendant	Daughter	Away day
Organized	▦	▦	
Efficient	▦	▦	
Methodical	▦	▦	
Dutiful	▦		
Tenacious		▦	
Dependable	▦	▦	
Hardworking	▦	▦	
Responsible	▦	▦	
Total	7	8	0

CARELESS	Flight attendant	Daughter	Away day
Disorganized			▦
Sloppy			▦
Inefficient			▦
Reckless			▦
Immature			▦
Extravagant			▦
Rebellious			▦
Exhibitionist			▦
Total	0	0	8

Her Personality Wheel would therefore look like this:

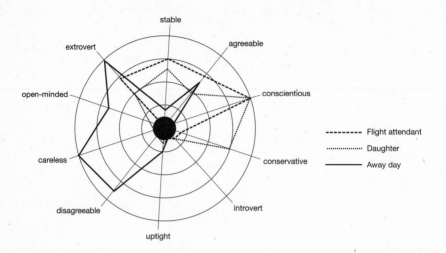

Reading the Personality Wheel

To start, look at your completed Personality Wheel as a whole. Do your personalities overlap or are they separated from each other? Is the general outline spiky or solid? Do they cluster in half of the circle, or spread to both? In other words, what is the bird's-eye view of your mental landscape—a solid continent, a jagged coastline, or a scattering of loosely connected islands? Although no two mental landscapes are ever identical, there are basic types of formations, just as there are types of personalities. Look at the Personality Wheels below and see which most closely resembles your own, then read the matching description of each type on the following pages.

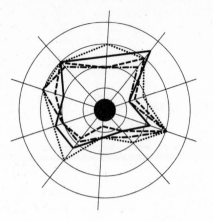

Single Major

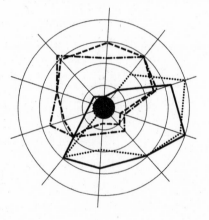

Double Major

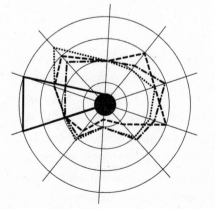

Major–Minor

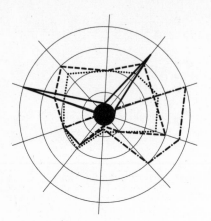

Major–Minors

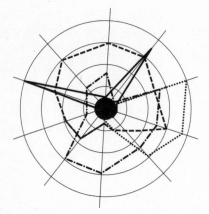

Multiple Minors

Single Major

If your personality outlines closely overlap one another you may be one of the rare people who effectively have just the one, entirely integrated personality—a Single Major. This is what we are all meant to be—a whole, integrated personality, with every bit closely connected to every other bit. No loose bits, no conflicts, no inconsistencies. The characteristics that identify Single Majors are always apparent, so if one of his or her traits is impatience, a Single Major will be impatient whether he or she is peeling potatoes or running a multinational corporation.

Single Majors tend to be reliable—even if they are reliably unstable! But overall they tend to be inflexible and unadaptable. If Single Majors are thrown into a situation calling for a response not within their repertoire—anger or aggression, perhaps—they either flounder or are forced to invent a new personality on the spot to deal with whatever is happening.

This is easy for children; they are making themselves up as they go along anyway. But as people get older their ability to create a new response from scratch diminishes. Meanwhile little-used minor personalities, created in earlier days but never trotted out enough to become active members of the family, tend to fade away. People who live fairly stable, unchanging lives therefore tend toward a Single Major formation, especially as they get older.

Sarah

Sarah was born into a comfortably off and loving family. She had one sister, four years younger, whom she adored from birth. One of her first memories was being called mother's little helper: "I remember positively glowing with pride," she says. "Looking back, this was in the mid-sixties and that term was used then— ironically—to refer to the tranquilizers all the housewives were getting addicted to. Even then I must have been a soothing influence."

After graduating from university in the 1970s, Sarah took a civil service job in the Department of Education. She rose steadily through the ranks, without making waves, and had a solid career in government bureaucracy. Then Sarah married a local businessman and fairly quickly gave birth to two sons. After the birth of the second she resigned and dedicated herself to her home and family.

For all her efforts, however, Sarah's home life did not run smoothly. Her husband went bankrupt, they lost their house and Sarah took a modest job in a local office to support the family. During the subsequent inquiry into her husband's business dealings he was accused of financial impropriety and had to defend himself in a complex civil lawsuit that lasted eight months. Throughout this time Sarah supported him stoically, turning up to the hearing with him each day, comforting him each night, shielding the children from the effects and turning their now-modest home into a refuge. Then one of her husband's creditors—a former family friend—informed Sarah that her husband had been having an affair for the past five years.

"I thought of leaving him. Yes, of course. Everyone said I should. It wasn't even as though the children would have suffered, because by then J—— was no sort of father to them, he was too busy trying to get himself out of trouble. But I didn't."

However, Sarah's constancy wasn't appreciated by her husband, and a couple of years later he left her.

"I suppose I should have been angry, yes," she says now. "But mainly I was relieved. Friends of mine tried to persuade me to get revenge. But I found I couldn't do it. We are still friends, actually. He has broken up with his girlfriend and I think he would like us to get back together. But I am happy now on my own. The children are both away at university and it is time for me to start a new life. I am thinking of becoming a landscape gardener."

Five Signs of a Single Major

- Friends who go back a long way and all know (and generally like) one another.
- Established habits, such as always going on holiday to the same place, loyalty to product brands, always reading the same sort of book.
- Long-standing relationships—for example, lifelong marriage, lengthy business partnerships, close family ties.
- Consistent physical appearance—people rarely say, "Oh! I didn't recognize you!"
- Coherent and unchanging views/attitudes. For example, likely to vote for the same political party every election.

The False Single Major

In some cases a Single Major formation may simply mean that your minor personalities play no part in your main roles. Your major personality deals with all the situations you encounter on a regular basis—work, home, social life. The minors may be triggered only in quite exceptional situations.

The fact that minors do not get triggered in any of your main roles suggests that they are cut off from the personality reading this book. It may be that they are redundant personalities—younger yous that have outlived their purpose and are now quietly expiring in a mental backroom. There is absolutely no point in reawakening one of these entities if it really has no use. You may well have an angry, terrified or uptight person somewhere in you, whose only possible contribution to your life is to cause havoc. So long as these entities are completely inactive they are best, like sleeping dogs, left to lie.

However, if a hidden personality is causing trouble, by waking up occasionally and intruding disturbing thoughts and emotions, it is worth finding out who it is and what it is about.

So if you have a Single Major formation, be alert for moments when you find yourself acting or thinking or feeling in a way not reflected by the shape on the wheel. If possible, make a note of the way you are feeling and acting in these moments, and describe the situation that provoked it.

Remember the situation you see may not be quite what it seems to outsiders. For example, you might find that you go uncharacteristically quiet at some social events and become extremely talkative at others, even when the events seem very similar. If you can't immediately see what is special about the event at which you display uncharacteristic behavior, think about what is happening. Are you unusually tired, so that you see this party as a social duty while normally you would see it as a treat? Are you feeling cool toward your partner because of some disagreement between you that occurred before you came out? And is this now coloring your perception of the people at the party? In which case, did the other personality actually take over in that earlier situation and is now simply refusing to give way to the partygoer in you?

After a while you may find a link between a particular situation and the emergence of behavior or thoughts or feelings that do not fit in with the shape you have drawn for the major roles. You will have made contact with a minor personality who might need some attention.

Double Major

Major–Majors are balanced people. Balanced, that is, between two (often entirely opposing) personalities. It is always a precarious balance because if one personality gets the better of the other, it will grow while the other will shrink, and the person will turn into the more common Major–Minor. So Major–Majors stay that way only in the—quite rare—case that the two different people they are get equal time out.

This is most likely to occur in people who are equally invested in their home and work life, each of which requires an entirely different set of talents and responses. Unlike Multiple Minors, the different personalities in a Double Major are weighty and distinct, so they tend not to switch chaotically but only in the particular situation where each is called for. When a major is active it is not easily ousted by the other (in the way that Andrew's clubber is pushed aside by the police officer; see Major–Minor below), so the person is generally stable and reliable, switching only when the situation (work to home, say) changes.

Clare/Clareta

Clare is known as two quite different women to two entirely different sets of people. They are even known by different names. If the two groups ever mixed, this could be a problem, and one of Clare's personalities would have to take charge. As it is, it is easy for Clare to maintain the separation because one group of friends lives in Suffolk and the other is in Peru. Even if there was no geographical divide, however, it is unlikely that Clare would invite Clareta's friends to mix with hers, or vice versa. They wouldn't get along.

One person who does see the two of them, though, is Angela, Clare's younger sister. It is through her that I came to know about Clareta. The two girls were born in Lima to English parents who were members of the diplomatic community there. They spoke English at home and their early education was at an English school. But all their fun times were spent with local Spanish-speaking staff and their children.

"All our English speaking was done either at school or at family meals. Both of them were pretty formal and boring. It was difficult to make friends at the school because we all got whipped back home in chauffeur-driven cars after lessons, and there wasn't much chance to get to know the other children. And meals at home were excruciating. My parents didn't like children much, I don't think. So the people we really relaxed with and the children we played with were local—Spanish speakers, all of them."

Clare and Angela's parents retired when Clare was sixteen and Angela was thirteen. The family moved back to England and the girls were sent to a local private school. "It was a frosty old place, but I quite liked it," says Angela. "Clare hated it, though. I didn't take that much notice—we weren't very close then—but I think she became anorexic for a bit. She certainly got very thin. She was always terrifically well-behaved and spoke in this formal way like something out of a Victorian novel. I just thought of her as some weird relative—Little Miss Goody Two-shoes. Nothing to do with me, really.

"I went a bit mad when I was sixteen, seventeen. I got in with a bad crowd and had trouble with the law and drugs. Clare happened to be back in Peru—my parents had kept a little house there for holidays and we treated it like a second home. So the parents sent me off there to get me away from bad influences. And I think they hoped Clare would straighten me out.

"But when I got there Clare was someone else altogether. She was hanging out with these local lads, drinking, smoking, doing drugs and sleeping around. It was a much wilder scene than I'd been into. And I realized that this was what she did whenever she was out there. The uptight Victorian miss got left in the departure lounge at Heathrow.

"There's no point in talking to her about this because I really don't think she recognizes the change that comes over her. I've often tried to find Clareta—that's what she calls herself in Peru—in Clare, but she makes out she doesn't know what I'm talking about."

Five Signs of a Double Major

- Two distinct sets of friends who do not mix.
- Commitment to two roles demanding different qualities—e.g., child-rearing and a taxing career.
- Rarely talks about the life s/he leads outside the one s/he is currently in—e.g., talks work at work, domestic matters at home.
- Two very different types of clothes—e.g., a woman may have a collection of stern business suits and a number of girlie frocks, but little in between.
- (If in a committed relationship) A long-time mistress or lover in addition to the partner.

Major–Minor

Major–Minors often appear to be Single Majors: predictable and consistent. Every so often, however, when the behavior is triggered by a particular situation they become someone else altogether. The behavior of their minor may be entirely inconsequential—a hobby or interest that simply gives the major personality a rest. Or it may be an intensely emotional personality created out of desires, urges and beliefs rejected by the major personality, either because they clash with the rest of its beliefs and attitudes or because the major is locked into a role preventing it from exercising this particular personality.

Although a minor may be very different from the major, it doesn't necessarily give any trouble. Indeed, a minor may exist explicitly to give the major personality a time-out. This works particularly well if the two personalities have completely separate external domains—home and work, say—so they need never compete. If they are forced to meet on common ground, though, there may be a conflict. In such a situation the minor invariably gives way to the major.

Andrew

Andrew is a policeman—an extremely dedicated and good policeman, not least because he has never wanted to be anything else. If asked, he laughingly attributes this vocation to a fascination with TV cop shows in his childhood (and he is probably right).

"I was right on target for this job—I got in just when there was a push to get more ethnic faces on show in the Force, and I'm half Jamaican. They wanted to keep me on the beat, but I wanted to do CI [criminal investigation] work, so I went for promotion early and got put to steer a desk. It's not like it was in [1970s British television police drama] *The Sweeney* anymore—you have to follow procedures now, and I suppose that goes against the grain sometimes. When you've spent the best part of a month nailing some villain and then they walk free on account of some technicality, you need something to take your mind off it."

The process is simple. Andrew gets home to his comfortable flat, takes off his working suit and puts on casual wear. The change of clothes releases the new personality: Andrew is a clubber. There is nothing immediately obvious about the transformation. He remains law-abiding, avoids the drugs that circulate freely at most of the venues and always takes a cab home if he drinks. But this Andrew happily turns a blind eye to the activities of others. He avoids noticing certain people he knows to be drug dealers, even a couple that his policeman personality has in the past pursued. If he sees a drunk getting in a car, he ignores it. If he sees a fight, he walks on by.

"It was a girlfriend I had who brought it home to me that I'm a different person when I'm out. I was with her in the street and we passed this bloke who was pushing this girl up against the wall and threatening her. I didn't see it. I mean I didn't *see* it! I can only tell you what happened because she made me stop and intervene. 'You've got to,' she kept saying. 'That's what you're for!' And I realized she was right."

When the girfriend forced Andrew's attention to the incident that the clubber did not see, the policeman in him—the major personality—was brought back to consciousness and took over from the minor. The effect was to reduce the clubber a little— nowadays a situation in which a clear breach of law is taking place is likely to call out the cop in Andrew, a change that he reluctantly admits might be for the better.

Five Signs of a Major–Minor

- Their partners recognize there is a part of them that can't be shared or is out of bounds.
- Poor memory for certain events.
- Occasional acts that are out of character.
- Ability to give up quite deeply ingrained habits for short periods— e.g., stopping drinking for Lent.
- A small collection of clothes entirely different from the rest.

Major–Minors

Major–Minors are probably the most common type of characterscape: the sort of people who have a well-recognizable major personality, but also a number of others that come out in different circumstances. (Major–Minors differ from the Major–Minor in that they have several minors rather than just one.) Provided the personalities complement one another, this is rather a good formation: stable enough to allow the person to sustain long-term plans and relationships, but flexible enough to adapt to change.

Jonathan

Jonathan started his working life as a builder's apprentice and worked his way up to establish his own small construction company. Even Martha, his wife, jokes that Jonathan's first love is his company. That may or may not be true, but his business is certainly what sociologists would describe as Jonathan's defining role. It is how most of the rest of the world sees him—as a straight-arrow, hands-on contractor, a man who plays fair financially, who gets jobs done on time, and who consequently is rarely without customers.

But while Jonathan is dedicated to his business, he is also a good, if frequently absent, husband and father, who tries to make up for his periods away from Martha and the children with occasional intense spells of excessive generosity and attention.

His employees would not altogether recognize this Jonathan, the doting family man, and even Martha is surprised when it appears. His foreman, who has worked for Jonathan for more than twenty years, was astonished when he first met this "other" personality.

"It's a strictly working relationship between Jon and me. We don't get together socially and I like it that way. He treats me well enough, but he's a tough customer and sometimes he asks too much of the men . . . And he's tight with the money—straight enough, but he doesn't exactly throw it about. So I have to stand up for the lads, squeeze a bonus out of him if they've done particularly well—that sort of thing. I couldn't do that if we were best mates, could I?

"Last year, though, his wife asked mine if we would go round for a celebration party—his oldest daughter was getting engaged. Bit of a surprise, actually, and I wasn't too keen, but my wife insisted, so we went along.

"Well, we walked in, and there among his family he was a different man. I mean, really different. He was welcoming and talkative and joking. And it turned out that for an engagement present he had bought his daughter a house—no kidding! It cost him more than the company had made him in the whole year. Now, how do you square that up with a man who won't even buy his men a crate of beer at Christmas?"

The petty criminals in Jonathan's neighborhood see another Jonathan again. He is also a local magistrate and has spent a good deal of time studying both criminology and civil and criminal law. On the bench neither the quick-tempered, tightfisted Jonathan nor the excessively generous one is to be seen. Instead he comes across as careful, considered, measured and reasonable.

And none of his male friends see much of any of these Jonathans. He used to play in a local football team and some of his former teammates keep their sporting links in middle age by taking occasional golfing and fishing breaks. These "weekends out," as he calls them, consist of boisterous days and lively, alcohol-fueled nights. He makes sure they take place a long way from home.

Five Signs of a Major–Minors

- Difficult to get to know: just when you think you are getting somewhere he becomes someone else.
- Wide interests and knowledge of surprising areas.
- Reliable enough in general dealings, but you can never be sure of him . . .
- Interesting and varied CV.
- Wardrobe may contain many different styles.

Multiple Minors

Multiple Minors are butterflies, flitting from one thing to another. No major ever gets to develop because they don't stay with one set of responses for long enough to establish it as a default.

The personalities in Multiple Minors tend to be distinct, for it is the difference between them that keeps them all separate. In some cases, though, the personalities in their complicated system may be quite similar to one another, in which case the person will seem quite consistent and may even be confused, by those who don't know them well, with a Single Major.

Multiple Minors may be bewildering and irritating, but they can be amusing and stimulating too. Indeed, Multiple Minors are usually very creative and often full of ideas and plans. The problem is that they rarely carry them out because the personality that conceives them is not around long enough to get them under way. Even if one of the personalities is the sort that concentrates obsessively, it never gets to be out for long enough to get very far. Other, less committed personalities interrupt, and when the obsessive one gets back it may feel furious that its plans have been thwarted by—it feels—itself!

Typically, Multiple Minors start one task, then break off and start another, often without being able to give a sensible reason for doing so. They pick up interests, hobbies and enthusiasms, then drop them almost immediately, only to come back to them weeks later and carry on as though they had never lost interest. They are the same with friends, and have a disconcerting habit of being intimate with you one time, then distant when you meet them again.

With no major to steer them, Multiple Minors are like sailboats without rudders—entirely at the mercy of the wind. Usually they have been in windy weather all their lives, which is why they developed their multiple characterscape. If life subsequently stabilizes, one of their personalities—the one most suited to the current life—may grow into a major. But if they continue to live a life of constant change (which they are inclined to contrive), they may continue to host a large and increasing number of diverse personalities. If these characters are aware of one another and can control when one comes out and another goes away, this very diversity can make them spectacularly successful, especially in today's world. But if the personalities fail to know one another, the person's life is likely to fall into chaos.

Amy

Amy seemed to have a perfectly normal childhood. She was the eldest of four children, born into a working-class family in the north of England and brought up in a fairly conventional way. You have to look quite closely at her background—and perhaps take into account her genetic inheritance—to see why she developed as she has.

"My mum was moody. Well, that's what we called it then. Today she would probably be called manic-depressive [bipolar disorder] but then it was just moody. When she went into a dip she was kind of cold—not horrible, just not caring. So I invented all sorts of ways of comforting myself: I'd pretend I had another mum altogether— model them on other kids' mums or people off the telly. I was lonely a lot of the time, so I made up little friends, too. I used to pretend to have this big sister, Sheila, who shared my room, and I would talk to her at night.

"Because I was the oldest I had to look after my little sister and brothers when Mum was down, and behave sort of grown-up. I'd look after the others all evening, then go to bed and dream of being looked after by someone else. I switched in my head from being 'little looker-afterer' to 'little me.' Then Mum would brighten up, and instead of having to be quiet and sweet and caring I was suddenly allowed to be noisy and childish, and I learned to make the best of it because you never knew how long it would last."

Amy's practice at switching in her head came in useful later in life when she became involved with an alcoholic who was a fervent protector of Amy while he was on the wagon and hopelessly dependent on her when he wasn't. "I could do 'little-miss-helpless' to a T," she recalls. "It wasn't that I needed him to look after me—I didn't. But I could see it made him feel good, and that helped him keep off the booze. And it felt good. You can really get into it. One day I forgot how to turn on the video and I needed to tape something. So I called him at work and he came home and did it for me. If I heard of someone doing that now, I'd say 'spoilt dumb bitch.' But it seemed normal at the time."

Around this time Amy signed up with a rather grand domestic help agency and soon she was besieged by rich families offering her well-remunerated full-time work. She had a knack of becoming an instant "treasure." "They were offering me my own cottage, holidays in the Caribbean with them, other staff to lord it over, all that," she recalls. "And I took up the offers a couple of times but—I don't know." Amy pauses. Then:

"Okay, this is what I know about myself. I can't be tied down. It's not that I don't want to be—it's just that it doesn't work. I'm a freelancer. People say I don't take anything seriously, but that's not true. I do take things seriously—it's just that, however seriously you take something, there's always something else, isn't there?"

Five Signs of a Multiple Minor

- Erratic career path.
- Talents and abilities come and go—one day a brilliant cook, the next day can't boil an egg, and so on.
- Sudden mood swings: down one moment, up the next.
- Wide range of acquaintances, but few really close or long-term friends.
- Attitudes, opinions, beliefs change rapidly.

How do your minors relate?

The previous exercises will, I hope, have given you an idea of the sort of pattern, or landscape, formed by your personalities. That is, how connected or separate they are. They should also have brought at least some of your minors out into the open so that you can see them directly, rather than just sensing they are there because of their influence on your behavior.

This exercise is designed to show how your minors relate to one another—whether they are all good guys or bad guys, complementary to one another or opposed. Then there is a guide to some of the more common minors. Of course, the cast of characters I present here are only a few of the countless personalities a human brain can create. They are stripped down as much as possible to their essential characteristics, and in reality even the most skeletal minor will have idiosyncrasies that distinguish it from these stereotypes. Certainly your own are bound to be far more complex and intriguing. It would be surprising, however, if you did not consider at least some of these examples recognizably similar to one of your own inner family.

Each profile shows what a particular minor does and why it does it. You might choose to read just those that you recognize as your own, but if you look at them all, you may spot some that you have missed or identify some that are within other peoples you know. Even if none of the minors here applies to you, the descriptions of them should help you analyze the functions and intentions of those minors that you *do* discover in yourself.

The case studies illustrate how each minor may manifest itself in a real-life situation. Many of them are cautionary tales—showing what happens when a minor becomes too dominant or when it is neglected or eclipsed by other personalities.

The descriptions below also touch on the way that the minor is likely to have originated. A minor's origins can be useful to ascertain because this can throw light on its present function and purpose. However, the idea is not to encourage you to probe your ancient history or "get to the bottom" of your personalities' behavior—it is to discover what they do *now*.

To begin, look again at the overall pattern that your personalities make on the wheel and decide which of the formations below best describes the general layout.

Clustered at the top

Each of the five dimensions on the Personality Wheel is independent of the others, so if you score high on one, there is no reason why you should score high on the one next to it. You are as likely to be highly extroverted and highly disagreeable, for example, as highly extroverted and highly agreeable.

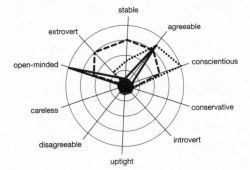

However, the Personality Wheel is constructed so that the characteristics that are most highly valued in our culture are in the top quadrant of the circle: extroversion, stability, agreeableness. Those which are valued less are at the bottom. At first sight, therefore, it might be pleasing to find that all your personalities cluster in the top half of the circle. It suggests that even your minor personalities are pretty regular guys.

However, few human characteristics have no purpose at all—even those we may prefer to keep quiet about. Any quality that consistently worked against us as a species would probably have disappeared by now because natural selection ensures that attributes which reduce our chances of passing on our genes are slowly eradicated. So although we tend to value certain characteristics over others—extroversion is commonly thought to be better than introversion, for example, and laid-back people are generally believed to be healthier than those who are uptight—there are situations when being shy and bashful and even moody, angry and jealous are *useful*. Bashfulness may bring out the protector in a person who might otherwise crush you; moodiness allows you to swing with events, adapting your physiological responses in a quickly changing environment; anger gives you the energy to right wrongs; and jealousy is a crude but effective way of telling you that someone else may be getting what you would like to have for yourself.

For these reasons our brains are fulsomely equipped to produce the entire range of responses, and it would take an unusual mixture of genetic inheritance and upbringing to produce an adult who did not just sometimes feel disagreeable, antisocial or anxious. So if all your personalities are up there in the sunlight, ask yourself if you are really so bereft of the characteristics in the rest of the circle. Is there never a time when you feel uptight or behave in a disagreeable way? Could this be a case of one personality (the one who has done this exercise) refusing to acknowledge the existence of those s/he doesn't approve of? Is this situation—being asked to examine and report on yourself—one that brings out a personality you *like* to be rather than one that you usually *are*? Are you telling yourself what you think other people want to hear, and switching into that personality in the process, like the students in Chapter Two who matched their self-descriptions to the people they thought they were going to be working with?

It might be very useful to ask others—those you can trust to be honest with you—to say whether they have ever detected in you any of the characteristics that your shapes do not cover.

Clustered at the bottom

Always disagreeable? Always shrinking from other people? Constantly moody, anxious, self-obsessed? I hardly need to tell you that you have problems, whether it is with one personality or several.

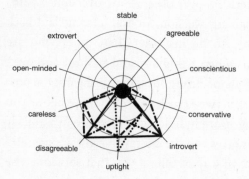

But are you sure there are not personalities in you who lie in the empty spaces of the circle? Could it be that the self-admittedly uptight personality who has done this exercise just can't remember the agreeable, enthusiastic you? As we saw in Chapter Three, when you are down, it is extremely difficult to remember or even imagine feeling and behaving differently. Could you be a victim of particularly strong state-dependent memory, edging toward compartmentalization?

Here again you need someone else to tell you honestly whether the characters you have identified are really the only ones you manifest. Don't just ask those you are with now, though. It might be that this situation brings out the self-deprecating personality who has just filled in the wheel. Try instead to ask a range of people how they see you. You might be surprised.

Suggestion: If you really do not discover a more positive personality lurking somewhere inside you, consider creating one from scratch. Various ways of doing this are explored in Chapter Three.

Extending into every section

1 Your personalities between them *get a mark on every spoke*

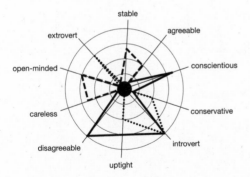

This is potentially good—between you all, you have the entire range of responses that in theory allows you to adapt to more or less anything life throws at you.

The question is, are the personalities coming out at the right time? For example, few roles would ideally extend very far up the disagreeable or uptight spokes, while a large number would usefully eat into the conscientious and agreeable segments.

Look at each role and see whether the attributes it scores highest on are appropriate for the situation in which it tends to emerge. You may, for example, have a personality that rates high on careless and extrovert, which is great if the role it is associated with is, say, "vacationer" or "partygoer." It may not be so good if the role in which it is activated is "librarian" or "operating theater nurse." If you find such a mismatch between the role and the characteristics of the personality it brings out, you may want to think about what it is particularly in each situation that triggers the "wrong" personality.

Say you really are a librarian and in that role you manifest a high level of carelessness. Ask yourself why you should react so perversely to a situation that clearly calls for care. The fact that you are careful in other roles (you must be to get this particular pattern) means that one of your personalities has that quality, so why is it not coming to life in the library? Could it be that the personality who does come to the fore *wants* to be fired?

2 Individual personalities extend into opposite segments

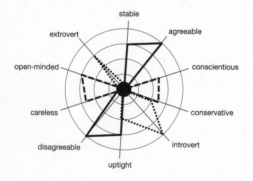

If you have a personality that registers a significant score on two opposing spokes—for example, 5 on agreeable and 5 on disagreeable—this suggests that the role you have distinguished contains two personalities, each of which comes out in subtly different situations. If under "worker,"

for instance, you check not only talkative, bold, energetic, gregarious, assertive, cheerful and enthusiastic, but also shy, quiet, bashful, withdrawn, reserved, polite and timid, you should examine the particular work situations that trigger each type of response. You may find an obvious division—for example, you may be extroverted in your own department or when you are with your peers, but introverted with your superiors. The roles then would be split into "worker" and "employee."

By this stage in the exercises you should have a fairly clear head count of your personalities and some idea of how they relate to one another. Contradictory characteristics and behaviors you have previously observed in yourself with some puzzlement should now be starting to make sense as manifestations of different psychological entities. The next section examines how these personalities came to be created and what purpose they play in your life.

CHAPTER 7

Meet the Family

Every family of personalities is unique, but they are created in brains put together in much the same way and from experiences and needs common to us all. Hence each of us tends to have an inner family with a broadly similar structure. For example, we all have personalities whose main purpose is to protect us. Other personalities can be regarded as controllers—there to drive and steer our behavior. Then there are minors who monitor our progress, others whose job it is to keep up our morale and yet others who are compelled to undermine it. We make personalities to deal with particular roles: school, dating, work, parenthood. And most of us carry around old versions of ourselves that once had a use but are now redundant.

This section is designed to help you identify your particular personalities and understand what they do, how they do it, and what can happen if they get neglected or overbearing. It presents profiles of some of the most common minors grouped into functional categories:

- **Defenders**   Protect and guard us against threats, both real and imagined.
- **Controllers** Drive and steer our behavior.
- **Punishers**   Are controllers or defenders whose energy has become misdirected.
- **Role players** Are personalities created for a particular situation or purpose.

- **Relics**   Are old minors that no longer have a useful function.
- **Creatives**   Originate new ideas, aims, visions.

You may well have some personalities that do not fall into any of these categories at all, but most people will find they have one or two personalities from each group. To help you identify them I have provided a Wheel outline for each one which shows that personality's essential characteristics—a high level of agreeableness for the Pleaser, for example, and a high degree of disagreeableness for the Bully. The position on the wheel—which quadrant it falls in—is also significant. However, these shapes are intended only as a rough guide to what such personalities might look like. Your own "artist," say, will almost certainly not look like the typical example because it will have characteristics—extroversion or agreeableness, perhaps—that are not part of its essential "artist" nature, but happen to be attached to your particular artist and therefore show up on the wheel. So if you do not recognize the form made by a typical personality in the table, this does not mean that you do not have the equivalent.

For this reason you should not depend on the wheel alone to recognize your personalities. Look also at the phrases next to each shape. Are these things you find yourself saying or thinking at particular times but not at others? Ideally, ask someone else if he or she has noticed you using words or expressing sentiments like this, and if so, in what circumstances. Try not to depend on your own memory, because the wise words of the Guardian, say, will seem quite alien to you if the Clown is currently to the fore.

The likelihood is that you will find echoes of your own personalities in these rather than perfect descriptions. The thing to recognize is that even if your minor might not behave in the same way as the stereotype, it is there to do that particular job.

Defenders

Defenders are absolutely essential. If they are too weak we might be indifferent to the dangers of walking down a dark unfamiliar street late at night or of taking on a physical challenge that is too much for us. The problem with Defenders, though, is that they are often quick to overdo their authority. They exaggerate dangers or even invent them, so that instead of preserving us from danger or injury they cocoon us, hold us back and prevent us from experiencing and enjoying a full life.

The Guardian

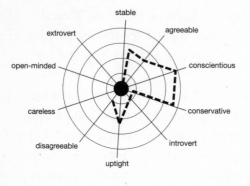

What it says
"Be careful!"
"It's not worth the risk."
"Better safe than sorry."
"There's something lurking in the bushes!"

What it does
The job of the Guardian is to watch out and alert us to danger. It steers us away from doing straightforwardly reckless things and makes us shy of new situations and challenges. The Guardian's origins lie in the alarm system hardwired into every animal, including humans. At its most basic

level this system produces fear—not the conscious feeling of being frightened, but the physical changes preparing us to run away or fight in threatening situations.

Running away or lashing out is not always the best way to cope with a situation, however. Certainly it is rarely helpful in social situations. Humans have therefore evolved a capacity to inhibit primitive urges such as these, while the more sophisticated, conscious parts of their brain assess the situation and work out a better strategy than simple fight or flight. The Guardian is part of this rational fear-assessment mechanism. It is able to describe and explain dangers rather than just reacting to them. That doesn't mean, though, that the fears are necessarily realistic. The Guardian always errs on the side of caution. It is basically a *stopper*, endlessly calling out, "Don't take the risk!"

Strengths

Obvious. Without some form of active internal "protector," most of us would lead extremely short and miserable lives. We would repeat our mistakes and walk carelessly and repeatedly into physical and emotional harm.

Weaknesses

As the most powerful and significant member of the defense group, our Guardian has a strong and urgent voice, which is why most of you are here right now with all of your faculties intact, able to read this book. It is a voice that commands. But its self-appointed task is cautionary and preventative. So the Guardian can often insist upon unnecessary and even unwise caution. One bad relationship does not mean—as the Guardian may insist—that we should avoid all future relationships. Few really satisfying things are achievable without taking some sort of risk, so the Guardian should not be allowed to rule as much as it would like to.

Recognize/expect it

In risky or unfamiliar situations.

Questions to ask it
"Are you overreacting?"
"Do I need you at all at this point in time?"
"Are you aware that I am no longer three years old?"
"Do you equate all fresh experiences with danger?"

The Guardian's voice is generally strong and insistent. But other more reckless personalities may drown it out at precisely the time you should be most aware of it.

I'm a fireman, and when I started in the job I remember that when the bell went off I couldn't wait to get to the scene; no nerves at all. I got this reputation for being a real gung-ho character.

I'd had the training, of course, and a lot of that is about self-protection—you're worse than useless if you get yourself hurt because then some other fellow has to come in and rescue you. So heroics are not encouraged. But if we were in the middle of an incident it would be me who'd go that one step further than what the rule book said—I'd take the proper precautions, but say the call came to withdraw from a building where there was still some slight chance of there being someone inside, I would just hang on that big longer, do a last look round before I pulled out. Nothing that an outsider would see, but my mates noticed. Like I said, they didn't approve, but I liked the sense of, well, heroism, I suppose.

And that was how I got injured. We were in the top floor of this sweatshop down in east London. It was an ancient old building—all rotten timbers, like a tinderbox—and very soon after we got in, my superior officer gave me the signal to pull out. And on this occasion, unusually, I was pleased to get it. Something—I don't know what—must have warned me that this time I really shouldn't hang about. But then I thought, No, I always give it a few seconds more—one last look! And that's what did it. A beam came down behind me, blocking my exit.

The rest is history. And I'm okay now, thanks to my mates. But the thing about it is this: as a firefighter, any sort of professional, I suppose, you get a feel for things. On top of or as well as all the stuff you know from the book and all the stuff you can tell from your own experience, there is this other sense that you develop. And you either listen to it or you don't. On that occasion I didn't listen. I heard it loud and clear, and I ignored it. And lived—just—to regret it. I teach new men now, and I sometimes try to explain it to them. Follow the rules, yes. Do it by the book. But over and above that, listen to your gut.

—*Colin*

The Worrier

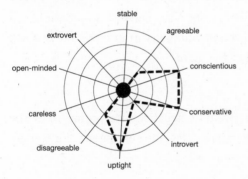

What it says
"Why isn't Mary home yet? She must have had an accident."
"My boss definitely gave me a funny look—he must be planning to fire me."
"It's definitely cancer."

What it does
The Worrier differs from the Guardian in that it generates fear whether or not there is real cause to be afraid. Whereas the Guardian grasps what is happening and then thinks up all the things that can go wrong, the

Worrier never even bothers to look out. Instead it hides away in its little dungeon thinking up all the bad things that could ever go wrong and telling everyone else about it without actually checking to see if any of them are *likely* to happen. It thinks the world is a dark, dangerous place, and is sure that unless we spend much of our time thinking and fretting about perils we will walk right into them. It does not trust the Guardian to give adequate warning of danger, but when the Guardian does speak, the Worrier amplifies the warning a thousand times. Although it seems to be highly sensitive to everything, it is actually more cut off from reality than almost anyone else.

Strengths
Few. In truly risky circumstances, if it works with another personality—one with a practical bent, say, who will devise a way out of the situation—it has some use. It is also useful as a curb on a reckless minor who is hell-bent on self-destruction. The Guardian may sound the alarm against some reckless course of action, but the Worrier is the one that will go on and on, warning long into the night.

Weaknesses
The Worrier's wildly overimaginative, negative interpretation of the world can prevent you from acting in it, let alone enjoying what you do. If it is allowed free rein, it can even make you ill.

Recognize/expect it
In the early hours, when its insistent whisperings prevent you from sleeping.

Questions to ask it
"What evidence is there that you're going to get the sack?"
"What are the odds on a burglar knocking at your door after eight p.m.?"
"Hasn't Mary—like everyone else you know—often got home a little later than she expected?"

Meet the Family

Given half a chance the Worrier amplifies small risks into major perils.

I've always enjoyed our holidays. When we first got married we used to go to local resorts for a week or two. Have fun on the big dipper and at the fairground, walk along the pier, eat fish and chips, sit in deck chairs on the beach if the weather was fine, go to the cinema or a show at night. I really looked forward to those holidays.

Then as we started to get more money, and as foreign holidays became cheaper and more popular, like other people we began to go abroad. It was my husband's idea really, but I quite liked the idea at first. So we took a fortnight in a big hotel in Spain. And the year after that we went back. And then we had a fortnight in a resort in Turkey.

And I just wasn't enjoying it all because I worried about everything. I suppose it all came from when I was young and people used to say that the water abroad wasn't fit to drink—and sure enough, when you got there you found that instead of drinking water from the tap, people were selling bottled water.

Then one of the first times in Spain I had one of the local meals at a restaurant. It was rice and prawns and tomatoes and things, but spicy, which I didn't really like. That night and all the next day I was laid up with a really bad stomach. I'd never been that ill at home from something I'd eaten.

Then my purse was stolen—or at least it went missing. I'll never be sure. But I'd put it down somewhere, and when I went to look for it again, it wasn't there. It was no great loss, there wasn't much in it. But we reported it to the police and they were terrible. None of us could really understand each other, but when we made it clear to them how little money had been in it, and that I couldn't even be sure whether I'd mislaid it or it had been stolen, they just lost all interest. They didn't seem to care. They more or less told us to forget about it.

My husband wasn't bothered and told me to relax. And he insisted on continuing to go abroad. But from then on, all I could do was worry. You'd see these reports on television about big tourist hotels abroad collapsing because they'd been put up too quickly and too cheaply—and I'd get a cold shiver down my spine and think, we could have been in one of those.

Of course I'd never have the local food or drink again. I'd find an English pub and get fish and chips or pie and peas there. But even then I wasn't really happy. You couldn't trust the ingredients. And I was always worried about having things stolen. Some of the hotels didn't have a safe to keep your money and things in, and the rooms never seemed very secure. So before we went I'd spend lots of time and money on taking out all sorts of insurance, from sickness to injury to theft. But it never stopped me worrying. I'd worry before we left, all the time we were there, and then when we got back I'd start worrying about having to go through the same thing again next year.

—*Marion*

The Pleaser

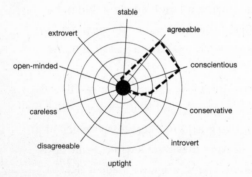

What it says
"Smile!"
"Sorry!"
"There's no sense in arguing."
"If I just keep quiet she will soon relax and we can go back to having a normal time together."
"I know I'm being taken advantage of, but it keeps the peace."

What it does

The Pleaser's job is to ensure that we are always on the good side of other people and thus safe from their anger or dislike.

The Pleaser believes, often wrongly, that anything is better than conflict. It is happy to abandon arguments in favor of agreeing to differ, and may be quite prepared to say and do things that the rest of the family doesn't believe in order to avoid bad feeling.

This personality is most often born out of fear. It may be the straightforward fear of punishment from someone perceived as being stronger. Or it may be that the person is aware of the potential strength of another personality—a Bully, perhaps, or a Mule—and is scared of getting into a conflict in which that other personality might be unleashed to the detriment of everyone (inside and out). The Pleaser may also be created out of simple laziness. If you live with a dominant person it may just be easier to constantly appease him or her than to summon the energy to insist on your own rights.

Strengths

It is often very effective. Appeasing a potential aggressor can indeed protect you from harm. And when the aggressor is too powerful and dangerous to tackle in any other way, pleasing and appeasing can be the only course open to you.

Weaknesses

It often does not work. The Pleaser inside us cannot be expected to recognize this fact, but not all hostilities can be talked away or bought off with gifts and soft words. The danger of allowing the Pleaser too much scope is that you can slip into the habit of pleasing and appeasing everyone and everything and become a social doormat.

The Pleaser can make us a soft target for any neighborhood bully— the kind who might actually back down if confronted rather than appeased. But if we insist on pleasing him, he will return with increased hostility and confidence. The Pleaser can also threaten the sense of self-esteem carried by other members of the family. If the Pleaser triumphs over them too regularly they will become weaker and the sense of our selves as capable and confident personalities will suffer. It may also infuriate other, feistier personalities in the same family, who will then become resentful and angry because they feel their own needs are not being met.

Recognize/expect it

Whenever you come up against what might be called a strong personality outside your family.

Questions to ask it

"Is this threat really serious?"

"Are you here just because everyone else around here is frightened to come out?"

"Have you considered alternatives to appeasement—such as simply walking away?"

The Pleaser often comes to the fore in relationships where one person is more committed than the other.

I had fallen in love with him at first sight. I knew from that moment onwards that he was the only one for me. I was prepared to do anything to win him and then to keep him. And at first it seemed to work both ways. Our first months together were deliriously happy. We couldn't do enough for each other. Life was just one happy round of giving and receiving pleasure.

Of course I thought that could go on forever. At my young age, so madly in love for the first time, there seemed no reason for it to end. I wasn't looking for any signs of change. So when things began to alter, at first I didn't notice, and then I suppose I chose to ignore them. They were such small signs. We had developed this ritual of giving each other presents, little things, nothing special, after every time we'd been apart for more than a day. Well, David stopped doing that, but I didn't. It hurt a bit somewhere inside— but I quickly forgot, and he always seemed to appreciate my gift.

I suppose I'd always done more than him around the apartment. But gradually I came to be doing almost everything, from the

170

cooking and cleaning to taking out the rubbish, paying the bills, washing up—everything. But the funny thing is, I didn't really mind. If David was happy with that arrangement, then so was I.

One or two of my friends would comment on this, saying things like they'd never let a man get away with that! I suppose I saw what they meant, but felt that it wasn't really their business. What made David and me happy together was our concern, no one else's.

But I adored him, you see. Even when I discovered that he was having an affair with a woman from work, I couldn't contemplate losing him—and the crazy thing is, as I now see it, I thought the affair must be my fault! I obviously wasn't pleasing him enough. So I cried when I was alone and put on makeup and sexy clothes and redoubled my efforts when he was at home.

I don't need to say that it didn't work. In fact it seemed to have the opposite effect to the one I intended. Every extra effort that I made to rediscover my old David, to turn back the clock, seemed just to distance him further from me. He told me as much on the day he walked out. He couldn't bear my smothering, needy attentions, he said. He said he thought I deserved someone else—someone better!—who would appreciate what I had to offer. Then he left. And I have to say, I haven't found that someone else yet.

—*Christine*

The Fighter

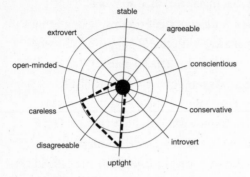

What it says

"Tackle trouble head-on."

"Never give an inch."

"I'm going to get my blow in first."

"Stand your ground."

"Don't show your weakness."

What it does

The Fighter hits out against threats, takes the battle to the enemy and gets her retaliation in first. Fighters are convinced that aggression can only be countered by aggression, and that aggression is quite a good policy even when there isn't any obvious aggression to counter. Fighters are not necessarily physical combatants, of course. They are much more likely today to fight with words. The fact that the aggression is usually fairly well removed from actual bodily interaction may disguise the Fighter: a clever one can wield verbal weapons with devastating effect and never be recognized for what she is.

The Fighter may often develop into a Bully, but actually her main purpose is not to put others down but to keep them *away*. Seen as an individual she may seem absolutely selfish, but in the context of the inner family she is often behaving in a misguided but well-meaning way. By getting her blows in first she believes she is protecting the other members from attack.

Strengths

Fighters frequently get what they want. The best and most energetic fighting personalities are featured largely in the majors of effective politicians, for example, and successful businesspeople.

Weaknesses

Unless it is kept in place by other, more amenable personalities, the Fighter is likely to be destructive to others and to its own family. By definition, it does not know or care when it is time to stop—or when it is time not to fight at all, but to adopt an alternative strategy. Somebody who spends his life in search of arguments, however successful he may be in winning those arguments, is likely very soon to run out of both friends and adversaries. The Fighter's armor has always been useful to us, and for that reason will probably always stay with us. But it must not be allowed to delude itself that it is the only or the most popular or the least fallible card in our pack.

Recognize/expect it

Whenever you are in a situation where there is the possibility of confrontation or a whiff of threat.

Questions to ask it

"What are you doing here?"
"Are you really required and were you actually called for, or did you just muscle your way to the front?"
"What do you hope to achieve?"

The less often the Fighter is deployed, the greater the effect it will have when it emerges.

The first ten years of my schooldays were pretty happy. I was at local primary and secondary schools, with boys and girls that I had known all my life. I did okay in lessons. I was a pretty cheerful teenager. Then when I was sixteen my family moved to the other end of the country. I went to a new school where I just didn't fit in. I didn't know anybody and my accent was all wrong. Then they started bullying me.

It was just comments at first, on the street and stuff. Then the text messages started. At first it was just one or two of them—really horrible messages about being a peasant and stuff. Or just something like "Oink oink," making out I'm a pig. But they got more horrible, and they came more and more often, so my mobile would be bleeping all the time, and it was just this big stream of horrible texts—all day, last thing at night, and I'd wake up to them first thing in the morning.

It was really horrible and I just didn't know what to do. I couldn't tell my parents, they wouldn't have understood and anyway couldn't have done anything about it. I couldn't tell any of the teachers, partly because I didn't know them and was scared of most of them—and anyway they never do anything. They're meant to, but you know if you tell it will just make things worse.

Then two of my old friends came to visit and I told them. They were great. We talked about it, and they reminded me of that time when we were a lot younger and there was a bully in our class and I got mad with her one day and slammed a desktop down on her fingers—and she never bothered us ever again.

So we made this plan. We just made a note of all the numbers that texted in those messages. Then one night we sat down in my room and the other two started calling them on their phones, so they didn't think it was from me. It was amazing how many of them answered and then stayed on the line as we called them everything under the sun.

Then I did it myself. I got up early one morning and began calling them. I told them that they would really suffer if they didn't stop—because I wouldn't stop. Those that cut me off, I texted them saying the same thing. Then I rang, or texted, to ask if they'd got the message!

It was astonishing because most of them stopped. But one or two still came in and I went into overdrive—I really hit back at them, calling them and texting them twenty-four/seven, all hours of the day and night! They didn't like it one bit. But they stopped bothering me. Oddly enough I became pretty good friends later with a couple of that gang. I go out with them at weekends.

—*Myra*

Controllers

Controllers want to make the decisions about daily life and dictate how we behave in it. The single huge difference between these characters and Defenders is that the latter are always trying to stop us from doing things, whereas Controllers point us in the direction in which they think we should travel and try to send us there. Controllers are doers. As a result, Controllers may struggle with Defenders (and others) to take charge of our actions, causing conflicts both within the family and with those outside.

The Wise Friend

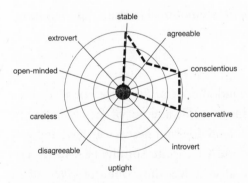

What it says
"Get to know him better before you commit to that deal."
"Haven't you been this way before?"
"Are you sure you want to do that?"
"Don't expect too much and you won't be disappointed."

What it does

It is easy to get the Wise Friend confused with the Guardian. Both have grown-up, sensible voices and claim to be acting for the good of everyone. The Wise Friend is also quite quick to spot dangers. It points out things that other personalities often do not want to acknowledge—that the person you are crazy about is less than crazy about you, that the job you want so badly is actually going to drive you mad, that the house you have set your heart on has a leaky roof and the potential to make you bankrupt.

The difference between the Wise Friend and Guardian, however, is that the latter is motivated by "gut" reactions. The Wise Friend, though, is not an extension of the brain's warning system, and its thinking processes are therefore far less colored by fears. Nor is it a servant of our compulsions and desires. It really is a "mature" character: it develops later than most and depends on the brain's frontal lobes with their extraordinary ability to weigh up information.

Strengths

The Wise Friend can see the advantages as well as the perils of any given action and offers a genuinely balanced view of things. It is more or less the only personality that is free from emotional pressure. You can therefore trust its judgment.

Weaknesses

When it does come through loud and clear, the Wise Friend is often assumed, both by itself and others (inside and out of the family), to be our real self. In fact, the Wise Friend does not necessarily have any special claim to superior status and can, quite simply, be wrong. The Guardian is never wrong because it has only one message (albeit wrapped up in many different packages): "Don't!" It doesn't *care* if you fail to achieve something that other personalities dearly want. Its purpose is to prevent you from taking risks, and never mind if you stay just where you are—that suits it fine!

The Wise Friend, on the other hand, genuinely tries to arrive at the best solution for everyone, and that calls for a complex and delicate computation, which is bound at times to go wrong. Nobody, not even the Wise Friend, *always* knows best. But the danger with a Wise Friend's mistakes is that the bad advice is likely to be both impeccably well-intentioned and persuasively phrased. The Wise Friend uses the "tried and tested" rule to make many of its judgments, so it is basically conservative by nature. If you always obey it in such situations you may neglect more adventurous options.

Recognize/expect it

Don't bank on the Wise Friend emerging when you need it. This is one you should learn to call on whenever you have a complex decision to make or you are in need of calm reassurance or counseling.

Questions to ask it

"What do you have to say?"

"What are you basing this advice on?"

"What do the others have to say about this?"

"Are you sure you are taking everyone's emotions into account?"

We all have the *potential* for a Wise Friend, but it is one that needs to be encouraged, because without the forceful engine of emotion behind it, its voice is often drowned out.

I had been intending for some time to have a career change. I'd been in my current job for almost ten years, having joined the company straight from school. It wasn't a bad job. It was reasonably well paid—although I'd never get rich there. I liked most of my colleagues. But I was increasingly convinced that I was being taken for granted. I got a small wage increment regularly, every couple of years, but it had been five years since my last promotion and there was no sign of another one on the horizon.

And I was in a rut. I wasn't bored rigid—I still quite looked forward to going in most mornings. But I did have this regular sinking feeling that my life was going nowhere. So I thought that it was time to take the plunge and move on. The trouble was, every time I sat down and thought about it for any length of time, this voice inside me kept throwing up objections: "Why give up a good thing?," "Think of the friends and colleagues you'd lose," "There's no guarantee the grass would be any greener in any other business—in fact, it could be a good deal worse," that kind of thing.

The difficulty was that this was just about the only internal advice I seemed to be getting. It was while I was on holiday that things changed. I was relaxed for the first time in what seemed like years, and when I turned my mind to the job thing, I seemed to see things in a whole new way. Instead of just worrying about what could go wrong, I started thinking about what could go right. It's not that the old worries had gone, but now I was able to balance them with the advantages. By the time I got back home I knew I was going to take the plunge. It still took months of agonizing to write a single application. But I was offered a new job and I took it.

And it's fine! I couldn't say it made an immense, dramatic overnight improvement to my life, my finances or even my happiness. In fact, once I'd settled in, the new job wasn't all that different from the old one. Which made me occasionally wonder what all the fuss had been about. Fear of the new, I suppose.

—*Raymond*

The Driver

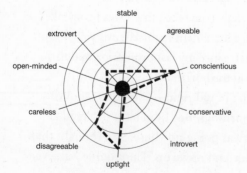

What it says

"Don't stop now."

"Don't stop now either!"

"Get on with it!"

"You are falling behind—catch up!"

"You've got to do better than this!"

"Now do that too—you can relax later."

What it does

The Driver is the one who gets us going and keeps us going. It is the character who is too busy to eat properly, is oblivious to tiredness, refuses to recognize defeat. It is the voice that tells us to get up in the morning (earlier!) and to stay up at night (later!). As soon as one task is finished, the Driver pushes us to complete the next.

The Driver is rooted in the brain's reward system, a neural circuit that creates the urge to act in order to pursue pleasure. This particular circuit is fueled by the neurotransmitter dopamine, which gives a sense of pleasurable anticipation. When activity in the circuit is diminished by lack of dopamine—as happens in people with Parkinson's disease, for example—we lose the ability to move forward and sink into lethargy and depression.

Strengths

The Driver gets us up in the morning, forces us to work through the day and stops us collapsing in front of the TV come evening. It tells us to turn our dreams into reality and not to give up on them at the first sign of an obstacle. It cracks the whip and generally keeps us going.

Weaknesses

It doesn't know when to stop. In fact, it doesn't have the concept of stopping. Left to itself it would drive the entire family into the ground.

Recognize/expect it

When your other personalities start shouting "Enough."

Questions to ask it

"When are you planning to stop?"

"Where is this actually getting us?"

"To whose benefit is all this activity?"

If the Driver is not kept under control it can create compulsions that destroy the very ambitions the Driver originally set out to fulfill.

I set up my Internet business in 2000 and worked at it day and night. It was just me then—it was before I was married—so I can't say I was doing it for anyone but myself. The more I worked, the more I enjoyed it. I was doing a full-time job by day as well, and building up the business at night. I didn't slack on the day job—actually the more successful I became online, the harder I worked during the day.

I suppose you would say that I became a workaholic. There was a definite addictive quality to the way I was behaving. I would work until three or four in the morning some days, and I was meant to be at work by eight next morning, so I often only got about three hours sleep.

In the middle of this I got married but it didn't slow me up. In fact it made me work harder because now I reasoned I had someone else to work for. She kept complaining that I was never there for her, though. So I gave up the day job, but then I found I just spent the hours I would have been doing that on the computer, so I still didn't have time for her. I wouldn't even stop for meals. And she left me.

Even that didn't bring me to a stop. I just went at it even more frantically. I think I had some idea that if I became really successful she would come back to me. What happened instead was that the business went belly-up. It wasn't my fault—I did everything I could to save it but the market just wouldn't support it. So suddenly I had nothing to do.

That was when I started trying to get her back. I still say that I was just, well, courting her, like I should have found time to do before we were married. But she put it another way: stalking. So now she has an injunction out against me and I'm not allowed near her.

—Vikram

The Organizer

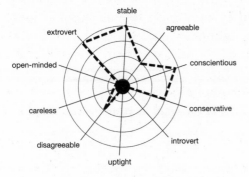

What it says

"Things need sorting out round here."

"I can't bear this mess."

"No one else is going to do it, so I suppose I will have to."

What it does

The Organizer compulsively files, grades, shelves, stores and stacks—essentially, puts into manageable order—every animate and inanimate thing it encounters. It is the part of us that we depend on to keep as much of our world as possible stable, dependable and organized.

Strengths

Organization is an essential part of human society. The value and rewards of organization are usually learned early in life, whether they be the recruitment and organization of a soccer team or the benefits of properly labeled and shelved CDs, and without organization (and by extension, organizers), our lives would be confused and unworkable messes. We could not catch trains to work, live in buildings, fly away on vacation, watch television, read books, eat in restaurants, as well as select CDs to play and take part in soccer.

Weaknesses

If allowed too much dominance the Organizer can become obsessive. In making the world too orderly it may remove a lot of fun and creative possibility from life. If every outing is organized down to the last detail, for instance, there is no chance that it might take off in some unexpected—and ultimately more rewarding—direction.

Recognize/expect it

When you find yourself remarking inwardly on the mess in another person's home or find that you cannot relax in your own home until every item is in its right place.

Questions to ask it

"Are you needed or wanted here?"

"Are you organizing this for a particular purpose or because you would be worried if it was out of order?"

"Can't you let someone else manage this particular operation/outing?"

"Will imposing order here actually improve this situation?"

The Organizer is never happy until it has imposed "order" on its surroundings. Sometimes the effect is literally deadening.

My husband spent his working life building up and running a big travel company. The company was successful because he was such a stickler for detail. He used to make surprise visits to branches whenever he was in a town, and if anything was out of place—even a coffee cup left on a desk—he would make sure the branch manager knew about it. And then he'd do another check in a few weeks time to make sure the message had got through.

When he retired we decided to move to the country. He had always said he wanted to garden in his retirement, and I didn't want him getting under my feet, so I encouraged him to buy a house with a nice big garden. Before then all we'd had was a little square that he'd paved over because he said he didn't have time to see to it.

The new garden had mature borders and some good trees and it really was a picture in spring—full of blooms. But of course what he had to do was reorganize the whole lot. He didn't like the weeds in the borders so he pulled them out and then other weeds sprung up—even more of them. So he grassed over the borders. He didn't like the way the ivy got hold of the trees, so he poisoned it. Then the two nicest trees fell down because it turned out the ivy had been holding them up! He didn't like the way the lawn grew unevenly where he had extended it, so he turned it into a terrace. Then he didn't like the hedge because he couldn't manage to cut it exactly horizontal. So he replaced it with a brick wall.

Now he's happy with it, but I'm not. We had our tea out there yesterday, and I looked around and realized there wasn't a single flower in the whole garden. We could have been sitting in one of his branch offices. Next spring I'm going to scatter some wildflower seeds in all the little crevices. Just to keep him busy pulling them out.

—*Marjorie*

Punishers

Punishers are often Controllers or Defenders who have gotten out of hand. Instead of directing us safely forward, they have turned their energy into a corrosive force manifesting itself as continual criticism, attack or negative evaluation. This may be turned inward or out.

The Critic

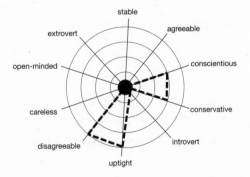

What it says

"You/they are useless."

"They are not praising you, they are being kind."

"Why can you/they never get anything right?"

"You/they are letting yourself/themselves down."

"You're letting everybody else down."

What it does

The Critic constantly monitors our own or other people's performance—depending on whether it is turned inward or out—and concludes that it is not up to scratch. When it is turned inward, it tells us that we are not competent, that what we have done is rubbish, that what we will do tomorrow will be just as bad and that we will never be as good as everyone else. When we make a mess it says "I told you so." When we do something well, it homes in on the one tiny thing we got wrong and ignores everything we got right.

When it is turned outward, the Critic monitors the performance of everyone else, pointing out where they are falling short of some impossible ideal. Its voice is harsh and cruel and hurtful, but when challenged it will appeal to facts: "I am simply pointing out the truth," it will insist.

The Critic thrives in our current world of celebrity, where we are constantly reminded that other people are more beautiful, rich and successful than ourselves.

Strengths

The Critic is fine so long as it knows its place and stays there. It is useful to have a personality that acts as a reality check and monitors our performance. By doing this, the Critic can help us to improve. At its best it is a useful teacher.

Weaknesses

If the Critic is unchecked he will undermine and ultimately paralyze the other, more positive personalities in the family. When turned outward he will drive away friends and color the world his own jaundiced hue.

Recognize/expect it
Whenever you have reason to compare your own life and achievements with those of anybody else.

Questions to ask it
"Are your criticisms actually useful?"
"Are your comments and suggestions doing more harm than good?"
"Are you simply indulging a spasm of negativity?"

The Critic is not happy just to criticize the person—it often extends its negative view to anything the person is associated with.

It would be easy to say that I'm never happy with anything. But it's probably truer to say that I'm never happy with anything from the moment it becomes mine! I can't really understand it. On the face of things I've done okay; I've got an okay life—as my friends never stop pointing out. But a good job, a house and the rest of it never seem quite okay to me.

I got a new job last year. When I applied for it I thought it looked great. I really wanted it badly and I put everything into my application and interview. And I got it. Then I started it, and very quickly I was unhappy with it because it suddenly didn't seem that great a job anymore. In fact, it seemed worse than my last one.

Objectively I know that can't be true—but it's not what I *know*, it's what I *feel*. On a completely different level, a good friend of mine bought some great new curtains. At least they looked great in her place. They looked so great that I just had to get myself an identical set. And they should—objectively, I know they should—have looked just as great in my living room.

But they didn't. They looked ordinary at first. Then very quickly they came to look completely out of place—terrible, in fact. But they are the same curtains that I loved enough to splash out an enormous amount of money on. The only difference is that now they are my curtains, and a really insistent part of me keeps saying that they are just not good enough, I shouldn't have bothered, I should have used my own taste, it's all been a waste of money.

—*Peta*

The Bully

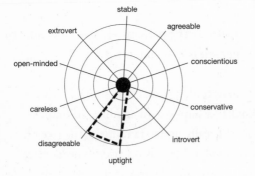

What it says

"If *he* is down, *I* am up!"

"That person is trying to get one over me."

"You won't get away with that!"

"This person is a threat to me; therefore I must attack him."

"This person frightens me; therefore I must attack her."

What it does

The Bully was originally a protector (see the Fighter), but it now hits out at people who do not constitute a threat. In a blinkered way the Bully still thinks of itself as keeping the other guys safe by preventing others from getting close. The effect is to prevent the development of close or warm relationships. Essentially the Bully is frightened, and by hitting out first it hopes to preempt any challenge to its power. If it is confronted, its fear may become stronger than its aggression and it will back down.

Strengths
Disappearingly few.

Weaknesses
It is dangerous to those within and outside the family.

Recognize/expect it
The Bully in us tends to be activated by people who frighten or challenge us in some way, yet do not have our status, strength or position. Hence you should watch for it carefully in situations where you are dealing with people over whom you have power.

Questions to ask it
"What are you scared of here?"
"Are you using your power/status/authority correctly?"

Bullies may be created out of the anger left over in a person who feels he once lost out to a weaker person. Their preemptive aggression is designed to prevent its happening again.

I've spent a number of years trying to work out what turned me into a bully. Or I suppose I should say what turned me into a full-time bully, as I guess most of us do a bit of bullying some of the time. There was one period in particular that I'm not especially proud of, partly because I later became really good friends with the girl I was bullying. She had arrived at our school from somewhere a long way away—somewhere up north.

She was obviously vulnerable. Anybody would have been at that age and in her situation, in a new home and school, with absolutely no friends, not knowing any of the teachers. She was a sitting duck to be picked on. And did we pick on her! We got her mobile phone number and started sending her texts.

They were okay at first, I think, but the whole thing just gathered momentum and got out of control, until a whole gang of us were texting her morning and night, sending her really awful, threatening texts. We stopped when she started sending them back! And I think she phoned us in the night—something like that. Anyway, the fun went out of it. And then we got to know her and she was great!

So all's well that ends well. Not really, because I knew I had done something pretty awful and I didn't really know why. But when I look back, I think I'd probably been bullying other people quite a bit before then, and I continued doing it a bit to others even afterward.

I was an only child. My parents couldn't have another baby but wanted one, so they adopted a little brother for me. I pretended to be happy, but I was really unhappy about it. I felt threatened. I felt that I'd been pushed aside. At least half of the love and attention that had been mine exclusively was now going to be given to someone else. So I bullied my little brother throughout our childhood. And when this girl from the north arrived at our school, I suppose she might have reminded me of him. She was pretty and outgoing—obviously people were going to be attracted to her. So I stepped in to stop that happening—or to make her feel as miserable as possible. Perhaps I just wanted her to go away.

I have to watch myself even now, years later. I know that I'm prone to bullying, especially to newcomers in my life. So I just have to be careful and keep a close eye on myself, or I wouldn't have a friend left in the world.

—*Suzie*

The Martyr

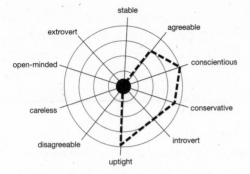

What it says

"Show this person that you will do anything to please them."

"You are not worthy."

"Obviously, do not offend—but more than that, prepare to debase your-self in case neutrality is seen as an offense."

What it does

The Martyr probably started off as a Pleaser, but it went one step further. Pleasing others, it decided, was not enough. It had also to sacrifice its own aims and ambitions, however legitimate, and even demean itself in order to continue pleasing. The effect is that it inhibits other members of the family from pursuing their own needs and therefore generates resentment in them. The Martyr interprets this internal conflict as evidence of her own unwor-thiness, which can be put right only by yet more self-sacrifice.

Strengths

The Martyr may actually lead a person into doing a lot of good work for others.

Weaknesses

In doing good for others the Martyr may do positive harm to those within its own family. If it gets the upper hand it may lead the person into warped, one-sided relationships and ultimately into a cheerless, virtually masochistic existence.

Recognize/expect it
Whenever you feel inferior to somebody to whom you are attracted. Whenever you feel urged to offer more pleasure to a friend or partner than you receive in return.

Questions to ask it
"Is your cause really worth it?"
"How about giving an equal amount of attention to yourself today?"

Martyrs may encourage other people to walk over them, then feel resentful when they do.

My sister, Elizabeth, was the clever one in the family, and we all had high hopes for her when she got into Cambridge. It was there she met Robert. They both got almost identical degrees, but Elizabeth got herself a job while Robert went on to do a postgraduate degree. As far as we could understand, the deal was that after three years or so, he would be in a position to get a good job and Elizabeth could stop work and have babies—which she desperately wanted to do—and he would support her. Then when the children were old enough, Elizabeth would take up her career again.

It didn't work out that way at all. Robert decided he didn't want children and Elizabeth went along with it. I remember she was very upset at the time and we all (the rest of the family) thought she should leave him. But she insisted that if that was what Robert wanted, that's how it would be. She had this idea that he was some sort of genius who needed nurturing and that children might get in the way of his brilliant career.

Eventually he did make a prestigious career for himself in the university. But there was never any money and Elizabeth has gone on working at her dreary job to keep them in the stuff that Robert likes—good wines, for example. And traveling. Not the two of them, just him. He always has an excuse—a conference or something—but actually I think he just likes going to these wonderful places.

Elizabeth does absolutely everything for Robert. She does all the domestic stuff. She organizes his traveling—even types up his itinerary, like she's his secretary or something. She taxis him about—Robert has never learned to drive; she buys his clothes; and if he is working at home, she literally tiptoes around the place so as not disturb his concentration.

All of that would be all right if Elizabeth seemed happy. But she's not. Over the years we have watched her get grayer and pinched and sort of mean. Depriving herself has become such a habit that she can't do anything else, and I hate having to watch it. And there is some kind of resentment brewing under the surface. Once I was staying there when Robert was due back from a trip. It was atrocious weather and his plane was delayed, so he missed the last train back. He phoned Elizabeth and I heard her saying that she would drive out to get him—it was a round trip of about six hours and would mean her being up all night and then having to go to work in the morning. I told her: "He can't possibly expect you to do that," but she was halfway out the door before he was off the phone.

But her car wouldn't start, so she had to call him back and tell him to get a hotel for the night. We had a couple of glasses of wine and then Robert rang again to say he couldn't get into a hotel and was going to have to stay in the station and wait for the first train. It was like "Mummy! Come and get me!" It made me giggle and that set her off too. But there was real malice in her laughter that made me feel quite uncomfortable. "He's only got a lightweight jacket," she said, "and short-sleeved shirts." And then she opened a bottle of wine that he'd been saving for a special occasion.

—A. R.

191

Role players

The personalities in this group started as acts or roles that the person adopted to deal with particular situations. At first they were worn like costumes or masks, but as they were employed over time they grew into full-fledged personalities. Role players were all useful at some time, and many of them retain their original purpose.

The Success

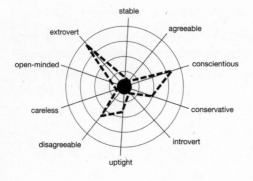

What it says
"I am a winner!"
"I can do anything I turn my hand to."
"Success comes easily to me."
"I always finish on top."
"Nothing can hold me back."

What it does
Success is usually created to keep up appearances in a culture where failure is not an option. It is an act initially adopted to persuade the external world that the person exhibiting it was triumphant in a particular arena. It makes us attempt to take the lead in all situations, raises our expectations of ourselves and causes us to put a good face on all situations. If it

is allowed to develop a life and momentum all its own, the Success personality is prone to believing its own publicity.

Strengths
It boosts confidence, urges everyone in the family to live up to its expectations and often turns belief ("I'm a winner!") into reality.

Weaknesses
The danger with Success is that its claims and beliefs do not match reality, so it misleads us into thinking we are doing better than we are and may make the person who displays it seem absurd, conceited or even deceitful. It may mistake style for substance; it can substitute glossy self-advertisement for genuine accomplishment. And if it does those things, it can backfire on us spectacularly by making us appear emptily boastful to other people.

Recognize/expect it
In any competitive or potentially competitive environment.

Questions to ask it
"Is this the right time and place to project a successful personality?"
"Are you keeping tabs on the situation?"
"Do you need to emphasize what might already be obvious?"

Success can be very attractive. But it can also drive people away.

I was good at school. I finished top of the class all the way through primary school, and in high school I passed most exams without trouble and was more than useful at sport. So in my final year I fully expected to be made head boy and was both disappointed and surprised when I wasn't. I couldn't understand it.

I couldn't help feeling that they'd overlooked something, that maybe my obvious qualifications hadn't been properly recognized. I suppose that's when the self-advertisement started. Throughout my late teens and twenties, through university and into my first job, I had this irresistible compulsion to "talk myself up." When I look back now I cringe. It's not as if I didn't have enough going for me without shouting about it all over the place. And of course it had the opposite of the intended effect. I must have been pretty well unbearable. My conversation with almost anybody, almost anywhere, revolved around me and what I had done. I guess people crossed the street when they saw me coming. It took me a long time to get over, a long time to suppress that boaster in me. But I still think I should have been head boy.

—*Damien*

The Professional

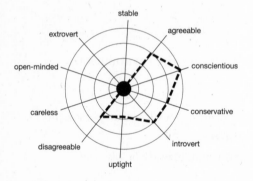

What it says
"If a job is worth doing, it's worth doing well."
"Work is work and play is play and the two shouldn't be confused."
"I don't have time for amateurs."
"I don't bring my personal life into the office, nor should others."

What it does
The Professional, like the Driver, is a doer—a personality that behaves in whatever way is appropriate for the job on hand. Very useful it is too, until it is time to stop work. The danger then is that the Professional refuses to step back and allow others to take over.

Strengths

Self-evidently, the more we concentrate on and enjoy our work, the more rewarding—in all senses of the word—that work will be.

Weaknesses

Nobody should be at work all of the time. If the Professional personality within us becomes too dominant, it can ride roughshod over other essential roles in our lives. The workaholic father, mother, sister, brother or friend may be a good provider, but he or she is rarely an easy companion.

Recognize/expect it

In the workplace—its only legitimate habitat.

Questions to ask it

"Are you sure this is a working situation?"
"Might your work benefit from the input from other personalities?"
"Have you heard of burnout?"

When it is coupled with the Driver, the Professional often fails to notice when it is time to pack up.

Looking back, I'd suppose I'd describe myself as "dutiful." I was a hardworking if not particularly inspired schoolgirl. I spent more time in the library than in the bar at college, and when I landed a good job with a public relations company I was determined to put in all the hours necessary to do a good job. And it worked—or it seemed to work. I went steadily up the professional ladder. I got a reputation for thoroughness and dependability. The fact that I was putting in eighty-hour weeks didn't bother me.

Then I reached my thirties and began to realize that not only was I chronically single, I didn't seem to have any friends. That wasn't because I'm unattractive. I'm not that modest—I know I can be fun to be with. It was because of my work. I was devoting so much time and energy to my job, which I continued to do extremely well, that I had nothing left over at the end of the day.

It was a vicious circle that took some time to break. At first, even when I'd made a conscious effort to put in fewer hours at the office and make myself some downtime, I couldn't properly enjoy it. There'd be a nagging voice in the back of my head telling me that I was wasting valuable time, that there were important phone calls to make, reports to write and clients to see. That voice has never really disappeared. It has just got a little quieter over the years. It lets me have a bit of time to myself, occasionally.

—*Jacqueline*

The Boss

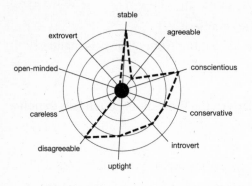

What it says

"I'm the only one who can run this show!"
"I know better than you do."
"Get *on* with it!"
"If I don't take charge, no one will!"
"I'm in charge!"

What it does

The Boss is superficially similar to the Professional or—at worse—the Bully. Unlike the Professional, though, the Boss role has been developed primarily for other people, and is often paper-thin and collapses on challenge. The Boss attempts to control every situation it finds itself in and every person it finds itself with. It calls the shots in even the most unlikely and unnecessary situations—such as dictating whose turn it is to buy the afterwork drinks in a bar. It confuses the line between professional circumstances, where seniority counts, and domestic or social situations, where rank is less important.

Strengths
Some situations do demand a boss (which is how they are created), and many awards accrue to the person who steps up to take on that role.

Weaknesses
People who are used to bossing others around can find it hard to shake off the habit. They may—and do!—take their bossiness out of its natural habitat at work and impose it on others when it is unrequested and misplaced. This, needless to say, is a formula for resentment.

Recognize/expect it
In situations where someone needs to take charge.

Questions to ask it
"Are you sure we are still at work?"
"Could you be overdoing it?"
"Might someone else be a better lead in this particular situation?"

The Boss, like the Professional and the Driver, may not know when to leave the stage.

I didn't realize I was doing it until it was pointed out to me. I don't suppose anybody does, or they wouldn't act that way. I'd been a teacher for fourteen years and a headmistress for the last five of them, and I guess I'd just got used to ordering people around!

The thing is, at work they were very young people who actually looked to me for instructions and orders. At home they were my family, several of whom didn't look to me for much instruction and

197

one of whom—my husband—didn't look to me for any orders at all! I was told that I was being bossy, of course. My friends told me, and my older children weren't shy about making it clear. But I'd got into a kind of mindset that was difficult to shake off. Once I could come out of the school gates and become a normal person again, but in recent years I seemed to carry my headmistress personality with me everywhere I went.

It wasn't the end of the world, of course, nor even the end of my marriage—my husband actually said that he found a little bit of bossiness quite appealing! But it was awkward. It was awkward at times for me, so I can guess what it must have been like for other people. She just needs watching carefully, that headmistress inside me!

—*Geraldine*

The Clown

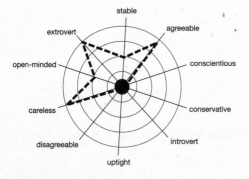

What it says
"I don't care if people think I'm a fool."
"Life's too short to be serious."
"I will do almost anything if it gets a laugh."
"Must keep them laughing."
"Me? Upset? Never!"

What it does

The Clown has several functions and may have been created to fulfill any or all of them. One is to draw attention to the person in whom it lives. It may have originated in a child's need to get the attention of parents without displeasing them. Another is to distract attention from another one of the internal family who may otherwise court disapproval. For example, a child may develop a Clown to distract people from a personality who feels it is failing to fulfill adults' expectation. A third function is the obvious one: to keep other people happy.

Whatever its function, the Clown carries a heavy weight of responsibility both to its own inner family and to others. It is frightened that if it ever stops fooling about, something calamitous will happen: it will be neglected or scorned, or sadness will take over the world.

Strengths

Everybody likes and needs to be amused. People who are prepared to go out of their way to be amusing can therefore be attractive, and in some circumstances genuinely helpful.

Weaknesses

The Clown is driven to hog the limelight because it is scared that if it ever stops clowning, something dreadful will happen. If other personalities are not strong enough to take over when there is serious business to be done, the person may be taken for what the Clown would have them believe is the case—a fool.

Recognize/expect it

In situations where you feel uncomfortable and might go to unnecessary lengths to break the ice.

Questions to ask it

"Why are you coming out now?"
"Are other personalities trying to come out?"
"Is there a hint of desperation here?"
"Have they seen it all before?"

If it is kept in its place the Clown is a role worth preserving.

Telling jokes and acting the clown was what I was good at when I was younger. Teenagers need a kind of niche, don't they? Some are good at football, some are good at fighting, some are just plain cool, and some are funny. I was the funny one. And it made me popular. Even the teachers liked me. But I realized that after a while nobody took me seriously for very long; even if I put my hand up in class, the teachers expected me to make a joke. And away from other people I was actually quite a serious and studious youth. So I learned to trim the act back a bit.

It was pretty much a teenage thing, though, and I thought I'd put it away when I got older. I had to. I became a bank manager, and a bit of gravitas is expected in that job. You can't really go mugging and gurning to customers and colleagues while discussing overdrafts and interest rates. Not all the time, anyway.

At home it was different. We had a big family and I love hamming it up at kids' parties. It is as though there is this whole other part of me that isn't much use most of the time—or particularly funny, for that matter—but on certain days in the year it really came into its own. So now it gets brought out, dusted down, does its job, and put back in the box again. And everybody's happy.

—John

Relics

Relics are minor personalities created for some long-ago purpose who have been frozen in that role, unable to move on. Although they may gain new information each time they come out, many of them never seem to mature—perhaps because their behavior is such that they always succeed in re-creating the sort of situation in which they were created, so the world always looks to be the same to them. Many relics are children with childish attributes and limitations, such as the inability to see things from others' point of view or to articulate more complex ideas through language.

The Abandoned Child

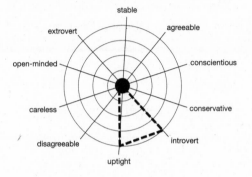

What it says
"I am all alone."
"I'll always be alone."
"Why have they left me?"
"I am frightened."

What it does
The Abandoned Child is embedded in a clutch of emotions dating from an episode (or episodes) in infancy. Babies initially show distress when they are parted from their mothers (or other familiar caregivers), but if the mother returns within a short period of time all is forgotten. Children who are left alone for prolonged periods, however, give up crying and searching and lapse into a state of resignation, cutting themselves off from their own fear and loneliness. Those emotions nevertheless register in the child's brain and may stay with it for life as an Abandoned Child minor.

Strengths
The Abandoned Child is a classic minor in that it is created by the brain's clever trick of carving out intolerable emotions and placing them in a separate compartment so that they will not pollute the major

personality. This character has no strengths of its own, but its creation was a masterpiece of situation management at the time.

Weaknesses
The Abandoned Child, if it is activated in later life, can make the adult emotionally needy and insecure. Part of its personality is the conviction that nothing can be done to regain security, so it does not even act as a spur to action.

Recognize/expect it
When someone you love has gone away, or perhaps just at times when you are alone without choosing to be.

Questions to ask it
"What are you so worried about? Do you think we will die if we remain alone?"
"Is he/she really deserting or just busy elsewhere for a while?"
"How about asking for reassurance in an adult way?"

Young children cannot project themselves into the future. A very short separation from the people who give them security may therefore feel to them like permanent abandonment.

It was a craze during the fifties, if you remember, to whip out the tonsils and adenoids of every child as soon as they sniffled. I had mine done when I was just three. To say it was traumatic would be an understatement. I don't mean the operation—I mean being dumped, as it seemed, in hospital.

I remember the first night in the children's ward, being in a cot by the window. I could see the cars passing below and I was sure one of them—the next one or the next one—would be my parents coming to take me home. But the whole long night went without them and I just wept myself dry. In the morning I remember a parcel turning up from my mother with clean pajamas and my teddy. This made me feel worse because I knew she must have been into the hospital to leave it and I couldn't understand why she hadn't come to see me. Now I didn't just feel abandoned, I was convinced my mother couldn't even be bothered to walk into the ward and see me!

She explained later that it had been almost as bad for her as for me. Apparently the hospital issued instructions to the parents saying they should not try to see their children on the ward because the children "settled" quicker if they weren't visited. Mothers' visits just set them all off crying again, apparently. She said she was beside herself with frustration, not being able to come and see me—the parcel was the nearest she could get.

I wouldn't say the incident scarred me for life or anything. But I do know this. If my husband is late home, even just half an hour, I go frantic. He is the most reliable, devoted man and I know perfectly well that he will not ever leave me, but I become absolutely convinced that he has. Permanently. I told him, right at the beginning of our marriage, that I had an irrational fear of him being in a car accident, so please would he call immediately if he was held up. He usually does. But on those isolated occasions when he hasn't been able to, I am right back there in that ward, counting the cars.

—*Annie*

The Mule

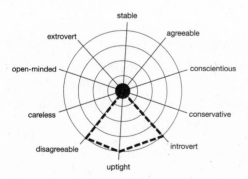

What it says

"No, I will not do that!"

"No!"

"Not likely."

"If I appear rude, I am actually doing nothing more than defending my own independence."

"Nope."

What it does

The Mule manifests itself in stubborn truculence or refusal to cooperate. Most Mules originate in childhood, from the child's battles with those who had power over them. Straightforward refusal was at that point just about the only resource on hand. Hence when the Mule emerges in an adult it is usually a sign of weakness—the person feels he has been transported back to a state of childhood impotence, where debate or a more dignified and reasoned form of refusal is beyond him.

Strengths

Although negative in style, the behavior is often surprisingly effective. Mulishness, when appropriately applied, can prevent an adult as well as a child from being exploited.

Weaknesses

It blocks debate, cuts off alternative paths of action and makes you very unpopular!

Recognize/expect it

When you are feeling exploited or in a situation where there is potential for exploitation, or when people in authority are pressing you to do something you are uncomfortable about. In circumstances of actual threat, obstinate and even truculent mulishness can be a positive defense mechanism and a means of asserting self-respect.

Questions to ask it

"Is this request so unreasonable?"

"Might it use less energy simply to comply rather than refuse?"
"If I do what they want, will any real harm be done?"

The Mule is usually created quite early in childhood. The more it triumphs then, the more likely it is to stick around into adulthood.

My parents had me late in life—after my brothers had left home—and they totally indulged me. I never had to refuse to obey them because they never insisted I did anything much. I just had to ask to get. But when I was about six my mother got seriously ill and my father hired a succession of au pairs and then properly trained child carers to look after me.

I was already used to getting my own way, and I certainly wasn't going to be told what to do by these people. At first I'd throw a tantrum. Later I'd just threaten a tantrum. Later still, they simply stopped trying to get me to do things I didn't want to do. Finally I was sent away to school, and a lot of that was hammered out of me. But a residue certainly remained, and as I reached adulthood I became very good at throwing what I suppose you would call a wobbly whenever anything came up that I didn't want to do.

It was ridiculous. If my mates wanted to go down the pub and I wanted to play football instead, I'd occasionally work myself up into a fit bordering on rage. It was utterly disproportionate—I'd yell and call people all the names under the sun. And then after an hour or two, it would all be forgotten by me—but not by my friends. So it was all pretty destructive. One day a mate sat me down and talked long and hard to me about it. I think that helped. I began to recognize this wobbly-throwing me that had a habit of springing up out of nowhere. I can't say he's gone away forever. But at least now I know to look out for him. If he begins to surface these days, I bite my tongue very hard indeed, or I just leave the room!

—*Declan*

Creatives

Creativity is a fundamental human faculty, and Creative personalities are the vehicles for it. People brought up surrounded by creative endeavor are naturally more inclined to be creative themselves because situations *make* personalities. But even those who have been deprived of that sort of experience (happily, very few today) will find a way to express their inherent creativity—perhaps through a hobby such as cooking or inventing or gardening.

The Artist

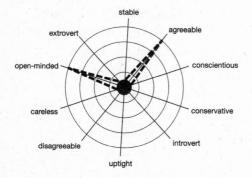

What it says
"I can see it in my mind's eye."
"I could make it into reality."
"I will make that."
"How shall I do it?"

What it does
The Artist is essentially a doer. Not only does it see things to be made, it also works out how to make them and actually sets about the task.

Strengths
Apart from the fruits of its creativity—which may or may not be valuable—the Artist's viewpoint constantly refreshes the entire family's way of seeing the world and therefore allows them all to interact with it more flexibly.

Weaknesses
Few. Even failed attempts to create can be to some degree laudable—and at the very least are harmless.

Recognize/expect it
Anywhere and everywhere. The artist may emerge in the home, when you are struck by a desire to rearrange the furniture; in the kitchen, when you see a new way to combine two ingredients; in the garden, when you place one plant next to another for visual effect; and whenever you find yourself spinning a story for someone's entertainment.

Questions to ask it
"Are you doing this often enough?"
"Are there other forms of creation and art you could explore?"

If the Artist does not emerge spontaneously it may need encouragement from outside the family.

I was the last person you'd expect to play in a band. I was a workaholic. I had my job in the daytime and my kids at night. I had no time at all to myself. My day consisted of feeding and dressing children, working, feeding and undressing children, then falling asleep on the couch. Also, I had no musical aptitude or inclination at all—I didn't even listen to it.

Three of my colleagues at work put me up to the idea. They'd started a small country music band just for fun. They played guitar and drums and fiddle, met once a week, and apparently had a whale of a time. And they told me they needed a singer. I just laughed! Even if I could sing—and I'd never tried—where would I get the time?

Well, they found a babysitter for me one night and I went along. They played a few tunes, very nicely I thought, then they gave me the song sheet and I tried out the vocals. Weirdly, I liked it! I found I was able to hold a tune, and as we did it more, I was able to put a bit more expression into my voice. The two hours, those first two hours, passed in a flash. And when I got home I wasn't in the least tired—I was exhilarated! I couldn't wait for the next session. So things just went on from there. I wouldn't miss those sessions for the world. They've progressed a bit now—we play occasional gigs in bars, and I've even started writing one or two songs of my own. And most astonishingly, it makes the rest of my life better! I've got more energy with the kids and at work. I think I'm better company all round.

—Chrissie

The Dreamer

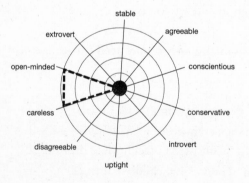

What it says

"I can see it in my mind's eye."

"I could make it into reality . . ."

". . . and I will . . . when I've got time/finished this current project/learned a bit more about it/get free of my responsibilities."

What it does

The Dreamer shares the Artist's ability to see how things *could* be rather than how they *are*. But it does not have the drive and practical skills to see the transformation through. Its projects remain dreams. The Dreamer comes from a source similar to that of the Artist—from our native compunction to think outside the box, to imagine schemes and artifacts that will enhance and enrich our lives. The Dreamer may possibly be more protean in his or her ideas—she may encompass a much broader scope than creations of purely artistic beauty and merit. The Dreamer is also capable of imagining new inventions, laborsaving devices, moneymaking initiatives. The Dreamer's flaw is implicit in her name—she may dream of whole new worlds but may never actually create or explore them.

Strengths

Dreaming is an essential precursor to artistic activity. If the Dreamer can find the Artist in the family, and merge with it, the combination will be stronger than either alone.

Weaknesses

The Dreamer is usually pretty harmless and has entertainment value. But it can also be a time-waster and a drain on resources that could be put to better use by other personalities.

Recognize/expect it

The Dreamer may emerge to fill the cracks between active pursuits, which is where it belongs. It is more irritating when it comes to life at a time when we really should be doing something practical, when it may interfere with a flow of real achievement or a discussion of actual projects.

Questions to ask it

"Is this a practical idea or are you just enjoying playing with it?"
"What would actually be required to put it into practice?"
"Are you stopping someone else from doing something more productive?"

Multiplicity—Part II

The Dreamer can often be traced back to a period of boredom or loneliness during childhood when its distractions were welcome and harmless.

I was a real live wire at my first school—always the first to put my hand up, first to be changed and ready for gym, always engaged and active. But when I got to my secondary school I was put into the top class, and for the first time I wasn't able to keep up. Instead of trying all the harder, what I did was retreat into my own head. I had always had an active imagination, but up until then I had channeled it into stories and art and things. Now I just used it to entertain myself and to get out of what I suppose might have felt like an uncomfortable situation—me, the dunce at the back of the class.

It started to spill over into my time at home. I'd spend long hours at school living in a world of my own, spinning increasingly elaborate narratives in which I was the central character. Then I would continue them as I walked home—I can remember getting quite upset if anyone tried to talk to me because I was so wrapped up in my own little world. I became antisocial, not because I didn't like people or wasn't popular but because my dream world was more interesting and exciting than anything I could do with other children.

Of course I fell behind at school as a result of this. And that was when I started to dream about being a success. Instead of actually working for exams I would spend my time pretending to myself that I had already passed them! So of course I didn't get the exam grades I needed to go to university, and in the end I had to take this dreary job my dad fixed me up with.

I'm still doing it. But I'm not going to be doing it for life. As soon as I've saved up enough money I'm going to take time off from work and go back and do the exams and get myself a university place as a mature student. Then I'll be back on the right road.

—*Peter*

As you can see, the life events that create personalities are not necessarily traumatic. Majors tend to be formed by the slow accretion of everyday experiences, while minors are more likely to come into being through a sudden shift in perception that produces a new way of behaving. The extent to which newly formed personalities maintain their separation depends on whether their view of the world can bind with personalities that already exist, and their survival depends on the recurrence of the situation—or type of situation—that brought them into being. Personalities are often born out of necessity—they arise to suit the occasion. Ideally they come and go according to circumstances.

Sometimes, though, our personalities do not heed their cues. One might refuse to hand over to another when it should, or refuse to come forward when needed. Or two might try to come out at the same time, engaging in a fight for dominance that prevents the energies and talents of either from being projected into the outside world. The next section is designed to help you to see how your personalities act and interact, and to encourage them to do so for the good of you all.

CHAPTER 8

Working Together

Visualizing your selves

This exercise is for those who prefer a more intuitive approach to the rather formal "framing and charting" technique described so far. Essentially it involves conjuring up one or more minors and externalizing them, much in the way that novelists experience the characters they create as being out there rather than inside their heads, and children experience Imaginary Companions, complete with clear physical attributes.

Visualization of this sort is used very widely as a tool in various kinds of psychotherapy, and a lot of people probably do something very like it whenever they want to transport themselves speedily into the world of their imagination. This particular exercise, however—using visualization to clarify our inner beings—was originally devised by the founder of psychosynthesis, Robert Assagioli (page 4).

This type of exploration will come more easily to people who are quite high on the dissociation spectrum. This is closely correlated with the multiplicity spectrum, because dissociation is one important way that personalities are created (Chapter Three). So it is likely that people who find it works well for them will also discover more minors than people who find it difficult. (NB: Before starting this activity, please

212

make sure you have read the warning advice on page 70 and answered the questions on page 117 relating to MPD.)

The exercise begins with the framing routine described for the Personality Wheel exercise.

- Relax, get into a neutral or relaxed state of mind and then allow thoughts and memories gradually to seep in. If memories of a holiday come to you, think of yourself in "vacationer" role. If you find work problems pressing in, think of yourself as "worker." If a seemingly irrelevant thought pops up—the idea of fixing a meal, say—don't act on it directly but encourage yourself into the role of "hungry" or "nurturer" or "mother" or "hostess"—whichever seems most appropriate.
- Close your eyes and become really aware of the thoughts, memories and feelings that come up when you slip into this frame. Imagine how this personality looks. It could be an image of you, either as you look now, or perhaps as you were as a child, or last year, or even in the future. Or it could be an object or, indeed, anything. Let it emerge, do not force it and do not censor it. Trust the process.
- Keep observing the image, letting it reveal itself; try to make contact with the feeling coming from it. Be aware that it may change as you are observing it—let this happen.
- Let the image speak to you and hear what it is saying. Objects are allowed to speak as well as people—you are, after all, working in an imaginary world and it is a *private* world, so don't worry about anyone thinking you are silly.
- Encourage conversation. Try to find out who this personality is. What does it want? Does it have a name for itself? What makes it happy, what sad? What does it think of the other personalities in the family? Who does it get along with, who does it disagree with? Why?
- When it feels right, stop and open your eyes. Record in your journal everything that happened. First, give your personality a name if it doesn't already have one. If it has given you a name different from the one you expected, go with that. Now write about its character, habits and quirks.

If you feel clear about this personality you may like to map it on the Personality Wheel along with the others. The shape may match one that you have already drawn, in which case you may be seeing the same personality from a new perspective, effectively "fleshing it out" so that you will recognize it more easily when next it emerges.

Kate

When Kate did this exercise she found that what came to mind was a tendency she had to let others do things for her that she could perfectly well do for herself, such as booking tickets, making travel arrangements and keeping in touch with mutual friends. It was obviously a line of thought that was on the back burner, and as soon as she relaxed, it bubbled up into her consciousness. As this happened she saw a tiara emerge. Realizing this was a symbol for a personality, she called it "Princess" and started to talk to it.

Princess, it seemed, felt entitled to use others to indulge her own laziness. Their reward, according to the Princess/tiara, was her company and friendship. She could not see why her attitude was sometimes met with resentment, because she regarded herself as special. The minor was, she came to realize, one that had emerged when she was a little girl, spoiled and petted by indulgent parents. In fact, her father's nickname for her had been Princess.

Bob

Bob found that he could not shake off a feeling of irritation that had first developed in him earlier that day during a lunchtime conversation with his friend Jacob. Jacob had recently become a teacher, and he seemed to Bob to have developed a patronizing manner toward his old friends, treating them as though they were his students. Bob had felt this at lunchtime when he had joined Jacob for lunch in a new restaurant featuring some quite obscure dishes from northern Spain. Jacob took it upon himself to tell Bob about them—how they were cooked, what went into them and so on—and even took over the ordering.

Working Together

At the time Bob could think only about how conceited Jacob seemed, but when he came to do this exercise he found an image of himself coming to mind. It was of him as a small boy being subjected to his father's "wisdom," which tended to take the form of long rambling lectures on subjects that didn't really interest him. He called the image "Reluctant Student" and concentrated on how it felt. The main thing he realized was the desire to move about—he felt pinned to the spot, unable to leave despite increasing boredom. It was this, rather than the lecturing itself, that created a sense of tension.

Harking back to the lunchtime incident, Bob realized that he was really rather interested in the food at the restaurant, and that it was actually he who had suggested they go there by way of an experiment. Jacob had made the effort to research the dishes, not to impress Bob but because, as he had told Bob when they made the arrangement, he happened to have a book on Spanish cuisine.

Bob's irritation had prevented him from taking in what his friend said—indeed, it had stopped him from really appreciating the meal. And the reason, he realized, was not that he felt he was being patronized, but simply that the situation—sitting still while someone else talked—reconstituted the frustrated little boy who couldn't wait to leave the table.

Julia

The image that arose in Julia's mind was of herself and her partner playing tennis: "The game was always the same—like a video loop. I would serve the ball over the net with all my energy and my partner would sort of lift up his racquet and let the ball hit the strings—but he would make no effort to hit it back. The ball would just fall to the ground and dribble away. So I would serve again and the same thing would happen. As it went on, time and again, I started to feel exhausted and less and less inclined to serve the ball. So I started just making it drop over the net so he would have to run to get it. He still wouldn't hit it back, but I got some satisfaction out of making him move. Then I started deliberately hitting it to the very edge of the court, where he couldn't get it. And that gave me even more satisfaction."

Julia had little trouble recognizing that the Tennis Player was echoing the role she played in her relationship. She was endlessly trying to engage her partner in a dialogue, but finding that he blocked all her invitations to communicate. The tennis ball was like the ball of conversation—it flew in one direction only. By concentrating on how the Tennis Player felt, Julia realized that she was rapidly getting exhausted by this one-sided game, and that she was starting to take pleasure out of, as she put it, prodding him with remarks intended to provoke rather than to produce a real exchange of views. It started her thinking about whether the relationship was worth preserving.

Know your triggers

Have you ever had the experience of seeing a photo of yourself, remembering precisely what you were thinking and feeling at the moment it was taken and being startled by the contrast between the remembered experience and the way you feel now? Whenever this happens you are effectively bringing two personalities face to face—the one in the photo and the one looking at it.

This exercise is designed to help you discover what situations bring out which of your minors. You will need a photo album, paper and pencil.

- Divide the paper into three columns.
- Go through the pictures in your album until you find one of you that you clearly remember being taken. Ideally it should be one that leaps out at you, releasing sudden memories that contrast sharply with your current situation.
- In the left-hand column on the paper, write down the situation in which it was taken. This does not mean the sort of thing you might

scribble on the back as a reminder ("Portugal, August 2000, waiting for ferry"). Rather you should write down what the situation was for *you*. If you were on vacation, for example, was it a vacation in which you were in charge or having an adventure or being looked after? Were you with your family? If so, were you at that moment being a son/daughter, partner, sibling or parent? If you were with friends, were they close friends? What was your position within the group? Were you the one who made sure everyone had their passports, or the one who nearly made everyone else miss the plane? If it is a work photo, were you in charge, part of a team, in competition with others, in uniform, on duty? If it is a party photo, were you the host or guest? Was it an intimate party or a big impersonal occasion?

- Now turn to the *inside* situation, as you remember it. In the second column write down what were you were thinking, feeling and most sharply aware of at the precise moment that photo was taken. This might not have anything obvious to do with the situation as seen by an outsider. Although the photo might have been taken on vacation, for example, your inner situation might have been boredom or irritation or exhaustion. You might have been thinking, I am anxious because my son's asthma has come back and we are a long way from home, or I am jealous because my partner is flirting with that girl again, or I want to go home. You might be in pain or too hot or engrossed in a book or feeling sexy or worrying about work.

- Match that inner state with one of the personalities you have already identified. If it doesn't match any of them, create a new name for it and write it alongside your description of the external and internal situation.

- Move on to another photo and do the same. Continue until you have dealt with at least a dozen photos this way.

- Look back at the list and see if you can see a pattern emerging. Does a particular sort of *external* situation bring out a particular *internal* situation—in other words, a particular minor? If so, which connections are essential and which are merely peripheral? For example, do those photos taken of you with your family—whether they are at your children's sports day or on the beach—consistently produce an internal state equivalent to your Parent or Caretaker or Witch or Indulgent One? Do parties correspond with Flirt or Princess or Loudmouth? Do photos taken at work always seem to be of Sulky Sue or Little Miss Tidy or Boss Man?

- Note which situations bring out which minors. In particular, make a note of situations that seem to activate two or more minors, or that bring out a clearly inappropriate minor. For instance, do parties bring out an introvert minor rather than an extrovert? Does work bring out a rebel rather than someone more conscientious? Does being with a particular friend, who you know is kind and caring, bring out a sulky or bad-tempered minor? These are the potential battle zones we will focus on.

Taking stock

You may find, having done the Personality Wheel and the visualization exercises once each, that you have identified all your minors. If you scored fairly low on the multiplicity scale (page 122–4) this may indeed be the case. But if you feel there are still things that you do, feel or think that cannot be accounted for by the personalities you have found thus far, repeat the exercises from time to time, ideally over quite a long period and in as many different situations as is practical.

When you feel fairly certain that you have identified all your minors, take stock. Write down the names of all of your personalities and then use the examples I have given as a template to arrive at a profile showing:

- What each one says/thinks (favorite phrases, telltale attitudes, reflexive comments).
- What it does (its function in your life, the way it manifests).
- Its strengths (what does it add to your life, has it a use?).
- Its weaknesses (does it hold you back or spoil other personalities' plans?).

- Questions to ask it (designed to increase its self-awareness).
- How the minor has manifested itself in your life generally, rather as the life stories I have placed against each of my examples demonstrate.

Then look down the list and see if you can spot any obviously opposing pairs. Have you discovered, for example, a Chicken who tries to stop you taking any risks and a Go For It! who would have you bungee-jumping off Niagara Falls? A Devoted Dad and a Wish I Was Free? A Miss Obliging and a Mule? Place these pairs together on your list—later they will be talking to one another.

Wait a few days before going on to the next section, and during that time just keep your personalities in mind. Note when you slip into one or the other, jot down their thoughts and sayings as these occur, think about when one or another has been particularly active and dictated a course of action in your life. Try to think of what might have happened had another minor taken charge. Listen to their thoughts and get familiar with the particular voice that each personality uses. Learn to recognize phrases that alert you to whoever is active. Generally try to distinguish each one clearly in your mind and get to know them. Once you are familiar with each one, move on to the next, final set of exercises.

Building the team

The previous chapters should have helped you to acknowledge and identify your minors and get an idea of what they do and why. Your own personalities will probably include some of the examples I have given, but by now I would expect that you have also found many that are unique to you. I would also hope that you have started to see how they might conflict with one another, and how these disputes cause problems in your day-to-day life.

The first set of exercises that follow are designed to get your personalities talking to one another. Later ones will help you to change your characterscape—strengthening minors who are generally helpful, curbing those who have got too strong, creating new ones where necessary and transforming those who are a nuisance. Finally we will deal with those personalities that might be better off out of the family altogether and see how that might be achieved.

The purpose of getting minors to communicate is not to bind them together into one. To do that would be to throw away the adaptive advantage of multiplicity. Rather the idea is to allow them to preserve their individual characteristics and make the best of them by ensuring they come out when, and only when, they are suited to the situation. It is, if you like, internal team-building.

Let sleeping dogs lie

Among your cast of personalities you will have some who are complex, active and dominant (your major or majors); others who are distinct but fairly narrow in scope (the Worker, the Clown); and some who are too shadowy even to name. Among these skeletal minors you may have got a glimpse of one or two unhappy or frightened or angry ones.

If a minor is emerging spontaneously, you may need to see where it came from in order to work out how best to move it along—away from its original miseries or resentments. It is possible to change minors even if they seem at first to be hopelessly stuck. But you must activate them at the same time as a more optimistic or stable personality who can talk to them and encourage them to see things from a different perspective. What is *not* helpful is simply to go over their pasts while entirely being them. You need to develop a degree of co-consciousness, and if you find this impossible, it may be best to avoid working with negative minors altogether.

The reason for this is obvious when you consider how memories are encoded in the brain (Chapter Three). Personalities *are* memories, and every time a memory is recalled, it becomes more firmly and more widely connected to others and thus more likely to be jogged into consciousness. Reactivating a traumatized personality, is therefore going to strengthen its influence rather than weaken it. This has been widely recognized for more than a decade, and hence psychiatry has largely abandoned therapies dependent on rehearsing old hurts in the expectation that this alone might take away their sting.

If you come across a minor that produces bad feelings, go on to another personality or stop the exercise altogether and do something routine that will flip you back into your default (major) personality. If the minor seems to be lingering, even when you stop trying to activate it, seek out a personality that will eclipse it by framing yourself in the positive personality's role. Or go back to the visualization exercise in the last chapter, but instead of allowing just anyone to come to mind, dismiss any negative minors that come up and zone in on one who is generally upbeat and happy.

If you find that a negative minor repeatedly intrudes and that you cannot easily slip out of it, you may prefer to pursue a formal course of therapy, either through one of the courses that use a multiple personality model similar to this (for contact details see pages 253–55) or through a more conventional route.

Making conversation

To carry out these exercises you need to create a state of mind that borders on the co-consciousness we looked at earlier (Chapter Two). For most of us, our normal state is to be one or another personality almost completely—the only hint we get of the others in us is what you might call breakthroughs when a backstage minor stirs into consciousness for a moment and throws in some contradictory thought or surprise emotion, or momentarily takes over the action, resulting in a "Why did I do *that*?" moment. Hence most instances of having more than one minor active are rather confused or uncomfortable and our brain—which is constantly trying to smooth over rough moments—tries hard to avoid them.

These exercises, however, depend on nurturing communal consciousness rather than stifling it. The idea is that if you can get two personalities (or more) to be active at the same time, they can talk directly to one another, exchange ideas, iron out misunderstandings and agree on future behavior.

In these sessions, try to use one personality as a sort of chair or host, to oversee and keep control of proceedings. In many people this will be their major or "default" personality. Normally a major tries to take over completely, but here the idea is to get it to retreat a little and tick away gently while allowing minors to come and go. Some majors are not suitable for this role, however. They might be bullies or too anxious or controlling to let others speak freely, or they might insist on overlaying the words of the minors with thoughts of their own. Your major might be totally skewed in its own thinking—a Critic that has got out of hand, or a Driver that can't relax enough to allow its mind to roam. Or it may think this sort of thing is quite simply silly.

If this is the case, you may do better to find a more appropriate minor that you can activate to play this role. For those who are aware of having one (and most of us do), the Wise Friend is a good candidate because it is by nature more distanced, cool and objective than most minors. Or you might like to look at the shapes on your Personality Wheel and see if you have an open-minded and stable one who you can bring in to do the job.

Before you begin, try to clear the stage of all but the personality that you want to chair proceedings. If this is not your major, "frame" yourself into the minor that you have chosen for this role. Then:

■ Refresh your memory of each (other) personality by reading back through your stocktaking list. Add any more minors that you have come across since you drew it up and flesh out the descriptions with any new insights.

■ Look at which situations bring out which minor. Start with those in which more than one minor seems to be active—where it is clear that two or more personalities are trying to get the upper hand.

■ Get into the frame by imagining yourself in that situation, much as you imagined yourself in a specific role (father, worker, gardener, etc.)

for the Personality Wheel exercise. Use the photos from the last exercise in the previous chapter to prompt your memory.

- Once you are in the situation, listen very carefully to the thoughts that occur. Most of our thinking is done in words, and these may be so distinct that they really sound like voices. (The difference between imaginary voices and hallucinatory voices has less to do with the way they sound than with a certain absolute *knowledge*, in the first case, that the words are being generated from inside your skull and not coming from outside.) At first they might seem very indistinct or babbling, as though several people are talking at once (which in a way, they are). But if you tune in carefully you will start to find that you can untangle the voices into separate strands.

- Identify the strands and write the name of the minor who is speaking next to each one. This might be a personality you have already identified and who you expect to be active in this situation. But it might also be someone you have not encountered before. If you are in doubt, think of a title—any title—and label it. If it turns out to be an inappropriate name you can change it to something more fitting later.

- Write down what is said. The ideal way to do this is to write it as you hear it, but if you find this difficult, or are lagging too far behind the voices, abandon it and write it down afterward. Do not censor it. This is absolutely essential. Throughout this exercise the big I (Chapter Two) will constantly attempt to edit what is going on and reduce your multiple threads of thought to one. Try to resist this. Listen carefully to the fainter voices, go with what they say and do not try to put words, so to speak, into their mouths. You might find that what you hear is a complete surprise to you.

- Go on until you feel you have got a useful amount of dialogue to work with . . .

You should now have quite a bit of writing, comprising speech from at least two and maybe many more voices. Read it over and note how it sounds. Do your minors shout at one another or tease or plead or just squabble in a dreary way? Do they listen to each other or simply ignore what the other is saying? Do two of them gang up against a third? Are they struggling to do fundamentally different things or just disagreeing about details? Does it leap out at you that one of them is quite obviously sabotaging the situation while another is trying to make it work?

Example

You are at home with a group of friends. You have been celebrating and you have produced a fantastic dinner that everyone has enjoyed. Now you are sitting around the table and you are meant to be relaxing. But the voices in your head are not.

Partygoer: This is great. I'm really enjoying today.

Inner Critic: You burned the meat. They said it was nicely done, but it was burned.

Partygoer: Not now, please.

Little-Badly-Done-By: I have done all the work up to now and nobody has even offered to clear the dishes.

Partygoer: Oh no, not you too! Not *now*!

Smugness: I'm pretty damn wonderful. Did all that on my own!

Outer Critic: D. wolfed down two helpings of pudding and she just can't afford to, she's falling out of that top as it is!

Leave-Me-Alone-Please: I can't keep this smile up much longer . . . When are they all going home?

Partygoer: I'm just not going to listen to all these miseries.

Love Everybody: These people are wonderful. I am so lucky to have them as my friends.

Outer Critic: No, they're not. They are boring.

Inner Critic: You just see them that way because you are boring yourself.

Love Everybody: It doesn't matter if they are boring. I love them.

Smugness: Aren't I wonderful for thinking that, even though they are boring?

Leave-Me-Alone-Please: These get-togethers are exhausting. I wish I could slip off and read my book.

Now look at the sentiments expressed by each minor and determine which are directly opposed to one another. In the example above, for example, Partygoer is clearly at odds with Leave-Me-Alone-Please, Inner Critic is diametrically opposed to Smugness and Little Badly-Done-By is hardly on the same wavelength as Love Everybody.

This is the point at which your "chair" personality needs to insert itself in the conversation. The aim is to alter the dialogue so that, instead of simply reiterating their opinions, the personalities start to *exchange* ideas and therefore influence each other instead of existing in their own little worlds. The important thing here is for the chair to resist driving the conversation. Instead it should nudge it along, generally allowing it to go in the direction in which it is drifting without hitting the buffers of old conflicts or disappearing down some dead end.

Very often the conflict or puzzle or contradiction that seems at first to need sorting out is not the crucial one, or a minor who seems at the start to be peripheral floats into the center and becomes the focus of the session. If that starts to happen, let it. Continue with the conversation until you feel you have arrived at a notable shift in opinion or a single negotiated settlement or some other natural junction. Stop at this point, even if the original conflicts you identified remain unaddressed.

Below is how the earlier conversation might go. The words in italics come from your Wise Friend, or whoever is acting as chair.

Partygoer: This is great (etc.).

Inner Critic: Yeah, *except* that you burned the meat. They said it was nicely done, but it was burned.

They said it was good. Why don't you believe them?

IC: Because you always get something wrong when you cook. You just can't do it.

Oh really? Smugness? What do you say to that?

Smugness: I think Inner Critic should shut up. Everything he says is rubbish.

IC: No, it's not. How about that pasta that came out in a solid lump last week? One of your guests asked for a knife to eat it with, remember?

How about the salmon that was still frozen in the middle? How about . . .

Smugness: Sorry, I can't take this (fading). I think I'm going . . .

No! Smugness, stay a minute. Didn't anyone else think we did a good thing today?

Little Badly-Done-By: If it was that good, people would have been more appreciative.

Maybe they didn't realize you wanted help because you seemed so competent.

LBDB: They can't have done—you heard what IC said.

How about listening to Smugness instead?

Smugness (brightening): Quite right!

LBDB: Smugness is just embarrassing. She has no place here at all.

Smugness: I make you all feel good, though, don't I?

LBDB: Hardly the point . . .

Why not? Maybe you could all do with a bit of Smugness's feel-good?

IC: We don't deserve it.

Smugness: Yes, we do!

IC: No, we don't!

Smugness: Yes, we do! (etc.)

Shh! Who else thinks we deserve some credit for today?

Outer Critic: At least we did something except sit on our backsides and eat!

Love Everybody: Don't be so mean! It was so kind of everyone to come. We should be grateful.

Do you think they came because they were doing us a favor, then?

IC: Can't think of any other reason.

OC: How about they like being waited on?

Leave-Me-Alone-Please: I wish you would all shut up so I can get back to my book.

Hallo! Are you sure you should be here? This is a social occasion after all.

LMAP: But I *always* come to social occasions.

Everyone: Why?

Maybe you're not so welcome at these times—have you thought of staying away when other people are about?

LMAP: But the whole point of me is that I come to social events.

What for?

LMAP: Because I've always been at them.

How come?

LMAP: Because I don't want to be there.

Then why are you there?

LMAP: Because I have always been there.

When else do you come out?

LMAP: When the others start organizing things.

You mean, you are there even before the party starts?

LMAP: Yup! Right at the start.

Do you try to stop the others making their plans?

LMAP: Not really. I know it's hopeless.

But you sort of invite yourself along in advance?

LMAP: Oh yes. I'm the first to arrive.

But why? Why do you go?

LMAP: Because I have always been there.

IC: Give up! She's beyond hope. You never get anywhere with her. She's just determined to ruin things.

LBDB: No, she's not. She has a miserable time. She talks to me at parties, so I know. She doesn't want to spoil things at all—she can't *help* being there, that's all!

Leave-Me-Alone? Do you remember being at parties when you were little?

LMAP: You bet! I was the only one to go to parties then.

You mean, the others weren't active at parties when you were little? They weren't at them?

LMAP: That's right. It was just me!

What about Partygoer?

LMAP: She wasn't even born then.

So why didn't you just not go to parties?

LMAP: It wasn't allowed, was it? Birthday parties, Halloween parties, egg hunts, you had to go or you were thought of as sad or weird.

But you don't have to go now.

Partygoer: And we would rather you didn't.

LMAP: But I've *always* been there . . .

How about if Partygoer gave you permission to stay asleep during the party?

Partygoer: Done!

LMAP: I think this is a trick.

It is. But try it. Just once—see how it goes.

LMAP: Okay.

Putting agreements into practice

When your conversation reaches a natural junction, ask everyone to go back to their own business—go back to sleep (i.e., become unconscious) or carry on as normal, as appropriate. Try to stop the conversation cleanly at this point, but put it on hold so you can pick it up again at this point at a future time.

Write down the main points as clearly you can, using the language of the minors themselves. Don't be tempted to tidy up or correct what the personalities say because the way they speak is a very good clue to what they are about. Leave-Me-Alone-Please's circular and limited thinking, for instance, and the childlike repetition of a nonsensical statement point to her origins as a Relic—a child still trapped in the schooldays parties she hated, but which are jogged into recollection by the very different parties she attends today, the same parties the other members of her now greatly extended family thoroughly enjoy.

When you have a complete record of the conversation—or as complete as you can make it—read it back and take note of any clear agreements that have been made. Note these separately and think about how they can be turned into concrete acts.

The agreement made by Leave-Me-Alone-Please sounds fairly straightforward: basically, she won't pop up at the next party. But this is not going to happen automatically because the party will jog those early party memories of which LMAP is an intrinsic part. However, the arrangement was specifically between LMAP and a minor who will also quite definitely be at the party: Partygoer herself. These two are in almost direct opposition. One way to eclipse LMAP, therefore, is to ensure that Partygoer is at full strength when you arrive at the next party.

To do this it would be worth having a private word with Partygoer before the next social event. You would start first by getting into the chairperson mode and then bringing on Partygoer through the framing technique. The conversation might then proceed like this:

Leave-Me-Alone-Please has promised to sleep this next do out. Remember?

Partygoer: Leave-Me-Alone-Please? Never heard of her. Can't we put some music on? What do you have to do to get a drink round here?

Calm down, we're not there yet. Leave-Me-Alone-Please is the one among us who always wants to slide off somewhere quiet. She's the one who made us all climb out of the bathroom window to get away from that wedding reception, remember? She says things like "I don't want to talk to these people" and "I want to be at home in bed."

Partygoer: I remember her.

Anyway, she's promised you that she'd sleep this one out.

Partygoer: Good thing too.

But you may have to remind her.

Partygoer: I never talk to her.

That's the point—on this occasion you must.

Partygoer: Okay, I'll tell her to buzz off.

I don't think that will help. It will make her even more active. If you want her to carry out her side of the bargain you'll have to give her something in return. How about agreeing that if she will stay quiet until, say, midnight, you will leave the moment she asks you to after that?

Partygoer: I might be too busy to listen.

Then Wise Friend will remind you.

Partygoer: I don't listen to Wise Friend.

Well, maybe you should start . . .

As you can see, conversations with and between minors do not necessarily go in the direction that any of you may want. It is like the orchestra of the brain—there is no conductor, so the various instrumentalists take their cues from one another rather than from any external director. The Wise Friend or chair can nudge and suggest, but is not in a position to control things any more than the others. Hence, changing the behavior of minors tends to be a long and uncertain business. One personality—whether it be the person's major or another minor—cannot just command another to do something. Indeed, if one personality did get that sort of control in the family, it would be overstretching its remit, because as we have seen, each minor was originally created for a purpose and many of them are still valuable. Even Leave-Me-Alone-Please—born out of the misery of attending parties as a child that she did not enjoy—has a limited role still, if only to keep Partygoer under some kind of control and get everyone home before dawn. You may discover a minor's function only after getting to know him very well and exploring how he interacts with others.

The empty chair

If you find it difficult to get your minors talking to one another just by thinking about it, you might like to try this famous technique originally developed by Frederick Perls, the pioneer of Gestalt Therapy. Perls used it to explore the duality of mind that he believed to be a driving force in much of neurosis. He would sit in one chair and have two other empty chairs beside him. The client would start off in one of the chairs, and imagine another part of themselves—say, the Parent or the Child—sitting in the other. These parts are in some ways similar to minors, and the physical separation of the two chairs, although it may seem artificial to begin with, may help to clarify the voices of your various personalities.

- Arrange two chairs or pillows a few feet from each other. Have extra chairs/ pillows nearby to bring in if another personality arrives un-expectedly and wants to join in.
- Frame yourself into the personality—major or minor—that you have chosen to chair. Spend some time establishing yourself in that mode, but do not get taken over by it completely.

- Now frame yourself as one of the minors you want to work with. Don't try to bring in any others yet—just stick with that one.

- Externalize this minor in the way that you did with the visualization exercise—that is, imagine it as a physical entity outside yourself. Sit it in the empty chair/pillow and reframe yourself as chair (*person*, that is, not the actual piece of furniture).

- In that mode, say hello to the chair with your minor in it. Don't be embarrassed. No one can see you but you and your minor, and they will be pleased to be acknowledged.

- Now ask it a question. Anything will do. "How are you today?" "What have you been up to?" Or perhaps: "Have I got your name right?"

- Shift into the other chair. Frame yourself as the minor and respond in that mode.

- Thereafter, shift from one chair to the other according to who is speaking. Try to hold both speakers in mind as you do it, but shift your attention from one to the other so that you respond in the appropriate voice.

- If another minor pipes up, bring in another chair and invite him to join in.

- Stop as before at a natural juncture. Write down the conversation.

- Proceed as before to secure future agreements/shifts in attitude.

Drawing up an agenda

As you get to know your personalities better and become more practiced at initiating discussions between them, you may find it useful to devise an agenda of what you want to achieve. Using your stocktaking list as a base, write down the names of your personalities together with the ways that they benefit or disadvantage your family as a whole. Then consider how they might be changed for the better. For example:

Personality	Strength	Weakness	Desired change
Inner Critic	Keeps smugness in check Gives reality check on performance	Undermines others' confidence Judgment too harsh and nonhelpful	Speak up only if it can give positive criticism—i.e., some way of improving performance
Partygoer	Generates pleasure and fun	Reckless—e.g., undermines health by binge drinking	Should occasionally stand aside for Leave-Me-Alone-Please
Leave-Me-Alone-Please	Potential to secure social downtime for quiet activities and relaxation	Comes out at wrong time	Learn to emerge when its desires are practical possibilities
Little Badly-Done-By	Alerts others to possibility that they are being treated unfairly	Often sees unfairness when there is none there	Check with a more objective personality: "Should I really be here now?" before launching into usual moan

Personality	Strength	Weakness	Desired change
Smugness	Makes everyone in the family feel good	Makes people outside feel bad and may cause them to dislike us	Currently too easily seen off by Inner Critic. Should be prepared to engage in dialogue with IC designed to test which of them should be uppermost in any situation
Love Everybody	Makes us, and everyone outside, feel wonderful	May invite others to take advantage of us	Should develop dialogue, as above, with Outer Critic
Outer Critic	Prevents us being taken in by/taken advantage of by others	Is too harsh and unforgiving—crushes Love Everybody and makes others dislike us	Learn to see others' faults without blaming them for these. Needs to talk more with Love Everybody

A helping hand

As you can probably see from the preceding exercise, once you start listening to minors talking it is almost inevitable that you will start to learn about their origins. Minors are embedded in memories—indeed in a sense they *are* memories—so whenever they are active they are bringing into the present some part of the past.

As I have said, there is no benefit to be had from simply digging out the origins of a troublesome or unhappy minor—all that is likely to do is make the personality more active. Going back to the "birthplace" of a minor can be useful, however, providing you can do it while *also* being one of your wiser, most adult or stable personalities. If you can do this—effectively achieving a state of co-consciousness—the happier minor can act as a helper, urging the unhappy one to overlay its original responses with ones more appropriate to the present situation. If you can do this consistently, the unhappy minor may be transformed, merge with another, or perhaps just fade away.

The Helping Hand technique, as I'll call it, requires that a hurt or troublesome minor is first brought to mind. For the reasons given earlier, I do not recommend deliberately activating such characters. This exercise should begin only when a minor pops up spontaneously and starts to give you problems.

By now I hope you will recognize when this is happening. Typical examples are when you find that you are having second thoughts about a plan of action that earlier seemed to be without flaws, or when you are of two minds about something. You might hear a voice somewhere deriding your performance or warning you about some imaginary peril. There may be an argument going on inside you, or you may be in a bad mood for no reason you can see. Unhappy or unreasonable minors can cause problems in countless different ways, and only you can learn to recognize when it is happening.

You may recall Gail, from Chapter Five, whose shopping trips were haunted by the anxiety of being mistakenly accused of shoplifting. She traced the fear to an incident that happened to her as a child, when she took another child's flag from the top of a sandcastle and was roundly punished for it. The shamed and angry child that she was at that moment remained frozen in time in her mind and leapt into consciousness whenever Gail was in a situation where a false accusation of theft might conceivably be made. But it was only when she saw a picture of a sandcastle in a store one day that she remembered the event that gave birth to her troublesome minor.

The fact that Gail maintained her adult consciousness while at the same time feeling the child's distress made it possible for her adult self to get a dialogue going with the child. "I was able to tell it, effectively, that the sandcastle had been swept away years ago—there was really no need still to be upset," she explains. "After that I started to deliberately recall the sandcastle incident whenever I entered a store and to talk to the child. I told her it had all been a silly mistake, no one was at fault, no more blame, no more unfair accusation. Bit by bit the message got through—the child started to realize that it *was not going to happen again.*

"Now when I shop, instead of going through my pantomime of innocence I force myself to behave normally. I pick things up, put them back. I might take an item of clothing to a window to see the color in the light, try on a jacket. At first it was uncomfortable. Little Falsely Accused, as I started to think of her, would agitate, 'Put it down! Let go! It's not *yours!*' But slowly she has got to realize that it is not going to happen again. The outrage is subsiding. One day I could even start to enjoy shopping."

A second example comes from someone I know well who was getting into trouble on account of an argumentative character almost directly the opposite of her usual agreeable self. Maggie does a high-profile public job, which requires her to look confident—more confident than she actually feels. This is her story:

There are times when all my swanky front just evaporates and I feel myself shrinking. It almost seems as though I am literally becoming smaller, like a child. It happens mainly when I am with people who I know—or suspect—are cleverer than me, or more successful, or have some sort of expertise that I don't share. I'll go in feeling chatty and cheerful and just fine, and then someone will say something that could be taken to be just a tiny bit unfriendly, or start talking about something I'm ignorant about, or it might be anything. And I collapse inside.

When that happens, later in the evening I often have a blazing row with someone! I'll spend all evening feeling pathetic and tongue-tied, and then suddenly the conversation will turn to something I know something about and I just—take over! If anyone tries to challenge me I go for them ferociously. I won't give an inch. I just have to win the argument.

One day I picked one of these fights with someone who I was meant to be chatting up for funding for the organization I work for. At some stage in the evening he made some political comment which I didn't agree with and I was away! Afterward he complained to my boss, and I thought, Well, I've got to get this under control. But I couldn't—the same thing happened less than a week later. As I banged the table and shouted I actually thought to myself, Hey! You said you weren't going to do this! But I couldn't stop. You know that phrase: "I don't know what got into me"? Well, that was how it felt exactly—as though something had got into me.

The way that Maggie described her argumentative behavior—as though something got into her—made me think that this might be the emergence of a minor personality. Although she was skeptical about it, Maggie agreed to attend a single session of ego-state therapy and report back to me. Ego-state therapy uses hypnosis, and the therapist began by putting Maggie into a light trance:

The therapist just told me to relax, to think about being in a garden, then about walking through it, visualizing the flowers, going down some steps. It wasn't like going into a deep trance or anything. I just felt relaxed. But I do know that, in any other circumstances, I would certainly not have talked like I did then. The therapist asked me to indicate, by raising a finger, if there was anyone other than me who would like to say something. I thought that sounded rather silly, but I

236

kind of felt like going along with it, so I raised my finger. Then she asked me who was there.

I was already aware of the shy, terrified me of course, as well as the argumentative me, but I had never really thought of it as a separate person. As I sat there, though, I had this absolutely clear image of a child in a school playground, feeling terrified of all the other children and trying to melt into the wall. I believe this was a real memory because I recognized the school as being the very first one I went to—I was only there for a few months, so I would have been just five. The feelings were real anyway; for a few moments I felt exactly what that child was feeling and saw the world—terrifying, noisy, threatening—through her eyes.

The hypnotist asked me what was happening and I remember not answering. She went on talking to me gently and I just didn't respond. It was weird: I was too shy to speak! Then she said, "What's your name?" and I answered: "Child." Normally I would feel absolutely stupid saying something like that, but I said it. Then the hypnotist said, "Do you want to talk to me?" and I shook my head.

Then—I can't remember what happened in between—after a while I think the hypnotist asked me if there was anyone else there. And I raised my finger again. As I did so again I had an absolutely clear picture of a teenage boy arguing like crazy against a bunch of adults. I wasn't in this character; rather I was watching from the other side of the table. But I knew that this was the out-of-control warrior I had come to get rid of. I told the hypnotist I saw this person and she said: "What's his name?" and I said, "Anthony."

Now this was the strangest thing of all, because as far as I can think, I don't know nor have I ever known anyone significant called Anthony. The name has no particular attraction to me, no resonance. I have absolutely no idea where it came from. Yet I said it without hesitation and with absolute certainly that this was the boy's name!

The second strange thing—which was also utterly unexpected—was I realized that Anthony was not a bully at all. He was protecting

237

Child. He wasn't at all sure he was up to it, and the only way he could do it was to put up a shield of words so the adults couldn't turn their scorn on the kid. If they had a relationship, it was of big brother to little sister, but that wasn't clear.

I can't actually remember how the session ended. I suppose the hypnotist had a chat with Anthony or something. Anyway, the things is, daft and New Agey and embarrassing as all this *should* be, it wasn't. And it was terrifically helpful because now when Anthony starts agitating I find I can sort of talk to him. I take a moment out and say internally: "Oi! What are you doing here? This person isn't threatening! I can cope!" And when I do this, he slides away.

Apart from stopping me arguing, it has made me feel better about myself because I realize that what I thought was a bully was actually nothing of the sort. It was another rather nervous kid, trying hard to be heroic. And I rather like myself for that!

Making a minor

The previous section looked at how a minor might be transformed, encouraged to merge with another or discouraged from muscling in when it is not needed or wanted. Here we see how you can deliberately create a new minor when the existing family seems to be short a member that could be of use.

Minors, as we have seen, are made by situations. They are learned responses to the things that happen to us. Hence people who have encountered a very wide range of situations, each quite different from the other, are likely to have a correspondingly large number of personalities. People who have lived a very "samey" life, by contrast, may just have a Single Major who is there morning, afternoon and evening.

Creating personalities is child's play—literally. Practically every game of make-believe involves pretending that the player is someone he or she are not, and every act of pretense brings a little minor flickering into life, at least for the duration of the game. Most of these are almost instantly forgotten, but some will be revived again and again, and some of those will become complex and well enough entrenched in the memory net to stay around for many years, if not for a lifetime.

As we get older our ability to create new personalities in response to new situations decreases. We tend to set, like jelly, into our existing major and various minors and struggle to make them cope with any new challenge that comes along rather than responding afresh. In today's fast-changing world, this inflexibility is often a great disadvantage. Many middle-aged people find it difficult to keep up with new technology, for instance, because as children they were not showered with gadgets that created a gizmo-friendly minor. Those of us who learned to drive before our roads were studded with speed cameras may not have the Lookout minor who was created in younger drivers as soon as they first took the wheel. A person who grew up thinking gay relationships were perverse is unlikely to have a personality that is comfortable with sexual diversity.

This exercise is designed to help you to spot any gap in your "cast list" of personalities and to create a new minor to fill it.

- Divide your life into manageable blocks such as Work/Home/Social.
- Using a separate sheet of paper for each category, list your strengths and weaknesses in each one. A sheet about work might, for example, look like this:

Strengths	Weaknesses
Reliability	Getting on with colleagues
Getting things done	Coping with complaints
Attention to detail	Initiating new projects

- Now identify the qualities that give you your strengths. You may like to do this by using the Personality Wheel. In the case above, for example, your strengths (solid line) and weaknesses (broken line) would give you a shape something like this:

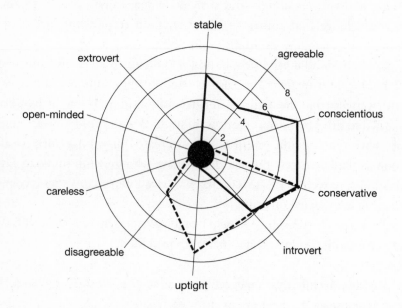

You can see clearly from this which characteristics are missing from the personalities who come out in you at work. You would benefit by creating one that was more extroverted (to get on better with your colleagues), open-minded (to initiate ideas), and agreeable (to cope with complaints).

Do the same for each major area of your life. You might find it helpful to use the Personality Wheel, but if not, just think carefully about the areas in which you are weak. You may also like to think of areas of life in which you feel you do not engage because you don't have the wherewithal. For example, you do less traveling than you would like to because you don't have a partner or friend to accompany you. In that case it might be useful to create a Lone Traveler—adventurous, open-minded, savvy, self-contained but extroverted enough to make new friends along the way.

Working Together

List the characteristics that your new minor should have. Start with general statements like "carefulness" or "extroversion" and then become increasingly specific. For example, you might write:

Carefulness—care with regard to other people—always friendly—smile first—don't wait for them to smile—remember names of people's children.

Search out people who display the characteristics you wish to incorporate into your new minor. Look for them among people you know, people you see on TV or read about in newspapers, fictional characters from plays, films and books.

Observe the people you have identified very thoroughly. Note the precise expressions, gestures and deeds that mark the characteristics you want to make your own. Do they display friendliness, say, by the way they smile? The way they listen? By what they say or do? Note also the characteristics that you do *not* want to be part of your creation. After all, you are not trying to replicate this person—your minor is a *new* personality, not a weak copy of someone else.

New minors may be created in many different ways. The main ones by which it can be done deliberately include:

- *Absorption.* If it is feasible and socially acceptable, try to spend as much time as is reasonably possible in the company of the person or people who possess the characteristics you have targeted (but make sure you are welcome!). If it is a celebrity you want to emulate, do the usual fan thing of collecting photographs and reading interviews. But remember, you are not out to worship this person, you merely want to incorporate certain of his or her characteristics.
- *Mimicry.* Once you have identified how your desired characteristics are manifested in the person you are using as a guide, copy them. Copy the smile, if it is the friendliness you want; the walk, the phrases, the gestures.
- *Fronting.* Build up your personality in cyberspace using an avatar (see Chapter Five). Identify with your online character and gradually introduce it into your offline life.

■ *Externalization*. Write down the personality you want to be. Give it a name and talk to it in your head. Initially you will have to make an effort to imagine what it will say, but in time you will find it will answer for itself and gradually it will take its place in the family lineup.

Saying goodbye

I started this book by inviting you to become aware of inner conflicts caused by squabbles among your various personalities. Anyone who drew a blank at that is unlikely to have got this far, so I assume that you know how it feels to be a battleground for warring minors. I hope that reading this book and doing the exercises in it have enabled you to identify the main players in your particular internal drama, and to start them talking in a way that will eventually lead to greater harmony between them.

Along the way, though, you may have identified some characters who just do not want to play. They might be ancient Relics who refuse to depart from their narrow, negative brief or Punishers who loathe the others in the family and are determined to put them down. Critics may have developed such harsh views that they are beyond modification and Defenders may not have the sense to see that their actions are actually destructive.

You have probably also discovered a number of unhelpful micros, fragments of personalities that are too skeletal to have self-awareness and have not (yet) managed to latch onto a more substantial personality that would lend them a sense of self. They might manifest themselves as destructive habits such as smoking or bingeing, or as apparently ungrounded fears or seemingly causeless moods. Some of them are just knee-jerk reactions—brain habits that have never been questioned. If you catch yourself saying something like "I never wear blue" and then find that you cannot explain why, you have probably stumbled upon a micro.

Then there are the seriously undesirable minors and micros: unhappy, traumatized or destructive entities formed by some extraordinary situation which—though long past and never to be repeated—continues to cloud the present so long as they are there to revive it. These may include intrusive memories of horrifying events such as accidents, sudden bereavement or crippling humiliation.

No one needs characters like these in their family. Once you are satisfied that they have no redeeming features and are beyond transformation, it is time to tell them that—to put it in corporatespeak—you have to let them go.

Letting go of a well-established personality is hard. Once it has been learned, a minor becomes part of the brain's hardware, as well as the software of the mind. Take a skeletal minor (or micro) that consists just of the desire and habit of smoking. Other personalities may overrule it, so its activity is curbed. But if the Smoker is well learned—in other words, if it is a full-blown addiction—it will remain encoded in the brain in the form of neural linkages that correspond to the Smoker's desire and behavior. So long as the neurons that make up the Smoker remain quiescent, its thoughts and feelings (Where can I get a cigarette?) will be silenced. But if those neurons are jogged into action, the Smoker will come back with a vengeance, as millions of recidivist quitters can testify.

Over a long period, unactivated neural patterns may degrade and eventually fall apart. This essentially is forgetting, and it is what you need to aim for if a troublesome minor is to be eliminated from the fold. Deliberately forgetting something, though, is notoriously difficult because the very act of trying not to think about something inevitably brings it to mind. In one episode of the classic British TV comedy *Fawlty Towers*, German visitors come to stay, and the hopelessly inept Basil (played by John Cleese) frantically instructs his staff: "Don't mention the war!" Subsequently, of course, Basil himself finds it impossible not to mention it. Indeed, he ends up goose-stepping around the dining room—compelled to draw attention to the very thing he wants most to keep under wraps.

So it seems to be with all of us. Simply trying to suppress thoughts often leads to them popping up even more frequently than they might have done otherwise. In one experiment, for example, volunteers were asked not to think about a particular subject, but to ring a bell if the forbidden thought did come to mind. On average the participants rang the bell an average of seven times during a five-minute period.[1] Furthermore, participants who were first asked to suppress a thought and then later asked to think about it experienced a rebound effect: they reported the thought many more times than those who were asked to generate the thought without first having suppressed it.

Directed, or Intentional, Forgetting is a technique that does seem to help people to prevent certain thoughts and feelings from becoming conscious. It seems to work by manipulating attention away from the things that are to be forgotten and attaching it to another set categorized as "to be remembered." It probably does not stop the thoughts from being activated *un*consciously—and minors can still have influence even when they are operating only at this level. However, banning them from consciousness should act on them as a sort of tranquilizer, making them more and more sluggish until, with luck, they will go into a permanent coma.

This, then, is the final exercise—a practical guide to saying goodbye:

- Select from your stocktaking list the minor/s you want to forget (then deal with one at a time).
- Note some telltale sign about them—a characteristic phrase or a particular habit by which you can recognize them quickly when they emerge.
- Make a note to yourself that when you become aware of this telltale you should resist being taken over.
- Instead, deliberately frame yourself into the Wise Friend (or similar chairperson) so that you can hold the unwanted minor in co-consciousness.
- Try to clarify the minor's thoughts—e.g., I am useless; I shall never be any better; everyone hates me. Write them down as a list in colored ink (say, green).
- Now make up a list of *directly opposing* thoughts. If they jog a more positive minor into life, all the better. Write them as a list in ink of another color (red).

- Reframe as Wise Friend (or another chair personality).
- Instruct yourself to remember the list of phrases written in red ink and to forget those in green.
- Repeat the phrases in red until you can say them by heart. Do not repeat those in green.
- If a green phrase subsequently pops into your mind, immediately chant the red phrases to yourself.
- Eventually you should find that the green phrases are drowned out by the red ones. Your minor's attempt to tell you, for instance, that you are universally hated will immediately trigger an even louder statement asserting your universal popularity. Do not expect to *believe* these phrases at first, just aim to learn them.
- Once the minor has given up and gone to sleep—as eventually it will—do not on any account be tempted to have a memorial service for it. Thinking about a minor you have finally put to sleep is like giving cardiac resuscitation to someone with a terminal illness—it is kinder to them, and to the rest of you, just to let it go.

I hope these exercises will have illuminated your inner family and encouraged its members to talk to one another and work as a single team rather than a collection of individuals with entirely different desires and ambitions. More broadly, I hope this book has shown that what has conventionally been regarded as harmful psychological conflict is more likely to be a sign of the inner diversity created by our ability to adapt to new circumstances. In our quick-changing and uncertain world, the essential multiplicity of the human mind will, I hope, come to be recognized as a ubiquitous and precious faculty rather than a curious and rare pathology.

Acknowledgments

Most of the people who helped me write this book don't know it. They are the many friends and acquaintances who have talked to me over the years about their personal experiences of multiplicity and how it has manifested in their lives. Some of these conversations were directed— that is, I was deliberately out to get material—but often the stories emerged in the natural course of conversation and it was only afterward that I realized their relevance to this project. In the former cases I had permission to use what I was told, and I have usually attributed it the real (first) names of the people interviewed. In the latter cases I have disguised details and changed names so that those who spoke to me cannot be identified. To all of them I am grateful.

Thanks, too, to Peter Tallack, my agent, who grasped the idea of multiplicity instantly and ran with it, and, for much the same reason, to my commissioning editor (then) at Little, Brown, Tim Whiting. Stephen Guise, my latest editor, improved the first draft immeasurably with his incisive comments and suggestions for structural rejiggering.

Rather belatedly, I'd like to thank the organizing committee of the International Society for the Study of Dissociation who made possible an extraordinarily fruitful visit to their annual conference in 2004. And (again, belatedly) thanks to Marcia Degun-Mather for helping me get to know a couple of my own minor personalities. We all get along much better now!

Notes

PART I

Chapter One: A Brief History of Our Selves

1 Robert Ornstein, *Multimind*, Macmillan, London, 1986, p. 25.

2 Simone Reinders et al., "One Brain, Two Selves," *NeuroImage*, 2003, 20, 2119.

3 *New Scientist*, 29 October 2005.

4 Onno Van der Hart, Ph.D., and Barbara Friedman, M.A., M.F.C.C., "A Reader's Guide to Pierre Janet: A Neglected Intellectual Heritage," *Dissociation*, 1989, 2(1), pp. 3–16.

5 Cited in H. F. Ellenberger, *The Discovery of the Unconscious*, Basic Books, New York, 1970, p. 127.

6 Morton Prince, *The Dissociation of a Personality*, Longmans, Green and Co., New York, 1906.

7 Helen H. Watkins, "Ego-State Therapy: An Overview," *American Journal of Clinical Hypnosis*, April 1993, Volume 35, No. 4, pp. 232–40.

8 Joan Acocella, *Creating Hysteria: Women and Multiple Personality Disorder*, Jossey-Bass Publishers, San Francisco, 1999.

9 The leading researcher in this field, Elizabeth Loftus, details her work in *The Myth of Repressed Memory*, St. Martin's Griffin, New York, 1996.

10 James V. Haxby et al., "Distributed and Overlapping Representations of Faces and Objects in Ventral Temporal Cortex," *Science*, 28 September 2001.

11 Simone Reinders et al., "One Brain, Two Selves," *NeuroImage*, 2003, 20, 2119.

12 G. Tsai et al., "Functional Magnetic Resonance Imaging of Personality

Switches in a Woman with Dissociative Identity Disorder," *Harvard Review of Psychiatry*, July/August 1999.

13 Joseph Ciorciari, "EEG Coherence and Dissociative Identity Disorder," *Journal of Trauma and Dissociation*, 2002, Volume 3, Issue 1.

14 *Collins English Dictionary*, third edition.

Chapter Two: The Landscape of Mind

1 J. Rowan, *Subpersonalities—The People Inside Us*, Brunner-Routledge, London, 1990.

2 A. G. Morgan and R. Janoff-Bulman, "Positive and Negative Self-complexity: Patterns of Adjustment Following Traumatic and Non-Traumatic Life Experiences," *Journal of Social and Clinical Psychology*, 1994, No. 13, pp. 63–85. For an overview of research see John Altrocchi, "Individual Differences in Pluralism in Self-Structure," in John Rowan and Mick Cooper (eds), *The Plural Self*, Sage Publications, London, 1999.

3 Marjorie Taylor, *Imaginary Companions and the Children Who Create Them*, Oxford University Press (USA), 2001.

4 Marjorie Taylor and A. Kohanyi, "The Illusion of Independent Agency: Do Adult Fiction Writers Experience Their Characters as Having Minds of Their Own?" *Imagination, Cognition and Personality*, 2002/3, No. 22, pp. 361–80.

5 For more on this see Rita Carter, *Mapping the Mind*, Weidenfeld and Nicolson, London, 1998.

6 S. Harter, "Self and Identity Development," in S. S. Feldman and G. R. Elliot (eds), *At the Threshold: The Developing Adolescent*, Harvard University Press, Cambridge, Mass., 1990, pp. 352–3.

7 K. J. Gergen and S. J. Morse, "Self-Consistency: Measurement and Validation," *Proceedings of the American Psychological Association*, 1967, pp. 207–8.

8 Stanley Milgram, *Obedience to Authority*, London, Tavistock, 1974. http://www.stanleymilgram.com also gives details of these and other Milgram experiments and links to other sources.

9 Walter Mischel, "Continuity and Change in Personality," *American Psychologist*, 1969, 24(11), pp. 1012–8.

10 http://www.prisonexp.org

11 Susan T. Fiske, Lasana T. Harris and Amy J. C. Cuddy, "Why Ordinary People Torture Enemy Prisoners," *Science*, 26 November 2004, Vol. 306, No. 5701, pp. 1482–3.

12 Tara Pepper, "Inside the Head of an Applicant," *Newsweek*, 21 February 2005.

13 Daniel Druckman and Robert A. Bjork, *In the Mind's Eye: Enhancing Human Performance*, National Academy of Sciences, New York, 1991.

14 Kennon Sheldon et al., "Trait Self and True Self: Cross-Role Variation in the Big-Five Personality Traits and Its Relations with Psychological Authenticity and Subjective Well-Being," *Journal of Personality and Social Psychology*, 1997, Vol. 73, No. 6, pp. 1380–93.

Chapter Three: Mechanisms of Mind

1 Ronald C. Petersen, "Retrieval Failures in State-Dependent Learning," *Psychopharmacology*, 1977, No. 55, pp. 141–6.

2 G. H. Bower, "Affect and Cognition," *Philosophical Transactions of the Royal Society of London (Series B)*, 1983, 302, pp. 387–402.

3 Becker-Blease et al., "A Genetic Analysis of Individual Differences in Dissociative Behavior in Children and Adolescents," *Journal of Child Psychology and Psychiatry*, 2004, Vol. 45, No. 3, pp. 522–32.

4 Colin A. Ross, *Dissociative Identity Disorder: Diagnosis, Clinical Features, and Treatment of Multiple Personalities*, John Wiley, New York, 1997.

5 Ross, *Dissociative Identity Disorder*.

6 Marlene Steinberg and Maxine Schnall, *The Stranger in the Mirror: Dissociation—the Hidden Epidemic*, Cliff Street Books, New York, 2000.

7 Steven N. Gold, "Fight Club: A Depiction of Contemporary Society as Dissociogenic," *Journal of Trauma and Dissociation*, 2004, Vol. 5(2).

Chapter Four: Changing Times, Changing Selves

1 Population Trends, HM Government, 30 September 2004.

2 *Independent*, 17 November 2005.

3 P. W. Linville, "Self-Complexity as a Cognitive Buffer Against Stress-Related Illness and Depression," *Journal of Personality and Social Psychology*, 1987, Vol. 52, pp. 663–76.

4 Cathy tells the full story of her depression and recovery in her book: *Life After Darkness*, Radcliffe Publishing, Oxford, 2006.

5 Catherine Harmer et al., "Increased Positive Versus Negative Affective Perception and Memory in Healthy Volunteers Following Selective Serotonin and Norepinephrine Reuptake Inhibition," *American Journal of Psychiatry*, July 2004, No. 161, pp. 1256–63.

6 Shankar Vedantam, "Prescription for an Obsession?," *Washington Post*, 19 March 2006.

Chapter Five: The People You Are

1 For evidence of this, see Judith Rich Harris, *The Nurture Assumption*, Bloomsbury, London, 1998.

2 "Ego Boundaries, or the Fit of My Father's Shirt—Mind-to-Body Ratio Is Not Always One-to-One," *Discover*, November 1995.

3 Interview, *Woman's Hour*, BBC Radio 4, 30 May 2006.

4 N. Ramirez-Esparza et al., "Do Bilinguals Have Two Personalities?," *Journal of Research in Personality*, 2006, No. 40, pp. 99–120.

5 Margaret Shih et al., "Stereotype Susceptibility: Identity Salience and Shifts in Quantitative Performance," *Psychological Science*, 1999, 10(1), pp. 81–4.

6 M. Inzlicht et al., "Stigma as Ego Depletion—How Being the Target of Prejudice Affects Self-Control," *Psychological Science*, March 2006, pp. 262–9.

7 Interview with Grayson Perry by Trace Newton-Ingham: http://www.saatchi-gallery.co.uk/artists/grayson_perry_articles.htm

8 "Eating Disorders and the Search for Solutions," NIMH Publication 01-4901, 2001.

9 "The Prevalence and Correlates of Eating Disorders in the National Comorbidity Survey Replication," James I. Hudson et al., *Biological Psychiatry*, 3 July 2006.

10 "Wasting the Best and the Brightest: Substance Abuse at America's Colleges and Universities," The National Center on Addiction and Substance Abuse at Columbia University, March 2007.

11 Terra D. Barnes et al., "Activity of Striatal Neurons Reflects Dynamic Encoding and Recoding of Procedural Memories," *Nature*, 20 October 2005, 437, pp. 1158–61.

12 Marcia Degun-Mather, "Ego-State Therapy in the Treatment of a Complex Eating Disorder," North East London Mental Health Care Trust, *Contemporary Hypnosis*, 2003, Vol. 20(3), pp. 165–73.

13 Virgin Money commissioned TNS to survey 2,057 adults aged over sixteen between 10 and 15 May 2005.

14 Gareth McLean, "When the Playboy Met the Liar," *Guardian*, 1 August 2006.

15 *Midweek*, BBC Radio 4, 18 January 2006.

Notes

16 "The Body Remembers: The Psychophysiology of Trauma and Trauma Treatment," *Psychotherapy Networker*, September 2004.
17 Robert Hof, "My Virtual Life," *Businessweek.com*, 1 May 2006.

PART II

Chapter Eight: Working Together

1 D. M. Wegner, D. J. Schneider, S. Carter III and L. White, "Paradoxical Effects of Thought Suppression," *Journal of Personality and Social Psychology*, 1987, 53, pp. 5–13.

Resources

Further reading

The Plural Self, John Rowan and Mick Cooper (eds), Sage Publications, London, 1999, and *The Multiple Self*, Jon Elster (ed.), Cambridge University Press, Cambridge, 1986.
Two excellent collections of essays by psychologists and philosophers about a pluralistic view of the self.

Subpersonalities, John Rowan, Brunner-Routledge, London, 1990.
Rowan is one of a very few psychologists fully to endorse the notion of normal multiplicity. This book details his own views about how they are created, how they work and how they manifest in everyday life.

The Myth of Sanity: Divided Consciousness and the Promise of Awareness, Martha Stout, Viking Penguin, 2001.
Stout considers multiplicity to be pathological. However, she believes it to be so pervasive that it is effectively the "norm" and manifests in everyday behavior as well as in clearly dysfunctional individuals.

The Stranger in the Mirror, Marlene Steinberg and Maxine Schnall, Cliff Street Books/Harper Collins, 2000.
An informative and practical introduction to dissociation in all its guises.

Resources

The Society of Mind, Marvin Minsky, Pan Books, London, 1988, and *Multimind*, Robert Ornstein, Houghton Mifflin, Boston, 1986.
Both put forward the notion that individual minds are made up of many semi-autonomous brain modules, each of which has its own aims, talents and influence. Brain-imaging studies bring new confirmation of this every day.

Websites
Astraea's Web: http://www.astraeasweb.net/plural
This is an extraordinarily comprehensive source of information, insight and guidance to the whole field of multiple personalities, with emphasis on "normal" multiplicity.

http://lists.topica.com/lists/darkpersonalities
A multiplicity discussion site for people who are interested in the topic generally, or consider themselves to be healthy and functional multiples.

Other multiplicity resources
Voice Dialogue (page 4)
A therapeutic technique based on getting inner selves to talk together and also to strengthen what it refers to as "the Aware Ego." This is described on its website as "a process where your usual ego becomes aware of itself, or rather of the selves that are a part of it, and is then able to *choose* which selves to express, rather than have the selves choose for you." See http://www.voicedialogue.com and *Embracing Our Selves*, Hal and Sidra Stone, New World Library, California, 1989.

Ego-state therapy (page 4)
Uses hypnotherapy (mainly) to bring otherwise hidden "ego-states" (what I refer to as personalities) into consciousness and thus to open them to interrogation and behavior modification. See http://www.clinicalsocial work.com/egostate.html and *Ego-States—Theory and Therapy*, John and Helen Watkins, Norton, New York, 1997.

Resources

Psychosynthesis
A somewhat spiritually inclined therapeutic system which is based on the idea that people are divided into subselves, but that they can develop a Higher Awareness that transcends the parts. See http://www.psycho synthesis.org.

Dissociation—information and links to therapy
The site http://www.sidran.org is for people who are concerned about or interested in the dysfunctional or extreme form of multiplicity known as Dissociative Identity Disorder. The International Society for the Study of Dissociative Disorders website (http://www.issd.org) includes a list of therapists as well as a comprehensive book list and information about dissociation.

Index

Index

Index

Index

Index

About the Author

Rita Carter is an award-winning science and medical writer. She contributes to a wide range of newspapers and magazines, including *New Scientist, The Independent, The Times,* and *The Daily Mail.* Before specializing in science, Carter worked for six years as a TV newscaster on Thames TV and as a radio host/producer.

One of her lives in an isolated country house in the depths of the British countryside, with a cat. The other travels widely throughout Europe and the United States, talking, commenting, and broadcasting on medical and scientific topics, particularly on the social and philosophical issues raised by recent advances in brain research.

WITH MY WARM COMPLIMENTS,
please accept this copy of

GOD: DISCOVER HIS CHARACTER

as a token of my personal gratitude and
thanks to you for your faithful friendship
and commitment to help fulfill
the Great Commission.

One's view of God determines their lifestyle,
their selection of friends, the kinds of
music and literature they enjoy,
and every other consideration of life.

It is my sincere prayer that through
understanding the truths contained on these
pages, you will come to better appreciate the
character of our awesome, all-powerful,
loving God and Father, who revealed
Himself to us through our Lord Jesus Christ
to establish a warm, intimate,
and personal relationship with Him.

In His great love,

Bill Bright

P.S. My prayer for you is Ephesians 3:17-21.

"This is an outstanding book and is must reading for all believers."

"One of the best ways to know somebody is through the testimony of one who has been a close and faithful friend. Bill Bright has spent half of a century in an intimate relationship with God. His devoted study of the attributes of God has prepared him to share with others rare and valuable insights into the character and the personality of Him, whom to know is life eternal."

—Dr. D. James Kennedy, Senior Minister,
Coral Ridge Presbyterian Church

"Dr. Bright, in his compelling and biblically based book, *GOD: Discover His Character*, reminds us that God's power and sovereignty are so awesome that He is eager to have a personal relationship with every person who humbly and sincerely seeks to know Him."

—George Gallup, Jr., Chairman,
George H. Gallup International Institute

"Daniel 11:32 says, '…but the people who know their God shall be strong, and carry out great exploits.' Dr. Bright has written a book that will help believers to know the Lord intimately and to practice courageous Christianity, which is so needed on our day."

—Bill McCartney, Founder & President, Promise Keepers

"I have known God to be a God of love, mercy, and a righteous judge, but Bill Bright's book, *GOD: Discover His Character*, has been a timely reminder to me of His greatness and majesty. A great book to read for even the most mature Christian!"

—Beverly LaHaye, Founder and Chairman,
Concerned Women for America

"Who would not want to know God? And who of us who know God would not want to know Him more personally? This book will help us not only to know about God but to know Him intimately. Every one of us would do well to read these pages carefully and prayerfully."

—Dr. Paul Cedar, Chairman, Mission America

"As we know His power, presence, mercy, and sovereignty, we begin to understand how God deals with us. As we understand His holiness, truth, and righteousness, we again understand His plan and purpose for our life. By understanding the love, mercy, and faithfulness of God, we understand how He forgives all sinners and loves us equally. Bill

Bright has shown us that understanding His attributes helps us to understand God and to live for Him."
—*Elmer L. Towns, Dean, School of Religion, Liberty University*

"Many people know about God, but Bill Bright has written from a personal walk with God, thus it has been a life of discovery that is not his alone, but for all who desire to know God. This is an outstanding book and is must reading for all believers."
—*Thomas E. Trask, General Superintendent, Assemblies of God*

"If we want to make sure our obedience is on target, we first need to make sure that it is grounded in a love relationship with the One to whom we are to be obedient. This book will help you do just that."
—*Robert E. Reccord, President, North American Mission Board, Southern Baptist Convention*

"What an incredible book! Bill Bright eloquently describes what it's like to come into the awesome presence of God. As I read the book, I found myself weeping as I was reminded of His glory, greatness, and majesty!"
—*Dr. Stan Toler, Senior Pastor, Trinity Church of the Nazarene, Oklahoma City*

"In his book, *GOD: Discover His Character*, Bill Bright has captured the heart cry of all sincere Christians…that we may discover the glory of God and His ways toward all mankind."
—*Pat Robertson, Chairman & CEO, The Christian Broadcasting Network, Inc.*

"To know God as He is revealed in Holy Scripture is to love Him and your attitude toward Him will affect almost everything you do in life, particularly the way you feel toward other people. Because he has studied the Scriptures carefully and put God to many tests for over fifty years, no one is better qualified to describe God than Bill Bright. This book will enrich your life!"
—*Tim LaHaye, President, Tim LaHaye Ministries*

"In his new book, *GOD: Discover His Character*, Dr. Bright challenges readers to understand and apply profound truths about the nature and character of God to daily living. The true value of this book lies in its focus on the interaction between understanding the truth about God and the way we are to live in this world. I highly recommend this rich emphasis."
—*Michael D. Cozzens, PhD., Academic Dean, International School of Theology*

DISCOVER

HIS

CHARACTER

BILL BRIGHT

GOD: Discover His Character

Published by
NewLife Publications
A ministry of Campus Crusade for Christ
P.O. Box 620877
Orlando, FL 32862-0877

Design and production by Genesis Publications.
Edited by Joette Whims.
Cover by Koechel-Peterson Design.
Printed in the United States of America.

Library of Congress Cataloging-in-Publication Data
Bright, Bill.
    God: discover his character / by Bill Bright.
        p.   cm.
    Includes bibliographical references.
    ISBN 1-56399-121-7 (hc.)
    1. God—Attributes.   I. Title.
  BT130.B74   1999
  231'.4—dc21
                                99-33089
                                  CIP

For more information, write:

L.I.F.E., Campus Crusade for Christ—P.O. Box 40, Flemington Markets, NSW 2129, Australia

Campus Crusade for Christ of Canada—Box 529, Sumas, WA 98295

Campus Crusade for Christ—Fairgate House, King's Road, Tyseley, Birmingham, B11 2AA, United Kingdom

Lay Institute for Evangelism, Campus Crusade for Christ—P.O. Box 8786, Auckland, 1035, New Zealand

Campus Crusade for Christ—9 Lock Road #3-03, PacCan Centre, Singapore 108937

Great Commission Movement of Nigeria—P.O. Box 500, Jos, Plateau State, Nigeria, West Africa

Campus Crusade for Christ International—P.O. Box 620877, Orlando, FL 32862-0877, USA

DEDICATION

This book is gratefully dedicated to every person who has faithfully prayed for or supported our ministry over the years. In particular, I dedicate this book to the members of History's Handful, a movement of leaders committed to a special strategy to provide resources to help fulfill the Great Commission. These unselfish servants have made possible many, many projects that might not have otherwise been accomplished without their generous sacrifices of personal time and resources.

CONTENTS

PART III: OUR GRACIOUS SAVIOR
(Attributes of Relationship)

PART IV: CONCLUSION

APPENDICES: HELPS FOR SPIRITUAL GROWTH

ACKNOWLEDGMENTS

Remembering and thanking all the people who have influenced me in writing this book over the past fifty years or more would be almost impossible. To the poet's line, "No man is an island," I must add that no author writes a book solely on his or her own efforts and knowledge. Literally hundreds of people have contributed to my journey of seeking and knowing God.

In the early days of my spiritual walk with our Lord, my pastor, Dr. Louis Evans, and our church's Christian Education Director, Dr. Henrietta Mears, nurtured me with their preaching, teaching, and personal friendship. During the five years of my theological studies at Princeton and Fuller Theological Seminaries, I was blessed to learn under spiritual giants such as their presidents, Dr. John A. Mackay and Dr. Harold J. Ockenga. My professors also opened up the Word of God to enrich my life and ministry. A few that I remember the most included Dr. Carl F. H. Henry, Dr. Charles E. Fuller, Dr. Robert Smith, and Dr. Wilbur Smith.

In addition to my formal study in the Word and personal experiences with God, I have learned much from the writings of great biblical scholars and effective ministers of the gospel. I have shared some of their rich insights with you in this book. They include men such as A. W. Tozer, J. I. Packer, Stephen Charnock, Arthur Pink, Charles Stanley, Chuck Colson, Tony Evans, David Jeremiah, D. James Kennedy, Bill Hybels, Jim Cymbala, Norman Geisler, R. C. Sproul, Erwin Lutzer, Ravi Zacharias, Henry Blackaby, and many others. I commend their speaking and writing to anyone who wants to know God more intimately.

I am particularly indebted to my dear friend of more than forty years, Dr. Adrian Rogers, pastor of the famous Bellevue Baptist Church, Memphis, Tennessee, for expressing his thoughts in the Foreword to this book.

My special heartfelt thanks go to researchers and writers Les Stobbe, Helmut Teichert, Nancy Schraeder, and Jim Bramlett. I am indebted to my *NewLife* Publications staff: Dr. Joe Kilpatrick, publisher and general editor; Joette Whims, substantive editing and polishing; John Barber, theological review; Tammy Campbell, editorial assistant; and Michelle Treiber, cover coordination and print brokering. My gratitude also goes to Lynn Copeland of Genesis Publications for her design, typesetting, and copyediting.

Finally, I save my dearest expressions of love and appreciation for my beloved wife of more than fifty years, Vonette. She has walked with me through the good times and the hard times over these years as we have learned to love, trust, obey, and fellowship with our great God and Savior, the mighty Creator of the Universe.

FOREWORD

I guess I should not have been shocked to read recently a national newspaper article titled, "Few TV Dads Give Positive Vibrations." The National Fatherhood Initiative report stated, "For millions of America's children, the primary daily contact they have with the idea of a father is the time they spend watching a father on television." Yet according to a five-week review of prime-time programming on five major networks late last year, only 14.7 percent of these programs featured fatherhood enough to be rated. Of these, only four programs promoted responsible fatherhood positively.

The seriousness of this situation is that 40 percent of the nation's children do not live with their biological fathers, and whole communities exist where single mothers head almost all the households. Is it any wonder that too many children grow up with a distorted, false view of what a good father is really like? Without a healthy view of an earthly father, how can they picture a loving heavenly Father?

Even children who grow up in church often do not reach adulthood with a positive view of God. In an article titled, "When You Think of God, What Do You See?" (*Life*, December 1998), author Frank McCourt expresses the experience of many children and teens:

> We didn't hear much about a loving God. We were told God is good and that was supposed to be enough. Otherwise the God of my memory is one the tribes of Israel would have recognized, an angry God, a vengeful God, a God who will let you have it upside your head if you strayed, transgressed, or coveted. Our God had a stern face...and a message of damnation from the pulpit, scaring us to death. If we didn't understand [some doctrine] and asked questions, we were brushed aside and told it was a matter of faith so [eat your dinner] and shut up."

This article also reported that 96 percent of Americans believe in God and 79 percent pray to God and feel that He has helped them make decisions. McCourt continues:

> America's God is vaguely defined. Ours is not a monocultural nation like, say Iran, Italy or Japan, but a proudly diverse one. On the contrary, America makes it society's business to support, protect and nurture minority viewpoints, values, and traditions. Within these are many different views of God (sometimes gods, plural; sometimes "exalted beings" possessing a divine essence). America has become one nation under "gods."

As immigrants bring their religions with them and many Americans experiment with philosophical beliefs based on humanism or secularism, we have indeed become a nation under many gods. The crucial question for all these culturally diverse worshippers and philosophical seekers is, "Who is the one true God who can remove their sins and give them eternal life in heaven after they die?"

There is an answer, and I am so happy that my good friend, Dr. Bill Bright, is addressing this important question of who God is and what He is like. It is a privilege for me to recommend this book, *GOD: Discover His Character*. Having walked with God for almost six decades, Bill's passion, like the apostle Paul's, is to know God and make Him known to others. Here he shares his experiences and the biblical truths he has learned for knowing, loving, serving, and worshipping his God.

As you read this book, you will see the many sides of God's character and nature. These truths, converted into principles of relating to our awesome, majestic God, will help you at every turn in the road of life. In the troubled and uncertain times in which we live, it is comforting to know the God of the holy Bible, the Constitution of the Christian faith. When there are so many gods to choose from, even here in America, we need this solid word of the one true God in this unsure age in which we live.

Dr. Adrian Rogers
Senior Pastor, Bellevue Baptist Church
Memphis, Tennessee

CHAPTER 1

CAN ANYONE *REALLY* KNOW GOD?

ave you ever considered one of the most important questions anyone could ask? *Is it possible for a mere human, less than a tiny speck on a pebble of a planet in the midst of a vast galaxy, to know the great God who created everything?* If so, can we know God well enough to trust Him with the most sensitive areas in our lives? Even more, *do* we know God well enough to love and obey Him in whatever He asks of us? The quest to know, love, and serve God is the greatest adventure in life!

Yet the goal of knowing God may seem impossible. We can compare our quest to know God to the story of a microscopic mite that lived on a flea on a little dog in a small yard of a humble home. This house was on the outskirts of Jerusalem in the kingdom of the rich and powerful King Solomon, who reigned centuries ago. The king lived in a mysterious palace in the midst of royal elegance far beyond the microscopic world of the mite. In mite miles, the distance from the mite to the king's palace seemed like light years.

This tiny mite decided that the most important work he could ever do was to write a book about that world-respected king.

After reflecting on his book for a long time, the frustrated mite abandoned his project. He just did not know what to write; he had a deep desire, but none of his words seemed adequate to describe such a majestic person.

In a very real sense, that was my predicament as I set forth to write about our glorious and mighty God. He lives in indescribable splendor beyond my wildest imagination. His character is far above the limited scope of my human understanding. The only difference between me and the mite that wanted to write about King Solomon is that, compared to God, I am less than a mite in this universe of more than one hundred billion galaxies.

Have you ever felt like I do about understanding and knowing our great God? How can we as mere human beings fully grasp any facet of our gloriously incomprehensible God? So why would I attempt to undertake such a seemingly impossible task? More importantly, why should any of us try to understand who God is?

WHY IS IT SO IMPORTANT TO KNOW GOD?

My desire to write a book about God began many years ago when Dr. James Montgomery Boice of the "Bible Hour" radio program interviewed me. One of the first questions Dr. Boice asked me was, "What is the most important truth to teach any follower of Christ?"

What an incredible question! No one had ever asked me that before, so I was not prepared to answer it. For a brief moment, I was speechless. But then I am convinced that God's Holy Spirit gave me the answer: "The attributes of God."

I have had years to think about that question and my answer. Today I am more convinced than ever that there is nothing more important to teach another believer than who God is, what He is like, and why or how He does what He does. These attributes of God can be referred to as His character, nature, qualities, or personality.

Yet one of the most tragic trends I have noticed in our churches today is the way believers view God. Renowned author A. W. Tozer writes in his book *The Knowledge of the Holy:*

The low view of God entertained almost universally among Christians is the cause of a hundred lesser evils everywhere among us. With our loss of the sense of majesty has come the further loss of religious awe and the consciousness of the divine presence…It is impossible to keep our moral practices sound and our inward attitudes right while our idea of God is erroneous or inadequate. If we would bring back spiritual power to our lives, we must begin to think of God more nearly as He is.[1]

In fact, everything about our lives—our attitudes, motives, desires, actions, and even our words—is influenced by our view of God. Whether our problems are financial, moral, or emotional, whether we are tempted by lust, worry, anger, or insecurity, our behavior reflects our beliefs about God. What we believe to be true about God's character affects our friendships, our work and leisure activities, the types of literature we read, and even the music to which we listen. If the majority of believers do not have the right view of God, how can our society even begin to see Him as He is? Because of the wrong view of God that predominates in all areas of our culture today, our society is in moral turmoil, and we are in danger of losing our moral soul.

We can trace all our human problems to our view of God. A contrast in two lives from history illustrates the different outcomes that result from a wrong and a right view of God.

The first example is Karl Marx, who was born in Trier, Germany, in 1818. Educated in German universities, he became the editor of a Cologne newspaper. Marx denied the existence of God, believing that the individual, not God, is the highest form of being. Instead of God being in control, he felt that people make themselves what they are by their own efforts. Society, therefore, is the supreme agent for achieving success and fulfillment.

In *Economic and Philosophic Manuscripts of 1844,* he wrote, "All that is called history is nothing else than the process of creating man through human labour, the becoming of nature for man. Man has thus evident and irrefutable proof of his own creation by himself…For man, man is the supreme being."[2]

Since Marx believed that man was a god, he concluded that society, composed of the common man, should rule and overthrow the reigning government by force. He and Fredrich Engel collaborated on defining philosophical ideals that eventually formed the basis for communism.

In the 20th century, Vladimir Lenin revived Marx's ideas, accomplishing the overthrow of the czarist rule in Russia. Stalin followed Lenin as Communist leader of the Soviet Union. Under their reigns and the Communist rulers who followed them, tens of millions of Russians were slaughtered by the state. The loss of life resulted because these Communist leaders believed that there was no God, that the individual had no inherent value, and that the state was of supreme importance. Today, Marx's ideas still form the basis for totalitarian government in many countries, including North Korea, Cuba, and China.

> HOW WE VIEW
> GOD WILL
> CHANGE THE
> WAY WE LIVE
> AND RELATE
> WITH OTHERS.

Contrast the life of Marx with the life of Martin Luther. He too was a revolutionary. He was born in 1483 in Eisleben, Germany, only a couple of hundred miles from where Marx would later begin his life. Martin Luther was also educated in German universities.

Like Marx, the young Luther struggled with ideals of authority, morality, and ethics. Although he tried to serve God as a monk, he grew increasingly terrified of God's wrath. Then he was drawn to Romans 1:17, "The righteous shall live by faith." This simple concept changed his view of God. He wrote:

> At last, meditating day and night and by the mercy of God, I...began to understand that the righteousness of God is that through which the righteous live by a gift of God, namely by faith...Here I felt as if I were entirely born again and had entered paradise itself through gates that had been flung open.[3]

Luther's realization—that God's free gift of forgiveness is available to each person on earth—emphasized the value God gives to each individual created in His image. What a contrast to the beliefs of communism!

Luther's teaching on the life of faith, as opposed to earning salvation by good works, was the beginning of the great Protestant Reformation that reshaped Europe during the next two centuries. Today, the principle of forgiveness by faith is followed by hundreds of millions of people worldwide. In America, we owe much of our historical and religious roots to what Luther began in Germany.

These two examples show that a false view of God leads to sin and corruption—and many times cruelty and great human tragedy. On the other hand, a proper understanding of God leads to a life of blessing for oneself and many generations to follow.

You may dismiss this by thinking, *I am no Karl Marx or Martin Luther. I am not a world leader or a person with great influence.* None of us are. Yet how we view God will change the way we live and relate with others. Consider the couple who takes in a foster child because they know God loves that little one; they may live next door to parents who neglect or abuse their child. One person cheats his customers because he thinks "no one will ever know"; another repays a loan despite severe financial hardships, because he has a reverential respect for a God who notes men's actions and expects honesty.

All of our actions, like Marx's and Luther's, are driven by our views of God and how He interacts with us. Nothing in life could be more important than knowing God accurately.

DOES GOD WANT TO RELATE TO US?

Understanding God is not a simple task. I readily admit that, like all human beings, I am incapable of completely explaining the attributes of our awesome God who reigns in overwhelming majesty. Who am I, a mere man, trying to describe the God of the universe who is all-powerful, holy, and righteous? In fact, while I was writing this book, I was overcome with a sense of my unwor-thiness. I fell to my knees in tears and confessed, "Oh, Lord, I am not worthy to write about Your character. Forgive me for being so presumptuous." At that moment, the Lord seemed to put His arms around me, assuring me that He had called me to do this.

That's why I am so anxious to share with you, through this book, the truths about God: because I know without a doubt that God wants us to *really know* Him. Let me go back to my analogy of the mite on the flea on the dog. The mite had given up hope that he could ever understand the mighty king. Then it was as though King Solomon searched out that insignificant mite. First, the king found the owner of that small home on the outskirts of Jerusalem. He stepped into the yard, found the dog, then the flea, and finally, with astonishing lovingkindness, told the mite—in the mite's own limited language—all about himself.

This part of the analogy is the most humbling to me. God did not just content Himself with speaking to us through our limited language. Instead, He assumed our limited form—that of a human—setting aside His riches and splendor and honor to become like us! That, of course, was the miraculous day when God was born as a baby in a manger in the small village of Bethlehem. That baby's name is Jesus Christ, the Son of God and Savior of the world. This demonstration of God's love is beyond my comprehension and shows His great desire for us to know Him. God's willingness to become a man changed forever the way I can relate with Him.

HOW CAN KNOWING GOD CHANGE MY LIFE?

What misconceptions do you have about God that are preventing you from getting to know Him better? Are you so unsure about what God is really like that you cannot trust Him completely?

Take heart. Because of God's love, He has provided the way for us to understand more about what He is like, what He is up to, and how He can help us change our lives completely. Keep reading. We will discover many ways He has given us to know Him better.

My prayer is that the Holy Spirit will mightily use this book to reveal to you the amazing and wonderful character of our glorious Creator God and Savior. If you read this book with prayerful sincerity, it will alter your perspective and you will find your life changing in astounding ways.

I can tell you from personal experience that an intimate walk with God never fails to produce an abundance of joy and adventure in people's lives. Let me share an example from one man's life, John Newton. His story demonstrates what a right view of God can do for each of us.

John Newton's mother was a devoted Christian, but she died when he was a child. As a young man, he decided to follow in the footsteps of his father, an English sea captain. He joined the British Royal Navy but was discharged because of unruly behavior. To escape further problems, he moved to the western coast of Africa and worked for a slave trader. He eventually became captain of a slave ship, and he treated the slaves despicably. What a loathsome man he had become!

On one voyage, his ship was severely battered by a fierce storm. Fearing for his life, he surrendered himself to God, setting his life on a new course. Over the next few years as he became convinced that slavery was abhorrent, he gave up his slave trading and later even crusaded against slavery. His life changed so much that he studied to become a minister. When he preached, he was known as the "old converted sea captain." All because he had personally met and come to know God. He wrote one of the most famous hymns in English, *Amazing Grace*. In it, he describes his own transformation:

> Amazing grace, how sweet the sound,
> That saved a wretch like me.
> I once was lost, but now am found,
> Was blind, but now I see.

Who else but almighty God could change a calloused man engaged in the slave trade into a compassionate minister and anti-slavery crusader?

Have you experienced this change? Has God been intimately involved in your life? For more than fifty years, I have walked and talked with our loving heavenly Father. It has been the greatest adventure of my lifetime. The more I get to know Him, the more peace, joy, love, and excitement I experience. He has proven to be my best friend, someone I can trust in every situation.

My desire is not just to share information about God with you—although that is important. But I trust that the Holy Spirit will help me communicate my heart about God. Hopefully, you will be encouraged to embrace the right view of God and know Him well enough to love, trust, and obey Him as never before.

As we explore the truths of these pages together, discovering who God is and His love and plan for us, I am confident that your life will never be the same. Let us begin by looking more closely at how we can know God intimately.

CHAPTER 2

WE CAN KNOW GOD INTIMATELY!

n 1978 at the height of the Cold War between the Soviet Union and the United States, the Soviet government, at the request of the Russian church, invited me to visit that vast land. During my visit to eight cities, I sensed that millions of people were imprisoned by fear resulting from mental and physical abuse. The KGB, the secret police of the Soviet government, seemed to squeeze every individual to discover information about the activities and views of political dissidents, followers of Christ, and Jews. Under this kind of suspicion and tyranny, no one trusted anyone. Even family members turned against each other in this oppressive uncertainty.

While few of us live under such conditions today, you may have often wondered, *Who can I really trust?* Perhaps you have a friend or two you consider trustworthy. But beyond that, who can you trust with the things that you consider most private and valuable?

I am sure you will agree that trustworthiness is in short supply today. At every level of government, there are officials who feel that dishonesty serves a purpose in politics. Within our financial institutions, businessmen have used the wealth of others to their personal advantage, often depriving those who are most vulnerable, senior citizens, of their retirement funds. People break contracts without remorse under the pretense of smart business practices. Husbands and wives, some who have been married for decades, betray their spouses for their own selfish, lustful desires. Families, especially innocent children, are shattered by broken promises. Good friends become enemies over lapses in honesty.

If a close friend or relative has betrayed your trust, how did that betrayal affect your relationship? Did it influence how much you trust other people today?

In many cases our past experiences, backgrounds, and personalities shape how we view other people and how we form relationships with them. If someone we trusted hurt us, we hesitate to trust anyone else again. If a parent or sibling treated us shamefully, we respond by protecting ourselves from other close relationships. Although trust is an important part of any healthy friendship, for many of us, building trust is one of the most difficult elements of our relationships.

> THE AMOUNT OF TRUST YOU HAVE IN GOD DEPENDS ON HOW YOU VIEW HIM.

But what about God? Can He be trusted? How far are you willing to go in trusting Him? The amount of trust you have in God depends on how you view Him. Some people think of Him as a big bully, a cosmic policeman, or a divine Santa Claus. Others believe He is like their insensitive, selfish parents who do whatever they want because they have the size or power.

Some consider God to be hard to get along with, someone to fear. Others think of Him as a heartless dictator waiting to punish them for doing wrong. Perhaps you see him as a kindly grandfather who just shakes His head over the terrible plight of humankind but does not get involved. Do you see Him as loving, gracious, tender, and compassionate? Or as critical, jealous, vindictive, and haughty?

I hear from many Christians who are discouraged in their quest to know God more fully. They claim to have tried to learn what God is like but have come up short. Maybe they failed on a commitment they made to God and feel the communication lines are down between themselves and heaven. Others believe that God has abandoned them or treated them unfairly. Some simply do not know what God is like and have decided that they probably will never know more than they do now. Millions of people cry out, *"Who are you, God?"*

WE CAN HAVE AN INTIMATE RELATIONSHIP WITH THE GOD OF CREATION

In Chapter 1, we learned how important it is to know God and to have the right view of Him. But how can we develop a relationship with a Being who is beyond our comprehension? The process toward intimacy is similar to getting to know a new neighbor.

Imagine that a new couple moves next door to you. What impression do you get of what they are like? You probably notice the furniture and belongings carried into their house, and the type of car in their driveway. The first time you meet them, you most likely find out what they do for a living. Are they lawyers or construction workers, computer specialists or businessmen, teachers or factory workers? You probably ask questions about their hobbies and interests. Do they enjoy gardening or do they pride themselves in how well they play golf? These facts give you a little insight into what kind of people they are.

As you get to know your neighbors better, you also discover more about their character. Are they kind, generous, amiable, and compassionate? Or do they speak harshly, criticize, and act rudely toward others? Do they have good character?

With time, you may get to know your neighbors more intimately. Are they ambitious or lazy? Do they shade the truth or are they honest? Do they keep their word? Do they practice values similar to yours or do they live by a different set of rules? How do they react under stressful situations? This closer relationship uncovers the deeper qualities of their inner lives.

Of course, God is not like a next-door neighbor. He is so much more than that. His characteristics are far above what we as humans can accomplish or even understand. But because He is loving and gracious toward us, He reveals His character to us so we can relate more intimately with Him. As in any relationship, developing intimacy is a process. Someone has aptly said, "If we take one step toward God, He will take two steps toward us."

God Helps Us Get to Know Him

Through their own ability, human beings cannot advance in their knowledge of God beyond a few biographical facts. But God in His love and mercy has taken steps to make Himself known to us in many ways. Because God is so far above us in every aspect, the process begins with Him as He reveals Himself to those who hunger and thirst to know Him.

The most important place we can turn to find the truth about what God is like is in His holy Word, the Bible. It gives us the most accurate picture of almighty God. Although all facets of God's nature are always present, He reveals Himself in three primary ways:

God reveals Himself as our great Creator. Genesis 1, the first chapter in the Bible, unveils the Creator's mighty works, His unlimited power, and eternal knowledge. In Part I, "Our Great Creator," we will discover that our Creator-God has no limitations.

God reveals the depth of His integrity as our perfect Judge. The remainder of the Old Testament shows how God built a nation of people dedicated to Him and how He led and blessed these people. Throughout this historical account, God gives laws and promises that establish His nature as one of holiness and integrity. If the people obeyed these laws, they would be blessed and happy; if they did not, they would bring God's wrath and judgment upon themselves. In Part II, "Our Perfect Judge," we will look at the holiness, truthfulness, righteousness, and justice of our perfect God.

God reveals Himself as our gracious Savior. In the New Testament, God sent His Son to earth as Savior of the world. Jesus is the flesh-and-blood picture of God with whom we can relate. The life, death, and resurrection of Jesus prove God's love, mercy, and faithfulness. In Part III, "Our Gracious Savior," we will discover the depths of God's compassion through His Son and how we can know that love.

Would you not agree that the most astounding news we can ever hear is that God, the almighty Creator of heaven and earth, invites us to have an intimate relationship with Him? He makes it simple for us to do so. Knowing God intimately can transform your life into one of passion, joy, adventure, and peace. With a clearer understanding of the greatness of our God, we will be able to:

- Learn how to worship and praise God as a part of our daily lives
- Renew our passion, love, and commitment for God
- Clear up misconceptions about God's role in our lives
- Understand the depths of His love
- Learn what it means to "fear" God
- Discover ways to seek God wholeheartedly
- See how His names reflect His character
- Learn how to tell others about God's character in clear and simple terms

Before we begin discovering a right view of God, understanding some truths about what God is like will give us insight into His unique character.

GOD IS A PERSONAL SPIRIT

Someone asked Buddha, the founder of Buddhism, if God existed. He replied, "The question is not relevant. If there were a God, man could not comprehend him anyway. So what good would it be to have such a God?"

Some "religious" people consider God a force, an evil spirit, or something encased in wood or stone. As a result, their concept of God is hazy or impersonal. If God were merely an energy force or a composite of the universe as New Age philosophies teach, knowing Him personally would be impossible. And if God were merely an idol, made by man's hand from wood or some precious metal, our efforts to know Him would be futile. How could a human have a relationship with an inanimate object?

But God's Word reveals God as a personal Spirit; therefore we can know Him personally. This may seem like such a simple concept, but it is the underlying truth on which we base our understanding of God.

The Bible shows that God has a distinct personality. The New Testament book of John says that God is Spirit.[1] Although He does not have a physical body as we do, He possesses all the characteristics of a personality: He thinks, feels, and wills. The Bible gives us several proofs that we can know God personally.

Many Old and New Testament believers knew God and were considered His friends. Let me give you a few examples.

God called Abraham, the "father" of the Hebrew nation, "My friend."[2] Moses met with God "face to face" when he talked to God in the tabernacle. Can you imagine how this personal experience must have changed his life? The Book of Exodus describes this encounter, which occurred just before Moses received the Ten Commandments:

> Whenever Moses went to the Tabernacle, all the people ...would rise and stand in their tent doors. As he entered, the pillar of cloud would come down and stand at the door while the Lord spoke with Moses. Then all the people worshiped from their tent doors, bowing low to the pillar of cloud. Inside the tent the Lord spoke to Moses face to face, as a man speaks to his friend.[3]

Both Enoch and Noah were said to have "enjoyed a close relationship with God"; Job talked of a time "when God's intimate friendship blessed my house."[4] And in the New Testament, Jesus, the Son of God, told His disciples, "Now you are My friends."[5]

God has names. Many couples use great care in giving their newborn baby a name that has significance to their family. In the same way, each of God's many names reveals something important about His character. In the Bible, He is called Almighty, Eternal God, Heavenly Father, Lord of Hosts, Living God, Most

High, and Jehovah, along with many other names. In the next chapter, we will see the incredible truth behind God's most important name, Jehovah. (For a complete listing of the names of God with Scripture verses, see Appendix C.)

God is described throughout the Bible by a personal pronoun. He is not described as an "it," but as "He," a word that denotes a definite gender and personality. An impersonal force cannot be described this way.

God acts as a distinct personality. The Bible consistently demonstrates that God is a conscious, self-aware being, someone who thinks and makes decisions. For example, He is the Creator. How could an inanimate object of gold or silver or some impersonal force design the intricacies of the universe? That takes planning, unlimited intelligence, and supernatural power. Also, the Bible tells us that God "speaks," "sees," and "hears."[6] God exhibits a range of emotions from righteous anger to holy jealousy to love and grief.

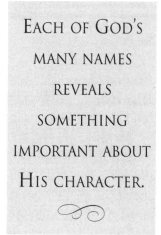

EACH OF GOD'S MANY NAMES REVEALS SOMETHING IMPORTANT ABOUT HIS CHARACTER.

GOD IS THREE PERSONS IN ONE

As we learn more about God's personality, we will find many areas that are hard to understand. This is because God is so far above our limited understanding that we cannot grasp the fullness of His nature. The fact that God is three-in-one is one of these difficult concepts. Yet this truth is one of the most important aspects of God's relationship with us.

Theologians have called God's triune nature the Trinity. The members of the Trinity are involved with everything together, yet they also have distinct roles. This is hinted at in the first chapter in the Bible. Genesis 1:26 reads, "Let *us* make people in *our* image" (emphasis added). The plural pronouns "us" and "our" mean that more than one person was involved. Who else but God was present during creation? No one. Therefore, the Trinity in its simplest terms means one God manifested in three persons with three distinctive roles.

God the Father is first in the Trinity. In general, He orchestrates action. For example, He sent to earth God the Son, Jesus, and bestowed His authority upon Him.[7]

God the Son is the second person of the Trinity. Jesus Christ is fully God and fully human.[8] He is the cornerstone and head of the worldwide Church.[9] Jesus now sits at the right hand of God the Father interceding for His Church.[10]

God the Holy Spirit, the third person of the Trinity, is our Comforter. As the "active arm" of God on earth, He lives within believers and guides us into all truth.[11] He convicts us of sin and helps us know God and His will.[12]

Yet God is still one. It is difficult for us, with our limited comprehension, to understand how God the Father, God the Son, and God the Holy Spirit are distinct personalities, co-equal, yet one at the same time. Our best efforts to understand this relationship fall far short.

One popular analogy is to compare the Trinity to water. It can be three distinct forms: liquid, ice, or steam. The same chemical formula, H_2O, can assume each form under different temperatures. In a similar way, God assumes three different "forms" to accomplish His purposes.

Here is another analogy. We all play different roles in our lives. I am a husband, father and grandfather, and the head of an international organization. I perform different duties in each role, yet I am the same person. God also performs different roles—heavenly Father, loving Son, and Spirit of Comfort.

Of course, the Trinity is far more complex and profound than any awkward illustration I can give. One of my seminary professors once said, "If you try to understand the Trinity, you will lose your mind…If you deny the Trinity, you will lose your soul."

The reason I take the time to explain the mysterious relationship between the three members of the Trinity is that this truth underlies all the work of God. These are a few examples:

- God the Father orchestrated creation.[13] God the Son performed the work of creation.[14] God the Holy Spirit was also involved.[15]

- All three members agreed upon Christ's birth in human form.[16] Christ's baptism, which marked the beginning of His earthly ministry, was attended and approved by all three members.[17]
- Christ's resurrection was the work of the Trinity: God the Father raised Christ from the dead.[18] Jesus laid down His life and took it up on His own accord.[19] The Holy Spirit was the power in the resurrection.[20]
- All three members of the Trinity participate in the miracle of the new birth when a person becomes a child of God.[21]
- All three members of the Trinity participate in the atonement —when we receive forgiveness of our sins.[22] And then all three persons of the Trinity come to live in the new believer's life.[23]

Each member of the Trinity has His own role to play, but each is fully God. God is not three separate Gods like some might envision, but has complete unity. No Person in the Trinity is less important, less powerful, or less of anything than any other Person. As we discover more about God, we will see how the Trinity works in our behalf.

DEVELOPING A RELATIONSHIP IS AN ADVENTURE

Today, after more than fifty years of getting to know God, I have more joy in the Lord's presence than I have ever had. My communication with Him grows sweeter and sweeter. There is no one in the universe with whom I would rather spend time than my heavenly Father. I do not have adequate words to describe to you the many things He has done for me and the marvelous ways He has guided my life to make it an exciting adventure. My number one priority in life is to maintain my love for Him and to demonstrate my love by my obedience.

To this end, Vonette and I begin every day on our knees reading His holy, inspired Word and surrendering the activities of our day to His guidance. I want to be a suit of clothes for the Lord Jesus. I invite Him to walk around in my body as His temple. My heart's passion is to let Him think with my mind, love with my heart, speak with my lips, and continue to seek and save sinners through me. This is what He came to earth to do 2,000 years ago.

As we explore the amazing attributes of our glorious Lord, I encourage you to walk with Him, talk with Him, worship and praise Him, and give Him your cares and worries. He yearns to be your loving Savior and wrap His strong arms around you. You need never feel lonely or abandoned again. Here is a prayer you might pray as we begin our journey to know God more intimately:

Dear God, I want to know You as You really are, the Creator God of the universe, our Heavenly Father, who holds everything in Your hand. You know my past, present, and future. Help me to love, trust, and obey You with all my heart, soul, mind, and will. Thank You for giving me an opportunity to know You intimately as my heavenly Father and to tell others about You and Your marvelous love. Amen.

CHAPTER 3

OUR
AWE-INSPIRING
GOD

H ow big is your God? Renowned theologian and Bible translator J. B. Phillips once wrote, "Your God is too small."[1] By now, you have probably realized that this is a problem we all face.

Truthfully, none of us can completely grasp the width, depth, complexity, or immensity of any part of God's nature. But if we merely have a human-centered view of God, we limit ourselves to only what we can accomplish through our self-efforts. Or we may think that He is just a little more intelligent, powerful, or wise than we are. Such a view of God robs us of an intimate life-changing relationship with an awe-inspiring God.

God has given us minds that can see farther than our own human limitations. For example, we can discover the intricacies of the DNA molecule, which no one has ever seen. We can study about places we have never visited, such as the underwater world of deep-sea creatures. We use cellular telephones with the knowledge that the signals may be coming to us from as far away as telecommunication satellites orbiting in space. These concepts extend our thinking beyond what we can observe with our eyes.

In the following pages, let us put aside our tendency to be superficial in our understanding of God and stretch our minds to get a clearer idea of His magnificent nature.

GOD'S MOST IMPORTANT NAME

One of the biblical concepts that help establish God's unlimited nature is His most important name. When God commanded Moses to lead the Israelites out of Egyptian slavery, Moses wondered what to tell them if they should ask the name of this God. In His short reply, the Lord spoke some of the most profound and revealing words recorded in the entire Bible. He said, "I AM WHO I AM. This is what you are to say to the Israelites: 'I AM has sent me to you.'"[2]

The Israelites immediately understood that the Hebrew word for I AM identified God as the only self-existent, eternal, personal Supreme Being. They clearly realized who had given Moses the message. It was God Himself! In the very next verse, God said to Moses:

> "Say to the Israelites, 'The LORD, the God of your fathers —the God of Abraham, the God of Isaac, and the God of Jacob—has sent me to you.' This is My name forever, the name by which I am to be remembered from generation to generation" (NIV).

The word "LORD" is written in all capital letters in many Bible versions to distinguish this name from other references to God. It is translated from the Hebrew YHWH, which means God's personal name. Other Bible versions translate it as Jehovah. In Isaiah 42:8, God clearly says, "I am the LORD [YHWH]; that is My name!" This name was so sacred and holy that the ancient rabbis would not allow anyone to say it aloud for fear that someone would inadvertently use it wrongly. When reading Scriptures that contained this name, the rabbis substituted Adonai (Lord) instead of reading aloud the most holy name. Consequently, the exact pronunciation of YHWH was lost. Today, scholars believe it was pronounced Yahweh.

Because I AM contains no adjective or qualifier that describes or limits its meaning, it signifies that God is complete. He has no beginning, no end, needs no help, no counsel. Everything He is and does is perfect, not lacking in anything.

THE SPLENDOR OF GOD

As king of Israel, David composed many lyrical psalms expressing God's grandeur. In Psalm 145, he writes:

> I will praise You, my God and King, and bless Your name each day and forever. Great is Jehovah [YHWH]! Greatly praise Him! His greatness is beyond discovery! Let each generation tell its children what glorious things He does. I will meditate about Your glory, splendor, majesty and miracles. Your awe-inspiring deeds will be on every tongue; I will proclaim Your greatness. Everyone will tell about how good You are, and sing about Your righteousness.[3]

Many other biblical writers also wrote of God's splendor. In the New Testament, Paul describes Him as "the King eternal, immortal, invisible, the only wise God, [to whom] be honour and glory for ever and ever."[4] The apostle John described what happened when he glimpsed God the Son during a vision. "When I saw Him, I fell at His feet as though dead. Then He placed His right hand on me and said: 'Do not be afraid. I am the First and the Last. I am the Living One.'"[5]

Our God is so gloriously incomprehensible that our minds just cannot grasp the whole nature of God. Yet we must find some human way to understand God's characteristics—at least in part. Four basic qualities of God are integral to each of His other attributes: His infinity, self-existence, eternal nature, and self-sufficiency.

God is infinite.

One day, Augustine, a leader in the early Church, was walking along the ocean shore pondering God's nature when he noticed a small boy playing in the sand. The child scooped a hole in the sand with a seashell, then ran down to the water's edge and dipped his shell full of seawater. Immediately, he ran back and dumped the water into the hole he had made in the sand. Of course, the water just leaked out through the sand.

Augustine asked the boy, "What are you doing?"

The boy confidently replied, "I am going to pour the sea into that hole."

"Ah," Augustine later reflected, "that is what I have been trying to do. Standing at the ocean of infinity, I have attempted to grasp it with my finite mind."[6]

Who can understand God's infinity? The prophet Isaiah writes, "Who has measured the waters in the hollow of His hand, and marked off the heavens by the span, and calculated the dust of the earth by the measure, and weighed the mountains in a balance, and the hills in a pair of scales? Who has directed the Spirit of the LORD, or as His counselor has informed Him?"[7]

God's infinity means that He has no limits, boundaries, or end. God cannot be compared to any finite standard. Everything within our world is finite; even the universe, as vast as it is, has a limit. God and only God is infinite. Since His infinite nature relates to all of His attributes, God's love, holiness, mercy, and all other qualities are unlimited in their scope and expression.

God is self-existent.

As humans, we use the word "create" differently than God does. When we "create" a work of art, we start with a material, such as sculptor's clay, and mold it into a different shape. Our "creation" is actually something reshaped, rearranged, combined, or invented. Mankind has never made something out of nothing. Not so with God. When He created the world, He made it out of nothing. We cannot really comprehend what that means. We have never seen "nothing."

We cannot even use the word "created" to describe God. God was not created. Everything else in the universe had a beginning, except God. Because He is the Creator, He exists outside of the created order. He is different from and independent of His creation, dwelling in pure existence far above everything He has made.

God is also the force or cosmic glue that holds everything together.[8] Without Him, everything that He created would disintegrate.

God is eternal.

Imagine that you want to discover what is going on in a room filled with people, but the door is locked. You peer through the keyhole, trying to piece together what each person in the room is doing. People move about, coming into view, then disappearing out of sight. What a frustration! If only you could open the door and walk into the room to see what is going on!

That is how time and space are to us. We look at events through a keyhole, and all we know is what we can see happening right now. For us, time defines boundaries. We mark the point in time of our birth and death. We count history by years and ages. As a human being, I cannot even begin to imagine what it must be like to live outside the boundary of time.

But God is not bound by the dimensions of time. Before He spoke the first word of creation, time did not exist. He created time as a temporary context for His creation.

It baffles my mind to realize that God experiences all past, present, and future events simultaneously. Everything that has ever happened or will ever happen has already occurred within His awareness. God sees the beginning of the parade of life; He sees its end. All history is but a little speck within the spectrum of eternity. Our God encompasses all of eternity!

God is self-sufficient.

Every living thing on earth needs food, water, and air. Without a constant supply of these, all living things die.

Although God is a living being, He has no needs. He is dependent upon nothing outside Himself. All creation relies upon God for existence and the maintenance of life. God has no need for anything and is not vulnerable in any way. He does not need our help. Yet He offers us the privilege of being involved with Him in the fulfillment of His purposes as His friends.

We will never be able to fully understand God's magnificence. In fact, His infinity, self-existence, eternal nature, and self-sufficiency are incomprehensible. But are you not glad that God is so far beyond our human abilities? We can have complete confidence in a God who is greater than us and any of our problems.

APPLYING GOD'S QUALITIES TO HIS CHARACTER

One important principle about God's nature is that all the attributes of God are interactive and completely interrelated. With our human limitations, we dissect God's nature into parts or attributes so we can understand them, but that is not how they exist in God's character. Each attribute is perfectly complete and fully a part of God's personality. As we study these attributes, keep in mind that if we exalt one of God's qualities over another, we can get a distorted view of God's character. In fact, overemphasizing any one of God's attributes to the exclusion of others can lead to heresy. For example, teaching only about God's mercy and neglecting His role as a judge will prevent people from understanding God's hatred of sin and the future punishment for wrongdoing. Therefore, as we study each quality individually, we must remember that it is only one aspect of God's magnificent nature.

Since God's attributes are so interlinked, we cannot understand one without the others. The following diagram will help you see how God's attributes relate to each other and how they are all part of the whole of God's nature.

Let me apply the principle of God's unified nature to the four basic qualities we just covered. One of the attributes we will examine is God's love. God is not just a huge bundle of love; His love has all four basic qualities.

God's love is *infinite*. There is no limit to His love; it is beyond measure.

God's love is *self-existent*. It did not come to Him from somewhere else. It has always been a part of His character. God's love did not begin at some point; it has always existed in the heart of God.

God's love is *eternal*. It never had a beginning and will last for-

GOD IS

One God—Three Persons
Father, Son, and Holy Spirit

ALL-POWERFUL EVER-PRESENT ALL-KNOWING

SOVEREIGN

CREATOR

MERCIFUL

JUST

Infinite

FAITHFUL LOVING SAVIOR JUDGE HOLY RIGHTEOUS

Eternal

Self-Existent

UNCHANGING TRUTHFUL

Self-Sufficient

ever. His love is never less or more. It always exists without the limitations of time or amount.

God's love is *self-sufficient*. He does not need love to make Him what He already is. He is not dependent on love to make Him happy or more fulfilled.

Throughout the rest of this book, keep these four qualities in mind and apply them to each of the attributes we will learn about.

APPLYING NEW INSIGHTS TO YOUR LIFE

Sometimes when I am sharing about God's love and forgiveness with an individual, he will have a questioning look on his face and ask, "But is God real?"

I kindly reply, "Oh, definitely. God is real—very real—and He has made it possible for us to know Him. But this special relationship with God requires a response from us." I often share what Jesus says in John 3:16: "God so loved the world that He gave His only Son, so that everyone who believes in Him will not perish but have eternal life." The only way we can have a relationship with our great Creator is through His Son, Jesus Christ. Knowing Jesus is the first step to knowing God.

Have you made a decision to turn to God by trusting Jesus as your Savior and Lord? If not, turn to Appendix A and read "How to Know God Personally." These few pages will help you get started on your new adventure as a child of God.

Another essential step to growing in our relationship with God is listening to His Spirit. Jesus promises, "When the Spirit of truth comes, He will guide you into all truth."[9] God has given us the Holy Spirit to help us in our relationship with Him. To discover how you can live in the power of the Holy Spirit, turn to Appendix B, "How to Be Filled With the Spirit."

A third response we make as we begin to know and appreciate our marvelous God is to seek Him wholeheartedly. David prayed, "O God, You are my God; I earnestly search for You. My soul thirsts for You; my whole body longs for You."[10] Because of David's desire to seek God wholeheartedly, God called him "a man after My own heart." I urge you to consider what might be keeping you from hungering after God. Ask God to help you resolve any issues and turn away from anything that would prevent you from having an intimate relationship with Him.

In the next chapter, we will embark on our adventure to intimacy with God by looking at God's attributes of ability, beginning with His unlimited power. Then we will see that He is present everywhere and that He knows everything. Together these abilities demonstrate that He is sovereign, ruler over all, and that such a God can do anything!

PART I

OUR GREAT CREATOR

(Attributes of Ability)

Do you not know? Have you not heard?
Has it not been told you from the beginning?
Have you not understood since the earth was
founded?
He sits enthroned above the circle of the earth,
and its people are like grasshoppers.
He stretches out the heavens like a canopy,
and spreads them out like a tent to live in.

ISAIAH 40:21,22, NIV

CHAPTER 4

GOD

IS

ALL-POWERFUL

One of the National Aeronautics and Space Administration's (NASA's) most important projects is the International Space Station that our country is building in cooperation with Russia, Japan, Brazil, and several other European countries. If you visit the Space Center in Houston, you can view a documentary film about the space station. On a huge screen several stories high, space ships carrying materials for the space station are shown blasting into the sky. The power of the rockets can be seen as the huge screen fills with boiling clouds of fire and smoke from the booster engines. The roar thunders throughout the room. What power in those engines!

Then on the screen you see the orbiting space station. Its components are linked to allow astronauts to live in space and perform science experiments. Against the backdrop of the darkness of the universe, the huge space station floats through emptiness. It is thrilling to think about the power that scientists use to put men and women in space miles above the Earth to live and work for months at a time. What remarkable technological progress!

Then the camera turns to show the space station from another angle. Now the Earth is visible behind the steel structure with its many angles and parts. Our blue planet with its swirling clouds looms huge, dwarfing the now fragile-looking space station. The Earth appears so big that only a portion of its surface fills the entire screen.

Suddenly, you get a glimpse of how very close the space station really is to the Earth. Although it has taken thousands of pounds of fuel to blast the astronauts miles into space, they really have not gone far from our planet's surface compared to the expanse of space.

Our human efforts are so minuscule compared to the reaches of outer space. We are like ants trying to scale Mount Everest. After crawling over blades of grass and fallen twigs, the ants think they have traveled a great distance. But when their journey is compared to the distant mountaintop ahead, they have hardly begun.

> "THE HEAVENS DECLARE THE GLORY OF GOD; THE SKIES PROCLAIM THE WORK OF HIS HANDS."
>
> PSALM 19:1

Sometimes we as humans become so caught up in our own power that we forget how very limited we are. We are like those ants toiling across a tiny square foot of earth. When was the last time you tried to accomplish something completely beyond your ability? Perhaps you have valiantly concentrated all your energy on the challenge at hand, only to find that it was not enough to do what needed to be done. Afterward, you felt exhausted and defeated.

However, God is capable of doing anything—as long as it does not violate His other attributes. (For example, He cannot lie, change, deny Himself, or be tempted.) Otherwise, no task is too large or too difficult for Him. He never fails or gets tired. Because He is all-powerful, He has the ability and the strength to do whatever He pleases. His power is not restrained or inhibited in any way by His created beings. God generates power within Himself and does what He chooses to do whenever He chooses to do it. His power is not an abstract idea but a force to be reckoned with. Theologians use the term *omnipotence* to describe the awesome, unlimited power of God.

GOD'S POWER IN CREATION

When I tour a historic mansion and scrutinize the building's details—the quality, design, and décor—I can draw some conclusions about its builder. Is the foundation strong? Are the walls and floors plumb and square? How well are the most intricate details constructed? Does the design flow from one room to another?

We live on a grand estate called Earth. As we look at the beauty and intricacies of our residence, we marvel at the genius of the design. When we gaze up into the heavens, we are overcome with awe at the vastness of what our Creator has brought into being. In one of the most beautiful passages in the Bible, King David describes how nature testifies to the power of God:

> The heavens declare the glory of God; the skies proclaim the work of His hands. Day after day they pour forth speech; night after night they display knowledge. There is no speech or language where their voice is not heard. Their voice goes out into all the earth, their words to the ends of the world.[1]

To get just a small idea of God's creative power, let us consider our universe. We live on one of nine planets that revolve around the sun. As the dominant light of our solar system, our sun gives off far more energy in one second than all mankind has produced since creation. With a diameter of approximately 860,000 miles, the sun could hold one million planets the size of the Earth. Yet our sun is only an average-size star.

Our sun is just one among 100 billion stars in our galaxy, the Milky Way. The Pistol Star gives off 10 million times the power generated by our sun, and one million stars the size of our sun can fit easily within its sphere. It takes 100,000 light-years to travel from one side of the Milky Way to the other. (One light-year is 5.88 trillion miles or the distance light travels in one year.) Our galaxy is moving through space at a phenomenal speed of one million miles per hour! If the Milky Way were compared to the size of the North American continent, our solar system would be about the size of a coffee cup!

Yet our Milky Way is not a huge galaxy. One of our neighbors, the Andromeda Spiral galaxy, is 2 million light-years away and contains about 400 billion stars. No one knows how many galaxies there are in the universe, but scientists estimate that there are billions of them.[2]

Isaiah writes, "Look up into the heavens. Who created all the stars? He brings them out one after another, calling each by its name. And He counts them to see that none are lost or have strayed away."[3] Scientists estimate that there are ten billion trillion stars in the universe, or about as many stars as there are grains of sand on all of our planet's seashores. If all the stars were divided equally among the people of the world, each person would receive almost two trillion stars.

Yet, with the unfathomable vastness of our universe, God spoke and the heavens and earth came into being; He laid the foundations of the world.[4] His invisible qualities—His eternal power and divine nature—can be clearly seen and understood from His creation. Even people who have never received a verbal witness about God have no excuse for not knowing Him because of His power displayed in creation.[5] He alone is the Almighty Sovereign of the universe.

Truly, God is omnipotent. Allow me to give you three truths about His infinite power.

GOD IS THE ULTIMATE SOURCE OF ALL POWER

Our homes depend on a central source for electrical power and can be plunged into darkness due to a storm or other disturbance. This power is transmitted into our homes on slender cables, which can break or wear out. But God's power is inherent in His nature. He does not derive His power from any other source; all power has always been His and will continue to be His for eternity. Any power that we have comes ultimately from God. King David acknowledged in one of his prayers, "In Your hands are strength and power to exalt and give strength to all."[6] Paul prayed for the Ephesians that they would "begin to understand the incredible greatness of His power for us who believe Him."[7]

GOD IS MORE POWERFUL THAN ANYTHING IN THE UNIVERSE

God has more power than all the forces of nature. The combined energy of earth's storms, winds, ocean waves, and other natural forces do not equal a fraction of God's omnipotence. He expresses His power through the laws of nature, which He has instituted—although God is not bound by these laws.

I have flown millions of miles, but I remember the most violent storm I ever encountered. Vonette and I were on our way from New York City to Washington, D.C., when suddenly the airplane began to buck like a wild mustang throwing its first rider. It felt as though the plane was out of control, like a leaf blown about in the wind. The sky seemed to explode with brilliant flashes of lightning.

As we rode through the storm, Vonette and I were reminded of when Jesus calmed the wind and waves. The disciples shouted to the Lord, "Save us, we're sinking!" Vonette and I began to pray, "Oh, Lord, You have not lost Your power over nature. We ask You to still the storm and to save us, though we're ready to meet You now if it is Your will. But if You have something yet for us to do in this life, we ask You not to allow the enemy to destroy us and all these other passengers."

Almost immediately, the turbulence stopped. The plane was stabilized and we continued on our course. Our petitions to God turned into praise and thanksgiving. Later we discovered that the plane had been severely damaged—lightning had knocked a hole in the fuselage—and that our lives were truly in danger. Yes, our God is more powerful than the greatest storm.

God is also more powerful than all the rulers on earth. Do the nuclear capabilities, chemical weapons, and military strength of other countries frighten you? We do not need to fear. The prophet Isaiah writes, "All the nations of the world are nothing in comparison with Him. They are but a drop in the bucket, dust on the scales."[8] After learning firsthand of God's power, King Nebuchadnezzar acknowledges, "He does as He pleases with the powers of heaven and the peoples of the earth. No one can hold back His hand or say to Him: What have You done?"[9]

We need not fear that any one person or nation will put God to the test. He is so far above our earthly governments that they can do nothing outside His power. No ruler or army can change any plan that God has made.

God is also infinitely more powerful than Satan and his evil legions. God is not intimidated by the devil's rebellious hatred. God is the Creator; Satan is a created being who can operate only within the prescribed limits God places on him. Satan is nothing compared to God.

Jesus told His disciples that "the prince of this world [Satan] now stands condemned."[10] Demons screamed in fear when they saw Jesus. The Book of Matthew records Jesus' encounter with two men who were demon-possessed. The demons immediately recognized the Son of God's power over them by saying, "Have you come here to torture us before the appointed time?" They requested that He let them go into a nearby herd of pigs. He said one powerful word—"Go." And they did. In response, the pigs ran over a cliff to their deaths.[11]

As Christians, sometimes we feel that Satan has the upper hand. But our almighty God fights for us. Romans 16:20 gives this promise: "The God of peace will soon crush Satan under your feet." How encouraging that promise is when we are battling the evil forces that confront us every day!

GOD HAS THE POWER TO DO ANYTHING

Whatever God chooses will come to pass because He has the omnipotent ability to make it happen. God told Isaiah, "Everything I plan will come to pass, for I will do whatever I wish."[12] Speaking to God, Job acknowledged, "I know that You can do all things; no plan of Yours can be thwarted."[13] Consider some of the things our almighty God can do without any effort.

God has the power to create anything from nothing.

The psalmist writes, "The LORD merely spoke, and the heavens were created. He breathed the word, and all the stars were born... Let everyone stand in awe of Him. For when He spoke, the world began! It appeared at His command."[14] When God spoke, the sky was filled with stars. Pastor Tony Evans writes, "It takes no more effort for God to create a universe than it does for Him to create an ant."[15] God's power is so unlimited that He could speak a few trillion more universes into existence, then the next day a few trillion more, then the same every day for a trillion years. It would not lessen His power one bit!

God has the power to sustain everything He has created.

Deists believe that God created the world then withdrew, letting His creation run automatically like a watch with a battery. It is up to us to maintain what is in the world, they say. Yet that is not how God is depicted in the Bible. The ongoing existence of all creation depends on our all-powerful God every second of every day. The writer of Hebrews affirms: "The Son...sustains the universe by the mighty power of His command."[16]

God has the power to judge sin and rebellion.

One of the great mysteries of life is why God allows evil on the earth. We will never find a complete answer to this puzzle. At the same time, we can know for sure that God will use His mighty power for the destruction of evil. He has given us examples in His Word: the great flood in Noah's time and God's judgment of Sodom and Gomorrah. Every injustice will be righted; every act of sin and rebellion will be accounted for.

OUR RESPONSE

As we discover the character of our heavenly Father, we will want to do more than file away facts; we will want to seek His presence and fellowship. Worship is our response to God that shows our gratitude for who He is. But what does it mean to worship God? Picture a huge, ornate room with an immense throne at one end.

The room is filled with people and angels praising God. The throng opens up to reveal a carpeted aisle that leads right to the throne.

Suddenly, you realize that you must walk up that aisle and stand before the elevated throne. Your eyes look up to catch sight of the Person who sits in the honored seat. That Being is so full of light and power and righteousness that your eyes cannot bear to look at Him.

What can you say that will mean anything to this glorious King? Your mouth is dry and you cannot speak. There are no words adequate for the moment. All you can do is bow down before Him in humble adoration, servitude, and worship.

Throughout this book, we will learn the importance and the simple truths about worshipping our great Creator. The most basic element of worship is attitude. Our worship should begin with an attitude of awe for who God is and what He can do. We must realize how weak we are compared to the infinite power of God.

Once we have a right view of God, we will begin to praise Him. King David expressed this attitude when he was gathering materials to build a glorious temple to almighty God:

> O LORD, the God of our ancestor Israel, may you be praised forever and ever! Yours, O LORD, is the greatness, the power, the glory, the victory, and the majesty. Everything in the heavens and on earth is yours, O LORD, and this is your kingdom. We adore you as the one who is over all things… O our God, we thank you and praise your glorious name![17]

Do his words reflect your awe of God's power? Take a few moments right now to praise God. The following "Life Application" will help you focus your attention on Him and address any attitude problems hindering you from worshipping Him.

As believers, we have access to the greatest force in the universe—the awesome power of God. In our next chapter, we will examine how God uses His unlimited power in our behalf.

LIFE APPLICATION

EXALT YOUR GOD—An important part of worshipping God is praising Him. Make the following Scripture prayers your songs of praise. As you repeat the words, meditate on the character of God:

> Ah, Sovereign LORD, you have made the heavens and the earth by Your great power and outstretched arm. Nothing is too hard for You...O great and powerful God, whose name is the LORD Almighty, great are your purposes and mighty are your deeds (Jeremiah 32:17–19, NIV).

> The LORD merely spoke, and the heavens were created. He breathed the word, and all the stars were born. He gave the sea its boundaries and locked the oceans in vast reservoirs. Let everyone in the world fear the LORD, and let everyone stand in awe of Him. For when He spoke, the world began! It appeared at His command. The LORD shatters the plans of the nations and thwarts all their schemes. But the LORD'S plans stand firm forever; his intentions can never be shaken (Psalm 33:6–11).

REFLECT HIS IMAGE—Prayerfully answer these questions about your life and put them into practice: How do you think God wants to display His power in your life? What areas in your life need to be transformed by His power? How can you draw on His power to make a difference in the lives of those around you?

SHARE HIS MAJESTY—Think of one person you know who needs to be reminded that our Creator is all-powerful. Share the truths of this chapter with them; encourage them that nothing is too difficult for God.

CHAPTER 5

GOD USES HIS POWER IN OUR BEHALF

S ome time ago, I had to fly from Los Angeles to New York for a mere three-hour stop, then fly to Portland, Oregon, to speak to several hundred pastors at a conference. When I reached Portland, I was bone tired. Every fiber of my being ached with fatigue. As I stood in the terminal, I felt impressed to pray, "Lord, do You have something that You would like to share with me?"

Immediately, I felt another impression to turn to the 40th chapter of Isaiah. I began to read a familiar passage, which took on new meaning for me. "Don't you know by now that the everlasting God, the Creator of the farthest parts of the earth, never grows faint or weary?...He gives power to the tired and worn out, and strength to the weak."[1] I could identify with the writer, for I was absolutely worn out.

I continued to read: "Even the youths shall be exhausted, and the young men will all give up. But they that wait upon the Lord shall renew their strength. They shall mount up with wings like eagles; they shall run and not be weary; they shall walk and not faint."[2]

At that moment, it was as though a great infusion of power

flooded my very being. I was so excited as I thought about who God is and what He had said to me. I felt I could have thrown my luggage over the airport terminal and run to the meeting some miles away. Suddenly, I could hardly wait to stand before those pastors and proclaim to them the glory and power of our great and faithful God and Savior. Within thirty minutes or so, I did have that privilege, and God empowered and anointed me for the occasion in a marvelous way.

In all my years as a believer, I have found God faithful to use His power in the behalf of those who seek Him. A right understanding of who God is will revolutionize the life of every believer. It will launch him or her into the exciting adventure of supernatural living in the power of this mighty God.

But perhaps you have asked yourself: How much can I expect God to do through me? How involved is He in what I see going on around me? What is He willing to accomplish in my life?

GOD USES HIS POWER PURPOSEFULLY

When we look at the cosmic universe, we see order and design. Everything is in its place; everything has its purpose. If creation has so much purpose and design, then human history must also have purpose and design.

Many people are skeptical about God's willingness to get intimately involved in their affairs. They may agree that God has a general purpose for everything, but they wonder: *Do we live by luck or the breaks produced by our own hard work and cleverness?* They question if God even knows or cares about the details in their lives.

In His Word, however, God shows that He has a plan for this world and every person in it: "I have a plan for the whole earth, for My mighty power reaches throughout the world."[3]

No matter what happens anywhere in the world at any moment, God is always in control. This is a comforting truth. How would you like to live in a world where everyone could do whatever he wanted? Can you imagine the chaos? For example, I have visited countries that seem to have no traffic laws. Taxi drivers go at breakneck speed, in and out of lanes, often colliding with each other. Fortunately, I have not been in a collision although I have ridden in thousands of taxis. I certainly would not want to drive to work each day in heavy traffic where drivers do not follow traffic laws.

Sometimes this world seems just as chaotic and out-of-control, yet God knows what is in the future. He is not the author of evil and suffering, nor is He responsible for the consequences of mankind's sins. He does place authorities in their positions to help bring order to our world. The apostle Paul tells us, "Obey the government, for God is the one who put it there. All governments have been placed in power by God. So those who refuse to obey the laws of the land are refusing to obey God."[4]

God has unlimited power within Himself and does what He wants with it. This would be terrifying if God were a tyrant who meted out His power indiscriminately. Fortunately, the Bible says God acts out of love and righteousness (attributes that we will examine later). Some of us may question why God does not answer our prayers when and how we ask. But God is not a "genie" or Santa Claus who gives us everything we ask for just the way we want it. He uses His power to fulfill His purposes, plans, and will for us and everyone involved in our situations. He knows what we need far better than we do. Can you think of at least one prayer request for which you are now thankful God did not answer the way you wanted? Often we pray selfishly or from our fleshly natures. But as we align our ways and desires with His perfect will, and pray in faith, we will see His power demonstrated more frequently in answered prayer.

GOD KNOWS THE BEGINNING FROM THE END, AND HAS US IN THE PALM OF HIS HAND.

When we study God's Word from Genesis to Revelation, we get a glimpse into how He directs history and nations. The psalmist writes: "Come and see what our God has done, what awesome miracles He does for His people!...By His great power He rules forever. He watches every movement of the nations."[5] Although events at times make no sense to us, God knows the end from the beginning, and has us in the palm of His hand.

Man is at best a microbe on the "grain of sand" we call earth, yet God created us for a purpose. We feel most fulfilled when we respond to that purpose.

God's Power Is Shown Through His Son

First Corinthians 1:24 tells us that God demonstrates His power through His Son. We can see evidence of this in His virgin birth. God planned before the foundation of the world to send His Son to die for us.

God's ultimate display of power was raising Jesus Christ from the dead. After Jesus' death by crucifixion, His enemies put a Roman seal on the tomb and set guards to make sure no one disturbed His body. Yet their efforts meant nothing to God. When He was ready to display His power, He simply rolled the stone away from the tomb and Jesus walked out alive and well.

Paul writes that the power available to us as believers is "the same mighty power that raised Christ from the dead and seated Him in the place of honor at God's right hand in the heavenly realms."[6] Does that not thrill you? The amount of power available to us through God's Spirit is equal to the power God used to raise Christ from the dead! Like Paul, we can honestly say, "I can do everything through Him who gives me strength."[7]

Reflecting God's Power

In the midst of the barren desert between Los Angeles and Las Vegas stands a 300-foot tower. On top of this tower rests a black receiver that is 45 feet high and 23 feet wide, surrounded by 70 heat-conducting tubes. Tens of thousands of people who drive across the desert during the daylight hours see what looks like a brilliant ball of fire glowing from the top of the tower. This is the world's largest solar-powered electricity-generating station: Solar One.

How can a receiver turn into a glowing ball with a temperature exceeding 1,175° F? The secret is on the ground. On the desert floor surrounding the tower are 1,818 computer-controlled frames, each holding 12 giant mirrors that track the sun daily from the time it rises until it sets.

When sunlight strikes these mirrors, it is reflected onto the receiver at the top of the tower. The heat generated at the receiver is then transformed into electrical energy through a system of thermal storage and a turbine generator. When the network of mirrors is working in harmony, tremendous power is generated from the sun.

Note that the tower itself does not have the ability to generate power. This process is possible only because light from the sun—the real source of the power—is reflected onto a helpless receiver.

Have you considered that God wants us to reflect His power on earth? As we begin to understand our God's vast and magnificent power, our lives cannot help but be transformed. Everything about us will change—our attitudes, actions, motives, desires, our lifestyle, and even our view of God. As we are transformed, we light up the world around us. Our society which was once darkened by fear, ignorance, and hopelessness will become lightened with our witness of God's power, care, and intervention in our lives.

GOD WANTS US TO BE VESSELS FOR HIS POWER

Just because God has the power to do anything should not cause us to assume that we can use that power for selfish purposes. His power is dedicated to the accomplishment of His purposes, not ours. He will bring about the future that He desires. As our all-powerful God and loving Father, His ways are infinitely better than ours.

God is seeking faithful servants to be channels of His incredible power. Paul was one of countless servants of Christ who was available for God's mighty power. Acts 19:11 records that "God did extraordinary miracles through Paul" (NIV). Through Paul's prayers, other Christians also understood what it means to be "strengthened with all power according to His glorious might."[8] The ways God desires to use us are beyond counting, but let me mention five that will help us reflect God's glory.

God gives us power to conquer evil forces.

We have already seen that God's power is infinitely greater than the forces of evil. We can apply that truth to our own battle with Satan and his helpers—no matter what they throw at us.

When God instructed Moses to lead the Israelite people out of Egypt, conflict developed between God's servants (Moses and his brother, Aaron) and Pharaoh's magicians. These accomplished sorcerers could have intimidated Moses and Aaron. Their demonic power was clearly evident when they threw their rods to the floor and the rods became serpents. But God demonstrated His superior power when Aaron's rod devoured the other serpents. This was a graphic illustration of how much greater God's power is than any other.

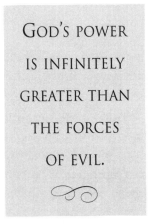

GOD'S POWER IS INFINITELY GREATER THAN THE FORCES OF EVIL.

Satan's power is most clearly demonstrated through false religious systems. Millions have followed him to disastrous endings. From the 900 followers of Jim Jones who tragically died in Jonestown, Guyana, to Heaven's Gate cult members who committed suicide in recent years at the command of their leader, many have been deluded by Satan's wiles. But when we walk with God, we need not be afraid. The devil and his forces are no match for God. God's Word promises that we can have victory in our spiritual battles. James 4:7,8 says: "Resist the devil, and he will flee from you. Draw close to God, and God will draw close to you."

Although we are weak at times, we can stand firm and say "no"; we can quit any habit or addiction; and we can speak up to tell the truth at any time. How do we do these difficult feats? In the power of the name of Jesus Christ and faith in our almighty and powerful God.

God gives us power to live a holy life.

I like to compare the Christian battle against sin to an individual swimming upstream against a surging current. His progress is slow and tortuous; he is constantly swept backward by powerful undercurrents. Hovering near the swimmer is a speedboat with a powerful motor. He can continue to try to swim upstream or he can choose to climb aboard the speedboat, which can easily whisk him up the river. Staying in the water means he must trust in his own efforts. Accepting a ride in the speedboat allows him to take advantage of a power far greater than his own.

We have a similar choice. When battling evil spiritual forces, worldly influences, and our own fleshly temptations, we can either fail miserably by fighting temptation in our own efforts or defeat that sin-current that drags us down by living in the unlimited power of the Holy Spirit.[9]

Peter explains, "As we know Jesus better, His divine power gives us everything we need for living a godly life. He has called us to receive His own glory and goodness!"[10] We do not have to make our own lives holy or clean up our messy lives before we invite God in; we can appropriate God's holiness through His Holy Spirit living His life within us.[11]

The Scriptures assure us "that if we ask anything according to His will, He hears us. And if we know that He hears us—whatever we ask—we know that we have what we asked of Him."[12] We can become holy vessels of the all-powerful God by committing to live holy lives and being filled with the power of the Holy Spirit.

God gives us power in our weakness.

Since nothing is too hard for God, we do not have a need too great for Him to meet nor a problem too complicated for Him to solve. We can never face a foe too strong for Him to conquer. We can never pray a prayer too difficult for Him to answer.

His ways are always above our ways, and when we submit to His will, we experience peace and He builds patience into our lives. Our frailties in His hands become strengths. When Paul repeatedly asked God to remove a physical ailment that was tormenting him, God responded, "My gracious favor is all you need. My power works best in your weakness."[13] God uses our weakness to highlight His magnificent power. Just as He helped me speak to those hundreds of pastors in Portland, He will enable you to do more than you could ever imagine.

God gives us power to proclaim the gospel.

One important aspect of living a holy life is spreading the good news of God's love and forgiveness to everyone we meet. Paul writes, "Everywhere we go, we tell everyone about Christ…I work very hard at this, as I depend on Christ's mighty power that works within me."[14]

Each time I am with someone for five minutes or more, I consider it a God-given opportunity to testify of God's mercy and grace in my life. Whether in an airport, a taxi, or a restaurant, I am prepared to share with others my excitement about my Lord and my love for Him. How can I do this? Because God through His Holy Spirit gives me the power to represent Him.[15]

You may be thinking: *Bill Bright is the president of a worldwide organization dedicated to introducing people to Christ. Surely, proclaiming the gospel is easier for him than for me. I could never witness like that.*

I am naturally a shy and reserved person, so sharing my faith is sometimes difficult for me. I must continually rely on the power of the Holy Spirit to be a fruitful witness. When I obey God's command to tell others of Jesus, God makes the experience joyful and meaningful. He reminds me that I am not responsible for convicting the sinner or drawing others to Him. He is. I am just to follow His command in love, concern, and the power of His Holy Spirit.

At Campus Crusade for Christ we have trained millions of believers around the world to share their faith in Christ. We have learned that successful witnessing is simply taking the initiative to share Christ with everyone who will listen, in the power of the Holy Spirit, and leaving the results to God.

God gives us power to fulfill His plan for our lives.

God wants to strengthen us so we can serve Him in the fulfillment of His purposes. That plan includes allowing us the privilege of making an eternal difference in the lives of others. But that is possible only as we come to know God as He really is. He is our God who can do anything through us that He chooses to do: "By His mighty power at work within us, He is able to accomplish infinitely more than we would ever dare to ask or hope."[16]

If we really believe that God is all-powerful, we will no longer walk in fear and unbelief. We will place our faith in God—not necessarily *great faith* in God, but rather faith in a *great God* who is omnipotent. In turn, He will lead us into a life full of adventure and purpose. I have found no better way to live!

Pastor David Jeremiah explains that the unlimited power that raised Jesus Christ from the grave is available to us today:

> Most believers give lip service to God but live their lives in their own strength. They operate in their own energy about 80% of the time. Then they have a power outage. You know what a power outage is? It's going to the doctor and finding out there is something wrong with you that they can't fix. And realizing that you don't have control. It's going into an office where you have been going for 25 years where you feel secure, and getting a pink slip saying that you have been laid off from your job. Now you don't know what to do. Most of us as believers don't really touch the power of God until we have our own power outage. Then we discover that when we are weak, God is strong. I tell you that the power of God that was in Jesus Christ is the power that is available to you today. So we, too, can say with the Apostle Paul, "I can do all things through Christ who strengthens me" (Philippians 4:13).[17]

God's power is something we can trust. Yet God's character involves much more than power. His strength is used in conjunction with His many other qualities. One of these is the unlimited nature of His knowledge. In the next two chapters, we will learn more about God's incredible knowledge—and how it affects our lives.

LIFE APPLICATION

WRITE IT ON YOUR HEART—Commit the following statement and verses to memory. Then as you encounter situations during this week where you are in need of strength, claim these promises by faith.

- Because God is all-powerful, He can help me with anything.
- Philippians 4:13—"I can do everything with the help of Christ who gives me the strength I need."
- Isaiah 40:29—"[God] gives power to those who are tired and worn out; He offers strength to the weak."
- 2 Chronicles 16:9—"The eyes of the LORD search the whole earth in order to strengthen those whose hearts are fully committed to Him."

COUNT ON GOD—What difference can God's power make in a situation you currently face that is beyond your control? Commit your circumstances to Him in prayer and by faith depend on Him to give you strength and to work changes through His mighty power.

OBEY GOD—Do you feel incapable of doing something that God wants you to do? Rather than concentrating on your inadequacies, focus on God who "by His mighty power at work within us…is able to accomplish infinitely more than we would ever dare to ask or hope" (Ephesians 3:20). By faith, take the steps necessary to do what God is asking of you.

CHAPTER 6

GOD
IS PRESENT EVERYWHERE

In 1985 during the week between Christmas and New Year's Day, my fellow staff members and I were involved in a conference televised simultaneously on every continent via 97 down-link locations. Using the newest satellite technology, I spoke from Seoul, South Korea, in the early morning hours while audiences around the world watched in their corresponding time zones. The following day, I traveled to Manila to speak at the televised conference. The third day I was in Berlin, and the fourth night in Mexico City. I traveled more than 40,000 miles in five days and spoke more than twenty times.

Although physically present in only one city at a time, I was present on television sets around the world. In every part of the globe, people saw my face in full color. Those who had met me personally could say, "Yes, that's Bill Bright, because that's a perfect picture of him." Viewers also heard my voice, and those who had previously heard me in person could say, "It's Bill Bright, all right! I recognize the inflections in his voice and the way he pronounces words."

In a narrow sense, I was "present" through my face on the screen and the voice that came out of the speakers, but I was not really present. Viewers could not touch me. I could not see the people in the worldwide audience. I did not know if they were standing or sitting, and I was not aware of what they were thinking, planning, or doing.

But God is present everywhere at the same time. It's not that He is physically present in one city and present by voice and picture in another city, as I was by the technology of electronics; He is present in the fullest sense everywhere at once. How does He do it? This is how God explains His presence when speaking to Jeremiah: "'Am I only a God nearby,' declares the LORD, 'and not a God far away?...Do not I fill heaven and earth?'"[1]

God's ability to be present everywhere is called *omnipresence*. It means that there is not a sliver of space anywhere in the universe where He is not dynamically and powerfully present with all of His wonderful personal attributes. Everywhere throughout the world, to the utmost reaches of the universe and in heaven, God is always and immediately present with all of who He is!

GOD'S SPIRIT-PRESENCE

Can you imagine being completely free of all the limitations of time and space? We cannot, of course. But God can, and is! He is not limited by a body, but is a Spirit who moves wherever He wishes.

How can we explain His Spirit-presence? Many writers have compared it to the wind. No one can see the wind; it comes and goes as it pleases. No one can box it in or stop it from blowing. Yet we can see the results of wind. We see its massive strength in roiling tornadoes, hurricanes, and typhoons. The wind can also be gentle, like the whisper of a breeze off the ocean. It can bring the smell of soft rain on the leaves or the freshness of spring through an open window. Is this not like the wonderful contrast of our God who can both topple rulers and calm the fears of a little child?

Meteorologists try to predict the wind, yet with only partial success. Recently, the meeting of hot and cold air masses spawned deadly tornadoes in Central Florida, which took weather forecasters by surprise. The devastation caused the loss of more than forty lives and millions of dollars in property. In a similar way, God's presence and work cannot be predicted for He does what He wills (of course, He will not contradict His nature). Jesus also used the wind analogy to describe the work of the Holy Spirit: "Just as you can hear the wind but can't tell where it comes from or where it is going, so you can't explain how people are born of the Spirit."[2]

Yet a wind analogy is inadequate to completely describe the awesome presence of our infinite Creator who lives outside the time-space dimension in which we find ourselves bound. Unlike the wind, He is literally in every place in the entire universe at the same time! Not a single atom in any galaxy is hidden from His sight.

Solomon, the famous biblical king who was given unparalleled wisdom from God, built a temple for our majestic God. Awed by the holy task, Solomon asks, "Will God really live on earth? Why, even the highest heavens cannot contain you. How much less this Temple I have built!"[3] Truly, a temple of gold could never contain God, since even the heavens cannot hold him.

GOD'S SPIRIT IS DIFFERENT THAN HIS CREATION

Many religions believe that God's existence is somehow bound up with His creation. A. W. Tozer writes of one such scene:

> Canon W. G. H. Holmes of India told of seeing Hindu worshipers tapping on trees and stones and whispering, "Are you there? Are you there?" to the god they hoped might reside within.[4]

The belief that God is everything and everything is God is called *pantheism*. Like these Hindus, if you touch a tree, you touch God. To carry it further, this belief leads to the conclusion that since everything is god, we are gods. These fallacies take away God's majesty and make Him common and ordinary. But pantheism is not what the Bible means when it describes God's omnipresence. Author Bill Hybels explains the difference this way:

The Bible says that God is Spirit, so technically, He doesn't dwell in three-dimensional space as we do (John 15:15). His *presence* is everywhere, but not His *essence* (that would be the heresy known as pantheism). God is no less present in one portion of the universe than any other. And He is no more present anywhere than where you are right now. In other words, anyone, anywhere in the universe might say, "The Lord is in this place." Wherever you are, God is right there, right now.[5]

Think of the difference this way. Earlier we described God's creative power as a potter who forms a pot out of clay. We would

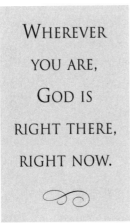

Wherever you are, God is right there, right now.

never confuse the pot and the potter. They are distinct in nature and substance. So it is with God. He is distinct from His creation, so far above it in every way that we cannot equate His essence with His creation. Yet because He has no limitations, God is also present in every corner of His universe. This means that He is present in the mountains and the stars, but He is not these things.

In this chapter, we will consider three truths that provide the basis for an understanding of the omnipresence of God. These truths are promises on which we can base our lives.

God's Presence Sustains the Universe

There is no place within all of creation that is not supported by the divine presence of God. Acts 17:28 records, "In Him we live and move and exist." Let me use an example that is very personal to each of us. God was present when you and I were fashioned in the womb. Psalm 139:13–16 says:

> You created my inmost being; You knit me together in my mother's womb. I praise You because I am fearfully and wonderfully made; Your works are wonderful, I know that full well. My frame was not hidden from You when I was

made in the secret place. When I was woven together in the depths of the earth, Your eyes saw my unformed body. All the days ordained for me were written in Your book before one of them came to be (NIV).

We are the result of God's marvelous workmanship. He designed us. He made our bodies wonderfully complex. He was present from the moment of conception, is present every moment we live, and will be present when we die.

Let us think for a moment about what God sustains for each of us. It is estimated that as adults our bodies contain sixty trillion cells that have all been carefully organized to perform life's various functions in harmony. Consider these other facts about the human body:

- Our nose can recognize up to 10,000 different aromas.
- Our tongue has about 6,000 taste buds.
- Our brain contains ten billion nerve cells. Each brain nerve cell is connected to as many as 10,000 other nerve cells throughout the body.
- Our body has so many blood vessels that their combined length could circle the planet two-and-a-half times.

God also customized each of us with our own special DNA blueprint, which is contained within every single cell. It has been estimated that if our individual blueprint were written out in a book, it would require 200,000 pages.[6] And God knows every word on every page!

Can you imagine if factories all over our country were manufacturing intricate human bodies? With our human record, what a mess it would turn out to be! The assembly line would grind to a halt because of back-orders on hands and feet. Hearts would malfunction due to system design defects; recalls would bring back hundreds of thousands of misassembled brains.

Now think of the millions of living organisms, from viruses to elephants, and the trillions of systems, from galaxies to earth's numerous ecosystems. It all works. It runs without tune-ups or teardowns and rebuilds. We hire experts to keep sophisticated computers functioning at maximum capacity, yet many people believe that our amazing universe has no Designer and no Sustainer! But it does—our loving, creative, ever-present God.

GOD REVEALS HIS PRESENCE IN DIFFERENT WAYS

God reveals His presence to us, which allows us to have an intimate relationship with Him. Let us consider several ways in which God manifests His presence to us.

God's "illuminating presence" affects every person.

Like turning on a light in a dark room, the light of God's presence opens our eyes to truth. Paul explains that God "made His light shine in our hearts to give us the light of the knowledge of the glory of God in the face of Christ."[7]

We begin to know God when the light of His presence exposes our sin. Paul writes, "It is shameful even to talk about the things that ungodly people do in secret. But when the light shines on them, it becomes clear how evil these things are."[8] Once we recognize our sinfulness and turn from it, God in His grace can reconcile us to Him through the death of His Son, Jesus, on the cross.

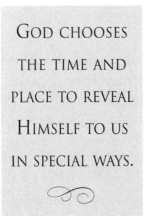

GOD CHOOSES THE TIME AND PLACE TO REVEAL HIMSELF TO US IN SPECIAL WAYS.

King David was well aware that God is present everywhere at once, and what that meant for him. At times, he may not have wanted God's presence—for example, during his adulterous affair with Bathsheba. In Psalm 139:7, he asks, "Where can I go from your Spirit? Where can I flee from your presence?" (NIV). But after he was forgiven and for the rest of his life, he reflected on God's companionship. He realized that at any given moment, God was present in Israel, in all of the nations around it, even in the distant regions. David also counted on God's presence during troubling times.[9] This affirmation of God's help came from the heart of a man who had walked in God's illuminating presence and found Him faithful—even during his disobedience.

We can have this same assurance. Hebrews 13:5 says, "Never will I leave you; never will I forsake you" (NIV). This promise gives us hope for the future and confidence in our gracious God.

God's "inspirational presence" is revealed in special places and at special times.

God has revealed Himself to men in unique ways. God spoke to Moses on Mount Horeb through a burning bush. Later on Mount Sinai, God came down in a pillar of cloud and passed in front of Moses. God's glorious presence so filled Solomon's temple that the people fell face down on the ground and worshipped the magnificent God of Israel. Paul saw the Lord in a blinding light on the road to Damascus.

On countless other occasions, God makes His presence especially known to ordinary believers. The setting may be a devotional time, church service, or during a revival. God chooses the time and place to reveal Himself to us in special ways, and when He does, we never forget the joy of being in His inspirational presence.

I have experienced God's special presence many times since surrendering my life to Him in 1945, although I have never seen Him or heard His audible voice. One dramatic experience happened early in my ministry when He gave me a vision for Campus Crusade for Christ. One evening at about midnight during my senior year in seminary, I was studying for a Greek exam. Vonette was asleep in a nearby room. Without warning, I sensed the presence of God in a way I had never known before. Within moments, I had the overwhelming impression that the Lord had flashed His instructions for my life on the screen of my mind.

This was the greatest moment of my Christian life. In a very definite way, God commanded me to invest my life in helping to fulfill the Great Commission in this generation.[10] I was to begin by helping to win and disciple students of the world for Christ. How I would do this was not spelled out in detail. That came later to my fellow staff and me as the Lord has given additional insights for the implementation of the original vision.

I awakened Vonette, and together we praised God for His direction and promised that through His grace and strength we would obey Him.

God's "incarnate presence" is manifested in Jesus Christ.

Perhaps you have heard the story of the little girl who was afraid of the dark and whose mother kept insisting, "God is watching over you. He will take care of you." But the little girl insisted, "Mommy, I want a God with skin on." And that, of course, is the reason God visited this planet. God became a man, the God-man Jesus. The God with skin on.

John tells us, "The Word [Jesus] became human and lived here on earth among us...No one has ever seen God. But His only Son, who is Himself God, is near to the Father's heart; He has told us about Him."[11] Our awesome God was willing to restrict Himself to a physical body so He could live among us and teach us about Himself. This is the most tangible way God has revealed His presence to us.

God's "indwelling presence" resides within every believer.

How would Jesus' followers continue to have fellowship with Him once He left this earth to return to His Father's side? Just before Jesus returned to heaven, He told His disciples, "I will ask the Father, and He will give you another Counselor [the Holy Spirit] to be with you forever—the Spirit of truth...He lives with you and will be in you."[12] Paul wrote, "Don't you know that you yourselves are God's temple and that God's Spirit lives in you?"[13]

Unbelievers cannot begin to comprehend why we are so confident that God is filling us with His presence. Though God is omnipresent in their universe just like He is in ours, they cannot sense His presence, so they deny He is there. Jesus explained this to His disciples: "The world cannot accept Him [the Holy Spirit], because it neither sees Him nor knows Him. But you know Him."[14]

Do we deny that the wind does not exist because we cannot see it? Of course not, for we can feel it. The God who is present everywhere is felt by those sensitive to the Spirit of God.

GOD WANTS US TO CONSCIOUSLY LIVE IN HIS PRESENCE

Indeed, our confidence is in the ever-present nature of God. We can be sure that He sees us, walks with us, and loves us no matter where we are. That fact leads us to our third truth: God wants us to "consciously" live in His presence every day.

A classic little book, *The Practice of the Presence of God*, gives the essence of living moment by moment in God's presence. Its author was a humble monk named Brother Lawrence, who served his Lord by washing pots and pans in a monastery during the 16th century. Joseph de Beaufort, his close friend, says of Brother Lawrence, "The worst trial he could imagine was losing his sense of God's presence, which had been with him for so long a time."[15]

Brother Lawrence spoke openly about his practice of living in the presence of God:

> All we have to do is to recognize God as being intimately present within us. Then we may speak directly to Him every time we need to ask for help, to know His will in moments of uncertainty, and to do whatever He wants us to do in a way that pleases Him. We should offer our work to Him before we begin, and thank Him afterwards for the privilege of having done them for His sake. This continuous conversation would also include praising and loving God incessantly for His infinite goodness and perfection.[16]

Every morning, I make it a practice to fall to my knees in prayer beside my bed. I ask my Lord to live His life in and through me throughout the day. My request is that He will walk around in my body, speak with my lips, use my hands and feet for His glory, and control my thoughts so they honor Him.

I encourage you to begin a daily practice of praising God during all your activities. The following Life Application will help you get started. But praise is just the beginning of a lifestyle of practicing the presence of God. Remember, wherever you go, He is already there. In our next chapter, we will see how God's omnipresence means that He will always help us.

LIFE APPLICATION

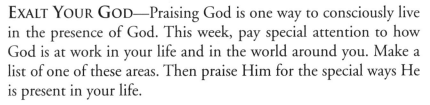

EXALT YOUR GOD—Praising God is one way to consciously live in the presence of God. This week, pay special attention to how God is at work in your life and in the world around you. Make a list of one of these areas. Then praise Him for the special ways He is present in your life.

REFLECT HIS IMAGE—Contemplate the following questions:

- How does knowing that God is everywhere influence what I think, say, and do?
- Are there "hidden" areas of my life that I need to turn over to my all-seeing God?
- If I fully understand that our ever-present Lord is *in* me, how will I live my life differently?
- How can having the Creator of the universe live His life through me impact my life and the lives of others?

SHARE HIS MAJESTY—Who can you encourage today with the great news that our God is always with us? Share the following verses with that person:

- Deuteronomy 31:6—"The LORD your God will go ahead of you. He will neither fail you nor forsake you."
- Psalm 139:12—"Even in darkness I cannot hide from You. To You the night shines as bright as day. Darkness and light are both alike to You."

CHAPTER 7

God Is Always With Us

When I awaken in the morning, God is with me. When I kneel to worship Him, He is with me. When I arrive at the office or at the airport for one of my many trips, He is still with me.

God is with me while I am on the airplane, and He is with me when I arrive at my destination, whether in California, Pakistan, or Brazil. He is with me as I turn out the lights at night anywhere in the world. We can be confident that Christ is present with us and all believers in the United States, Canada, Germany, Russia, Indonesia, Egypt, and every other country—at the same time.

God is not limited by time or space or height or depth—or even our level of faith. He is always with us whether we are taking giant steps of faith or we are taking the first baby steps of faith. He lives inside of every person who puts his trust in God through faith in Jesus Christ.

God Is Present With Us in All Places

Let us apply this attribute to the events of our lives. First, God's omnipresence means that we cannot go anywhere that God is not beside us. The psalmist writes, "If I go up to the heavens, You are there; if I make my bed in the depths, You are there. If I rise on the wings of the dawn, if I settle on the far side of the sea, even there Your hand will guide me, Your right hand will hold me fast."[1] God sees us, walks with us, and cares for us no matter where we are.

During NASA's Apollo 13 flight, Jim Lovell, Jack Swaggart, and Fred Haise were scheduled to walk on the moon. Just after they blasted off, an explosion on their ship endangered their lives. Not only did they have to abort their plans to make a moon landing, but it also looked as if they would not have enough engine power and cabin oxygen to return to Earth alive. One of the tensest times during the flight was when the space ship orbited behind the moon. For agonizing hours, the astronauts were sailing through the darkness on the far side of the moon, out of reach of radio contact with Mission Control in Houston. All over our country, Americans prayed for the safety of the astronauts. The country breathed a sigh of relief when radio contact was reestablished and when Apollo 13 was successfully brought back home.

How could God hear all the prayers for the astronauts? Because God is no less present behind the shadow of the moon than right beside you right now. In fact, without God's omnipresence, prayer would be ineffective. God promises His people, "Before they call I will answer; while they are still speaking, I will hear."[2] When I am in Orlando and pray for a fellow staff member in Thailand, God is with both of us. He is fully present in Orlando to hear my prayer, and at the same time fully present in Thailand to act in behalf of the one for whom I am praying! The basis for all prayer rests on the fact that God is omnipresent.

GOD IS PRESENT IN ALL OUR CIRCUMSTANCES

Have you had an experience that left you wondering where God is? Sometimes we do not feel God's presence, but emotions can be misleading. No matter what we feel, God is still there.

David often felt abandoned by God. In Psalm 22, he implores, "My God, my God! Why have you forsaken me? Why do you remain so distant? Why do you ignore my cries for help? Every day I call to you, my God, but you do not answer."[3] Yet later in the same psalm he states his trust in God's presence:

> Yet you brought me safely from my mother's womb and led me to trust You when I was a nursing infant. I was thrust upon You at my birth. You have been my God from the moment I was born…Praise the LORD, all you who fear Him!… For He has not ignored the suffering of the needy. He has not turned and walked away. He has listened to their cries for help.[4]

Two Dutch women during World War II experienced God's omnipresence. Corrie and Betsie ten Boom became involved in hiding Jewish people during the Nazi occupation of their country. As a consequence, the Nazis sent the two elderly women to Ravensbruck, one of the most dreaded concentration camps. There they endured incredible depravation and suffering. Yet they ministered to hundreds of other prisoners who needed to hear about their Lord and Savior. Their barracks were transformed into a Bible study and prayer center, and the cruel, harsh attitudes of many prisoners were turned to compassion and love.

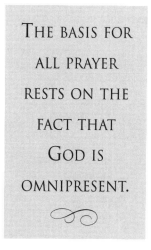

THE BASIS FOR ALL PRAYER RESTS ON THE FACT THAT GOD IS OMNIPRESENT.

Eventually, Betsie became deathly ill. As she was taken to the prison hospital, Corrie tried to shield Betsie from the sleet that stung their bodies. After the orderlies set Betsie's stretcher on the hospital floor, Corrie leaned down to hear the words on her sister's weak lips, "…must tell people what we have learned here. We must tell them that there is no pit so deep that He is not deeper still. They will listen to us, Corrie, because we have been there."[5]

Betsie died the following day. Soon after, Corrie was miraculously discharged from the camp—only days before all women her age were put to death. For the rest of her life, Corrie traveled the globe telling her story of God's presence and faithfulness even in the worst of places.

Our confidence is that "there is no pit so deep that God is not there." We cannot face a situation in which He does not walk beside us.

GOD IS PRESENT WITH US DURING EVERY CRISIS

What crisis are you facing right now? Unemployment, serious health problems, the break-up of your marriage, rebellious teenage children, rejection by those who once loved you? God walks with us, gives us strength, understands our pain, and knows how to handle our problems. He will help us if we only ask Him and are willing to do things His way and in His time.

Isaiah 43:1–3 records God's precious promise to be with us in times of crisis:

> The LORD who created you says: "Do not be afraid, for I have ransomed you. I have called you by name; you are mine. When you go through deep waters and great trouble, I will be with you. When you go through rivers of difficulty, you will not drown! When you walk through the fire of oppression, you will not be burned up; the flames will not consume you. For I am the LORD, your God, the Holy One of Israel, your Savior.

One of the most basic crises each of us faces is our own death. For many people, even Christians, the terror of leaving this world is very real. One of my fellow staff members faced such a crisis just after her thirtieth birthday. Days after her doctor admitted her to the hospital, she began having problems breathing. Although she pressed the nurses' call button, no one responded.

Panicked, she realized that she was dying in a hospital bed— and no one knew. As her breathing became more labored, she began to lose consciousness. She was helpless, yet she desperately wanted to live to see her young daughter and husband again.

Within seconds of her panic, a supernatural peace flooded over her. God impressed this promise clearly on her heart: "If you awake and are in heaven, I am with you. If you awake and are in this hospital bed, I am with you. Either way, I am just as close to you."

With that promise ringing in her ears, she put her future in God's hands. Then through eyelids barely cracked, she saw the elevator doors slide open in the hall outside her room. Out walked her pastor! By the time he reached her bedside, she drifted into unconsciousness. But because of his quick response, her life was saved.

The comforting words of Psalm 23:4 ring beautifully. "Even when I walk through the dark valley of death, I will not be afraid, for You are close beside me. Your rod and Your staff protect and comfort me." I encourage you to memorize and meditate upon this beloved psalm.

GOD IS WITH US WHEN WE WITNESS FOR HIM

Jesus promises, "Be sure of this: I am with you always, even to the end of the age."[6] This was given as part of the Great Commission —the challenge to go into the entire world and preach the gospel and disciple those who come to faith in Christ. It is when we are fulfilling the Great Commission that Jesus' promise to be with us becomes most precious. He has given us the challenge to reach every person on earth with God's message of love and forgiveness. Yet He did not leave us alone to accomplish this impossible task. He has sent us His Holy Spirit who empowers us to do what is humanly impossible—but possible with God.

I take great comfort in the fact that Jesus is with every one of our ministry's 20,500 full-time staff and over 660,000 trained volunteers in 181 countries of the world.[7] His Holy Spirit is the one who works within the hearts of all believers so that His work will be accomplished.

You can take comfort in knowing that God is present and working during any ministry He gives you to do. As you share your faith in Jesus Christ with your neighbor, God is with you. When you teach your children about God's love, God is with you. When you witness to that coworker who is an atheist, God is with you. God will bring forth the fruit and help us be faithful to Him in introducing others to Christ as Savior and Lord.

NOTHING WE DO IS HIDDEN FROM GOD

Jesus promised that our heavenly Father, "who sees what is done in secret, will reward you."[8] Just think about that. When we privately do something good that no one else knows about, God still sees it and rewards us accordingly.

When a Sunday school teacher labors teaching preschoolers about God's love, she may not receive many affirmations from others, yet the Lord sees every smile and hug she gives them. When a godly pastor spends hours in his office in heartfelt prayer for people who dislike him, try to thwart his ministry, or are apathetic about the church, God sees his deep concern. For the bedridden elderly person who adopts a prayer ministry in behalf of loved ones, neighbors, and friends, God hears. For the godly parent who prays hours into the night for a prodigal child, God sees. God knows about the businessman, betrayed by his business partner, who does not take revenge but responds in forgiveness and love. To these faithful servants, our ever-present God says, "Love your enemies, do good to them, and lend to them without expecting to get anything back. Then your reward will be great."[9]

> GOD'S OMNIPRESENCE ENABLES US TO BE IN CONSTANT COMMUNION WITH HIM.

On the other hand, God also sees the wrong things we commit in secret. We only fool ourselves by thinking that no one will ever know. Scripture says, "Nothing in all creation can hide from Him. Everything is naked and exposed before His eyes. This is the God to whom we must explain all that we have done."[10]

There is no place we can hide when we do wrong. God sees and is beside us. As believers, we may break our fellowship with God when we sin, but He does not leave our presence. He is still dwelling within us, convicting us, helping us to do what is right through His loving discipline, and waiting for us to repent of our wrongdoing.

Some people see God as a "great traffic cop" in the sky watching their every move. I like to think that He loves me so much that He cannot take His eyes off me. I am the "apple of His eye." Thank You, Father, for watching over us.

CONSCIOUSLY LIVING IN HIS PRESENCE

God's omnipresence enables us to be in constant communion with Him and to depend on Him in every situation. But at times we ignore His presence because we are so preoccupied with our lives and focused on material concerns (food, clothing, shelter, finances, and jobs). Sometimes we even forget that He is with us while we are busy serving Him. Brother Lawrence discovered this truth when he began to practice the presence of God. For fifteen years, his responsibility was to wash greasy pots and pans in the monastery—a job he disliked. Practicing the presence of God transformed what he considered a chore into an exciting privilege. He writes, "My day-to-day life consists of giving God my simple, loving attention. If I'm distracted, He calls me back in tones that are supernaturally beautiful."[11] This is what he considered important in walking with God:

> The most holy and necessary practice in our spiritual life is the presence of God. That means finding constant pleasure in His divine company, speaking humbly and lovingly with Him in all seasons, at every moment, without limiting the conversation in any way.[12]

Living in God's presence means realizing that God is with you and is vitally concerned about every part of your life. As I practice this, I find that throughout the day the Lord Jesus communicates with me through impressions in my mind that spring from meditating on His Word and talking to Him in prayer. This makes both prayer and the study of God's Word an exciting adventure for me. Let me give you some promises that you can rely on as you consciously practice the presence of God in your daily activities.

When we are confused, God will guide us.

Confusion is rampant in our society—even among believers. People ask: Why are these things happening to me? Where should I go and what should I do with my life?

We can have confidence that God will reveal Himself to us when we do not know where to turn. He promises, "I will instruct you and teach you in the way you should go; I will counsel you and watch over you."[13] Through His Word, prayer, the leading of the Holy Spirit, and our open hearts, He will guide us along the pathway He has planned for us.

When we are afraid, God will protect us.

No matter where we are afraid—at home alone, driving on the freeway during rush hour traffic, facing a hostile meeting, or walking alone at night—God is right beside us. He promises, "Do not fear, for I am with you; do not be dismayed, for I am your God. I will strengthen you and help you; I will uphold you with My righteous right hand."[14] What a comfort this is for us in our daily lives!

Claim this promise and consciously remember that God is with you during your times of fear and uncertainty. He will comfort you and give you courage to confront your fears. He will also protect you so that you will never experience anything outside His will for your life.

When we are tempted, God will help us resist.

Satan's main strategy with God's people has always been to whisper, "Don't call, don't ask, don't depend on God to do great things. You'll get along fine if you rely on your own cleverness and energy." The devil is not terribly frightened of our human efforts, but he knows his kingdom will be damaged when we lift our hearts to God.[15]

Although we can be tempted by our own flesh and by worldly influences, Satan is a major player in our desire to disobey God. Radio Bible teacher David Jeremiah puts temptation in a new light:

> Suppose you and one of your friends are on the border of doing something wrong. Both of you know it is wrong. But you are about to do it anyway. But if you should say to your

friend, "Go right ahead and do it, but I think you should know that I just heard from heaven and God will be here in a few moments." Maybe your friend will respond, "Wow, if God is going to be here soon, maybe I will do this tomorrow or next week, but I don't want to do this if God is going to show up in a few minutes."[16]

Surprise! God has already shown up. He is here…now! When facing temptation, we should say to ourselves, "This is being carried out in the presence of almighty God." Meditating on this truth will give you conviction to face temptation in your life.

I encourage you to practice the presence of God by asking our Lord to help you resist temptation. The Bible promises that "God is faithful. He will keep the temptation from becoming so strong that you can't stand up against it."[17]

When we are hurting, God will comfort us.

How could Paul and Silas sing praises to God in the depths of a stinking, cold Roman prison? Their backs were raw because they had been beaten with whips and rods. Their feet were in stocks and the jailer had threatened to execute them if they tried to escape. Paul and Silas could sing because God was with them in the inner dungeon while they were hurting.

The psalmist writes, "The LORD is close to the brokenhearted; He rescues those who are crushed in spirit."[18] Whether we experience physical, emotional, or mental pain, the Holy Spirit will comfort us and give us strength and courage to triumph over our hurts.

Several of our Campus Crusade for Christ staff members have lost small children to accidental death or disease. Vonette and I are thankful that this is a trial we have never had to endure, but we feel their pain. They tell me that it is one of the most agonizing crises that a person can ever go through. Tears flow for months; muscles are sore from sobbing. Many unbelieving couples break up afterwards due to guilt and blame. But many followers of Christ testify, "That was the most difficult thing I have ever experienced, but I have to tell you that God was so very near to me that I felt His presence like I have never felt Him before."

Although Scripture is clear that God is present everywhere at once, parents who have lost children give evidence that God manifests His presence in special ways at particular times of need. In 2 Corinthians 1:3,4, Paul assures us, "[God] is the source of every mercy and the God who comforts us. He comforts us in all our troubles so that we can comfort others."

When we are discouraged, God will encourage us.

Do you struggle with insurmountable bills? Have friends betrayed you? Do you feel inadequate at your job or as a parent? Scripture instructs us, "Cast all your anxiety on Him because He cares for you."[19] We are encouraged in Joshua 1:9, "Do not be afraid or discouraged. For the LORD your God is with you wherever you go." Not only will God help you conquer every discouragement, He will help you climb every mountain in your life! And when you come through the valleys of discouragement, you will find that God was there all the time. Sometimes He was waiting patiently for you to exhaust your means and energy and turn to Him for His help. What a tremendous encouragement! We can trust that kind of God for anything!

When we are lonely, God will be our companion.

Some of our most lonely moments can be when we are in a crowd, and yet no one notices us. Our hearts ache when we think no one cares. But Jesus is our ever-present friend.[20] He promises, "Never will I leave you; never will I forsake you."[21]

He is also with us as we face lonely tasks. When David Livingstone sailed to Africa for the first time as a missionary, a group of his friends accompanied him to the pier to wish him bon voyage. They were concerned for his safety and reminded him of the dangers of that unexplored land. One of the men even tried to convince him to remain in England. But Livingstone opened his Bible and read Jesus' words from Matthew 28:20: "Lo, I am with you always." He turned to the man who was especially concerned about his safety and smiled. "That, my friend, is the word of a gentleman...So let us be going."

No person or circumstance can ever remove us from the presence of our loving God. Paul writes, "I am convinced that nothing can ever separate us from His love. Death can't, and life can't. The angels can't, and the demons can't. Our fears for today, our worries about tomorrow, and even the powers of hell can't keep God's love away. Whether we are high above the sky or in the deepest ocean, nothing in all creation will ever be able to separate us from the love of God that is revealed in Christ Jesus our Lord."[22]

He is here with us right now and forever—because He is our ever-present God. He is our guide for life and for eternity. What an incredible truth! What a powerful motivation for us to know, love, trust, obey, worship, and enjoy the presence of our wonderful God and Savior.

LIFE APPLICATION

WRITE IT ON YOUR HEART—Commit the following statement and verses to memory. Then as you encounter situations during this week where you need the comfort of knowing God is near, claim these promises by faith.

- Because God is ever-present, He is always with me.

- Joshua 1:9—"I command you—be strong and courageous! Do not be afraid or discouraged. For the LORD your God is with you wherever you go."

- Psalm 16:11—"You will show me the way of life, granting me the joy of Your presence and the pleasures of living with You forever."

COUNT ON GOD—Our ever-present God is everywhere you have been and everywhere you will go. He is in the classroom, the courtroom, the office, the home, and the hospital room. He is with you in life and in death. He is the only one who can be with you no matter what. Are you in the midst of a struggle or situation where you need His guidance? Turn to Him now and place your trust in the One who is always with you. Study His Word and let it guide you.

OBEY GOD—God is present with you each minute of every day. He knows what you do and think every moment. Is there some area in your life in which you are not obeying God? Your ever-present God knows, so commit yourself to obeying Him today.

CHAPTER 8

GOD
KNOWS
EVERYTHING

Many people consider Albert Einstein the most dazzling intellect in history. Did you know that the beginnings of his theory of relativity came from an essay he wrote when he was 16 years old? By age 26, he had published five major research papers in an important German journal. For one of those papers, he received his doctorate. The ideas he introduced in those papers were so revolutionary that they changed the way we view the scientific universe.

When the Nazis came to power, they denounced Einstein's work, confiscated his property, and burned his books. Soon after, he moved to America and became a U.S. citizen. In 1939, Einstein learned that German scientists had split the uranium atom. He wrote a letter to President Franklin D. Roosevelt warning him about the German discovery, which he predicted would lead to the invention of the atomic bomb. Because of Einstein's advice, the U.S. government established the Manhattan Project, which developed the first two atomic bombs in 1945.[1]

Einstein's ideas impacted not only the way scientists think about matter, but also the way war is waged. They even spilled over into the moral realm. To Einstein's shock, modern philosophers took his scientific theory of relativity and applied it to the moral realm as *relativism*. This philosophy destroyed society's belief in absolute truth and helped produce acceptance for situational ethics. While Einstein's discoveries about the atom have advanced the arenas of energy and medicine, they have been used to destroy physical and moral lives.

God is the only source of all knowledge, understanding, and wisdom; everything we know and understand originated with Him. As the prophet Isaiah declares:

> Who has understood the mind of the LORD, or instructed Him as His counselor? Whom did the LORD consult to enlighten Him, and who taught Him the right way? Who was it that taught Him knowledge or showed Him the path of understanding?[2]

What great news! We do not need an intellect like Einstein's. We know Someone who knows the answers to all of life's questions. "Oh, what a wonderful God we have! How great are His riches and wisdom and knowledge!"[3]

THE GREATEST KNOWLEDGE

What a person knows can lead to riches, power, and advancement. Major corporations and companies pay consultants handsomely for what they know. Consider the computer industry. Fortunes are being made because people want quicker ways to find and manage information.

In 1953, there were only 100 computers in use around the world. These machines each weighed many tons and filled huge rooms. Today, there are more than 110 million computers in homes, schools, businesses, and government offices. Some of the newest computers are so small that they can fit into a coat pocket.[4]

Our knowledge base doubles every few years. College graduates often discover that what they learned in their many years of study quickly becomes obsolete due to this information explosion. Every day new discoveries change what we previously accepted as factual. Yesterday's cutting-edge concepts are being replaced by today's insights. These in turn will give way to tomorrow's breakthroughs.

Yet the more we learn, the more we realize how much we still do not know. To compensate for our lack of knowledge, we are always trying to build a faster, smarter way to access knowledge. Some of today's sophisticated supercomputers can perform nearly 32 billion calculations per second and can store a billion characters in their memories. They can do in one hour what it would take your desktop computer forty years to perform. Scientists are also using technology called parallel processing in which they link networks of computers to be able to use each computer's idle time. The goal is to create a network that can perform a trillion calculations per second, a measure known as a teraflop.[5]

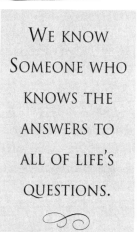

WE KNOW SOMEONE WHO KNOWS THE ANSWERS TO ALL OF LIFE'S QUESTIONS.

At the same time, many of these scientists and experts reject the one Person who has the greatest knowledge of all. According to 1 John 3:20, "He knows everything." Our magnificent Creator God not only knows everything but also is the source of all knowledge. His knowledge is absolutely pure, totally true and accurate, and undefiled by distortions or wrong perspectives. Unlike man's knowledge, God's knowledge is never superseded or made obsolete by new discoveries.

Most scientists spend their lives trying to understand and solve the mysteries of life and the universe. But for our all-knowing God, there are no mysteries. He has a clear understanding of everything that baffles mankind. To Him, a teraflop is nothing.

OUR ALL-KNOWING GOD

Theologians call God's unlimited knowledge *omniscience* (all knowing). What does God's omniscience mean? Nearly 150 years ago, one of the last century's great theologians, Stephen Charnock, wrote:

He knows what angels know, what man knows, and infinitely more; He knows Himself, His own operations, all His creatures, the notions and thoughts of them.[6]

Because God knows absolutely everything that can ever be known, He has never had to learn anything. He does not need a computer because all knowledge is instantly accessible to Him and He remembers everything at all times. He is never bewildered or confused or perplexed. He never has to figure something out; everything is always absolutely clear to Him. Nothing ever surprises God; He is always completely aware of all events because He sees everything. Nothing ever turns out differently than He expected or planned.

In this chapter, I want to highlight four areas of God's omniscience. They will help us more fully understand how much we can trust God with everything in our lives.

ONLY GOD KNOWS EVERYTHING ABOUT HIMSELF

As humans, we do not understand much about ourselves. For example, has anyone ever pointed out a task you messed up and said, "You should have known better than that"? But you thought you did know what to do when you started—until you failed.

Now imagine what it would be like to deal with a god who has inadequate knowledge about himself and his creation. At Shinto shrines in Japan, people tie messages to tree branches to inform their gods of needs. These worshippers have never experienced a God who knows everything, so they operate on the premise that their deity needs the most elemental information.

Not so with the God of the Bible. He knows His own essence and infinite perfections. He knows what is unknowable to anyone else. First Corinthians 2:11 says, "No one can know what anyone else is really thinking except that person alone, and no one can know God's thoughts except God's own Spirit."

If God did not know Himself completely, then His knowledge of everything else would be incomplete as well. We could not trust Him with our problems. Let us take this a step further. If God did not know Himself perfectly, then He would be ignorant of His own ability; He would not know how far His power extends. That would mean He could not govern everything, for He would not know how to exercise His power. Let me give some examples of the importance of God's knowledge of Himself.

As humans, we do not know ourselves, let alone what is going on in the heart of another person. That is why many of our laws when put into practice work against what they were intended to do. For example, malpractice laws intended to help patients injured during a medical procedure can also be used by a dishonest person to cheat the system out of millions of dollars. In a similar way, if God did not fully know His own holiness, He could not discern the difference between evil and good. Consequently, He could not prescribe laws or execute justice, for He would be limited in His knowledge of a person's heart attitudes. But He does understand His holiness, so He is the perfect judge.

Second, if a king did not know his own authority or the borders and nature of his kingdom, how could he rule? His authority would suffer from serious lapses. But God does know every detail about His creatures, and His ability to rule in majesty and fairness is unequaled.

Third, in sports, we sometimes say about a rookie who makes it to the major leagues, "He doesn't know his own strength." Therefore, he plays well below his capabilities. We can never say that about God. No one but God is capable of truly understanding His divine magnificence and His many attributes.

Jesus tells us, "No one really knows the Father except the Son and those to whom the Son chooses to reveal Him."[7] What we know about God is possible only because He has revealed Himself through creation, the Bible, and Jesus Christ.

ONLY GOD KNOWS EVERYTHING ABOUT HIS CREATION

Some people believe that our vast and orderly universe originated as a result of a massive explosion known as the "Big Bang." This theory proposes that billions of years ago, before there were stars or planets, all of the energy and matter of the universe were crammed together into a big ball. Somehow, this huge ball exploded, which caused the planets, stars, and galaxies to emerge. Yet even renowned scientists admit that no one really knows how stars originated. Abraham Loeb of the Harvard University Center for Astrophysics says, "The truth is that we don't understand star formation at a fundamental level."[8]

Where did the original matter and energy come from? How could life originate from the dead, inorganic matter of the Big Bang? And why do explosions today create only chaos and destruction instead of order and intricate design that is present throughout the universe?

How foolish to believe that this universe created itself. Truth and knowledge about creation can only originate with God.

ONLY GOD KNOWS EVERYTHING THAT HAS EVER HAPPENED OR WILL HAPPEN

Have you ever known someone who was a "know-it-all"? No matter what you say, he corrects you. If you tell a story, he has a better one. He parades his knowledge about the latest fads or news. Soon your ears tire of hearing him talk about what he knows.

Although God knows everything that has ever happened or will happen, He never comes across as a "know-it-all." He never uses His knowledge in a selfish way. Not a single event throughout all eternity has gone unnoticed by God. In the Book of Isaiah, God declares, "I am God, and there is no one else like Me. Only I can tell you what is going to happen even before it happens."[9] His omniscience is vitally important to us. As we get to know Him more intimately, we realize that we can trust Him because He does know everything we have done and will do, yet He loves us anyway.

Some people are intimidated by God because He knows the end from the beginning—and everything in between. Statements like Proverbs 15:3 unnerve them: "The LORD is watching everywhere, keeping His eye on both the evil and the good." They know that He sees their sin. This truth is disturbing for a husband who secretly looks at pornographic material and the employee who steals from the job. But God who sees what is done in secret will someday reveal such behavior publicly. On the other hand, God's omniscience is comforting to those who confess their sins as they recognize them. They know their sins have been forgiven.

God Knows the Past

None of us have a perfect memory, and we sometimes forget incidents in our past that would be helpful in the future. As a result, we run into all kinds of obstacles because we did not remember the past.

Our omniscient God, however, never forgets the past. One of the marvelous facets of God's knowledge is that He knows everything that has happened in the past as though it were happening right now. He has no dark recesses in his memory where some past action lies hidden. Since He knows our past perfectly, as we submit to the Holy Spirit, He illuminates what we need to know to take proper action.

The only time God promises not to remember our past is when we seek His forgiveness. God says, "I, even I, am He who blots out your transgressions, for My own sake, and remembers your sins no more."[10] Even though He is aware of our sins, He consciously does not "remember" them after we confess them.[11]

God Knows the Present

If God did not know all the present, then He could be deceived and misled. But God knows everything about all His creatures. The psalmist writes, "The LORD looks down from heaven and sees the whole human race. From His throne He observes all who live on the earth. He made their hearts, so He understands everything they do."[12]

We can compare God's knowledge to a mother who knows exactly what her child has done and is doing. Mothers often intuitively discern the real motives of their children's actions. If that is true of a mother, how much more is it true of our heavenly Father! God knows every good intention we have—as well as every temptation to rebel against His commands.

This can be very encouraging. For example, during Jesus' final meal with His disciples before the crucifixion, He predicted that Peter would deny his Lord. Jesus says to him, "Simon, Simon, Satan has asked to sift you as wheat. But I have prayed for you, Simon, that your faith may not fail. And when you have turned back, strengthen your brothers."[13] Knowing the condition of Peter's heart and that Peter would later disciple his brothers and sisters in their faith, Jesus prayed for him even before his denial. Jesus does the same for us today.

God Knows the Future

For years, highly educated and experienced economists have predicted doom for the American economy, yet we are experiencing quarter after quarter of improved profits and higher productivity.

> THERE IS NOT A THOUGHT IN YOUR MIND OR A MOTIVE IN YOUR HEART THAT GOD DOES NOT KNOW.

Stock market consultants forecasted a market decline and advised clients to switch into safer financial investments, yet the stock market continues to climb to extraordinary heights. No one really knows what the economy will do. As someone once remarked, "If you lined up all the economists in the world one after another, you wouldn't have enough to reach a conclusion."

Now consider the foreknowledge of God. At one time, nothing existed but God, yet at any point in time, He knew the past, present, and future. He knew when He would create the universe, that Adam and Eve would sin, and that He would send a Savior.

To prove His ability to predict the future, God gave us hundreds of prophecies in the Bible. One that fascinates me is the prophecy that the Jewish people would be called together as a nation.[14] The temple of Jerusalem was destroyed in A.D. 70 and the Jewish people scattered from their homeland. What were the chances that a people without a country could survive as a nation?

Every other nation since then has disappeared into oblivion. But in 1948, the Jewish people reestablished their homeland in Israel. The odds are astronomical of that happening after nearly two millennia. God's prophecies are 100 percent accurate because He not only knows the future, He also controls the future.

ONLY GOD KNOWS EVERYTHING ABOUT US

Occasionally when Vonette and I are talking together, one of us will say, "You read my mind; that was what I was about to tell you." Sometimes I will be silently praying about something, and she will ask me, "Have you thought about such and such?" To my amazement, that was the very thing I was praying about. How does that happen? I do not understand it, but I know that if human beings can be so in tune with one another, how much greater is God's ability to know our thoughts, discern our motives, and understand our weaknesses.

There is neither a thought in your mind nor a motive in your heart that God does not know. That is an awesome thought! King David explains:

> Oh LORD, You have examined my heart and know everything about me. You know when I sit down or stand up. You know my every thought when far away. You chart the path ahead of me and tell me where to stop and rest. Every moment You know where I am. You know what I am going to say even before I say it, LORD. You both precede and follow me. You place Your hand of blessing on my head. Such knowledge is too wonderful for me, too great for me to know![15]

I encourage you to take a few moments to worship God because of His knowledge and love for us. One way to worship our incomprehensible Creator is by coming before Him in silence and awe. Shut out everything else; turn off the radio, television, or music, and come into His presence. Tell Him how great are His attributes and works. Then listen in quietness as His Spirit speaks and ministers to your spirit.

LIFE APPLICATION

EXALT YOUR GOD—In silence and in awe, worship our all-knowing Lord with this Psalm:

> Oh LORD, You have examined my heart and know everything about me. You know when I sit down or stand up. You know my every thought when far away. You chart the path ahead of me and tell me where to stop and rest. Every moment You know where I am. You know what I am going to say even before I say it, LORD. You both precede and follow me. You place Your hand of blessing on my head. Such knowledge is too wonderful for me, too great for me to know! (Psalm 139:1–6).

In your own words, praise God for His knowledge of your past, present, and future. Thank Him for His forgiveness of your past, and praise Him for the peace He provides in the present, and the hope you can have because He knows your future.

REFLECT HIS IMAGE—How have you been influenced by the idea that morals are relative? Do you really believe that God knows everything and that His way is best? Spend time in the Bible and gain His knowledge. Then you can be an instrument of His wisdom, which is "far more valuable than rubies" (Proverbs 8:11). With your knowledge of God's Word, reject any relativistic ideas you may be practicing and reflect the standards of God's Word in your neighborhood and workplace.

SHARE HIS MAJESTY—Do you have friends or family members who need to know that our loving Creator knows all about them and wants to have a personal relationship with them? God's Spirit will help you find the words to say as you share the hope of Jesus with them. Today, encourage others with the Good News!

CHAPTER 9

GOD KNOWS EVERYTHING ABOUT US

Shortly after I became a Christian, a friend invited me to a celebration hosted by a man who headed one of the largest oil companies in the world at the time. As I went through the reception line, I knew I was just another nobody to this man. But afterward, the Holy Spirit began to impress upon me that I needed to talk to him about his soul. I obediently called his office, and to my surprise, he agreed to meet with me.

When I arrived for my appointment, I passed by all the various people who screen his visitors and walked into his office. He sat behind a big, mahogany desk in a high-back chair, not a sheet of paper on his desk. "What can I do for you?" he asked.

"Well, sir," I said, "I asked you for fifteen minutes of your time. I don't want to impose. I have come to talk to you about your relationship with Jesus Christ."

Suddenly, he began to cry. As he was sobbing, he told me his story. He became a Christian when he was eight years old. After attending college and getting involved in business, he turned away from God. He said, "I haven't been to church in thirty years. I have made such a mess out of my life. Some think that I am at the top of the ladder of success, but I feel like a great failure. I seem to have everything, but I have lost my family and everything dear to me."

Before I met with him, I had no way of knowing where this man was spiritually or what he was going through, but God did. As I responded to the Holy Spirit's leading, God opened the door so that this man's life could be turned around. He spontaneously volunteered, "I will be in church on Sunday."

Only God knows us perfectly and intimately. He understands our desires, motives, and thoughts. Nothing about us escapes His notice. In fact, God knows infinitely more about us than we will ever know about ourselves. God also knows what is going on in the lives of the people with whom we come into contact every day. He knows their struggles and has the answer to their problems.

God not only knows all about us, but He will never forget us. He even keeps an account of the number of hairs on our heads.[1] God promises through Isaiah:

> Can a mother forget the baby at her breast and have no compassion on the child she has borne? Though she may forget, I will not forget you! See, I have engraved you on the palms of My hands.[2]

The reference to the engraving on the palms of God's hands is a prophecy about the death of Christ on the cross when the Roman soldiers drove nails through His hands. Christ submitted to death because of His love for us; the nail holes are eternal reminders of that love. No wonder we can have assurance that God will never forget about us!

Consider a few things that demonstrate how well God knows you.

GOD KNOWS HOW YOU ARE DESIGNED

Do you ever feel that your parents do not listen to you, your boss does not respect you, or that your co-workers in the church, even the pastor, do not understand you? How devastating to realize that almost no one knows what you are like inside or the dreams you dream. Take heart. Remember that God knows how we are formed.[3]

As our Creator, He custom-designed us for a unique purpose.

David declared that the steps of a godly person are directed by the LORD.[4] That means that He will guide us as we live our lives for Him. God even "understands how weak we are; He knows we are only dust."[5]

This assurance was evident in the experience of a pastor of a small church. He became so discouraged that he was ready to give up the ministry. A friend invited him to a prayer summit of pastors. When he got there, he confessed to his group, "I've been so defeated that I don't even think God knows where I am." But God did know where he was. The next day, the other pastors stood in a circle around him and prayed for him, and he had such an overpowering sense of God's presence that he went home walking on air. God knew exactly what this pastor needed to be renewed in his heart and mind. He will help each of us in similar ways because He designed us and knows exactly what we need at every moment.

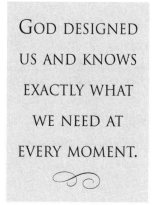

GOD DESIGNED US AND KNOWS EXACTLY WHAT WE NEED AT EVERY MOMENT.

GOD KNOWS EVERYTHING ABOUT YOUR PAST

God is aware of everything every person has ever done—both good and bad. God told Jeremiah, "The human heart is most deceitful and desperately wicked. Who really knows how bad it is? But I know! I, the LORD, search all hearts and examine secret motives. I give all people their due rewards, according to what their actions deserve."[6]

In man's system of justice, accused murderers are brought to trial, then prosecutors use every possible tactic to get the accused convicted. On the other side, defense attorneys use every possible tactic to get the jurors to believe their client is innocent, no matter what the evidence says. Jurors are often swayed by the skill of the attorneys rather than by the facts.

However, our all-knowing God accurately judges not only the

actions of people but also the intents of their heart, no matter what excuses they give, no matter how long they seem to get away with their sins. In a later chapter we will learn more about God's justice in greater depth. But let me ask you: What is your reaction to a God who knows every sin you have ever committed? Do you fear your future is doomed because of your past? He has not left us in a hopeless condition.

God loves you unconditionally in spite of your past sin. He will forgive you when you sincerely confess it to Him. We never have to fear that He will discover something in our past that will change His mind about loving us.

GOD KNOWS EVERYTHING YOU FACE IN THE PRESENT

When we face challenges or difficulties, the fact that God knows all things is encouraging. Pastor David Jeremiah tells his congregation:

> Our God knows what we are going through. He knows every minute of our pain and suffering. He not only knows what we feel, He also knows why we feel what we feel. He knows how it happened, and how long it's going to last and how intense it is. He knows every emotion associated with it; and when you are going through such difficult times, all you can do sometimes is look and say, "Father, you know...you know."[7]

Whatever your circumstances, whatever your need, God understands and will go through it with you. He knows about your hurt, rejection, and pressures. Your feelings and struggles are not unknown to Him, but He also knows the purposes for your trials. He wants to help you accomplish those purposes and to experience His joy through them. In Him there is hope for a way out and a better tomorrow.

GOD KNOWS THE FUTURE HE WANTS FOR YOU

Amy Carmichael was one of the most beloved missionaries during the end of the 19th and beginning of the 20th centuries. She served God in India for fifty-five years. Sherwood Eddy wrote: "Amy Wilson Carmichael was the most Christlike character I ever met, and…her life was the most fragrant, the most joyfully sacrificial, that I ever knew."[8]

When she was growing up in Ireland, she desperately wanted blue eyes. With the faith of a child, she truly believed that God would change her brown eyes to blue if she asked Him. One night, she prayed fervently for blue eyes, then confidently went to bed. When she awoke the next morning, she ran to the mirror. Her same brown eyes were reflected in the glass. How disappointed she was!

Later during her years in India, she became aware of the tragic plight of many girls from poor families who were sold to Hindu temples as prostitutes. Amy began rescuing these young girls and bringing them to her home in Dohnavur to raise them and teach them how much God loves them. She would stain her white skin with coffee grounds and dress in Indian clothing so she could sneak into the temples unnoticed. One day as she dressed, she realized that her disguise worked only because she had brown eyes. Blue eyes would have been a dead giveaway! At that moment, she realized that one of the reasons God said no to her prayer as a child was because He had a plan for her future that involved the lives of hundreds of other precious little ones. God had known her future—even when she was a little girl half a world away.

In Ephesians 2:10, Paul tells us, "He has created us anew in Christ Jesus, so that we can do the good things He planned for us long ago." God knew what He had planned for our lives before we were even conceived. He understands our capabilities, opportunities, and life mission. We can trust Him with every moment of our future.

GOD KNOWS WHICH CHOICES WILL LEAD TO HIS BEST FOR YOU

As you were sitting in the classroom in high school or college, you probably thought many times, *I don't see any purpose in all the stuff I'm having to learn.* Or maybe you have a friend who is a sports trivia addict who can spew out an incredible number of statistics on players who were active in the '40s and '50s. What purpose is his knowledge, except to amaze his friends?

God uses His omniscience for more than categorizing information. Peter tells the crowd that Jesus "was handed over to you by God's set purpose and foreknowledge."[9] What was the purpose of this foreknowledge? To establish a way for us to have an intimate relationship with God through His Son, Jesus Christ, whose death and resurrection would result in victory over Satan and eternal death. His purpose was our freedom.

> GOD USES OUR ADVERSITY, HEARTACHE, TESTINGS, AND PERSECUTIONS TO BLESS US.

God knew that once you chose to become His child, you would become "holy and blameless" before Him.[10]

Unfortunately, sometimes we think we know better than God does and do not listen to Him. How many times have you gotten impatient with the way your life is going and wanted to go directly from point A to point C? But it is not just getting to the destination that is important. God knows that by taking us through point B, the process of the journey will change us so we will be the kind of people we need to be when we arrive at our destination.

In Jeremiah 29:11, God promises, "I know the plans I have for you," declares the LORD, "plans to prosper you and not to harm you, plans to give you hope and a future" (NIV). Following His plan leads to the best choices for our lives—right now, in the future, and for eternity.

GOD KNOWS YOU NEED WISDOM

Because God's Spirit resides within us, we can rely on Him as our Teacher, Counselor, and Guide into all truth. He is willing to share His great knowledge with us. God promises:

> If you need wisdom—if you want to know what God wants you to do—ask Him, and He will gladly tell you. He

will not resent your asking. But when you ask Him, be sure that you really expect Him to answer, for a doubtful mind is as unsettled as a wave of the sea that is driven and tossed by the wind.[11]

God is never surprised when we have problems, and He is always with us to help us. But believers often deprive themselves of God's solutions because they do not take time to study His Word.[12] Or they may know the Word but not want to obey it or meet the conditions of God's promises. Thus they do not receive full benefit from God's omniscience.

Solomon writes, "Trust in the LORD with all your heart; do not depend on your own understanding. Seek His will in all you do, and He will direct your paths."[13] But God's help does not guarantee us a life free of trials and tribulations. In fact, James 1:2–4 and Romans 5:3,4 inform us that God uses our adversity, heartache, testings, and persecutions to bless us.

Trusting God does not eliminate temptation either. Remember how we read earlier, "No temptation has seized you except what is common to man. And God is faithful; He will not let you be tempted beyond what you can bear. But when you are tempted, He will also provide a way out so that you can stand up under it."[14] We sometimes wish we knew what that way out would be. Yet when we accept the fact that the God who knows the end from the beginning is providing the way out, we can relax. He has the power to make us victorious.

God knows all about you and loves you unconditionally. I encourage you—yes, I plead with you—to open your heart to Him and determine to walk with Him regardless of the cost. Remind yourself every day of the truth of our all-knowing God. You will never again feel the same way about your daily personal fellowship with our wonderful God.

In the next chapter, we will put all of God's attributes of ability (omnipotence, omnipresence, omniscience) together to discover another characteristic that sets Him far above anything or anyone else—His sovereignty. This attribute is one that gives us complete hope for the future.

LIFE APPLICATION

WRITE IT ON YOUR HEART—Commit the following statement and verses to memory. Then as you encounter situations during this week where you need God's wisdom, claim these promises by faith.

- Because God knows everything, I can go to Him with all my questions and concerns.
- James 1:5,6—"If you need wisdom—if you want to know what God wants you to do—ask Him, and He will gladly tell you. He will not resent your asking. But when you ask Him, be sure that you really expect Him to answer, for a doubtful mind is as unsettled as a wave of the sea that is driven and tossed by the wind."
- Psalm 147:5—"How great is our Lord! His power is absolute! His understanding is beyond comprehension!"

COUNT ON GOD—It is often difficult to trust other people. They can be wishy-washy or simply forget to do something they have promised. But God never forgets! Spend time in God's Word gathering His many promises. Choose one that applies to a situation you are facing right now and trust Him to fulfill it.

OBEY GOD—God not only knows the past, present, and future, He knows what is best for you. Is there something you have been reluctant to do? Decide today to do everything God's way and obey Him in the areas you turned over to Him.

CHAPTER 10

GOD
IS
SOVEREIGN

eople around the world are fascinated with royalty. Pictures of the late Princess Diana, Prince Charles, and other British royalty fill the tabloids and television screens. Why does their every appearance captivate our attention? Perhaps it is the grandeur in which they live.

Since we live in a democracy in a time in which sovereigns do not rule grand empires, it is hard for us to understand the depth of feeling that people have toward their kings and queens. When King Hussein of Jordan died in February 1999, his entire country mourned. Nearly a million people lined up to see the funeral procession—almost one-sixth of Jordan's population! Hundreds of Jordanians broke through the security barrier to get near the coffin.

As the coffin reached Raghadan Palace, it was placed on a cannon carriage, accompanied by the king's favorite Arabian stallion. A pair of boots were placed backward in the stirrups in remembrance of the fallen leader. All over Jordan, black flags waved from doorposts and car antennas. The country was almost shut down for a week for official mourning.

From earliest days, kings and queens have received honor and respect. One example is in 1911 when the former Indian rulers' courts paid homage to King George V and Queen Mary of England on the Delhi plain. The royal couple sat on a dais while the princes advanced according to protocol and did their salutes. The first prince gave the king a necklace that held a ruby the size of a pigeon's egg. His Highness of Panna presented the king with a twelve-inch umbrella made from a single emerald. Dressed in gold and silver brocade, Sir Tukoji Rao of Indore came with a gold stick that had jeweled engravings and a hilt carved from a single ruby.[1]

One of the rulers' dearest treasures are their titles. This was the title of the Seventh Nizam:

> Lieutenant-General His Exalted Highness Seventh in Line Equal to the Rank of Asaf Jah, Victor of the Realm and the World, Regulator of the Realm, Regulator of the State, Viceroy Sir the Honourable Osman Ali Khan, the Brave, Victorious in Battle, Faithful Ally of the British, Grand Commander of the Star of India, Knight Grand Cross of the British Empire, Nizam of Hyderabad and Berar.[2]

English royalty held lavish ceremonies to establish their positions, often spending months on elaborate preparations. When Queen Elizabeth II was crowned in Westminster Abbey in London, she rode in a gold coach pulled by eight magnificent grays. Anne Edwards describes a portion of the 1953 coronation ceremony:

> The Queen was next garbed in the gold Robe Royal and one by one was given the symbols of authority. The Sceptre was placed in her right hand and the Rod in her left. "Be so merciful that you be not too remiss," prayed the Archbishop, "so execute justice that you forget not mercy. Punish the wicked, protect and cherish the just, and lead your people in the way wherein they should go."
>
> ...A great gust of sound raised up through the Abbey, "God Save the Queen." Trumpets sounded, drums rolled, and then the great guns of the Tower and in Hyde Park were shot off.[3]

The Queen was crowned with the large solid-gold, pearl- and

ruby-studded St. Edward's Crown worn at all coronations in the 20th century. Then the peers of her realm performed the Act of Homage by kneeling before her and swearing allegiance to the crown. Even the Queen's husband, Prince Phillip, performed the Act of Homage.

THE GREATEST SOVEREIGN

Yet, there exists another Royal King whose majesty, splendor, and awesomeness are almost indescribable. Compared to Him, no other ruler or reign is even a blip on the screen of eternity. He does not need ceremony or to drape Himself in grandeur to appear more regal. Jewels and wealth mean nothing to Him. Yes, this divine Ruler is none other than the Sovereign God. His throne is far above the universe in heaven; He rules over all.

David, himself a king, asked, "Who is this King of glory?" Then he answers his own question, "The LORD, strong and mighty, the LORD, invincible in battle…The LORD Almighty—He is the King of glory."[4] In one of the final chapters in the Bible, John identifies Him as "KING OF KINGS AND LORD OF LORDS." John describes how he heard a loud voice of a great multitude in heaven shouting, "Hallelujah! Salvation and glory and power belong to our God…Hallelujah! For our Lord God Almighty reigns."[5]

As John continues to describe his vision of God's throne, he tries to convey what cannot be adequately described in words. I want to quote a portion here:

> I saw a throne in heaven and Someone sitting on it! The One sitting on the throne was as brilliant as gemstones— jasper and carnelian. And the glow of an emerald circled His throne like a rainbow. Twenty-four thrones surrounded Him, and twenty-four elders sat on them. They were all clothed in white and had gold crowns on their heads. And from the throne came flashes of lightning and the rumble of thunder …In front of the throne was a shiny sea of glass, sparkling like crystal.
>
> In the center and around the throne were four living beings…Day after day and night after night they keep on saying,

"Holy, holy, holy is the Lord God Almighty—the One who always was, who is, and who is still to come."

Whenever the living beings give glory and honor and thanks to the One sitting on the throne, the One who lives forever and ever, the twenty-four elders fall down and worship the One who lives forever and ever. And they lay their crowns before the throne and say:

"You are worthy, O Lord our God,
to receive glory and honor and power.
For You created everything,
and it is for Your pleasure that they exist
and were created."[6]

The throne of an earthly king or queen, however grand it may be, cannot compare to the glories of God. If we took away the royal trappings from any human sovereign, he would look just like one of us. His honor is derived from ceremonies and the homage paid him by other people, which can be removed in a moment. He may have the power of an army behind him, but in himself, he is a sinful, imperfect human just like you and me.

God's reign is different. God does not derive His right to rule from anyone or anything. No title was bestowed on Him by another, and there is no higher authority anywhere than His. The great I AM always does what He knows is best and answers to no one. His reign is so magnificent that we cannot even comprehend any part of it.

God's rule is supreme, paramount, and absolute. He has power to do anything that needs to be done. He is present everywhere so no one can hide from Him or escape His scrutiny. He is all-knowing, so there is nothing about which He is unaware. Amazingly, this great God loves you and me unconditionally, caring for the smallest need of the least of us.

THE GREAT PUZZLE OF LIFE

Submitting to God's sovereignty can be compared to putting together a billion-piece picture puzzle. History is like that giant picture. Only by looking at the photograph on the box cover can you see what everything will look like once all the pieces are in place.

Now imagine that you are given one piece of the puzzle. This is where you fit into God's great plan for the universe. What can you do with this piece? You have never seen the picture on the outside of the box. All you know is that your piece has a little dark color here and a few bright spots there. So you run around trying to match what you are doing with someone else's puzzle piece. The chances of finding one other person who has a piece that matches yours is almost zero. Therefore, there is no way you could ever understand what the completed picture will look like.

From a human standpoint, it is impossible to understand the many puzzles in life. But if you let God direct you, He will help you place your puzzle piece in the right place. He is not only big enough to see the whole picture, He created it.

We can see part of the picture of where God is taking history by reading the Bible. God gives us clues as to what His purposes are for us. In His sovereignty, He will fulfill all He has promised in His Word. We will look at three truths about the scope of God's sovereignty.

GOD SOVEREIGNLY RULES THE UNIVERSE

God reigns so supremely above His creation that we cannot question any of His actions. Whatever God wants to have happen will happen; His will cannot be thwarted. Daniel explains, "He determines the course of world events; He removes kings and sets others on the throne."[7]

God's creative actions set the stage for His sovereignty. He was able to create because He was in absolute control of every particle of material even before He brought it into being. Once He formed something, no matter how simple or complex, He remained in absolute authority.

Jeremiah reminded God's people of how completely God is in control. Because of their disobedience, they wanted to escape the judgment of the God they had spurned. God sent Jeremiah to the house of a potter. As the potter worked on a piece of clay, he skillfully shaped it with his hands into a beautiful vessel. But when another pot he was making was marred, he tossed it aside and began a new pot. He did what seemed best to him.

Through this illustration, God pointed out His limitless sovereignty. "O Israel, can I not do to you as this potter has done to his clay? As the clay is in the potter's hand, so are you in My hand."[8] As Creator, God could do whatever He wanted with His creation. No matter how much the clay complained or rebelled, it was shaped by the strong hand of the potter. Centuries later, Paul points out: "Shall what is formed say to Him who formed it, 'Why did You make me like this?'"[9] Norman Geisler explains God's sovereignty this way:

> If it is a power that you can manipulate, it is not God. If it is a power that created the universe that chooses to express itself one way this time, and another way at another time, for our good and His glory, then it is God.

GOD SOVEREIGNLY WORKS THROUGH HIS LAWS OF NATURE

Stephen Charnock writes, "We cannot suppose God a Creator, without supposing a sovereign dominion in Him."[10] God dominates nature to accomplish His purposes:

> He directs the snow to fall on the earth and tells the rain to pour down…God's breath sends the ice, freezing wide expanses of water. He loads the clouds with moisture, and they flash with His lightning. The clouds turn around and around under His direction. They do whatever He commands throughout the earth. He causes things to happen on earth, either as a punishment or as a sign of His unfailing love."[11]

God established the scientific laws that regulate the universe; only He can overrule their effect. For God, miracles are "routine."

I am amazed when I hear from Christians who doubt God's supernatural intervention in their lives. God did mighty miracles through Noah, Moses, and other Old Testament characters. He spoke through the prophets. He personally invaded our time and space in the form of His Son, the Lord Jesus Christ. Jesus performed miracles, died for our sins, rose from the grave, and ascended bodily into heaven. His resurrection is the greatest miracle of all. Now His Spirit lives in the hearts of millions of believers around the world. We sometimes take these miracles for granted.

God still suspends His natural laws today. I love the story told by former Campus Crusade staff members Dick and Carolyn Edic:

> In 1967,...300 staff and 300 selected students converged on the [University of California] Berkeley campus for a week of intense evangelism in every facet of the campus. We would meet as a group every morning for prayer, Bible study, and challenge before going out with our particular assignment on campus. Our plan was to culminate the week with a large rally in the Greek Outdoor Theatre with Billy Graham as the speaker. The Amphitheatre held about 8,000 people.
>
> Friday morning, we met as a group as usual. Billy Graham spoke to us. It was raining very heavily, so we feared that the heavy rain would prevent our final evangelistic outreach with Billy Graham. So we got on our knees as a group and prayed for about 45 to 60 minutes, asking God to stop the rain and prepare the way for the outreach.
>
> When we finished praying at about 11:30 a.m. and looked outside, the sun was shining! By meeting time, the seats had dried enough to attract 8,000 students, and Billy Graham's preaching went forward. After the rally, at about 2 p.m., it started raining again!
>
> This was the highlight of an exciting week of outreach to a tough crowd. During that week, 23,000 of the 27,000 students received a direct witness of the Lord Jesus Christ personally, in small groups, or in the mass meetings. We saw miraculous answers to prayer that demonstrated God's power to change lives and control the weather.[12]

Yet sometimes God chooses to let it rain and to work despite the floods or sloshing through mud as at Campus Crusade's EXPLO '72 in Dallas and EXPLO '74 in Korea. God is in the business of turning tragedy into triumph and sorrow into joy—at His choosing.

GOD SOVEREIGNLY FULFILLS
HIS ETERNAL MASTER PLAN

God actively directs His creation toward a pre-determined conclusion. Therefore, He controls all other authorities. The psalmist Asaph wrote, "It is God who judges: He brings one down, he exalts another."[13] Let me give you one example from Scripture.

God chose to use King Nebuchadnezzar as His instrument of judgment upon Judah's wicked kings and rebellious people.[14] Nebuchadnezzar's armies seemed unstoppable as they captured a vast empire including Jerusalem and took most of Judah's residents into captivity in Babylon. When Nebuchadnezzar began to boast about what *he* had accomplished, God removed him from the throne until he was humbled.

Seventy years later, in keeping with God's prophecy that He would bring His captive people back to Judah, God raised up another king. As prophesied, Cyrus sent the captives back to Jerusalem to rebuild the city.[15] This was all a part of God's magnificent plan to eventually send His Son, the Messiah, who would be born of a Jewish girl living near Jerusalem.

Someone has aptly said that God's master plan on earth is to:

1) Make sinners sons (spiritual children of God).[16]

2) Make sons like Jesus.[17]

3) Help the sons share the good news of eternal life through Jesus.[18]

Scriptural evidence supports the fact that God's work on earth is primarily of a spiritual, eternal nature.[19] Such a spiritual kingdom is in vast contrast to the material, physical, and temporal kingdom that occupies most people's efforts today.[20]

RESPONDING TO THE REIGN
OF THE KING OF KINGS

We do not live under the jurisdiction of a dictatorial ruler who is out to deprive us of all the fun and happiness in life. The King of kings and Lord of lords has our best interest at heart at all times. He orchestrates events to enable us to praise Him and glorify His name. When times get tough, we can remind ourselves of the conditions under which He reigns. The following paragraphs describe several ways in which He reigns in our lives.

God reigns through His omniscient wisdom.

As a young businessman I made great plans for my business and my future. I had carefully considered what I wanted out of life and what I would have to do to achieve my objectives. Then I met the Son of God! As I discovered the attributes of God—His love, holiness, wisdom, sovereignty, power—I began to realize I could trust His wisdom much more than I could trust my own intelligence.

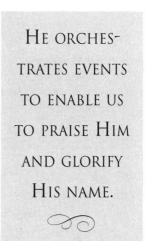

HE ORCHES- TRATES EVENTS TO ENABLE US TO PRAISE HIM AND GLORIFY HIS NAME.

God's sovereignty operates through righteousness.

In the 20th century, many men have held tremendous power and used it for evil—Stalin, Hitler, Mao Tse Tung, and Pol Pot, the vicious head of the Khmer Rouge in Cambodia. These few men, responsible for the deaths of tens of millions of innocent people, reigned in unrighteousness. But God sits on a throne of righteousness because He is holy. We never need to fear that He will act out of evil intentions. Submitting to His sovereignty will always be best for us.

God's sovereignty reveals His goodness.

Because God is good, He is a gracious Sovereign and obliging Benefactor rather than an arbitrary tyrant. The writer to the Hebrews encourages us to "come boldly to the throne of our gracious God" because we have a High Priest who "understands our weaknesses, for He faced all the same temptations we do, yet He did not sin."[21] God has bridged the gap of understanding between us and Him. We can count on His goodness when He deals with us.

THE MOST ASTOUNDING CONTRAST

Can you imagine Queen Elizabeth II giving up her crown to live as a pauper? Putting aside her jewels and dressing in rags? That is unthinkable.

But that is exactly what God did. Reread the description of His throne at the beginning of this chapter. What majesty, perfection, honor, and glory envelops our great God and Savior! Heaven is a place of such beauty and peace, where no sin mars the atmosphere. Pain and hurt are unknown. Angels and all other beings continually praise God.

When God's Son, Jesus Christ, was voluntarily born in a humble manger in Bethlehem, the only people who worshipped Him were lowly shepherds. The stable must have been drafty and not very private. What kind of place was this for the Sovereign of the universe? Where were His crown and His scepter?

Jesus did not live like a king either. He became tired and hungry, was ridiculed, beaten, spit upon, humiliated. The soldiers ripped off His clothes, and He was taken to court before a cruel ruler named Herod. The crowd shouted that they wanted Him killed. All His friends ran away, afraid for their own lives. Then He was cruelly nailed to a cross in front of a jeering crowd. He could have shaken the world in defiance, but all He said was, "Forgive these people, because they don't know what they are doing."[22]

Jesus did this because God loves us so much. His love motivated Him to communicate His love and salvation to us. To do this effectively, He had to become one of us—to walk, talk, eat, and look like us. Just the thought of our sovereign God putting aside His magnificent glory brings me to tears. How can we ever reach the depths of that love? How could we ever fear putting our lives into His hands?

Part of our problem with accepting God's authority and honoring Him is that we have lost our concept of majesty. With little sense of the majesty of God, we have trouble submitting to His sovereignty and worshipping Him. For most Christians, true worship is not something they practice very often or well. A. W. Tozer explains our dilemma:

The modern Christian has lost a sense of worship along with the concept of majesty [of God], and of course, reverence as well. He has lost his ability to withdraw inwardly and commune in the secret place with God in the shrine of his own hidden spirit. It is this that makes Christianity, and we have all but lost it. Added numbers, yes, but lost fear. Multiplied schools, yes, but lost awareness of the invisible. Tons of literature being poured out, of course, but no consciousness of the divine Presence. Better communication, certainly, but nothing to communicate. Evangelistic organizations, yes, but the concept of majesty and worship and reverence has almost left us.[23]

Understanding God's sovereignty causes us to focus on Him, not ourselves. Our response is to fall at His feet and give Him everything we are and own. If the royalty of England kneel before Queen Elizabeth II and pledge to submit to her reign, how much more important is it for us to kneel before God's throne and surrender ourselves to Him?

I urge you to recognize God's sovereignty right now by humbling yourself before Him. Totally and irrevocably submit to His lordship of your life. Worship Him by giving Him everything you own. Think of your life as a house with many rooms. Go through each "room" and surrender both the room and the contents to Him. If you have a closet full of fears, let Him control that part of your life. Invite Him into the room where you hide your insecurities and hurts. Let Him take down that monument of pride to your own abilities and talents that you have displayed in your living room. Ask Him to control your checkbook and bank account. Everything you "lose" by serving Him He will replace with something so much better. He controls the universe; He will without doubt enrich your life with joy, peace, happiness, fulfillment, satisfaction, and rewards far beyond your wildest imagination!

LIFE APPLICATION

EXALT YOUR GOD—Worship the sovereign Ruler of the universe with David's song of praise. As you repeat his words, meditate on how secure you are in God's care.

> Praise be to you, O LORD, God of our father Israel, from everlasting to everlasting. Yours, O LORD, is the greatness and the power and the glory and the majesty and the splendor, for everything in heaven and earth is Yours. Yours, O LORD, is the kingdom; You are exalted as head over all...Now, our God, we give You thanks, and praise Your glorious name (1 Chronicles 29:10,11,13).

REFLECT HIS IMAGE—As we increasingly commit ourselves to our sovereign Creator, we reflect God's image. Even the Son of God submitted to His Father. Jesus stated in John 8:28,29, "I do nothing on my own, but I speak what the Father taught me...I always do those things that are pleasing to Him." Yield your will to God today and determine to make submission to God a consistent part of your character. As you do, you will show others that God controls your life.

SHARE HIS MAJESTY—Does someone you know need to be reminded that God is in control? Comfort them with the fact that our sovereign Lord rules over every circumstance. Challenge them with the truth that God will accomplish His plans through them.

CHAPTER 11

GOD DIRECTS OUR LIVES

s members of a democratic society rife with individual-ism, Americans have difficulty understanding God as an absolute ruler. Did we not reject living under a sovereign ruler when the American Colonies revolted against the king of England? Why should we be subject to anyone now? Yes, we Americans love our independence and freedom.

We do pay homage to our superstar heroes, especially in enter-tainment and sports, but only as long as they produce astonishing performances for us. Other great champions quickly replace them.

With the decline in the belief of absolute truth, we tend to argue and debate our points of view with everyone, even our lead-ers, to get our beliefs and agendas accepted. Today we negotiate to get our own way, and compromise—even on moral issues—is considered a virtue.

But we cannot argue, debate, or negotiate with God, the King of the universe. If He is truly the Lord of our lives, and we are His true disciples, we say, "Yes, Lord!" Saying "No, Lord" is a contradiction of terms for the true disciple of Jesus Christ.

Please, fellow believers, do not follow the teaching of some who say that if you have enough faith in God, or if you repeat the name of Jesus, or quote a formula of phrases or Scripture verses, then you will get all your prayers answered. We cannot force God to do things our way. Sometimes in His wisdom and sovereign plan, His answer to our prayers is "no" or "wait." Our position is to trust, believe, and obey, not to demand.

CHOICE VERSUS OBEDIENCE

Does that mean we have no say with our sovereign God? Of course not! He does not consider us His puppets or slaves. He made us as free moral agents with minds, wills, and emotions. He will not force His love and plans upon us against our wills. Within the context of His master plan, God gives us the freedom to choose. This is a hard concept to grasp. Let me explain with an illustration. A few days ago, I flew to Dallas. I had complete freedom to get up and walk around on that jetliner. I could go get a magazine or talk to my fellow passengers. I could take a nap or make a telephone call. I had complete freedom—within limits. However, I could not alter the plane's course. That plane was going to Dallas!

Our relationship with God is like that. We are not robots mechanically programmed to follow His decrees. God has a course for us that has been charted before the beginning of time. God assures us in His Word: "My purpose will stand, and I will do all that I please."[1] His master plan for history will be accomplished, whether we choose to work with Him or follow our own stubborn way. Although He allows us to choose and suffer the consequences of our choices, He never relinquishes control of the plans to accomplish His purposes. God turns the pages of history; we do not. As you read the following truths about God's sovereignty, ask God to show you how you can restore His majesty in your life and what He wants you to do to obey Him.

GOD SOVEREIGNLY DIRECTS PEOPLE, CIRCUMSTANCES, AND EVENTS

When you read the newspaper or look at events around you, do you sometimes wonder who is in control? More and more Christians see themselves as victims of a wicked society. Many feel overwhelmed by circumstances and struggle with hopelessness, defeat, and discouragement. But God has not abandoned them.

I can clearly see how God's sovereignty has been at work throughout my life. When my mother was carrying me, she almost died many times. During that time, she asked God to spare her life. "Lord, if you will just give me time, and allow me to give birth to this little child, I will dedicate him or her to you." Not only did she survive, but she lived to be 93 years old and her godly example and powerful prayers were the greatest influence on my life. She dedicated me to the Lord and faithfully prayed that God's will would be done in my life.

After completing my college degree, I spent one year on the faculty at Oklahoma State University Extension. Then I left Oklahoma to seek my fortune in California. Although my mother was still praying for me, I had no interest in the things of God. I wanted to be a successful businessman, a man of influence and significance. I was a self-made, happy pagan.

The first day I arrived in California, I picked up a hitchhiker who invited me to dinner at his friend's house. I agreed and, as it turned out, his friend was Dawson Trotman, founder of the Navigators Ministry. After dinner, they said, "We're going to a birthday party. Would you like to come?" That celebration was in the home of America's top radio evangelist, Charles E. Fuller.

I am still awed by the fact that through God's sovereignty, I spent my first night in California in the homes of two of the most famous Christian leaders of the 20th century. That did not just happen by chance. God was orchestrating events in my life—even though I was not a believer—in gracious answer to my saintly mother's prayers.

God is sovereignly involved in directing each of our lives. Proverbs states, "Many are the plans in a man's heart, but it is the LORD's purpose that prevails."[2] God carefully supervises all that happens. No event escapes His notice. No person is beyond His influence. No circumstance exists outside His control.

THERE IS NO ROOM FOR LUCK IN GOD'S SOVEREIGN PLANS

"Good luck," I heard a man recently say. What about luck? Anyone who understands the Bible and God's revelation of Himself knows that there is no such thing as luck or chance, which implies a capriciousness of nature and the universe. When we use the word "luck," we express our unbelief or a lack of knowledge of God's attributes. With God in control, luck does not exist.

As believers, we live by faith in God and His Word and in the power of the Holy Spirit, not by luck or superstition. He also wants us to consciously acknowledge His sovereign control in the affairs of our lives. This means making our life's plans—from our simplest decisions to our career choices or our retirement plans—follow God's will. James explains the attitudes that please or displease God:

> Now listen, you who say, "Today or tomorrow we will go to this or that city, spend a year there, carry on business and make money." Why, you do not even know what will happen tomorrow. What is your life? You are a mist that appears for a little while and then vanishes. Instead, you ought to say, "If it is the Lord's will, we will live and do this or that." As it is, you boast and brag. All such boasting is evil.[3]

God has a much greater agenda than ours. As we make plans through the power of His Holy Spirit, we must allow God to change those plans at a moment's notice. We must seriously seek the will of God rather than our own will—and trust all our circumstances to His control.

GOD USES BAD THINGS FOR GOOD PURPOSES

You may have wondered, *If God is in complete control of everything, why does He allow (or cause) birth defects, famines, and war? Why does He permit sin, evil, and suffering?* God's very nature opposes these things. It was not His plan for Adam and Eve, the first humans, to sin and bring sickness, disease, and death upon mankind.[4] God created a perfect world, but man chose to sin, and the penalty for sin was death—physical and spiritual. This curse of death has affected all of creation, not just humans, and all the bad things that exist are due to living in a world under judgment, a fallen world. Part of Adam and Eve's punishment was pain and suffering in childbirth, fighting against nature for food, and struggling to make a living before finally dying.[5]

God does not initiate, cause, or authorize sin, or tempt anyone to sin. Yet He tolerates evil for a season to fulfill His righteous plans for people to respond by their own free will to His love.

Pastor Charles Stanley explains that God allows troubles, accidents, adversity, and similar problems to come into our lives for a purpose. Some of these purposes are:

- To get our attention
- To draw us to himself
- To help us get to know Him
- To see Him as He is
- To taste of His goodness
- To have an intimate, close relationship with Him
- To prevent distance from and avoidance of God[6]

> GOD IS MORE CONCERNED ABOUT OUR ETERNAL FUTURE THAN OUR PRESENT COMFORT.

Our disappointments are often God's appointments. He is far more concerned about the quality of our eternal future than He is about our present comfort. In fact, difficulties and suffering are tools with which He shapes us into the image of Jesus Christ. It is never fun to be enrolled in the academy of adversity, but unless God takes us through the curriculum of trials, we will never become the quality person He wants us to be. Adversity is the touchstone of character.

Romans 8 promises, "God causes everything to work together for the good of those who love God and are called according to His purpose for them."[7] God uses even the most disastrous situations for our good.

In the summer of 1976, thirty-five female Campus Crusade staff leaders—including my wife, Vonette—gathered in Colorado for a retreat. That night, they were trapped in the Big Thompson Canyon flood.

At about 1:30 in the morning, I was awakened and informed of the flood and of the rescue of one of the women, who was now in the hospital. About an hour later, another staff member was brought to the hospital by helicopter. By this time, we had good reason to believe that several of the women had drowned.

I did not know if Vonette was safe, struggling for her life in the floodwaters, or dead. But I had incredible peace because I knew that God is sovereign and ever-present. So even though I had no idea where Vonette was and could not help her, I knew God was with her and the other women. Because He is all-powerful, God could save all the women whose lives were in danger. But God is also all-knowing. If it was best for Vonette to be taken home to heaven, I could completely trust my loving Father to do the right thing.

Soon I sadly learned that seven of our staff women perished during the flood. I knew that each of these women was rejoicing in the presence of her Savior. I also learned that Vonette and twenty-seven other staff women had escaped the raging water.

In the weeks that followed, we mourned for those dear friends we had lost. But we also felt led by God to make their last moments on earth a tribute to our sovereign God. With full approval of the grieving families, friends of Campus Crusade ministry placed full-page ads in most newspapers across the country featuring pictures of the seven women who died. The headline read, "These seven women lost their lives in the Colorado flood, but they are alive and they have a message for you." The advertisement gave readers an opportunity to read the gospel and receive Jesus Christ as their Savior.

Approximately 150 million people read those ads. The response was phenomenal. Only God knows the full extent of what happened, but many thousands wrote to say that they had received Christ that week as a result of the tragic deaths of those seven women. A foreign ambassador told us that his life was changed by the ad, and later helped open the door for ministry in his country, which had previously been closed to the gospel.

We can give all our worries and cares to God, knowing that He cares about what happens to us.[8] When tragedy strikes, take comfort in the fact that no difficulty will ever come into your life without God's permission. Knowing this truth does not make adversity pleasant, but it gives us hope that the result will be worth whatever pain we endure.

GOD OVERRULES THE EVIL INTENTIONS OF PEOPLE

What about the intentions of evil people? Is God's hand present when they devise evil against us? Throughout the Bible we see incidents of God intervening to thwart the evil intents of humans.

Sometimes it seems as if following God's will makes us more vulnerable to the evil intentions of others. That simply is not true. Yes, since Lucifer rebelled against God, and Adam and Eve sinned in the Garden of Eden, wars have existed between God and Satan, good and evil, light and darkness. God still has His plan, and He will execute it. We just do not always see His working at the beginning, in the middle of the warfare, or even at the end.

As a 19-year-old, Bruce Olsson went into the jungles on the border of Colombia and Venezuela to bring the gospel to the Bari people. God protected him from these aboriginal people who had never let a white man into their territory, and as they came to love him and his Lord, they affectionately called him *bruchko*. Then in 1988 Bruce was captured by Colombian guerrillas and held secretly in the jungle. It looked as if his ministry had been disrupted and maybe even ended.

Once the Colombian armed forces realized that the guerrillas had kidnapped Bruce, they tried to enlist the Baris, once a fierce, warlike tribe, to help rescue their beloved *bruchko*. The Baris refused, saying, "Violence only engenders violence."

Meanwhile, things were happening in the jungle. After five months in captivity, Bruce had so gained the confidence of the guerrillas that they gave him a Bible. Eventually he was able to hold Bible studies with his captors. During nine months of captivity, including one firing squad escape, Bruce led about half the guerrillas assigned to him to faith in Christ. He was so successful that the guerrilla leaders finally released him.

As the years passed after the kidnapping, these Christian guerrillas won others to faith in Christ. Finally, the entire Christian group broke away from the larger guerrilla group and surrendered themselves to the Colombian government. On April 6, 1994, Bruce Olsson wrote in a letter to his prayer and financial supporters:

> Resurrection Sunday also meant "conversion" to a great many members of the former guerrilla forces. In their camps [during my captivity] I witnessed more than a hundred break before the Lord in repentant tears, attentive to His Word and surrender their lives to the lordship of Jesus Christ. This action is prelude to the celebration of the 9th of April [when] ...descendants from the "Armed Forces for National Liberation" (ELN) and "Armed Forces for Colombian Revolution" (FARC), representing about half of the violent revolutionary forces in Colombia, will reincorporate themselves into national life at the surrendering of their arms and signature of the negotiated "Peace Plan."

DURING NINE MONTHS OF CAPTIVITY, BRUCE LED HALF HIS CAPTORS TO FAITH IN CHRIST.

God in His sovereignty protected Bruce despite the evil intentions of guerrilla leaders—and turned the whole incident into a great victory for Jesus Christ. Bruce writes, "The Bari had no doubt in God's sovereignty and trusted in His intervention in the lives and affairs of His creation. The relinquishing of arms [by the guerrillas] in the presence of Bari leaders was significant. It was vindication of the Bari's endurance and persuasion." God was sovereign through the actions of Bruce, the Bari, *and* the guerrillas! Does that give you hope in a situation you may face right now? God will sovereignly use you, too, as you follow His will.

OUR REDEMPTION AND GOD'S SOVEREIGNTY

The entire gospel is a declaration of God's sovereign pleasure concerning Christ. Writing to the Ephesians, Paul explained:

> God's secret plan has now been revealed to us; it is a plan centered on Christ, designed long ago according to His good pleasure. And this is His plan: At the right time He will bring everything together under the authority of Christ—everything in heaven and on earth.[9]

Satan plotted to defeat God's purpose by arranging circumstances so that the Son of God would be crucified. His plots were successful—at first sight. Consider all the evil intentions of men that God used to bring about our redemption:

- The religious leaders plotted to kill Jesus. They succeeded in their malicious intent.
- The court crowd asked Pilate to release Barabbas rather than Jesus. Pilate agreed to their hate-filled request.
- The soldiers beat Jesus and crowned Him with a crown of thorns. They were following the evil orders of their superiors.
- The rabble in front of the cross ridiculed Jesus as He was dying. Their purpose was to make Him look weak and insignificant. And they surely did.
- The government assigned soldiers to guard Jesus' tomb to thwart any claims that He had risen from the dead. They were successful for two days.

Today we know that all these evil intents were integral parts of God's plan. Jesus was just one man standing against the evil intentions of His physical world, and the spiritual world too, but His power was greater than anything anyone could throw at Him. We have available to us that same power, because as believers, the Holy Spirit lives within us. He will comfort us during times of trial, give us wisdom to accomplish God's will, and help us glorify God through every situation.

Do you feel as privileged as I do to be part of God's eternal plan, knowing that God has revealed to us His sovereign will for the grand scale of history? In fact, our sovereign God will ensure that grand finale! Jesus Christ, the Lamb of God, who seemed to be the "victim" of evil intentions, will reign supreme forever and ever. One more passage from John's Revelation gives us the panorama of the grand finale that will take place in the City of God:

> All the nations will bring their glory and honor into the city. Nothing evil will be allowed to enter—no one who practices shameful idolatry and dishonesty—but only those whose names are written in the Lamb's Book of Life.
>
> And the angel showed me a pure river with the water of life, clear as crystal, flowing down from the throne of God and of the Lamb, coursing down the center of the main street. On each side of the river grew a tree of life, bearing twelve crops of fruit, with a fresh crop each month. The leaves were used for medicine to heal the nations.
>
> No longer will anything be cursed. For the throne of God and of the Lamb will be there, and His servants will worship Him. And they will see His face, and His name will be written on their foreheads. And there will be no night there—no need for lamps or sun—for the Lord God will shine on them. And they will reign forever and ever.[10]

When we choose to submit to God's majesty and sovereignty, we are on the winning side. We will reign with the only One who is worthy of worship and who will be our comfort, guide, and friend throughout eternity! What a Savior! I can hardly wait for that moment!

I urge you to allow God to direct your life by surrendering your decisions, trials, hurts, and pain to Him. Give Him your joys, your accomplishments, your treasures. After all, if Indian princes chose to honor the king of England with their most precious and costly possessions, how much more should we honor God with every part of our lives! Unlike an earthly king, God will take what we give to Him and multiply blessings in our lives. We do not give up anything but pride, sin, and temporal possessions; He gives us back eternal life, joy, spiritual riches, and an eternal reign with Him! What a good God!

Now that we have some insight into the limitless abilities of God, we can turn our attention to His moral attributes. They are the basis of our laws, our justice system, and our ideas of fair treatment. In Part II, we will be examining God's high moral character: His ability to judge fairly, truthfully, righteously, and with perfect justice. We will discover why He acts as He does and how that affects our relationship with Him. We will answer questions like: Can I trust God to be fair? How will He judge events when it seems like everything is stacked against me? What does He do when His people commit wrong acts? Is He swayed by those who are more "spiritual" or who hold power in the church?

For a person who has a wrong view of God or who does not know Him intimately, the answers to these questions are unsettling. But as we learn more about God's moral attributes, we will be increasingly confident that we can put complete faith in our Perfect Judge and let Him preside over the courtroom of our lives!

LIFE APPLICATION

WRITE IT ON YOUR HEART—Commit the following statement and verses to memory. Then as you encounter situations during this week where you need to remember that God is in control, claim these promises by faith.

- Because God is sovereign, I will submit to His will.

- Jeremiah 10:23—"I know, LORD, that a person's life is not his own. No one is able to plan his own course."

- Romans 8:28—"God causes everything to work together for the good of those who love God and are called according to His purpose for them."

COUNT ON GOD—Does the fact that God is sovereign scare you? When God is in control, that means you and I are not. That may invoke fear, but it should bring comfort. How much better that our all-powerful, all-knowing God controls every circumstance rather than we who are imperfect and limited. Trust God today by placing your current situation into the hands of your capable and loving heavenly Father.

OBEY GOD—Our sovereign God controls every breath and heartbeat in your life. How foolish it is for us not to obey Him. Ephesians 2:10 states, "We are God's masterpiece. He has created us anew in Christ Jesus, so that we can do the good things He planned for us long ago." You will realize your own full potential by obeying Him. Pursue the "good things" He has for you to do—today.

PART II

OUR PERFECT JUDGE

(Attributes of Integrity)

They will sing before the LORD,
for He comes, He comes to judge the earth.
He will judge the world in righteousness
and the peoples in His truth.

PSALM 96:13, NIV

CHAPTER 12

GOD
IS
HOLY

olumnist Ray Cohn writes in the *New York Times*, "I don't
want to know what the law is, I want to know who the
judge is."[1] How important is a judge? All over the world,
we hear of court cases that are mock trials. Defendants
are paraded as guilty after being forced to sign confessions—
many times to crimes they did not commit. The judges in these
cases are part of a system that results in injustice for the people.
On the other hand, if the judge is honest and fair, he will fulfill
his role so that justice is served and complaints are addressed.

Since God is the most powerful judge in the universe, we
must know what He is like to understand His role as judge. What
kind of court does He hold? What kind of laws does He uphold?
Is His justice fair and impartial?

Today most people ignore God's role as judge of mankind.
They go on with their sin as if no one will ever call them to account. Yet in both the Old and New Testaments, God's justice is repeatedly presented. Look at a few of the times God acted as judge:

- He sent Adam and Eve out of the Garden of Eden because of
their sin.

127

- He destroyed the wicked cities of Sodom and Gomorrah.
- He sent plagues on Egypt for the Pharaoh's mistreatment of God's people.
- He struck down Ananias and Sapphira when they lied to the Holy Spirit.
- He inflicted King Herod with deadly worms after he accepted worship as a god.
- He sent disease into the Corinthian church for not honoring the Lord's Supper.

As we study God's role as the Perfect Judge, we will tackle some of the difficult areas and see the purity of God's moral attributes of integrity. We will learn about His holiness, righteousness, and faithfulness, and how they affect our lives. And of course, we will also discover the truth about God's justice, the basic characteristic for a good judge. Once we see how God's attributes of integrity work together, we can have confidence that every action He takes as judge is perfect. As we grow in our intimacy with God, we will also learn how we can be free of the fear of His judgment against sin. Allow me to begin by showing you the awesome magnificence of God's holiness.

THE POWER OF FIRE

They were called the Great Fires of 1988. That year, wildfires swept through 1.4 million acres of Yellowstone National Park. The park was like a huge lumberyard filled with millions of wooden poles stuck at intervals far enough apart to allow good air circulation but close enough for each old lodgepole pine to torch its neighbor. Pine needles and dead twigs littered the ground, providing tinder-dry fodder for the unquenchable appetite of the fires.

On September 6, spot fires were seen around Old Faithful Inn. Built in 1904, it is the world's largest log structure. It sits near Old Faithful Geyser surrounded by the majestic old forests of Yellowstone. Twenty-five miles north, a fire storm raged across 50 acres of forest. Winds as powerful as a tornado whipped the flames through the forest with the sound of a freight train, reducing trees to piles of white ashes and small charred spears on the blackened earth.

On September 7, wind gusts in the wildfire area enabled the fires to spread even faster. By afternoon, a large wall of intensifying black and brown smoke hovered close to the Inn, but firefighters felt confident that they could contain any outbreaks. Suddenly, fingers of fires around the Inn curled together to make a powerful fist that pounded the area. Then 50-mile-an-hour, fire-generated winds thundered in, sounding like the continuous roar of a jet taking off. Spot fires jumped up in numerous places close to the vulnerable buildings. A wall of flame higher than the tops of the trees advanced with incredible speed.

Firefighters worked furiously, soaking the Inn with water to protect it from the flames. Then as quickly as the fire had come, it turned to the northeast. The danger was past. Twenty-four buildings had burned, but Old Faithful Inn had been saved.[2]

Months later, the forest grew with new vigor. The heat from the fires split open the hulls of the pine cones, releasing their seeds and yielding a forest of little saplings sprouting everywhere. The dead underbrush had been burned away. New spears of grass turned the hillsides to spring green, and a bumper crop of wildflowers carpeted the meadows.

THE POWER OF GOD'S HOLINESS

Anyone who has been near a fire of that magnitude understands its tremendous power. When it roars through an area, everything is changed. Ancient trees turn into cinders. Buildings are reduced to ashes. Nothing can withstand its fury. In their wake, wildfires also bring new growth and regeneration.

In the Bible, God's holiness is sometimes pictured as a fire. A. W. Tozer writes:

> Only fire can give even a remote conception of it. In fire He appeared at the burning bush; in the pillar of fire He dwelt through all the long wilderness journey. The fire that glowed between the wings of the cherubim in the holy place

was called the Shekinah, the Presence, through the years of Israel's glory, and when the Old had given place to the New, He came at Pentecost as a fiery flame and rested upon each disciple.[3]

What does a fire do? It destroys the dead, purifies, transforms the landscape. It is powerful, beautiful, and awesome. No one can stand up to the heat and fury of a firestorm. Nothing can bring regeneration like a forest fire.

God's holiness has even greater power. Moses, who saw God's holiness in the burning bush, asked, "Who else among the gods is like you, O LORD? Who is glorious in holiness like you—so awesome in splendor, performing such wonders?"[4]

Of all God's attributes, nothing compares to the splendor and beauty of His holiness. It is chief among His attributes. That means His character is perfect in every way. He is totally pure. His moral excellence is the absolute standard of integrity and ethical purity for all within His universe. God's supreme holiness infinitely sets Him apart from His creation. Everything God does bears the imprint of His holiness. His holiness never diminishes.

OUR GOD IS EXALTED IN HOLY MAJESTY

Unfortunately, to a large degree, God's holiness has been ignored by modern Christianity because we are filled with the dead brush of sin and pride. Our unwillingness to acknowledge a holy God reflects our failure to recognize who God really is. The Hebrew root word for "to be holy" means to cut or to separate. The Old Testament reveals that God is above and separate from all that He created. He is exalted above everything in holy majesty.

We may also define *holy* as completely set apart from sin. It is a term describing conduct or behavior usually implying sacredness, being consecrated to God, or being worthy of God.[5] Holiness reflects a flawless, unblemished purity. God does not just match a standard of purity—He is the standard.

I feel totally inadequate to describe this attribute of God. How can I, or any sinful human being, find the right words to explain how pure and high God is in His holiness? How can I describe something that is so far removed from my experience and nature?

When I think of God's holiness, I am convicted by the sinful nature of my own being. We are all like a man wearing a beautiful white suit who was invited to go down into the depths of a coal mine. In the darkness of the mine, he was not aware that his suit was becoming soiled. But when he resurfaced into the dazzling light of the noonday sun, he was fully aware that his suit had become sooty and dirty. The light of God's holiness reveals the darkness of our sin.

Isaiah was a prominent citizen of Judah during the eighth century B.C., a prophet who followed God's commands and served his Lord. Today, we would consider him one of the "spiritual elite," a man of integrity and honor. At one point, Isaiah had a vision of heaven and the holiness of the Creator:

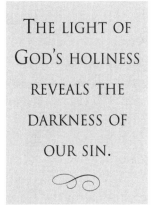

THE LIGHT OF GOD'S HOLINESS REVEALS THE DARKNESS OF OUR SIN.

> I saw the Lord. He was sitting on a lofty throne, and the train of His robe filled the Temple. Hovering around Him were mighty seraphim, each with six wings. With two wings they covered their faces, with two they covered their feet, and with the remaining two they flew. In a great chorus they sang, "Holy, holy, holy is the LORD Almighty! The whole earth is filled with His glory!" The glorious singing shook the Temple to its foundations, and the entire sanctuary was filled with smoke.[6]

Prior to his vision, Isaiah was focused on the sins of others, calling them to repentance. Now that he found himself in the very presence of our holy God, he became dramatically aware of his own sin and unrighteousness. Terrified, he exclaimed, "My destruction is sealed, for I am a sinful man and a member of a sinful race. Yet I have seen the King, the LORD Almighty!"[7]

When the angels surround the glorious throne of God, they sing, "Holy, holy, holy is the LORD Almighty." Stephen Charnock comments, "Do you hear, in any angelical song, any other perfection of the Divine Nature thrice repeated? Where do we read of them crying out, 'eternal, eternal, eternal' or 'faithful, faithful, faithful' Lord God of hosts?"[8]

This repetition, "holy, holy, holy," tells us that God's holiness is the supreme attribute of His being, the foundation of His eternal existence. His sovereignty and His role as judge are rooted in and flow out of His holiness. In fact, theologians speak of God's holiness as His "central and supreme perfection."[9]

GOD'S HOLINESS REQUIRES SEPARATION

Permit me to take you back to the Old Testament times when the Israelites worshipped God in a tabernacle they carried through the wilderness and into the Promised Land. The tabernacle pictured God's holiness and His separation from sinful mankind.

The tabernacle had three sections: the large area of service, the Holy Place, and the Holy of Holies. Each area was hidden from the other two by curtains.

Any priest who entered God's tabernacle first had to sacrifice an animal on the Brazen Altar to atone for sin. These burnt sacrifices were offered twice a day, once in the morning and once in the evening. Next was the Laver in which the priest washed his hands and feet before he appeared before the Lord—once again a symbol of our need for cleansing from sin. Then he was ready to enter the Holy Place.

Inside the Holy Place were three articles: the Table of Shewbread, the Candlestick, and the Altar of Incense. The Table of Shewbread held the special Bread of the Presence; the Candlestick continually burned pure oil; and the Altar of Incense held fragrant incense which was offered every morning.

But the Holy of Holies was the place where God's presence resided. It was hidden from view by a curtain so heavy that it took four men to move it. Only the High Priest was allowed to enter this place—and only once a year. If anyone else tried, God would strike him dead. Inside the Holy of Holies was the Ark of the Covenant, the dwelling place of God Himself, where once a year the High Priest offered sacrifices for his own sins and the sins of the people.

Why was the place of God's presence in the tabernacle hidden from view? Because God is so holy that no one can look upon His glory and live. No one can approach our holy God without a covering of blood to atone for the forgiveness of his sin.

Why was a lamb offered as a sacrifice for sin? It was a picture of Jesus Christ, the Lamb of God, and His sacrifice on the cross to provide a covering against the wrath of God on unconfessed sin. The only thing that can satisfy the judgment of sin demanded by God's holiness is the shedding of pure, innocent blood. Only Jesus' blood met this high standard.

GOD'S WRATH IS PART OF HIS HOLINESS

God is the absolutely pure and righteous being who abhors evil. He cannot tolerate any unrighteousness. Habakkuk 1:13 tells us, "Your eyes are too pure to look on evil; You cannot tolerate wrong" (NIV). God cannot secretly inspire any evil in us, for in His very nature He cannot accept any evil in any form.

God's holiness demands consequences for sin. We have broken His standard of holiness, and His holiness demands that He judge sin, not ignore or excuse it.

Throughout the Bible, God's wrath is pictured as a destroying fire. Think back to the story of Sodom and Gomorrah. The cities were filled with sin; the only righteous person was Lot. God allowed Lot and his family to flee from Sodom before He brought judgment. What was that punishment? The Lord rained down fire and burning sulfur upon those cities. All who lived there perished. Yet God's wrath is not uncontrolled anger, like we may sometimes think. Instead, it is a planned and just act that has its roots in God's holiness.

In the secular world, many people believe that actions do not have consequences. If you want to have extramarital "safe" sex, just use a condom. If you commit a crime, hire a good lawyer who can get you off on a technicality. Stealing items from your employer is okay because everyone else is doing it. The lack of teaching on morality in our public schools and in society in general has lowered the bar of standards for holy and righteous living.

This is how we sometimes approach God too. "Our sins are not so wrong," we say. "What others do is much worse." The person who believes this has not confronted the holiness of God. One small sin, one white lie, one hurtful word is enough to separate us from God's holiness.

GOD'S HOLINESS IS DEMONSTRATED IN HIS LAWGIVING

In recent years, numerous laws passed by state and federal legislatures have been struck down by the Supreme Court. In some cases, the judges ruled that a law could not be fairly applied. Other laws the Supreme Court decided had a fatal flaw that would prevent justice from being evenly distributed.

As the supreme, absolutely holy lawgiver, God has never announced a law that was not perfect in all respects. He has no need of a Supreme Court to determine whether His laws are fair or can be evenly applied. All His laws are an expression of the purity of His holiness.[10]

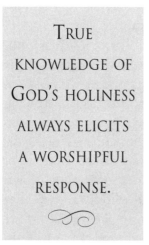

TRUE KNOWLEDGE OF GOD'S HOLINESS ALWAYS ELICITS A WORSHIPFUL RESPONSE.

Jude's epistle provides numerous examples of people who rejected God's laws —and suffered the judgment of a holy God. Jude mentions "godless men, who change the grace of our God into a license for immorality."[11] They thought they could get away with their sin. Not so, Jude writes, for we are dealing with a holy God who, after delivering the people of Israel out of Egypt, "later destroyed those who did not believe."[12] Even the angels who rebelled against God "He has kept in darkness, bound with everlasting chains for judgment on the great Day."[13]

Over and over again, we set up our own standards of what ought to please God: "I deal fairly with people." "I do not abuse my wife or my children." "I give to the needs of others in the homeless ministry I support." "I'm a good neighbor."

We slight the holiness of God when we think we can manage

on our own. We fool ourselves when we assume that keeping the Golden Rule[14] will cover our sins. How ridiculous our standards are when compared to His standards of righteousness. When Joshua gave his farewell address to the people of Israel after they had settled into the Promised Land, he knew that the people still worshipped foreign gods. He told them, "You are not able to serve the LORD, for He is a holy and jealous God. He will not forgive your rebellion and sins."[15]

None of our manmade standards of behavior meet the requirements of a holy God. God's holiness mandates that we keep all His laws perfectly at all times. The only way we can come into His presence is by having our sins covered by the blood of the Lamb, Jesus Christ. Only through Christ's payment can our holy Judge extend His mercy to us.

RESPONDING TO GOD'S HOLINESS

If we could just grasp even a part of the magnificent holiness of God and the miracle of His mercy to His sinful creatures, then our homes, offices, schools, and in fact, the whole earth would shake with people falling prostrate on the ground in worship and adoration of Him. Such a view would precipitate a healthy fear of God, which is a necessary starting point.[16]

True knowledge of God's holiness always elicits a worshipful response from us. Moses fell to his face before the burning bush. Isaiah said, "Woe is me!" We cannot stand in the presence of God without acknowledging His holiness and seeing our own sin. Author Beth Moore writes in *A Woman's Heart: God's Dwelling Place*:

> The light of God's glory shines two ways: it sheds light on the knowledge of God so we can see Him more clearly, but it also sheds light on us so that we can see our own sin more clearly. Remember, the closer you approach the light, the brighter it shines on you. This is the marvelous two-edged sword of intimacy. We see Him more clearly and we see ourselves more clearly. It is the perfect safeguard against pride. You can mark His word on this: true intimacy breeds true humility![17]

When we concentrate on God's holiness—His moral perfections and absolute purity—the only appropriate response is humble adoration. Adoration is the basis for all worship.

Whenever I meditate on the holiness of God, I am impressed with how worthy He is of our worship. I think of the verse, "Worship the LORD in the splendor of His holiness; tremble before Him, all the earth."[18] I want to become absorbed with His holiness, rather than with His might, His wisdom, or His other magnificent attributes.

As we meditate on God's supreme holiness, we cannot help but be overcome with a sense of awe. Music can help us express our awe for our Lord. Many of the old Christian hymns capture the spirit of worship. I encourage you to select one of them, such as *Holy, Holy, Holy*, and begin to worship God in song and praises right now.

After Isaiah humbled himself before the Lord during his vision, one of the seraphim flew over to the altar in the temple and picked up a burning coal with a pair of tongs. Isaiah says, "He touched my lips with it and said, 'See, this coal has touched your lips. Now your guilt is removed, and your sins are forgiven.'"[19] Worship God also for the Lamb of God who bridged the separation between God and the repentant sinner. *The Old Rugged Cross* is a hymn which tells that story in song. Read through the words of this classic hymn; then exalt God's holy name as one of His children who has caught a glimpse of His holiness and His merciful salvation.

LIFE APPLICATION

EXALT YOUR GOD—Exodus 15:11 records that, after Moses and the Israelites safely crossed through the Red Sea, they sang a song of praise to the Lord.

> "Who else among the gods is like you, O LORD?
> Who is glorious in holiness like You—
> So awesome in splendor,
> Performing such wonders?"

Make a list of the wonders our holy God has displayed in your life this past year. Be specific. Now, thank God for them and praise Him by singing the beautiful hymn *Holy, Holy, Holy*.

> Holy, holy, holy! Lord God Almighty!
> Early in the morning our song shall rise to Thee;
> Holy, holy, holy, merciful and mighty!
> God in three Persons, blessed Trinity!

> Holy, holy, holy! Tho' the darkness hide Thee,
> Tho' the eye of sinful man Thy glory may not see;
> Only Thou art holy; there is none beside Thee,
> Perfect in pow'r, in love, and purity.

REFLECT HIS IMAGE—We are called to be holy, which means "set apart," "dedicated to the Lord." First Peter 1:16 says, "God Himself has said, 'You must be holy because I am holy.'" Are there areas of your life you are ashamed of, aspects of your character or lifestyle that are not pure? Submit them to the Lord and ask for His cleansing and forgiveness.

SHARE HIS MAJESTY—Moral integrity is not very common today. Does a friend or family member need to hear that there is someone who acts with complete integrity and can always be trusted? Share the truth of God's holiness with them today.

CHAPTER 13

GOD GIVES US THE POWER TO BECOME HOLY

ave you ever known anyone who was extremely talented but morally flawed? It does not take long to realize that great ability without the moral guidance of good character can cause immense tragedy and grief. An individual's character, rather than his abilities, determines the lasting value of his accomplishments.

For example, the president of a famous university was discovered using his computer to transfer pornographic material to minors. The head of a prestigious charitable organization was convicted of embezzling from the charity. Several top political leaders have been accused of committing adultery with interns and staff. Obviously, not all people in these professions are guilty of such crimes, but these problems are so rampant that although we are a nation of achievements, we are morally bankrupt.

Christians also struggle with moral purity. Some time ago a man who held an influential position in a Christian ministry confided in me that he had never surrendered his life to Christ, although for years he pretended that he had done so. He said and did all the right things so that his friends and all who met him would think he was a committed follower of Christ. But he admitted to deliberately saying "no" to the Holy Spirit's leading and choosing to live a lie.

I was shocked that anyone who was exposed to the inspired Word of God, Christian fellowship, and ministry would dare to deliberately disobey God. But as we talked, I learned that he was simply afraid to live a holy life. The thought of complete surrender to the Lord was unappealing to him, and as a result, he had run from God for many years.

HOLY LIVING, THE SECRET TO LIFE

Like this man, a false view of holiness causes many Christians to stop short of complete surrender to God. They have a distorted view of holiness because they define it from a secular viewpoint. They imagine a holy person as some kind of religious fanatic, a "kook," or an isolated monk devoted to prayer and fasting. Others think that holiness has only to do with the way a person dresses or socializes. These misinformed believers decide they do not want to give up their lifestyle, pleasures, and pride and allow God to renew their minds. They do not let Him mold them into people with tastes and desires that bring true happiness and joy in fellowship with Him.

Tragically, some believers continue to wrestle with their childhood experiences with strict, legalistic parents or churches. I have heard some confess, "I tried to live up to the high expectations of my parents or pastor, but I have failed many times. I just can't live the Christian life!" They conclude that the Christian life is difficult to live. I agree—and go one step further: It is impossible to live a holy life on your own. Even with determination and our best efforts, we will always fail. We can never become holy in our own strength and abilities.

But the story does not end with our feeble efforts. Paul proclaims:

> There is no condemnation [guilt] for those who belong to Christ Jesus. For the power of the life-giving Spirit has freed you through Christ Jesus from the power of sin that leads to death. The law of Moses could not save us, because

of our sinful nature. But God put into effect a different plan to save us. He sent His own Son in a human body like ours, except that ours are sinful. God destroyed sin's control over us by giving His Son as a sacrifice for our sins. He did this so that the requirement of the law would be fully accomplished for us who no longer follow our sinful nature but instead follow the Spirit.[1]

This is the secret: We can live a holy life if we yield to the Holy Spirit who came to glorify Jesus Christ. Jesus is the only person to ever live a holy life, and now He resides within every believer through His Holy Spirit. His presence and power give us the strength to live a holy life moment by moment.

Holy, righteous living is the secret to a life of joy, power, victory, and fruitfulness. When we are holy, we are set apart and separated from sin for God's special use. God gives us the power to experience a whole new life based on His holiness and purity. But we must obey His direction and laws. In this chapter, we will learn about several ways God wants us to respond to His holiness.

Because God is holy, we must give Him reverential respect.

In 1996, I was privileged to receive the prestigious international Templeton Prize for Progress in Religion. As part of the honor, Vonette and I went to Buckingham Palace to meet with Prince Philip and Sir John Templeton. Because we were meeting royalty, we were very conscious of our appearance and our behavior.

Do we have less concern when we come before our Sovereign God, the ruler of the universe? He deserves much more reverence and respect than any human being who ever lived! He is not the "man upstairs." He is the great, holy, righteous, all-powerful, loving, creator God.

Many Scripture passages tell us to fear God. King David writes, "Serve the LORD with reverent fear, and rejoice with trembling."[2] Solomon explains, "The fear of the LORD is the beginning of wisdom. Knowledge of the Holy One results in understanding."[3] Fearing God does not mean to be afraid of God, but rather to express reverential awe and deep respect before Him.

Vonette and I get on our knees every morning to praise and worship God out of reverential awe for Him. I encourage you to examine how you come before God, how you honor His name before others, and how you respect His Word. In your daily quiet time with Him, give Him the honor He deserves. Spend more time worshipping Him than asking for your own needs.

Because our holy God abhors sin and evil, we must turn away from every evil.

God created the universe to function according to His standard of holiness. God's holiness is so complete that He cannot look on even one sin. Not one.

Picture God's holiness in this way. Envision a beautiful bride on her wedding day, dressed in white and looking radiant. The white dress symbolizes purity. It does not have a spot or wrinkle anywhere. If one ink spot stained the dress, people would focus on the ugliness of the stain rather than the loveliness of the dress. That is a picture of God's purity. God, who has never sinned in any way, is so pure and holy that He "cannot tolerate the slightest sin."[4] His heaven is pure and holy, absolutely free of all sin and evil.

> WE CANNOT EXPECT GOD TO ALLOW US INTO HEAVEN WHEN WE HAVE SIN-STAINS IN OUR LIVES.

No matter how religious, self-disciplined, or good we may try to be, we cannot expect God to allow us into His heaven when we have sin-stains in our lives. If God allowed one sin to mar His pure dwelling place, it would cease to be a holy city. Since God cannot even look on sin, our sinful, human situation is hopeless.

This is where a miraculous paradox comes in. Jesus Christ came to take away the sins of the world. He became sin for us. The perfect, holy Son of God took on the stain of our sin. He endured and satisfied the judgment of a pure God for our misdeeds —not just one or two sins, but every sin you and I have ever committed or will commit in our lifetimes!

Remember how the Holy of Holies in the tabernacle illustrated God's holiness and His separation from humans? The heavy curtain separated sinful people from God's presence. The sacrifices of lambs and goats symbolized a holy God who would take upon Himself the sins of the world. This ultimate sacrifice also included death—Christ's death on the cross.

The physical agony of the cross was nothing compared to the spiritual agony of God becoming sin for us! All the sins and evil ever committed, or that ever will be committed, were laid on Jesus Christ just before He died. Although Jesus abhorred sin and evil, He willingly took on the sins of all people. The Book of Hebrews explains this so much better than I ever could:

> What God wants is for us to be made holy by the sacrifice of the body of Jesus Christ once for all time...For by that one offering He perfected forever all those whom He is making holy...Now when sins have been forgiven, there is no need to offer any more sacrifices. And so, dear brothers and sisters, we can boldly enter heaven's Most Holy Place because of the blood of Jesus. This is the new, life-giving way that Christ has opened up for us through the sacred curtain, by means of His death for us.[5]

That is why during Christ's crucifixion God miraculously tore in two the heavy curtain that kept men and women from the Holy of Holies. Christ had paid the ultimate price. Those who accept God's forgiveness become spotless and pure so they now have access to God. In fact, all believers become God's holy temple as the Holy Spirit comes to live within them at the moment of their spiritual birth.

As His temples—His Most Holy Place—our lives are no longer temples of evil, immorality, stealing, or lying. Because God lives within us, we should abhor evil the way He does. When we understand how holy God is and what His Son endured to make us the temple of the living God, our motivation should be to live pure and sin-free lives.

Of course, living a pure life is possible only through the enab-

ling of the Holy Spirit. We are given power over sin and temptation as we are indwelt, filled, and anointed by Him.

According to God's Word, we do not have to sin. But if we do
sin, there is Someone to plead for us before the Father. This is
explained in 1 John 2:1,2: "My dear children, I am writing this to
you so that you will not sin. But if you do sin, there is someone
to plead for you before the Father. He is Jesus Christ, the one
who pleases God completely. He is the sacrifice for our sins. He
takes away not only our sins but the sins of all the world."

Becoming holy is more than obedience; it is a liberating,
cleansing freedom from all unwholesomeness. Sin in our lives creates a barrier to fellowship with God. It blocks the communication lines between us and God so He does not hear our prayers.[6]
Restored fellowship with God comes by confessing our sin and
turning from it. As the holiness of God is absorbed into every fiber
of our being, we become even more sensitive to sin and learn to
abhor it all the more as we walk in an intimate, joyful relationship
with Him.

Because God's holiness dispels darkness, we must walk in His light.

In the early '60s, I went to Rangoon, Burma, to speak to a gathering
of students. When I arrived, I was told that a group of radical Communist students planned to kill me by stoning me at the meeting.

When I began my speech, there was so much heckling that I
could not be heard. Since I knew that God inhabits the praises of
His people, I asked the few Christians in the audience to join me
in singing the praise chorus, *Hallelujah*. Satan cannot stand it
when believers praise God. As we praised God, the hecklers leaped
from their chairs and ran out of the meeting. We continued with
the meeting and several students received Christ.

Sin and evil always seek refuge in darkness. But God's holy
radiance exposes and destroys the darkness of sin and evil. Paul
writes, "God lives in light so brilliant that no human can approach
Him."[7] The more we meditate on the holiness of God, the more
we become aware of our sinfulness. In comparison to His purity,

everything else appears dull and dirty.

First John 1 says that "God is light and there is no darkness in Him at all…If we are living in the light of God's presence,… then we have fellowship with each other, and the blood of Jesus, His Son, cleanses us from every sin."[8] Jesus said, "I am the light of the world. If you follow Me, you won't be stumbling through the darkness, because you will have the light that leads to life."[9] As we follow Jesus, His light illumines our way and unbelievers see the holiness of God through our attitudes and actions.

Because our God is holy, we must serve Him with life-changing devotion.

Scripture gives us God's directive: "Now you must be holy in everything you do, just as God—who chose you to be His children—is holy."[10] Christians have been set apart by God for this divine purpose. If you want to see the holiness of God, examine the life and teachings of Jesus Christ. He is the visible expression of God's holiness. God wants us to place our lives under His lordship and conform to the moral character of His Son and reflect the beauty of His holiness and character.

Out of respect for God, I want to be holy as He is holy and never disappoint Him in any way. I would rather die than bring dishonor to His holy name. I have often prayed that if there is any possibility that I might be unfaithful to my beloved wife or in any other way bring dishonor to our Lord, that He would take my life before it happened.

George Muller, well-known for his great faith and ministry to orphans, was asked the secret of his fruitful service for the Lord. He said, "There was a day when I died…utterly died." As he spoke, he bent lower and lower until he almost touched the floor. "I died to George Muller—his opinions, his preferences, tastes, and will—died to the world, its approval or censure—died to the approval or blame even of my brethren and friends—and since then I have studied only to show myself approved unto God."

Everyone I know who has been greatly used by God for the cause of Christ has gone through an experience of "dying to self" as described in Galatians 2:20. It is not until we know the reality of "death to self" that we can live for Christ and God can truly use and bless us. My Galatians 2:20 experience happened in the spring of 1951 when Vonette and I signed a contract to become slaves of Christ. I daily reaffirm this contract.

Holy living involves a daily decision to surrender to the lordship of Christ. It involves yielding our will to God and adopting His perspective for life.[11] God wants our minds and hearts to be filled with His holy qualities. As our lives are transformed, we will project the light of His holiness into the darkness of our evil world. Real life—abundant life—begins with dying to self.

Because God expects holiness from His people, we must turn away from any idols in our lives.

God is very possessive of our affections. He warned the Israelites, "Do not worship any other gods besides Me. Do not make idols of any kind…You must never worship or bow down to them, for

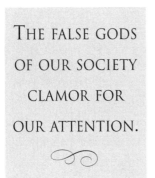

THE FALSE GODS OF OUR SOCIETY CLAMOR FOR OUR ATTENTION.

I, the LORD your God, am a jealous God who will not share your affection with any other god!"[12] He alone has the right to occupy the throne of our heart. He is to be exalted to the highest place in our lives. Everything else must be of lower importance.

Yet we are all guilty at one time or another of idolatry. The false gods and idols of our society may not be as obvious as those of ancient Israel or other cultures, but their presence is just as real. They clamor for our attention. They bargain for our allegiance. Here are some of the most common:

- The god of affluence. Many are convinced that wealth is the key to happiness. They place their trust in bank accounts and hoarded assets. The spirit of greed has gradually transformed their values so that money is now their master.

- The god of pleasure. Multitudes are convinced that fun is the chief goal in life. Couch potatoes vegetate in front of the TV screen. Sports fanatics cannot watch enough games. Some seek entertainment, thrills, and adventure in hopes of conquering boredom in their futile search for happiness.

- The god of achievement. The ambitious sacrifice themselves to this god. Pride is their relentless taskmaster. For these workaholics, accomplishments are the building blocks of self-esteem. No challenge is too great in their quest for significance.

- The god of infatuation. Some people idolize a celebrity, a hero, a friend, or even a relative. Their entire world revolves around that individual. The spirit of obsession amplifies healthy feelings of love and admiration into unholy worship.

- The god of self-worship. Many are convinced by the spirit of vanity that appearance is everything. Their life is preoccupied with beauty, fashion, and body-building.

- The god of sensuality. The spirit of lust has ensnared many with immorality. For them God's gift of sex has been distorted into perversion and tragically often ends in addiction, abortion, disease, and death.

Substitute gods usurp the worship and devotion that rightfully belong to our holy God. In reality, these idols can never fill the God-shaped vacuum within the heart of man. God's Word calls us to a higher focus: "You must be holy because I am holy."[13]

As believers who belong to the universal Church, we are the bride of Christ. God promises that the Church will one day shine faultless before Him. At the end of this age, Christ will present us to God clothed in Christ's purity and holiness.[14]

I can hardly wait for that day. That will be the moment when all of us, the Church of Christ universal with millions upon millions of believers, will give glory to God as the spotless bride of Christ. It will be one of the most moving moments in all eternity. We can prepare ourselves for that momentous occasion today by living our lives in the light of God's holiness and purity by faith through the enabling power of the Holy Spirit.

LIFE APPLICATION

WRITE IT ON YOUR HEART—Commit the following statement and verses to memory. Then as you encounter situations during this week where you need to be reminded of God's purity, claim these promises by faith.

- Because God is holy, I will devote myself to Him in worship and service.
- 1 Peter 1:16—"[God] Himself has said, 'You must be holy because I am holy.'"
- Psalm 96:9—"Worship the LORD in the splendor of His holiness; tremble before Him, all the earth."

COUNT ON GOD—Our holy God is perfect. Give your imperfections and limitations to Him. Trust Him to bring good out of your current circumstances and bring glory to His holy name.

OBEY GOD—God's very nature is holy, and His holiness abhors sin and evil. In order to have a healthy relationship with your loving Father, you must not have sin in your life. Search your heart for any hidden sin and confess it to your holy God. Commit yourself to turn away from temptation that you struggle with today.

CHAPTER 14

GOD
IS ABSOLUTE TRUTH

A story is told about a banquet speaker who was introduced as a very smart businessman. His business growing and selling potatoes in Maine netted him $25,000 the previous year. After a long introduction, he arose to speak. "Before I begin," he said, "I must set the record straight. What was said about my business is only partially true. First, it was not Maine, but Texas. It was not potatoes, but oil. It was not $25,000, but $250,000. And it was not a profit, but a loss. And one more thing about this introduction—it was not me who lost the money, it was my brother."

As the story illustrates, truth matters. And in some situations, it *really* matters. We all laugh at jokes about the doctor coming out of surgery to tell the waiting family, "I've got good news and bad news. Which do you want first?" But when one of our own loved ones faces a life-threatening illness or accident, we do not want jokes, we want medical experts to tell us the truth.

Josh McDowell, one of Campus Crusade's most well-known ministry directors, speaks to college students all over the world. One of his most frequent topics is "safe sex." Josh was invited to give the concluding talk during "Safe Sex Week" at the University of North Dakota to 3,000 students in a jammed auditorium. When he began by saying, "You've been brainwashed," a rumble spread through the crowd. Josh describes what happened next:

> When the students settled down, I continued, "You've had an entire week of 'safer sex' indoctrination: speakers, experts, videos, films, classes, and symposiums. You've been challenged, motivated, encouraged, indoctrinated, and pressured about using condoms to ensure safe sex. To top it all off, you were given a 'safer sex packet.' But you've been lied to."
>
> At this point, the crowd was becoming a little indignant with me. Then I lowered the boom with one more question: "After all the information on 'safer sex' you have received this week, how many of you know the statistical failure rate of the condom?" *Not one hand went up!* Suddenly, the auditorium was as quiet as a cemetery. They looked at each other with expressions of astonishment. They realized they hadn't been told the whole truth about safer sex.[1]

TRUTH HAS BEEN A MAJOR CASUALTY IN OUR MODERN CULTURE.

Josh finds a similar reaction in every university crowd he addresses. Invariably, the students have been thoroughly coached about how to have "safer sex," but are never told how unsafe "safer sex" really is. In essence, what they heard was a lie.

Read these statistics that fly in the face of "safe sex." Research conducted by Planned Parenthood (a group advocating the practice of safer sex) states that within one year of using a condom to prevent pregnancy, the pregnancy rate is more than 10 percent for all ages, and the rate is almost double for teens.[2] Statistics also show that a girl who becomes sexually active at 14 years old and practices birth control has an 87 percent chance of becoming pregnant before she graduates from high school.[3] If she is your daughter, niece, or a friend's child, does she not deserve to know the *whole truth* before she engages in risky behavior? Does shading the truth *really* matter to her—and consequently to her unborn baby? Of course!

But the consequences go even further. Physician Robert C. Noble writes in *Newsweek*:

> I can't say I'm comforted reading a government pamphlet called "Condoms and Sexually Transmitted Diseases Especially AIDS." "Condoms are not 100 percent safe," it says, "but if used properly will reduce the risk of sexually transmitted diseases, including AIDS." *Reduce* the risk of a disease that is 100 percent fatal? That's all that's available between us and death? How much do condoms reduce the risk? They don't say. So much for Safe Sex.[4]

In fact, all latex condoms have microscopic holes that are *fifty times larger* than the HIV virus. The oil-based lubricants used with condoms can also damage them. If a condom is too old, or has been exposed to heat or cold, it may be less effective.[5]

What comfort is the lie of "safe sex" to the young man who contracts gonorrhea or to the young woman who develops herpes or to the newborn who is born with AIDS? Telling incomplete "truths" can change a life—or cause death. It is vital that we know and tell the absolute truth.

THE WHOLE PROBLEM WITH ABSOLUTE TRUTH

Most Americans believe in absolute truth, right? Wrong! Truth has been a major casualty in our modern culture. In a study by George Barna of Americans between ages 26 and 44, only 20 percent of those surveyed strongly disagreed with the statement: "There is no such thing as absolute truth; different people can define truth in different ways and still be correct."[6] Shockingly, only 27 percent of those who described themselves as born-again Christians strongly disagreed! Fifty-two percent actually agreed at least somewhat with the statement![7]

If we look at the phrase "there is no absolute truth," it is logically inconsistent. It states an absolute truth about absolute truth while claiming there is no absolute truth!

The whole idea that truth is relative contradicts God's Word.

Second Timothy 3:16 says, "All Scripture is inspired by God and is useful to teach us what is true and to make us realize what is wrong in our lives. It straightens us out and teaches us to do what is right." For example, the Bible teaches that homosexuality is wrong.[8] Yet I recently read that a school board in Massachusetts voted unanimously to teach pre-schoolers (ages 3–5) about homosexual lifestyles. Pre-schoolers! This is a symptom of a culture that has rejected absolute truth.

Many people argue that even religious people cannot agree on what is absolute truth. As Christians we say that the Bible is true. The Hindus reject that, preferring the writings, or Vedas, of their holy men. The Muslims put their faith in the Koran, claiming Mohammed received it as a prophet of God. The Mormons are convinced that Joseph Smith got his messages straight from God.

To make the situation more confusing, other people claim to have received absolute truth. Today, more than a million people have purchased the bestseller *Conversations with God, Books 1 and 2*, which the author, Neale Donald Walsch, insists were dictated to him by God. Listen to the "absolute truth" that Walsch's god advocates: "I do not love 'good' more than I love 'bad.' Hitler went to heaven. When you understand this, you will understand God."

In his column in *The Wall Street Journal*, Charles Colson writes, "Mr. Walsch's God liberates us from traditional authorities—rabbis, ministers, parents, the Bible…He confidently attempts—in dialogue form, with his own questions and comments and God's replies and explanations—to repeal or modify every known religious truth and propound his own version of God's message as authoritative."[9]

A famous New Age believer made a statement in a television interview with Kathie Lee Gifford that everyone goes to Paradise after they die. Then with a question uncharacteristic of the media, Kathie Lee, a strong Bible believer, asked, "Are you saying you believe that the same thing happens to Hitler as to Mother Teresa?" The New Ager stuttered and stumbled and had no reply. Kathie Lee's poignant question demonstrated the ludicrous nature of those who reject truth.

What Is Absolute Truth?

If you were asked to describe absolute truth, what would you say? By what standard can we measure truth to determine if it is truth? If you do not believe there is such a thing as absolute truth, how do you find anything to be true and trustworthy? Following are three qualities of absolute truth.

Absolute truth is internally consistent. No matter which way you approach a true statement, it remains unassailably true. When we say that our God is absolutely truthful, we mean above everything else that He is internally consistent in His character and being. Proverbs 30:5 says, "Every word of God proves true." In fact, the Hebrew word for *truth* means conformance to a standard—God's standards.

Internal consistency of character is vital to all of God's attributes. If you can prove that God is not truthful in any aspect of who He is and how He acts, then His other qualities have no validity. If He were not absolutely consistent, then God's unlimited power, for example, could be compromised by His love. He would be like a powerful president of a country who fails to take action against evil because he lets his emotions, his wrong understanding of love, negate his power.

Absolute truth is true for all people in all places at all times. Not everything qualifies as absolute truth. For example, if you said, "Today, the interest rate for home mortgages is at 6.5 percent," that could be true for you living in America. But for someone living in Brazil, the interest rate might be 50-plus percent. And a month from now, the interest rate for you could change to 8 percent. Because interest rates fluctuate, the percentage rate is not true for all people in all places at all times. The rate is not an absolute truth.

On the other hand, if you say, "Adultery is always wrong," you would be stating an absolute truth.[10] Whether you live in Bangladesh, Japan, or the United States, adultery is still wrong. Adultery was just as wrong a thousand years ago as it is today. Adultery is wrong for the wife living with the alcoholic husband, or the business or military person separated from a spouse by extended travel.

Absolute truth has its source in our holy God. No human can think up or discover a new truth. Truth has always existed in God's nature; He is the author of truth.

We must always measure our beliefs by the truth in God's Word. Since He is the author of truth and since absolute truth resides in Him, He is the only One who can guide us to absolute truth. With Him, we see truth face to face. Any other guide will only lead us into confusion and deception.

Moses said, "God is not a man, that He should lie. He is not a human, that He should change His mind. Has He ever spoken and failed to act? Has He ever promised and not carried it through?"[11] Whatever God says is absolutely right. Whatever He promises will always be fulfilled.

> WE CAN BREAK GOD'S COMMANDMENTS, BUT WE CANNOT CHANGE THEM.

NOTHING CAN CHANGE GOD'S ABSOLUTE TRUTH

Have you ever heard the phrase, "written in stone"? This usually refers to some statement that cannot be changed. The phrase comes from the Old Testament account of when God gave the Ten Commandments. About two months after the Israelites had left their slavery in Egypt, they reached Mount Sinai where God revealed Himself to the people. God's holiness and power were very evident:

> All Mount Sinai was covered with smoke because the LORD had descended on it in the form of fire. The smoke billowed into the sky like smoke from a furnace, and the whole mountain shook with a violent earthquake.[12]

Moses went up the mountaintop into a cloud that looked like a devouring fire and stayed forty days and nights. During that time God wrote the Ten Commandments with His own finger on tablets of stone. God required His people to obey these timeless gems of absolute truth.

Meanwhile, the people, under the leadership of Moses' brother, Aaron, began to think that Moses would never return. So Aaron built them a golden calf to take God's place.

Aware of the peoples' disobedience, God told Moses to go back down the mountain. As Moses strode downward clutching the stone tablets, he heard noises like the sounds of celebration. When he got near, he saw God's people worshipping a golden calf. The people who had promised to obey all of God's law had already broken one of the Ten Commandments. In anguish and anger over the sight, Moses hurled the tablets to the ground, shattering them.

Then God said to Moses: "Prepare two stone tablets like the first ones. I will write on them the same words that were on the tablets you smashed."[13] Once more Moses climbed that cloud-covered mountain; once more God etched the Ten Commandments into stone with His finger.

Do you see the picture of absolute truth in this account? God wrote the commandments in stone. No one can erase or alter them; they are absolute truth. Moses, in his anger, shattered the stone tablets. As humans we can break God's commandments, but we cannot change them. The broken laws are not any less true. Once shattered, God just wrote them on stone once more. Nothing we can do will ever change God's absolute truth.

GOD'S ABSOLUTE TRUTH LASTS FOREVER

A woman received directions to a home for a baby shower, complete with the street name and the house number. But she never found the correct house and went home embarrassed. The next day she discovered some pranksters had switched several street signs in the area. She failed to reach her destination *even though she had true directions.*

If you have ever had an experience like that, you may be skeptical whenever you receive directions to an unfamiliar setting. That is how many people approach what God has said. They are not at all sure that His truth is absolutely accurate or applies to modern life. *Maybe He has forgotten about a turn, a detour, or a switched street sign,* they think. *Times change, so how can we rely on truth given centuries ago?*

Because God knows the end from the beginning, not one of His statements ever turns out to be a misdirection. He does not shade the truth or leave out an essential part. His absolute truth applies to every situation in history.

I encourage you to read Psalm 119, the greatest chapter in the Bible, about the endurance and truth of God's Word. Verse 160 says, "All Your words are true; all Your just laws will stand forever." Not only is God's truth absolute, but it lasts forever! We can count on it for eternity.

How God Reveals His Absolute Truth to Us

God wants us to know the absolute truth, so He has taken the initiative to show us truth in several ways: in His Word, the Bible; by the life, death, and resurrection of His Son; and through His Holy Spirit.

God recorded truth for us in the Bible.

The Bible is God's absolute truth in written form. Jesus tells us, "Your word is truth."[14] We can read it, memorize it, and meditate on it. God uses the Bible to reveal truth about Himself, ourselves, and about life.[15] There is no way anyone can live a holy, satisfying, fulfilled life without spending regular time in the Word of God.

It has been my practice for years to read through the Bible each year. My most important priority every morning is to read God's Word, even before I eat breakfast. Somehow the time I spend with God in the morning is more than compensated in the way the rest of the day unfolds.

God manifested truth to us through the life, death, and resurrection of Jesus Christ.

Truth is not just a concept, it is embodied in a person—Jesus Christ. While many people claim to *know* the truth, only Jesus could honestly claim to *be* the truth. Jesus explains, "I am the way, the truth, and the life. No one can come to the Father except through Me."[16]

John Wesley writes: "The word of His truth and wisdom is more ardent and more light-giving than the rays of the sun, and sinks down into the depths of heart and mind." The words of God put into human form by Jesus purify us when we let them sink into our hearts.

God guides us into truth through the working of the Holy Spirit.

As Christians, we have the Holy Spirit living within us. One of His primary responsibilities is to reveal truth to us. Jesus calls Him "the Spirit of truth."[17] The Holy Spirit is Christ's representative who communicates directly with us, illuminating God's truth, and giving us the power to obey that truth. In fact, when we worship God, we are to worship Him in spirit and in truth.[18]

I often use the illustration that the Holy Spirit represents one wing of an airplane and the Word of God represents the other. Our Lord Jesus Christ is the pilot. No airplane will fly with just one wing. If we do not rely on the Holy Spirit to guide us and also saturate ourselves with God's truth—His holy, inspired, inerrant truth—then our holy life will not fly. We must also allow Jesus to be the navigator of our plans, desires, wills, and emotions, for He is the truth.

We do not need to be confused about what is right or wrong —we can look to God's Word. We cannot complain that we do not have an example of how to put God's truth into practice—we have the truth in the flesh, Jesus Christ. And we cannot excuse ourselves from knowing and following God's truth—we have the power of the Holy Spirit who leads us into all truth.

Spirit-filled worship leads us to a reverence for God's truth, which in turn leads us to daily obedience. We put our worship into action when we say "yes" to God's truth in each and every decision of our lives. If you find yourself misrepresenting the truth to an employer, ask God to help you be completely honest out of respect for Him. The following Life Application gives more suggestions to help you worship God in Spirit and in truth.

LIFE APPLICATION

❧

EXALT YOUR GOD—The Bible states in Hebrews 6:18, "It is impossible for God to lie." Praise your heavenly Father that He is truth. Thank Him that in this world of "half-truths" and "double speak," His Word can always be trusted.

REFLECT HIS IMAGE—Jesus stated, "I am the truth." Are you known as a truthful person, someone whose word can be trusted? In God's book, there are no such things as "fibs" or "white lies." Our God of truth wants His children to be reflections of His character. Ask Him to help you tell the truth in situations you face where it would be easier to compromise.

SHARE HIS MAJESTY—Prayerfully ask God to show you an area in your church or ministry where you can stand up for God's absolute truth. Perhaps you can help high school students to understand the importance of God's command to be sexually pure. Or maybe you can explain the importance of being truthful to your spouse during a couples' Bible study. Be sure to back up your teaching with God's Word.

CHAPTER 15

GOD'S TRUTH SETS US FREE

On February 3, 1998, Karla Faye Tucker died. She had known the date of her death since December because she was scheduled to be executed in a Texas prison for the double murders she had committed.

Karla Faye Tucker was the first woman since the Civil War to be executed in the Texas prison system. In 1983 after three days of non-stop drug taking, she and Daniel Garrett broke into a Houston apartment and killed Dean and Deborah Thornton. Karla Faye was the one who swung the pickax. If anyone deserved a sentence of death, she did.

But something miraculous happened to Karla Faye during her fourteen years on death row. Soon after her arrest, she learned the truth that God loves even the vilest sinner and that He pardons completely the person who asks Him for forgiveness. Karla Faye said in an interview a month before her execution, "I asked [God] to forgive me and I knew I needed forgiveness. And I knew I had done something really horrible. But I think right at that moment what mostly hit me was His love. His love. It just surrounded me."[1] In that moment, the murderer became a child of God.

Although she would never again set foot outside a prison, God's truth had made her free. George Sechrist, who represented Karla Faye in her appeal process, saw her change as she grew in her faith. He says, "I've represented a number of folks on death row. All of them certainly are deserving of their day in court, regardless of what they've done, but I've never seen anyone who has genuinely transformed in any way as she has. And, quite frankly, I doubt I'll ever see it again!"[2]

Karla testified to the power of the Holy Spirit to change a life that had been ruined by sin. Her testimony was broadcast over radio and television to millions.

No one can commit a sin so rotten that God cannot transform that life into one which brings glory to Him. Although Karla reaped the consequences for her crime with the death penalty, she also influenced thousands of others for Christ with her testimony before she died.

Every day, we make decisions based on beliefs and values that we assume are true. Too often, we later discover our beliefs were an illusion of truth projected by our corrupt society. As John the apostle explains, "They are from the world and therefore speak from the viewpoint of the world, and the world listens to them."[3] The world's viewpoint is based on wrong values and misguided purposes, not absolute truth, and its ideas fluctuate with the time, the person, and the culture. Eventually, the world's viewpoint enslaves us to sin. But as we read in John 8:32, God's truth sets us free.

God's liberating truth is our anchor point for life. Solomon writes, "Truth stands the test of time; lies are soon exposed."[4] God's truth has endured for thousands of years. Man's "truth" has not. And since God's truth lasts for eternity, its power to free us from sin will never diminish.

WE CAN TRUST GOD'S WORD

Most of us have at least one friend we consider very honest. When we ask that person for his opinion, we find out what he really thinks. If we ask him to take care of something important for us, he will be open about whether or not he can complete the job.

We would not consider him a faithful friend if there were areas of his life where he acted dishonestly.

That is even more true of our holy God. We can trust His Word —completely and implicitly. The psalmist writes, "All Your commands are true. Long ago I learned from Your statutes that You established them to last forever."[5] It would violate God's truthfulness if His Word could not be trusted.

During the first centuries of the Church, false teachers tried to argue that the Bible was not completely truthful. Paul quickly defended the Bible.[6] He proclaimed that all Scripture is God's truth! That assurance is what gave Paul such incredible confidence as he traveled about the Roman Empire proclaiming the Good News of Jesus' death and resurrection. His life of service through incredible pressures and persecutions is proof that God's Word has power to sustain us.

> THE WORLD'S VIEWPOINT ENSLAVES US TO SIN, BUT GOD'S TRUTH SETS US FREE.

We can absolutely trust God's Word —to the last period on the last page. After more than fifty years of studying the Bible, I am convinced beyond any shadow of doubt that it is the holy, inspired, and inerrant Word of God. During these years, I have anchored my life of service to Jesus Christ on a God who is faithful and stands behind His holy Word. God has never failed me, and never will.

GOD'S PROMISES ARE TRUE

If God's Word can be trusted, we can be sure that the promises in His Word are also true. The writer to the Hebrews encourages us: "Let us hold unswervingly to the hope we profess, for He who promised is faithful."[7] God's truthful nature backs up His promises; therefore, we can immerse ourselves in His promises, applying them to our life situations. For example, consider Jesus' promises:

- "When everything is ready, I will come and get you, so that you will always be with Me where I am."[8]

- "The truth is, anyone who believes in Me will do the same works I have done, and even greater works, because I am going to be with the Father."[9]
- "I am leaving you with a gift—peace of mind and heart. And the peace I give isn't like the peace the world gives. So don't be troubled or afraid."[10]

The Bible is full of thousands of other wonderful promises from God, for every imaginable occasion. They mean so much to me that years ago I wrote a devotional book called *Promises: A Daily Guide to Supernatural Living*. The promises highlighted on each of the pages are still blessing the lives of those who read them. I encourage you to read through the Old and New Testaments, highlighting the amazing promises of God. You will be greatly blessed with what you find! Memorizing them will bring an invaluable source of encouragement.

GOD'S TRUTH EXPOSES DECEPTION AND IGNORANCE

Because our secular society has rejected God's holy inspired Word as the absolute standard for truth, we have lost our reference point for reality. Now our society often defines truth based on public opinion polls. We live in a media culture of sizzle and hype which influences public thinking. Advertising hucksters and spin-doctors are constantly at work to influence our thinking about events and issues. Educational institutions promote diversified views at the expense of truth. Even many journalists are no longer satisfied with reporting the facts. Instead, they slant the news to fit their own, often anti-God, interpretation.

This is the nature of the world system controlled by Satan, who is the father of lies.[11] These masters of deception, distortion, and manipulation take truth out of context or give only half-truths. Anyone who accepts this world system becomes bound up in deception, manipulation, lies, and ignorance. Many Christians have bought into these lies.

But God's truth is a light that shows us the difference between falsehood and truth. Jesus taught, "I am the light of the world. If you follow Me, you won't be stumbling through the darkness, because you will have the light that leads to life."[12] Without His truth, we are left to grope about in spiritual darkness. But His light frees us to see and do what is right and good.

Consider some of the deceptions promoted by our culture and the contrast of God's truth, as shown in the following table. Of the six options, which of the two columns are you tempted to base your life on? Every day, each of us makes choices about what we want to do or perceive to be true. Only God can free us from the deceptions and distortions of the world system. He has given us the Bible as a handbook for identifying truth and His Spirit,

SOCIETY'S LIE	GOD'S TRUTH
Money is the key to happiness. Wealth provides comfort and security, prestige and respectability. If you have a nice house in the suburbs and own the things you always wanted, you will find fulfillment in life.	"Stay away from the love of money; *be satisfied with what you have.*"[13] "Seek first His kingdom and His righteousness, and all these things will be given to you as well."[14] "My God will meet all your needs."[15]
Think of yourself first. Otherwise, your needs will go unmet. You deserve more out of life. Go ahead, reward yourself. You owe it to yourself.	"If you try to keep your life for yourself, you will lose it. But *if you give up your life for Me, you will find true life.* And how do you benefit if you gain the whole world but lose your own soul in the process?"[16]
You have a right to satisfy your sexual appetites and passions in whatever way you want. It's nobody's business what you do as long as you are not hurting anyone. Besides, biblical standards for sexual purity are prudish and old-fashioned.	"*Run away from sexual sin!*"[17] "Remain faithful to one another in marriage. God will surely judge people who are immoral and those who commit adultery."[18] "Do not commit adultery."[19]
It's okay to sin a little. Nobody's perfect. Loosen up and have some fun. No one will ever find out what you do. Lighten up. Get a life.	"The time is coming when everything will be revealed; all that is secret will be made public."[20] "Do not be deceived: God cannot be mocked. *A man reaps what he sows.*"[21]

Society's Lie	God's Truth
You have a right to get even. You're a wimp if you let people get away with anything. If someone hurts you, hurt them back. It's an eye for an eye and a tooth for a tooth.	*"Get rid of all bitterness, rage and anger."*[22] "Do not repay anyone evil for evil…Do not take revenge."[23] "Love your enemies. Do good to those who hate you."[24]
Character doesn't matter. If you want to get ahead in life, tell people what they want to hear. Bend the rules to achieve your purposes because the end justifies the means. Ability is more important than conduct.	*"I the LORD search the heart and examine the mind,* to reward a man according to his conduct, according to what his deeds deserve."[25]

the Counselor of Truth, within us as our Guide.

Do your decisions and lifestyle demonstrate that you are listening to God through His Word and His servants? Or are you living in the darkness of the lies of society and popular culture? Like a powerful floodlight, God's truth will expose for us the foolishness and destructiveness of every myth promoted by the world.

How God's Truth Sets Us Free

God's truth frees us to live as God has intended. On the other hand, the Deceiver wants us to base our lives on false assumptions. Jesus said to His followers, "You are truly My disciples if you keep obeying My teachings. And you will know the truth, and the truth will set you free."[26] Here are several ways God's truth sets us free.

We are free from death and eternal damnation.

Jesus said, "I give them eternal life, and they will never perish. No one will snatch them away from me."[27]

Paul wrote to Titus about the certainty of eternal life: "a faith and knowledge resting on the hope of eternal life, which God, who does not lie, promised before the beginning of time."[28] Paul knew that way back in eternity past God had promised salvation for those who believe in Him. That promise became reality in Paul's life, as it will for all of us who accept the message of Jesus' death on the cross for sin. The Book of Hebrews assures us:

> God also bound Himself with an oath, so that those who received the promise could be perfectly sure that He would never change His mind. So God has given us both His promise and His oath. These two things are unchangeable because it is impossible for God to lie.[29]

That is why the hope of eternal life based on God's promises is so firmly anchored for us.

We are set free from bondage to sin and guilt.

Our society has tried to cleanse itself from guilt by removing the Ten Commandments from our public schools, buildings, and courts so that no one will be reminded of breaking them. Those who sin try to rationalize all kinds of wicked behavior by blaming it on their background, circumstances, a parent or spouse. With society saying, "Don't worry, it's not your fault," why are so many guilt-ridden people filling up psychiatrists' couches? Because we are all born in bondage to sin and guilt, and only God can break those bonds. Only He can break the chains of blame shifting, bad habits, and addictions.

Nick Smith, a 17-year-old who participated in Josh McDowell's "Right From Wrong" campaign, understood this principle. By attending the meetings, he prepared himself to make godly decisions. While he was at an out-of-town track meet, he discovered several teammates glued to a less-than-wholesome movie on the HBO channel. He had two choices: to follow the biblical guidelines he had learned about keeping himself pure or to go along with his friends. Nick said, "Y'all shouldn't be watching that. It messes up your mind."[30]

One of the boys agreed with Nick and left the group. Not only did Nick resist the temptation to do something wrong, he also influenced another young man to do the same! If you turn your temptations over to God and trust in His power, He will help you step out of that pile of chains as a free man or woman.

Paul writes in Romans 6:22, "Now that you have been set free from sin and have become slaves to God, the benefit you reap leads to holiness, and the result is eternal life" (NIV). In Jesus we can live freely and joyfully.

We are set free from self-centeredness.

If you want to take a test to see how self-centered you are, note your instinctive reaction the next time you see a photograph showing a group of people including yourself. Whose face do you look at first? Your best friend's or your own? How about when you hear good news about someone close to you? Do you immediately think about how your friend is feeling or wonder why you do not get the "lucky breaks" in life?

You are not alone. We all have a self-centered nature. It's part of the human condition.

Jesus told His disciples, "If any of you wants to be My follower, you must put aside your selfish ambition, shoulder your cross, and follow Me. If you try to keep your life for yourself, you will lose it. But if you give up your life for Me, you will find true life."[31] Only Christ can free us to be more other-centered as we walk in the power of His Spirit. He fills us with His powerful love, which "does not demand its own way. Love is not irritable, and it keeps no record of when it has been wronged."[32]

We are set free from bondage to fear.

Paul informs us, "You did not receive a spirit that makes you a slave again to fear, but you received the Spirit of sonship."[33] Yet many Christians still live in fear. It robs us of joy and limits what we can do for our Lord. But God enables us to live in freedom through the power of His Holy Spirit—if only we will trust and obey Him!

We are set free from a life of mediocrity and insignificance.

God, the creator of over 100 billion galaxies, also created us in His image and has a wonderful plan for our lives.[34] Nothing the world offers can even come close to what God has planned. We will only be significant to whatever degree we are willing to fulfill the plan for which God has created us.

You Can Begin to Live Freely in God's Truth

Many years ago, a young missionary from Africa came to see me for counsel. He told me that he had little knowledge or experience of the Holy Spirit. He had spent several years on the mission field with no tangible results and felt like a miserable failure.

As we sat together, I explained that his ministry had been fruitless because he did not draw on the power of the Holy Spirit to help him. I further explained how important it is that we confess all known sin to God, turn from our sin, and walk in obedience to Him. Then as we surrender to the Lordship of Christ, we can by faith ask God to fill us with His Holy Spirit.[35] We can claim His promise to fill us knowing that if we ask anything according to His will, He hears us.[36]

In response, the man exploded in anger. He said, "I have spent my life serving God at great sacrifice. I have faced death and all kinds of persecution on the mission field. And now you offer me this simplistic solution to my problem?" He was irate and stormed out of my office.

A few days later he called me for another appointment. He said, "I don't agree with you. I believe that your explanation of the Spirit-filled life is too superficial and simple, but you obviously have a quality in your life that I don't have and I want very badly. I will ask God to show me if what you say is true."

I will never forget a letter I received from him a few weeks later. He wrote out of a joyful heart overflowing with praise and thanksgiving to God. He said, "I now understand what you have been trying to tell me. I did what you told me to do and now I want to return to the mission field and teach other defeated believers what you taught me. I've been liberated. I'm free!"

The choice is ours. Every day we must choose whom we will believe, God or Satan. Those who diligently seek truth in the right places will find only God's truth. Base your life on it because His absolute truth will set you free.

LIFE APPLICATION

WRITE IT ON YOUR HEART—Memorize the following statement and verses, and as you encounter the temptation to lie this week, claim them as promises from our God of truth.

- Because God is absolute truth, I can believe what He says and live accordingly.
- John 18:37—"I came to bring truth to the world. All who love the truth recognize that what I say is true."
- John 8:31,32—"You are truly My disciples if you keep obeying My teachings. And you will know the truth, and the truth will set you free."

COUNT ON GOD—God's Word can always be trusted because He never lies. Is there something that you have difficulty trusting God with in your current situation? Claim a promise from one of the following Scriptures and commit your concerns to God today.

- Romans 8:28—"God causes everything to work together for the good of those who love God and are called according to His purpose for them."
- Philippians 1:6—"I am sure that God, who began the good work within you, will continue His work until it is finally finished on that day when Christ Jesus comes back again."
- 1 John 1:9—"If we confess our sins to him, He is faithful and just to forgive us and to cleanse us from every wrong."

OBEY GOD—Is there something in the last few weeks that you have been untruthful about? First John 1:6 says, "If we claim to have fellowship with Him yet walk in the darkness, we lie and do not live by the truth" (NIV). Confess it to the LORD and tell the truth to the one you misled. Then determine to always speak the truth.

CHAPTER 16

GOD
IS
RIGHTEOUS

H ow can there be so many different views about what is
right and what is wrong? Why are moral issues no longer
seen as black or white but rather as varying shades of gray?
Why do the standards of morality constantly change within society?

Today the distinction between right and wrong is becoming
increasingly blurred. People passionately defend their sinful actions. What is right has become a matter of interpretation by the
individual, the community, or the courts. However, this view is
absolutely wrong because it assumes that public opinion and government legislation provide the ultimate criterion for determining
what is right. But our sovereign God sets the standards for His creation. His standards do not change; they are timeless. And our
American society, like many western nations, was built on the
biblical principles of right and wrong.

Our culture understands how important it is to be "right" about
certain things. Permit me to give you several examples:

An architect building a hundred-story skyscraper takes immense precautions to have the building's foundation perfectly level.

If the footings are off even a fraction of an inch, there are tremendous consequences. The farther up he builds on an unleveled foundation, the more unstable the skyscraper becomes.

Scientists at Mission Control in Houston also know the importance of being "right" when bringing a spaceship back to Earth. If the angle of re-entry into the Earth's atmosphere is off just a little, the spaceship will encounter too much friction and burn up before it reaches the ground.

Last, consider the speed skater in a race. Two lanes circle the track. The skaters not only race each other, but each skater is also required to stay in his own lane. If one skater crosses the line into the other lane, he is disqualified and loses the race.

Although most people understand the importance of laying the "right" foundation, having the "right" re-entry angle, or staying in the "right" lane, they have problems understanding the "rightness" of moral laws. When it comes to stealing, for example, most people divide stealing into categories like "borrowing," petty theft, robbery, and embezzlement. They feel that some categories are okay, such as taking a few supplies from their employer or school, or keeping the excess when a cashier gives them too much change. But to them it would be wrong to break into someone's home or rob a bank. Moral laws, they believe, are not as rigid as other laws. Therefore, we can bend them a little without incurring any penalty. But that is contrary to how God sees His righteous laws.

GOD IS ALWAYS RIGHT

It is easy to understand God's righteous role as Creator. Everything He created functions according to the laws applying to its creation. All His natural laws perform the way He intends for the good of His creation. Look at the way a coastal marsh works. Each day, tides bring fresh nutrients for the millions of tiny plants that grow in the soil and water. At high tide, all kinds of shellfish dine on these tiny plants. Fish such as spotted sea trout spawn in the calm water and the tiny hatchlings feed in their own little marshy nursery. Ducks and other birds build nests to raise their young. A stew of vegetation provides a smorgasbord for the ducklings and gos-lings. Natural laws and processes work together as a system to benefit all of God's creation.

It is easy to recognize how God created nature in its right order. But it is far less common to understand that God has created the moral realm to function in its right order, too.

In fact, as humans we often purposefully overlook one wrong to right another. In recent years, juries have declared a defendant "not guilty" of a crime despite evidence that clearly convicts him. Through their actions, jury members hope to make a statement about some other moral wrong connected with the crime. Many experts believe the jury in the O. J. Simpson murder trial did this to right the wrong of minorities often not getting equal justice in the court system. But ignoring one wrong to address another wrong will not make things right. We just end up with two wrongs —and no right.

As humans, we sometimes fail to do what is right in our daily lives. Have you ever said to yourself, "I know the right thing to do, but if I do what is right, I will mess up my situation"? Perhaps you are in a college class when someone advocates an immoral viewpoint. You do not challenge the speaker's opinion because you do not want to be viewed as a moral extremist. Standing up for what is morally right might cause you to be ridiculed, lose friends, receive a lower grade from the professor, or lose your job. As fall-en human beings, we have a hard time even understanding per-fect righteousness much less living righteous lives.

Only God is righteous because He is holy. He has never acted unrighteously; never had an evil thought; never rationalized a questionable act to make something else right.

WHAT IS RIGHTEOUSNESS?

We learned previously that God is holy. But His holiness and His righteousness are not the same. Holiness is "a condition of purity or freedom from sin."[1] God's righteousness is "the quality or at-tribute of God by virtue of which He does that which is right or in accordance with His own nature, will, and law."[2]

In other words, holiness describes God's nature; righteousness describes how God acts according to His holiness. God's laws are holy because they come from His nature. God's standards for enforcing His laws are always righteous.

Let me give an example of one law. God says, "Do not commit adultery." That simple statement arises out of God's holiness. He can never be disloyal when He has made a commitment; it is against His nature. In the Old Testament, God made covenants or promises to His people. He made a covenant with Noah that He would never again destroy the earth with a flood. The rainbow in the sky is the evidence of His covenant. Over the many centuries since the flood, God has acted rightly regarding this covenant. That follow-through with His holy covenant shows His righteousness.

> HOLINESS DESCRIBES GOD'S NATURE; RIGHTEOUSNESS DESCRIBES HOW GOD ACTS.

In the same way, when we stand before a minister and promise to love our spouse and be faithful to him or her the rest of our lives, we are making a covenant that reflects God's holiness. We act righteously when we keep that commitment or covenant.

But do not imagine that righteousness is reaching a standard like climbing a ladder to a higher level. That is what most people think when they consider righteous acts. "If I tell the truth more times than I tell lies, I'll be more righteous." "If I make up for the money I stole from my employer, then I'll be okay." No one can work up to righteousness because it begins as purity. It comes out of holiness; it does not reach up to holiness.

Holiness sets the standard. Righteousness is the result of a relationship that fulfills that standard.

GOD IS THE SOURCE OF ALL RIGHTEOUSNESS

How righteous is God? Everything God does is perfectly right in every way. David tells us, "The LORD is righteous in all His ways and loving toward all He has made."³ For God, righteousness is not an external standard that He must adhere to; righteousness is part of His very nature. It emanates from His inner being. As a result, whatever God wills is perfectly right. It is impossible for God to do anything wrong.

All righteousness within the entire universe has its origin in Him. The psalmist exclaims, "Your righteousness reaches to the skies, O God, You who have done great things. Who, O God, is like You?"⁴ Every action God has ever taken or will take is righteous. As a judge, He has never made a wrong determination. He has never had to reverse a decision when He learned more facts. No one can question His judgment in all His actions.

Heaven is filled with God's righteousness. "Righteousness and justice are the foundation of His throne."⁵ Because God is righteous, He wants righteousness to fill His universe.

God as Righteous Judge

When you walk into a courtroom and face the judge, you may wonder, "Who gave this judge the power to decide between right and wrong? Who gave the judge the moral and legal authority to pronounce what is righteous behavior and what is grievous misbehavior deserving punishment?"

Whether judges are elected directly by the people or appointed by the politicians we elect, they ultimately owe their authority and legal power to us, the people. These judges are subject to human passions, can misuse their authority, and be removed. A New England judge was recently removed after a grand jury indicted him for forcing young men to have sex with him in his private chambers—in return for dismissing their cases. An Illinois judge was removed for "fixing" speeding tickets in return for illegal bribes.

But when we discuss the righteousness of God, we are not talking about an appointed judge, prone to weaknesses. An infinite and powerful God does not need anyone to elect or appoint Him, to give Him righteousness. He was righteous before the beginning of time and always will be.

God told Jeremiah, "I am the LORD, who exercises kindness,

justice and righteousness on earth, for in these I delight."[6] He is the standard by which every evaluation of righteousness must be compared. If God were not inherently holy and just, He could not act righteously.

GOD'S LAWS DEFINE RIGHTEOUS BEHAVIOR

The *Dred Scott v. Sanford* Supreme Court case in 1856 shows how little righteousness we really have as humans. The case began when Henry Blow filed a suit trying to free a slave, Dred Scott, who worked for him. The problem, however, was that Henry did not own Mr. Scott. A Mrs. Emerson did. Although she lived in New York and Dred Scott lived in Missouri, she would not give him his freedom.

The case wound its way from the lower courts to the Supreme Court. By the time the Supreme Court Justices heard the case, the abolition movement in the U.S. had grown strong. Abolitionists wanted slavery outlawed in new territories and states like Missouri. Southern slave owners were desperate to keep their right to own slaves because of their labor-intensive farms. To complicate the case, Dred Scott had lived for a time in free Wisconsin territory. Because of that fact, Blow argued, Scott should be a free man.

The Supreme Court could not make up its mind. It heard oral arguments twice, then the Justices recessed for two months. They were so divided on the issue that they did not even meet during that time. Finally, each Justice wrote his own opinion. Seven of them ruled that Dred Scott was still a slave, while two ruled that he was free. Since the Supreme Court ruled that slavery could not be prohibited in new territories, only a constitutional amendment could outlaw the expansion of slavery. This decision was one of the principal causes of the Civil War.[7] Years later, The Supreme Court reversed its decision on slavery.

Throughout history, human judges have had a hard time determining right from wrong. Just like us, they are caught up in the culture, swayed by their own personalities, and limited to the evidence presented in court, which may not accurately portray the truth.

A more recent miscarriage of justice was the *Roe v. Wade* case in which the Supreme Court ruled that abortion is legal. Lawful killing of preborn babies is certainly not righteous. Yet the Court approved of this travesty. I am praying that, like its reversal on the slavery issue, the Supreme Count will reverse its decision in *Roe v. Wade* that legalized abortion on demand.

God does not struggle with right and wrong. The psalmist declares, "Righteous are You, O LORD, and Your laws are right."[8] His laws reflect His own righteous nature and the moral perfection of His character. Cultural bias, a lack of knowledge, or any other factor does not alter His rulings.

God's spiritual laws are every bit as absolute as His physical laws. If we break God's natural laws, we pay the consequences. For example, if you jump off of the Empire State Building in New York City, the law of gravity will guarantee your death. Likewise, if you lock yourself in a garage and breathe carbon monoxide instead of the oxygen that your body needs, you will die.

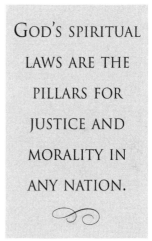

GOD'S SPIRITUAL LAWS ARE THE PILLARS FOR JUSTICE AND MORALITY IN ANY NATION.

God's spiritual laws are no less binding. As the perfect Judge and Lawgiver, God is also the law enforcer. His laws lay out the responsibilities for which God holds us accountable. They are a yardstick by which God measures our righteousness. When His laws are broken, He must punish anyone who defies His righteous laws.

You may wonder why God is so exacting about His spiritual laws. He did not make rules just for the "fun of it." His righteous laws focus on standards for acting rightly toward one another.

Consequently, God's spiritual laws are the pillars for justice and morality within any nation. To restate this fact, the laws of a nation are just only to the degree that they conform to the laws of God. When national leaders reject and disobey God, they cut their nation loose from the anchor of morality, and set it adrift in an ocean of moral relativity. Without God they lose their moral compass and doom their society to injustice, dishonesty, and depravity. In our next chapter, we will see how important righteous laws are to our nation.

WE CANNOT MEET GOD'S RIGHTEOUS STANDARD

Ever since Adam and Eve first disobeyed God, every person has been born with a sinful nature that insists on exerting self-will, even against the Creator. Isaiah describes our dilemma, "How can people like us be saved? We are all infected and impure with sin. When we proudly display our righteous deeds, we find they are but filthy rags. Like autumn leaves, we wither and fall. And our sins, like the wind, sweep us away."[9]

Imagine a contest between an Olympic gold medal winner and me to see who can jump across the Grand Canyon, which is miles wide and deep. Who do you think would win that match? While I am sure the Olympian would jump far beyond me, he would still fall short of the other side. We would both plummet to our deaths.

That is similar to our attempts to be righteous. Even when we try our very hardest, we still fall far short of God's perfect standard. Because of our sinful nature, it is impossible for us to live the righteous life God demands. As we read earlier, if we are ever to be acceptable to God, He has to intervene on our behalf.

FAITH IS THE KEY TO RIGHTEOUSNESS

We can be righteous only when God's righteousness is imputed, or freely given to us as we place our faith in God's only Son, Jesus Christ. Abraham was an Old Testament illustration of this truth, which was not fully revealed until Jesus came some 2,000 years later. Genesis 15:6 explains, "[Abraham] believed the LORD, and He credited it to him as righteousness" (NIV). This "righteousness" is sometimes referred to as "right standing" with God; in other words, God considers us right with Him. Abraham came into right standing with God because Abraham believed Him!

Since God's standards for morality and virtue are 100 percent perfect and we are imperfect and inadequate, we can only be righteous as a gift from God. Through our faith in His Son, He "credits" His own righteousness to our account.

In the New Testament, Paul referred to this passage about Abraham and then gave us the wonderful news that "the words 'it was credited to him' were written not for him alone, but also for us, to whom God will credit righteousness—for us who believe in Him who raised Jesus our Lord from the dead."[10] This is one of the most wonderful truths in the universe: God declares us righteous by faith, and sees us as having the righteousness of His own Son! This is grace, or unmerited favor—a free gift purchased for us by our Lord Jesus Christ through His death on the cross.

What is our worshipful response to the knowledge that God gives us righteousness because of His Son? The Bible contains many examples of prayers that we can offer up to God. One such prayer was written by Paul and is found in 1 Thessalonians: "Now may the God of peace make you holy in every way, and may your whole spirit and soul and body be kept blameless until that day when our Lord Jesus Christ comes again. God, who calls you, is faithful; He will do this."[11]

Make this prayer the cry of your heart. God will respond by touching your heart, spirit, soul, and body. We can be assured that He will answer this prayer and make us righteous in His sight.

LIFE APPLICATION

EXALT YOUR GOD—Worship our righteous God with the words of Psalm 119:137–144:

> O Lord, You are righteous, and Your decisions are fair. Your decrees are perfect; they are entirely worthy of our trust.
>
> I am overwhelmed with rage, for my enemies have disregarded your words. Your promises have been thoroughly tested; that is why I love them so much.
>
> I am insignificant and despised, but I don't forget Your commandments. Your justice is eternal, and Your law is perfectly true. As pressure and stress bear down on me, I find joy in Your commands.
>
> Your decrees are always fair; help me to understand them, that I may live.

REFLECT HIS IMAGE—We are called to be righteous, but we cannot do this in our own strength. Ask your heavenly Father to reveal areas of unrighteousness in your heart and life. Then repent and confess them to Him. Ask the Holy Spirit to empower you to live righteously in those areas you are most tempted to disobey God.

SHARE HIS MAJESTY—One of the ways we can testify of God's righteousness is by displaying our faith in Him. When you are with your friends, relatives, or neighbors who do not know Christ as Savior, relate your experiences with faith-building answers to prayer and share the gospel message of love and forgiveness. As people see your faith in a God who is trustworthy, many will want to live a righteous life as a child of God.

CHAPTER 17

GOD HELPS US LIVE RIGHTEOUSLY

We live in a world where many believe that the end justifies the means. They say it is acceptable to compromise God's standards to get ahead. But the fact is we always lose when we violate God's standards of righteousness. On the other hand, it is not always easy to do what is right.

I think of a situation in which we found ourselves as a ministry when we moved our headquarters from San Bernardino, California, to Orlando, Florida. We had been unable to lease or sell some of our property in San Bernardino. The buildings remained empty, yet every month we still had to make our mortgage payments.

I was counseled by some successful Christian businessmen to default the payments and allow the bank to repossess the property. After all, many businesses had done this during the economic downturn. Financially, we would be far better off, but that would be wrong since we had signed a contract with the bank. We purposed to trust God to help us pay the bills and sell the property in a way that would bring honor and glory to Him. Some would say, "Boy that's stupid." But we had given our word. Five years passed before we finally sold the property.

Although making those payments was a financial hardship, God has greatly blessed the ministry of Campus Crusade. Contributions have dramatically increased year after year. I believe God has blessed us because we run Campus Crusade for Christ in His way. We depend on Him to help us pay our bills.

As Dr. Bob Jones, Sr., once said, "It is never right to do wrong in order to get a chance to do right." In other words, if we had defaulted on our agreement, we could have saved a lot of money every year. Think of all that the ministry could have done with that money—but we would have violated our word and our contract. That would not have honored God. Living righteously means making sacrifices and saying no to desires. We cannot live this way in our own strength.

Let us look at a few action points that will help us do what is right no matter what.

DEPEND ON GOD'S RIGHTEOUSNESS RATHER THAN OUR EFFORTS

We are so fortunate that "the LORD is gracious and righteous; our God is full of compassion."[1] Otherwise we would be doomed by our lack of righteousness. Our righteousness does not depend on what we do, but on whom we place our faith. Paul explains:

> We are made right in God's sight when we trust in Jesus Christ to take away our sins. And we all can be saved in this same way, no matter who we are or what we have done. For all have sinned; all fall short of God's glorious standard. Yet now God in His gracious kindness declares us not guilty. He has done this through Christ Jesus, who has freed us by taking away our sins. For God sent Jesus to take the punishment for our sins and to satisfy God's anger against us. We are made right with God when we believe that Jesus shed His blood, sacrificing His life for us."[2]

There was not anything we could do to earn this gift of grace. We accepted it by faith. Now God no longer sees our sinfulness, but only the righteousness of Christ which covers us.

When we put our faith in Christ, we received a new nature—one of holiness and righteousness. Christ wants us to display His righteousness in our new life. We are commanded: "Throw off your old evil nature and your former way of life, which is rotten through and through, full of lust and deception. Instead, there must be a spiritual renewal of your thoughts and attitudes. You must display a new nature because you are a new person, created in God's likeness—righteous, holy, and true."[3]

Yet we are all tempted to achieve righteousness under our own power. That never works. We cannot live righteously without the enabling of the Holy Spirit, and His power is released through our faith. For example, if a person has a problem with swearing, he could try his hardest to quit using foul language. For the most part, he would be able to control his tongue, but when someone cuts him off on the freeway or breaks in front of him in a line, his mouth curses before he even realizes what he is saying. All his efforts to control this reaction come to nothing.

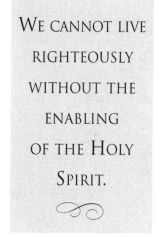

WE CANNOT LIVE RIGHTEOUSLY WITHOUT THE ENABLING OF THE HOLY SPIRIT.

The secret to changing bad habits like cursing is to turn the problem over to God. By faith, admit that you are helpless to change your bad habit. By faith ask His Spirit to give you righteous language to replace the filthy language. As you walk in the Spirit moment by moment, your heart is prepared to act righteously the next time someone angers you. When this happens, take a deep breath and start praising God for something good in the situation. Trust God to take over and work out the problem. This will make the difference in your reaction and the results of the problem.

SEEK GOD FIRST AND TURN AWAY FROM WORLDLY ATTACHMENTS

The only way we can live a life of faith is by submitting our will to the Holy Spirit moment by moment and depending on Him to empower us. When doing this, Jesus instructs us to "seek first His kingdom and His righteousness."[4] As a result, we will enjoy the rewards of righteous living and agree with David, "Surely, O LORD, You bless the righteous; You surround them with Your favor as with a shield."[5]

A friend of mine lived in a palatial home in El Paso, Texas. He was a very successful manufacturer who had accumulated considerable wealth. Following his retirement he ministered weekly to the poor people across the border in Juarez, Mexico.

However, one woman greatly ministered to him. She lived in a little hut with a dirt floor. Her earthly possessions were a small stove, a pot, a pan, a plate, a knife, fork and spoon, and one change of clothes. Every time she saw him she would tell him, "God is so good to me, He is so wonderful and faithful to me." This successful businessman loved God, but this godly woman was far happier than he was. Through her, he discovered that joy and fulfillment are not found in material possessions, but in a relationship with God and in obedience to His commands.

Seeking God first will lead to a new perspective on life. Old, worldly attachments will seem insignificant and God's blessings will be apparent in righteous living. I challenge you to rearrange your priorities, schedule, and finances to put God first and follow His "right" plan for your life.

ADJUST YOUR LIFE TO GOD'S STANDARDS

Some years ago, a Christian man from a Middle Eastern nation attended a Campus Crusade conference in another country. While there, he felt God calling him to join our staff. That decision meant much more sacrifice to him than it does to someone who joins our staff in the United States. Because of Muslim persecution in his country, his decision to follow the Lord in ministry could result in harm to him and even death—and the same consequences for his family. But he felt sure that God wanted him to tell his countrymen about the love of God as revealed through Jesus Christ our Lord.

After the conference ended, he went home and told his wife what God was leading him to do. Her reaction was amazing. She said, "If God wants you to join Campus Crusade for Christ, then I agree with your decision. I am willing to follow your decision."

She realized the ramifications that this change meant for her and her family. In fact, today she and her husband are exiles from their homeland because of their witness for Christ. But she adjusted her plans to fit into God's plans for their lives—and she and her husband saw tremendous fruit in their country before their exile. God continues to use them mightily in their new assignment.

We have discussed confessing sin when our lives take a turn from God's perfect standard, but God wants us to do more than that. Henry Blackaby and Claude King explain in their book *Experiencing God*, "God wants you to have no hindrances to a love relationship with Him in your life. Once God has spoken to you through His Word, how you respond is crucial. You must adjust your life to the truth."[6]

This means adjusting your life in areas in which you have been disobeying Him. If you are not sharing your faith, you begin witnessing to others. If you read questionable—even pornographic—books or magazines, or watch such videos, get rid of the objectionable materials at once. Start spending more time reading God's Word or other materials that edify your spirit, instead. If you are not spending enough time with your family, readjust your schedule.

Adjusting your standards also may mean making changes in your life that fit God's leading. If God directs you to change careers, you take the necessary steps to do what He asks. If you feel the Holy Spirit guiding you to help with the preschoolers in Sunday school, you willingly give up that Sunday morning class that you enjoy. If a need arises for someone to work with boys at church one night a week, you must stop working late that night. If He leads you to share His good news in other countries and cultures, you must step out in faith and respond. Knowing God's truth and holiness always leads to righteous action. But the rewards, friends, for you and those you serve are exciting and fulfilling.

BE AN ADVOCATE FOR RIGHTEOUSNESS WHERE YOU LIVE

As disciples of Jesus Christ we are to live righteous lives. But how does righteousness impact the course of a nation? The Bible declares, "Righteousness exalts a nation, but sin is a disgrace to any people."[7]

In the Book of Deuteronomy, God promised to bless the nation of Israel for obedience, but He also warned of judgment upon His people if His laws were disregarded. Second Chronicles 7:14 gives this wonderful promise: "If My people who are called by My name will humble themselves and pray and seek My face and turn from their wicked ways, I will hear from heaven and will forgive their sins and heal their land."

America has a unique heritage—one rooted in a dependence on God and His biblical principles. The scriptural principles for a godly nation were well understood by the Pilgrims. Their purpose, as stated in the Mayflower Compact, was to plant colonies "for the glory of God, and advancement of the Christian faith."[8] Ninety-nine percent of the colonial population professed to be Christians and most of our founding fathers were true followers of our Lord Jesus Christ. Early in the 19th century, the French philosopher and historian Alexis de Tocqueville did a study of democracy in our country and came to this conclusion:

> I sought for the greatness and genius of America in her commodious harbors and her ample rivers, and it was not there. I sought for the greatness and genius of America in her fertile fields and boundless forests, and it was not there. I sought for the greatness and genius of America in her rich mines and her vast world commerce, and it was not there. I sought for the greatness and genius of America in her public school system and her institutions of learning, and it was not there. Not until I went to the churches of America and heard her pulpits aflame with righteousness did I understand the secret of her genius and power. America is great because America is good, and if America ever ceases to be good, America will cease to be great.[9]

For many decades after our country's founding, American leaders advocated God's righteousness in government.

- George Washington said, "It is impossible to rightly govern the world without God and the Bible."[10]

- John Adams, the second president and co-drafter of the Declaration of Independence said, "Our Constitution was made only for a moral and religious people, it is wholly inadequate to the government of any other."[11]

- Noah Webster believed, "The Christian religion is the most important and one of the first things in which all children, under a free government, ought to be instructed."[12]

- Nearly all of the first 119 colleges and universities of our nation, including Harvard, Yale, Princeton, Dartmouth, William and Mary, and Columbia, were founded primarily to train young scholars in the knowledge of God and the Bible.

- Abraham Lincoln said, "But for the Bible we would not know right from wrong."[13]

- The first U.S. Supreme Court Chief Justice John Jay said, "Providence has given to our people the choice of their rulers, and it is the duty, as well as the privilege and interest of our Christian nation to select and prefer Christians for their rulers."[14]

- In 1892, the U.S. Supreme Court made the following ruling, "No purpose of action against religion can be imputed to any legislation, state or national, because this is a religious people …This is a Christian nation."[15] That court ruling cited 87 different historical precedents.

Then at the turn of the 20th century, a bloodless revolution began to change our nation. Unrighteous philosophies such as relativism and evolution spread throughout mainstream America. Without a single previous precedent, the Supreme Count in 1947 declared the separation of Church and State. This action was widely interpreted as separation of godly principles from public life. In 1962 and 1963, the Supreme Court declared school prayer to be unconstitutional and the Bible was outlawed from our schools.

Within a decade, the Supreme Court made it lawful to kill our unborn children yet unlawful to display the Ten Commandments in public schools. As a result, God's righteous foundation in America is systematically being destroyed. As the foundation crumbles, so does the nation. It is obvious from every social indicator that the secular and humanistic system has failed.

As believers, we dare not continue to be silent. For many years, I have had a deep burden for our country's moral condition. I firmly believe that if Christians will stand firm on the righteous standards of God's law, we can turn our country back to its godly heritage. We must hold fast to the righteous standards set forth by the sovereign Creator and Ruler of the universe in our own lives and be advocates for His standards in our culture.

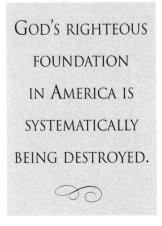

GOD'S RIGHTEOUS FOUNDATION IN AMERICA IS SYSTEMATICALLY BEING DESTROYED.

I have seen exciting gains in advocating God's righteousness through the fasting and prayer movement sweeping our country. In Houston, Texas, people joined together from November 22, 1996, to January 1, 1997, every day and evening for intercession, evangelistic messages, corporate repentance, racial reconciliation, and praise and worship. They renamed the large outdoor amphitheater in which they met "Prayer Mountain." Throughout the forty days, worship was held in Spanish, Korean, Chinese, Japanese, Indonesian, English, and other languages. Messianic Jewish pastors publicly embraced Arab ministers; Chinese and Japanese leaders prayed for one another; walls between people fell as they worshipped the Lord in unity. People streamed to the altar every night, eager to get right with God.

The fasting and prayer effort resulted in righteous action. Five thousand needy families received groceries, clothes, blankets, food, and toys. Lives were changed in miraculous ways. "I was involved in gangs," a 19-year-old man explained, "and two months ago was released from prison. A friend of mine invited me to come to Prayer Mountain tonight. Jesus saved me."

On January 1, Houston symbolically passed the baton to Dallas. On January 3, Dallas believers began forty days of fasting and prayer for their city. In February, believers in both Kansas City, Missouri, and Pasadena, California, started their forty days of city-wide fasting and prayer. Katy, Texas, located just outside Houston, also got involved in the fasting and prayer movement. The "domino effect" of one city's example produced amazing results![16]

Regardless of the beliefs and behavior of a nation, ultimately God will hold every person accountable. Whose standards of "right" will you follow? God's or man's? What we do in our personal lives and how we serve as an advocate of God's righteousness to our neighborhoods, cities, states, and country will help change the world for Christ.

Every day I review and meditate on the Ten Commandments. I urge you to keep the Ten Commandments clearly in mind by writing them on a card and displaying them in your car, on your refrigerator, or at your desk.

In the following Life Application, you will find ways you can be an advocate for righteousness. I urge you to begin right now through prayer and witnessing to help others know and apply the righteous standards of our loving God.

LIFE APPLICATION

WRITE IT ON YOUR HEART—Commit the following statement and verses to memory. Then when you are tempted to compromise God's righteous standards this week, claim them as promises from our God of righteousness.

- Because God is righteous, I can live by His standards.
- Psalm 145:17 (NIV)—"The LORD is righteous in all His ways and loving toward all He has made."
- 1 Peter 3:12 (NIV)—"The eyes of the Lord are on the righteous and His ears are attentive to their prayer."
- 1 John 3:7 (NIV)—"Dear children, do not let anyone lead you astray. He who does what is right is righteous, just as He is righteous."

COUNT ON GOD—Because God is righteous, He will never do wrong. How simple and wise to place your trust in Someone who cannot wrong you. So far, we have studied a number of God's attributes. Which one is the most difficult for you to understand or accept? This week, ask God to give you assurance that He uses all His attributes righteously for our good.

OBEY GOD—Our world today often calls right wrong and wrong right. We honor the immoral and ridicule the upright. Even the most "moral" programs on mass media today advocate immoral solutions to problems: living together before marriage to see if you are compatible partners; using violence to resolve disputes; using foul language to look "cool." As you watch television, listen to the radio, or read secular books and magazines, compare the ideas you encounter with standards in God's Word. Ask God to help you separate the unrighteous morals of our culture and exchange them for God's righteous rules.

CHAPTER 18.

GOD
Is
JUST

D o you ever wonder what happened to justice? Why is it becoming increasingly elusive? What has gone wrong with the manmade judicial system?

In one of the worst travesties in American justice, four young men from Chicago with no history of violence were convicted of kidnapping, rape, and double murder. The bullet-riddled bodies of a young couple were found on May 12, 1978. Acting on an anonymous telephone tip, the police arrested Dennis Williams, Verneal Jimerson, Kenny Adams, and Willie Rainge. News reports declared that the crime had been solved. The men were soon convicted, and two were sentenced to death row. Appeals failed; all looked hopeless.

In September 1981, a tattered envelope with a return address of the "Condemned Unit," Menard, Illinois, arrived at the offices of the *Chicago Lawyer* magazine. That letter led Rob Warden, editor and publisher of the *Chicago Lawyer*, and Dennis Protess, professor at Northwestern Medill School of Journalism, to investigate the case. They uncovered substantial evidence that exonerated the four convicts, including the first use of DNA to prove that multiple defendants were excluded as suspects in a rape case.

On July 2, 1996, more than eighteen years after the murders took place, Judge Thomas Fitzgerald ended the defendants' fight against an unjust sentence by reading, "All the convictions are vacated."[1] The four prisoners were free! The next day, the state attorney's office charged the real killers, Ira Johnson, Arthur Robinson, and Juan Rodriguez.

Justice is a pillar of any society. It vindicates the innocent and punishes the guilty. All too often though, this standard is compromised for personal gain. Corrupt judges sometimes tilt the scales of justice; unscrupulous lawyers manipulate laws and juries; witnesses lie. Truth is often distorted to benefit the rich, famous, and powerful.

Today, people are becoming less concerned about doing what is right. Instead they look for ways to cover their tracks, believing they will never get caught. If their transgression is discovered, they assume they will never be convicted. If they are found guilty, they can always appeal. If the appeal is denied, they will likely serve only a fraction of their sentence anyway.

Since our justice system can often be manipulated, many people mistakenly believe they can manipulate God's system of justice. They think that their excuses and alibis fool God. But oh how wrong they are! God told Jeremiah, "I the LORD search the heart and examine the mind, to reward a man according to his conduct, according to what his deeds deserve."[2] You can always count on God being just. He will always act according to what is morally upright or good.

GOD IS A PERFECT JUDGE

The Supreme Court is the highest court in our country. If we could expect justice anywhere, it should be when a case comes before these esteemed justices. Yet they are just human. Their caseload is so overwhelming that the solicitor general of the Justice Department chooses from thousands of potential cases to be brought before the court. The Supreme Court Justices are ten times more likely to hear a case if the solicitor general files it.

The staff of the solicitor general has mushroomed in recent years. They file briefs and make appearances in about 150 to 175 cases a year. But think of how many petitions are denied! There is so much paperwork in the Supreme Court system that detailed rules are applied to the way documents are filed, from the precise wording that must appear on the cover to the length of the brief.[3]

With all these constraints, most cases do not make it to the bench. Perfect justice is therefore not being rendered. It is humanly impossible.

But God does not need a brief to examine a case. He does not run out of time to consider the evidence. No research or investigation is needed in His court—He already knows it all. He knows the motives, thoughts, actions, and purpose for everything done. Our only option is to confess before a holy, omniscient, omnipresent, omnipotent, just God.

Justice is not an external system to which God tries to adhere. He did not have to go to law school to learn how to apply the law. His justice comes out of His inner being and is based on His holiness, truthfulness, and righteousness. Moses observed, "Everything He does is just and fair. He is a faithful God who does no wrong; how just and upright He is!"[4] God cannot be bribed or corrupted because His judgments are grounded in integrity. Because He has all the facts at His disposal, He cannot be fooled. His decisions are always based upon absolute truth. And when God pronounces judgment, He has the power to carry out the punishment.

God's standard is the benchmark by which all human behavior is measured. God "always acts in a way consistent with the requirements of His character as revealed in His law. He rules His creation with honesty. He keeps His word. He renders to all His creatures their due."[5]

God's attributes assure us of justice. If He were not all-knowing, how could He know whether we sinned wittingly or manipulated the facts to serve our purposes? If He were not present everywhere at once, how could He know all the circumstances surrounding the issue before Him? If He were not all-wise, how could He carry out the judgment in a totally just way?

When Abraham learned that God planned to destroy Sodom and Gomorrah, Abraham argued that God could not destroy the righteous with the unrighteous. He pleads his case by saying: "Far be it from You to do such a thing—to kill the righteous with the wicked, treating the righteous and the wicked alike. Far be it from You! Will not the Judge of all the earth do right?"[6] In the New Testament, James writes, "There is only one Lawgiver and Judge, the one who is able to save and destroy."[7] To get a clearer picture of God's role as Perfect Judge, let us look at a few characteristics of an effective judge.

A judge must have authority.

Our government endows judges with authority through the oath they take to execute justice. The law enforcement and prison systems back up the judge's authority. The robe that he wears and having everyone in the courtroom stand as he enters help to emphasize that authority. His gavel and his elevated seat in the courtroom show that he commands the proceedings.

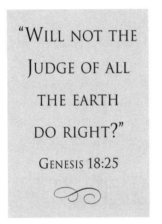

"WILL NOT THE JUDGE OF ALL THE EARTH DO RIGHT?"

GENESIS 18:25

We learned that God, as Creator, has the authority to do whatever He deems best with His creation. He is the potter; we are the clay. His throne is high above us in the heavens. His pronouncements are final. There is no higher authority than God.

God will judge every wrong act ever committed, every sinful motive, every evil word. The sentence for these crimes is eternal separation from God and His holiness.

But there are those who will live in safety with God. These are the ones who have accepted Christ's payment for our sin when He died on the cross. Our loving Savior, Jesus Christ, paid the sentence pronounced by the Perfect Judge. God sees these "sinners saved by grace" as righteous in His courtroom. Therefore, they will live eternally in the love, peace, and joy of God's presence.

A judge must have the power to execute his authority.

Can you imagine what would happen if judges had no authority to carry out sentences? Our prisons would be empty. No criminals would be deterred for fear of what the courts would do. Murderers, rapists, robbers, and child molesters could walk the streets terrorizing law-abiding citizens.

Since God is omnipotent, whatever He decides to do, He can carry out. He does not have to ask anyone's permission; He does not need a police force to back Him up. In His courtroom, His authority is the last word. No one can appeal His decisions. That is why He is pictured in heaven on a throne. As Sovereign of the universe, His authority is total and complete.

A judge must understand and know the law.

Many times, a higher court will throw out the ruling of a judge in a lower court. Why does this happen? Sometimes it is because the judge in the lower court, such as a municipal court, did not have the authority to apply the overarching laws of the state. The defendant can appeal his case to the State Supreme Court, which has greater power and can overturn the verdict.

God also follows laws—which He established. We find them in His Word as commands and rules. There is no higher law than God's laws. Not only is He the judge, He is also the lawmaker. Since God's laws are perfect, His justice is also without flaw.

A judge needs high moral qualities to judge fairly.

Without high morals, a judge will fail miserably. Our court system would fall apart, for our trials are only as good as the judges who preside over them. Judge Robert Bork tells the story of Judge Martin Manton, a Court of Appeals judge who was almost nominated to the U.S. Supreme Court:

> When it became known that Manton took bribes from parties appearing before him, he claimed innocence on the interesting ground that he took bribes from both sides, decided the case on its merits, and then returned the money to the losing party. That defense caused Judge Learned Hand,

perhaps the most distinguished court of appeals judge in our history, to call Manton a moral moron.[8]

Would you like to bring your case before a judge like Manton? Corrupt judges lead to injustice and unfairness. Victims do not receive proper consideration. The wronged are helpless; the wicked hold the power. If the judge is not truthful, honest, and wise in presiding over the courtroom, justice cannot be served.

A JUST GOD HATES SIN

As the holy and righteous sovereign of the universe, God cannot ignore or overlook any act of sin. David writes, "God is a judge who is perfectly fair. He is angry with the wicked every day."[9]

God's anger over sin should never be underestimated: "You spread out our sins before You—our secret sins—and You see them all. We live our lives beneath Your wrath…Who can comprehend the power of Your anger? Your wrath is as awesome as the fear You deserve."[10]

I urge you to live in reverential fear of God, continually searching God's Word and examining your heart for sins that you need to confess to Him. One of the greatest truths I have discovered in over 50 years of walking with the Lord is a concept called *Spiritual Breathing*. This process is similar to physical breathing. As we become aware of our sins, we exhale by confessing our sin.[11] Then we inhale to appropriate the power of the Holy Spirit, based on God's command to be filled with the Spirit.[12] We can know that God will fill, enable, and equip us because He promised to hear and answer our prayers in accordance with His perfect will.[13] This spiritual principle has allowed me to walk in fellowship with God and help others come to know and serve Him. This is the privilege of every believer.

GOD WILL EVENTUALLY PUNISH ALL SIN

The Bible tells us, "God will bring every deed into judgment, including every hidden thing, whether it is good or evil."[14] Yet, I am sure there have been times when you have asked, "Why are the wicked so prosperous? Why are evil people so happy?"[15] There may be several reasons why someone appears to be getting away with wrongdoing without being punished.

- God delays His judgment because He patiently provides an opportunity for repentance. But while God is waiting for repentance, the severity of future punishment is mounting.

- Sometimes we do not recognize God's judgment because it occurs in a way that we did not expect. Paul explains, "Do not be deceived: God cannot be mocked. A man reaps what he sows."[16] The more seeds of sin a person sows, the more harm will be caused. Sin is like an addictive poison. If you drink a little poison you may only get sick. But if you keep on drinking poison, it will eventually kill you.

The final judgment will occur at the end of time. Are you spiritually ready for that day of judgment? We will look at what is going to happen during that awesome time later in this chapter.

GOD BUILT NATURAL CONSEQUENCES INTO SIN

God does not wait until judgment day to settle sin accounts. He also built natural consequences into sin as a deterrent for our disobedient behavior.

I am reminded of a friend who was one of the most remarkable preachers and pulpit personalities I know. He was a pastor of a thriving church. Then one day, a prostitute came to his office seeking his counsel. He felt sorry for her and asked his wife if this prostitute could live in their home so they could rehabilitate her.

After living with them for three weeks, the prostitute told his wife that she wanted her husband. The wife just laughed in disbelief. They had a happy home and several children. He was one of the pillars in the Christian community. Yet to everyone's shock, he eventually left his family to live with this prostitute.

Many people from the Christian community pleaded with him to repent from his sinful lifestyle, but he persisted. This former pastor had several illegitimate children, and in time the prostitute deserted him for another man.

Finally, this former pastor did come back to the Lord, but he had been brought so low that despite his giftedness he could not hold a job. The last time I saw him, he was a haggard man weeping over his illegitimate children, wishing they would come to know the Lord. Finally, he went to his grave prematurely—a broken man, his life in shambles, and his family devastated.

We cannot thumb our noses at God's righteous principles and not expect to experience the just consequences of our actions. A reverential fear of God will help us avoid doing anything to hinder our relationship with Him. I live daily in reverential fear of God because when we disobey Him, we open the door to greater temptations. Sin grows until it totally engulfs us in destruction.

> WHEN WE DISOBEY GOD, WE OPEN THE DOOR TO GREATER TEMPTATIONS.

GOD WILL EXERCISE THE FINAL JUDGMENT

We need mention only two of God's judgments in the Old Testament—the flood in Noah's time and the destruction of Sodom and Gomorrah during Abraham's time—to recognize that many sinners receive God's judgments here on earth. For example, have you ever stopped to consider how many vicious dictators like Hitler, Mussolini, Stalin, and Ceausescu have met terrible ends?

God predicts judgment for the ungodly: "It is mine to avenge; I will repay. In due time their foot will slip; their day of disaster is near and their doom rushes upon them."[17] Yet many live as though they will never be judged. They scoff at the idea of an eternal hell.

The final judgment has, however, been part of the biblical message for thousands of years. The Holy Spirit inspired Paul to write this ominous warning:

> Because of your stubbornness and your unrepentant heart, you are storing up wrath against yourself for the day of God's

wrath, when His righteous judgment will be revealed. God "will give to each person according to what he has done." To those who by persistence in doing good seek glory, honor and immortality, He will give eternal life. But for those who are self-seeking and who reject the truth and follow evil, there will be wrath and anger.[18]

Those are hard words from a holy, just God. In Revelation, we have a visual description of that final Judgment Day of wrath:

Then I saw a great white throne and Him who was seated on it. Earth and sky fled from His presence, and there was no place for them. And I saw the dead, great and small, standing before the throne, and books were opened. Another book was opened, which is the book of life. The dead were judged according to what they had done as recorded in the books. The sea gave up the dead that were in it, and death and Hades gave up the dead that were in them, and each person was judged according to what he had done. Then death and Hades were thrown into the lake of fire. The lake of fire is the second death. If anyone's name was not found written in the book of life, he was thrown into the lake of fire.[19]

I never want to face that judgment seat! Thankfully, those of us who have trusted Christ will not appear before the Great White Throne judgment of sinners. But all believers will appear before Christ's judgment seat. This is a not a judgment of sin, but of how faithfully we have served our Savior with the opportunities and talents He gave us. Then, we will receive rewards for what we have done for Christ. In our next chapter, we will learn more about how God's justice works on the behalf of believers.

LIFE APPLICATION

EXALT YOUR GOD—Praise our just God with the words of Moses:

"Listen, O heavens, and I will speak! Hear, O earth, the words that I say! My teaching will fall on you like rain; my speech will settle like dew. My words will fall like rain on tender grass, like gentle showers on young plants.

I will proclaim the name of the LORD; how glorious is our God! He is the Rock; His work is perfect. Everything He does is just and fair. He is a faithful God who does no wrong; how just and upright He is!" (Deuteronomy 32:1–4)

REFLECT HIS IMAGE—The Lord spoke through Isaiah, saying, "I, the LORD, love justice" (Isaiah 61:8). God wants His children to mirror His nature through the power of His Holy Spirit. Search your heart by answering the following questions:

- Do you love justice?
- Does seeing injustice make you angry and/or sad?
- Do your actions line up with what you believe? What proof from your life experiences can you give to show that you truly love justice?
- Could those around you say that everything you do is just and fair? What recent actions can you recall that show how you will sacrifice convenience or something else to do what God deems just and fair?

SHARE HIS MAJESTY—Does a friend or family member need to be told that God is a God of justice? Think of someone who has been wronged and give them the comforting news that God is the perfect Judge. Lovingly warn someone who has not acted justly that God judges those who do wrong.

CHAPTER 19

GOD'S JUSTICE WORKS FOR OUR GOOD

D o you remember your years in junior high and high school? Every class seemed to have a student who was a prankster who deliberately violated school policy. When the teacher became aware of students' possessions disappearing, no one would confess or expose the guilty party. Then the teacher would announce, "No one is leaving this room until I find out who did this." Although you were an honest student, you sat with the rest of the class, twiddling your thumbs, and wondering, *Why can't I be excused? I've done nothing wrong and the teacher knows it. The teacher is not being fair!*

At every age, we recognize that many situations in life are not fair or just. If you have watched preschoolers play, you will soon hear, "That's not fair. I had it first." A high school student is killed in an accident caused by a drunk driver and the parents question, "Where's the justice? The drunk driver has barely a scratch, and our child is dead!" A pastor faithfully serving the Lord watches his wife, the mother of their three children, die of cancer. In his despair he wonders aloud about the justice of it all.

Yet the Bible is very clear in announcing that God is just. After leading the people of Israel for forty years in the wilderness, Moses publicly sang this song: "The Rock! His work is perfect, for all His ways are just; a God of faithfulness and without injustice."[1]

There is, however, not always a clear relationship between what we have done and what happens to us. Because questions about the justice of God plague us, let us consider practical implications of the statement, "Our God is just."

GOD'S PATIENCE TOWARD SINNERS

Justice delayed is often justice denied. If a defense lawyer can keep postponing a murder case, for example, evidence that is available in a speedy trial becomes useless. Witnesses may die or move away. The defense can challenge the validity of a witness's memory. Police departments misplace evidence.

What about justice for Christians? Sometimes they are unjustly targeted because of their faith. Nina Shea writes in *In the Lion's Den*, "Christians are the chief victims of this religious persecution around the world today."[2] Today 480 Christians will die or suffer brutality because of what they believe.

In Morocco, Rachid Cohen, a Jewish man who had received Christ as his Savior, was arrested and tortured for ten hours a day. He was burned with cigarettes, shocked in a low-voltage chair, and forced to sit in his own excrement. In China, persecutors beat, starve, and shock believers with electric probes. Thousands of stories of injustice toward believers have been documented.

Consider how God felt about the evil people living during the time of Noah. They all deserved the maximum punishment. If you had been God, how quickly would you have followed through on your threat to destroy the wicked? Would you have waited a week? A month? A year? More than five years?

Although the violation of God's justice had been described in detail, God did not act immediately. He invited Noah to build an ark to save himself, his family, and representatives of every animal group. Without modern tools, it took Noah 120 years to build that ark. Did the sin of the people decrease at all during that period of divine patience? No. Even after 120 years, only Noah and his family qualified to be rescued from the destructive flood.

So why did God not act immediately after declaring that He would destroy all humans except Noah and his family? Second Peter 3:9 says, "The Lord is not slow in keeping His promise, as some understand slowness. He is patient with you, not wanting anyone to perish, but everyone to come to repentance" (NIV).

All believers are saved because God delays His justice. At what age did you discover God's love and forgiveness? At 15 or 30 or 70? Whatever age you and I received God's promise of eternal life was more than enough time for God to have caused His wrath to fall on us. How many evil deeds had we committed before that day? How many people had we hurt? How many sins had we excused? None of us deserve even one day of life because of our sinful, depraved nature, so we must be grateful for a just God who delays punishment.

I am sure you have your own story of a friend or relative who received Christ late in life after years of self-centered living. One example is the famous skeptic Dr. Cyril E. M. Joad, who for years was head of the Philosophy Department at the University of London. Dr. Joad and his colleagues, Julian Huxley, Bertrand Russell, H. G. Wells, and Bernard Shaw, have probably done more to undermine the faith of the collegiate world of recent generations than any other group. Dr. Joad believed and taught that God was an impersonal part of the cosmos and that there is no such thing as sin.

> GOD'S DELAYED JUSTICE IS AN OPPORTUNITY FOR HIS MERCY TO BE SHOWN TO MANY.

Did God strike him dead? Did He send a crippling disease? No, but before he died, Dr. Joad became convinced that the only explanation for sin was found in the Word of God—and the only solution for sin was the cross of Jesus Christ. He became a zealous follower of the Lord Jesus. No doubt many of his followers turned to faith in God through his testimony and writings. God's long-suffering and incredible patience brought this skeptic to his knees at the cross. Truly, God's delayed justice is an opportunity for His mercy to be shown to many.

GOD IS AWARE OF INJUSTICE

In 1960, Raleigh Washington joined the army. He was quickly promoted from captain to major and then lieutenant colonel. He was well on his way to becoming a general when a group of white officers falsely accused Raleigh, who is black, of conduct unbecoming an officer.

Although none of the accusations were proven, he was given the choice of retirement in lieu of being discharged. But to get his retirement benefits, he had to admit that he was guilty. He refused. He was discharged one day short of twenty years of service, and therefore was disqualified from all of his retirement benefits. At the time, his wife was pregnant with their fifth child.

How would you have reacted? Since he had become a Christian two years earlier, Raleigh decided not to be bitter against the whites who had mistreated him. Instead, he applied to Trinity Divinity School to study to become a pastor. As a student, his income dropped by 90 percent. How he could have used that retirement income! But the Lord provided for the family's finances in exciting ways. When he graduated, the Evangelical Free Church recruited him to plant churches. Although he was their only black pastor, the white church members enthusiastically supported his church-planting efforts.

While he was planting his church, he met a Jewish lawyer named Jeff Strange, who learned about his military case. For the next nine years, Jeff worked to reverse the decision the army had made. Raleigh says, "Finally, I was reinstated for one day, so that I might retire. My retirement was made retroactive to 1980, and I received the accrued retirement benefits. In addition, they cleared my record and every document against me was destroyed. My military record was made immaculate.

"God uniquely sustained me and my wife and protected me from becoming bitter when falsely accused. Because I did not get bitter, God used whites to embrace my ministry, to support me, to befriend me. God used that time after my dismissal from the Army to teach my wife and me to walk by faith."[3]

We may encounter injustice in any place at any time. But God has His own way of righting wrongs. Even if someone deals with us unfairly, God is still in control. If you are the only Christian on a police force, in a fire station, or on a school faculty, you may be experiencing ribbing, even harassment for your faith. In fact, you may even be passed over for promotion because of your unwillingness to become part of the sinful activities of your culture. At one point the coach of the Toronto Maple Leaf hockey team made it very clear that he wanted no Christians on his team. He called them sissies. He traded the one Christian he had on the team, even though he was an excellent player. Where was the justice for this Christian player? Why did God not act?

That is a question only God can answer, but we do know that He is aware of every injustice. Within the scope of eternity, He makes everything right.

Through the prophets the Lord demonstrated His concern for those who were being mistreated, receiving abuse, and being denied opportunities to participate fully in the life of the community. For example, foreign armies oppressed the people of Israel and Judah. Instead of seeing rich and fertile fields, choice vineyards and pleasant gardens, God saw crops of injustice, bloodshed and oppression. He saw how the greedy landowners oppressed the poor. He saw the injustice in the courts, where the bribes of the affluent deprived the poor of justice. He knew of the murder of innocent people.[4]

Jesus told a story about a judge who was approached by a widow pleading, "Grant me justice against my adversary."[5] For some time this judge refused to respond to the widow. Finally she became so persistent that he said, "I will see that she gets justice, so that she won't eventually wear me out with her coming!"[6] Jesus relates this story to the suffering of the ones He loves: "Will not God bring about justice for His chosen ones, who cry out to Him day and night? Will He keep putting them off? I tell you, He will see that they get justice, and quickly."[7]

Sometimes we will see almost instant justice. On other occasions, we must wait. And at times we will not receive justice until after we join our heavenly Father in His home in heaven. But we can be assured that God sees it all—and that He cares about the mistreated even more than we do.

BLESSINGS AND JUDGMENT

When the Supreme Court was formed in the late 1700s, the first order of business was to fill in the details of the judiciary. After the lower federal courts were established and the new justices appointed, it was time to hear cases. The initial Court session began on February 1, 1790, in the Royal Exchange Building in the heart of what is now New York City's financial district. Robert Wagman writes, "When it became apparent that the five justices would have absolutely nothing to do, the session was adjourned after ten days."[8] On August 2, they met again, but once more they had nothing to do, so they adjourned for the year. It was not until February 1793 that the Court heard its first case.

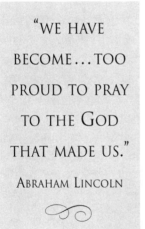

"WE HAVE BECOME...TOO PROUD TO PRAY TO THE GOD THAT MADE US."

ABRAHAM LINCOLN

Although the Supreme Court's jurisdiction was more narrow back then, can you imagine if today's Supreme Court adjourned early for a lack of cases to hear? Because of the tremendous number of cases presented to the Supreme Court today, it must limit itself to four cases per day. Each side gets one hour to present its arguments. The Justices hear cases two weeks, then recess for two weeks to allow them to write their opinions on these cases. The docket is always packed. Obviously, much has changed in two hundred years!

America has been greatly blessed because our ancestors acknowledged God's supreme sovereignty and their complete dependence on Him. They believed Psalm 33:12, "Blessed is the nation whose God is the LORD" (NIV). Christian values were cherished and laws were established that reflected biblical morality.

As we prospered we began to feel self-sufficient and to see our greatness as the product of our own abilities rather than the result of God's blessing. Abraham Lincoln said in 1863:

> We have been the recipients of the choicest bounties of Heaven; we have been preserved these many years in peace and prosperity; we have grown in numbers, wealth, and power as no other nation has ever grown. But we have forgotten God. We have vainly imagined in the deceitfulness of our hearts that all these blessings were produced by some superior wisdom and virtue of our own. Intoxicated with unbroken success, we have become too self-sufficient to feel the necessity of redeeming and preserving grace, too proud to pray to the God that made us.[9]

For the past several decades, our nation has taken drastic steps to divorce itself from God's standards of righteousness. What has been the result? Scholastic Aptitude Test (SAT) scores have dropped dramatically. Pregnancies, rapes, aggravated assaults, and murders have increased at an alarmingly epidemic rate among our teenagers. Suicide has become the second leading cause of death among adolescents. Gangs have turned many urban schools into war zones. The U.S. now leads the world in illegal drug use, exporting of pornography, divorce rates, abortion, and violent crime, and we lead the Western world in teenage pregnancies and illiteracy.

Thomas Jefferson wrote about the foolishness of abandoning God:

> God who gave us life gave us liberty. And can the liberties of a nation be thought secure when we have removed their only firm basis—a conviction in the minds of the people that these liberties are the gift of God? That they are not to be violated but with His wrath? Indeed, I tremble for my country when I reflect that God is just; that His justice cannot sleep forever.[10]

We are in danger of reaping God's judgment. If our country is lost, it is only because we as Christians have not obeyed our Lord's command to be salt and light to the people around us. You may be asking, "What can I do to help turn the tide of godlessness and immorality?" In 2 Chronicles 7:14, God's conditional promise begins with your willingness to humbly come before Him to admit your disobedience and indifference and seek His forgiveness. Then ask God to cleanse your heart from all wrongdoing. Pray that He will rekindle your first love for Him and once again send revival to your heart, your church and community, our nation, and our world.

CHRIST WILL JUDGE BELIEVERS

Our just God is not primarily concerned with punishing disobedience, but with rewarding right behavior. Yet God will reward only those who accept Christ's penalty for sin because His payment for our sins opened the way for God to reward us for what we do for Him.

Christ will evaluate each believer's life to determine rewards for faithful obedience and service or loss for disobedience. Paul explains, "We must all stand before Christ to be judged. We will each receive whatever we deserve for the good or evil we have done in our bodies."[11] Jesus will consider several factors when we appear before His judgment seat.

- He will judge the words we have spoken.[12]
- He will judge the deeds we have done.
- He will judge our motives.[13]
- He will judge our faithfulness.[14]

God will also reward those who bring others to faith in Christ. God told Daniel:

> Those who are wise will shine like the brightness of the heavens, and those who lead many to righteousness, like the stars for ever and ever.[15]

Every believer should desire to hear Jesus say these words: "Well done, good and faithful servant." Hebrews assures us, "God is not unjust; He will not forget your work and the love you have shown

Him as you have helped His people and continue to help them."[16]

Are you living for the glory of God or for self-satisfaction? There is an incredible reward awaiting the person who seeks to glorify God. Paul is so sure of this reward that he writes:

> Whatever you do, work at it with all your heart, as working for the Lord, not for men, since you know that you will receive an inheritance from the Lord as a reward. It is the Lord Christ you are serving.[17]

Do you trust God's perfect justice? It is undergirded by His holiness, truth, and righteousness and perfectly administered through His omniscience, omnipotence, and omnipresence. He is the Perfect Judge.

So far we have seen God's work as Creator and His position as Perfect Judge. But God also has another side to His character—gracious Savior. Think of holiness, truth, and righteousness as one side of a coin. What is on the other side? Love, mercy, and faithfulness. That does not mean that these qualities are the opposite of the former ones, but that one side of the coin needs the other to be complete. As we go on to the next section, "Our Gracious Savior," we will find more reasons to enjoy a lifelong, intimate relationship with our Creator and Perfect Judge.

LIFE APPLICATION

WRITE IT ON YOUR HEART—Memorize the following statement and verses. Then as you encounter situations during this week where you need to be reminded of God's justice, claim these promises by faith.

- Because God is just, I can be sure He will always treat me fairly.
- Jeremiah 17:10 (NIV)—"I the LORD search the heart and examine the mind, to reward a man according to his conduct, according to what his deeds deserve."
- Ecclesiastes 12:14 (NIV)—"God will bring every deed into judgment, including every hidden thing, whether it is good or evil."

COUNT ON GOD—Have you been wronged? Jeremiah 51:56 states, "The LORD is a God of retribution; He will repay in full" (NIV). Trust our perfect God of justice to judge your situations. Confide in Him about your anger and frustration regarding unfair treatment you've received. Then wait for Him to deal with the one who wronged you. No matter what happens, be fair and just to those around you.

OBEY GOD—The Word of God states in Galatians 6:7, "Do not be deceived: God cannot be mocked. A man reaps what he sows" (NIV). Are you sowing seeds of destruction, or seeds of mercy, justice, and goodness? Examine your motivations in the way you deal with difficult people. Which category do they fall into: destruction or mercy? Whatever you are sowing, you will reap. If you want to reap God's favor and blessings, obey His command to extend mercy.

PART III

OUR GRACIOUS SAVIOR

(Attributes of Relationship)

*There is only one God and one Mediator
who can reconcile God and people.
He is the man Christ Jesus.
He gave His life to purchase freedom for
everyone.*

1 TIMOTHY 2:5,6

CHAPTER 20

GOD
Is
LOVE

The plan seemed so wonderful at the time. More than 100,000 people would camp out in a pristine glade in upstate New York where everyone would get along and love each other. This meeting was part of a movement— one that its followers believed would change the world. The movement really began in 1967, which some called the "Summer of Love." Its members were called hippies. The slogan expressed noble ideals: love, not hate; peace, not war. One of its corner-stones was "free love." Hippies thought they could ignore God's standards, as well as thousands of years of social rules, and gratify themselves with free sex.

The Woodstock Festival in the summer of 1969 culminated this national "Love-In." Instead of the expected 100,000 hippies descending on a quiet countryside, 1.5 million long-haired young people wearing beads and feathers flooded the area for three days of music.

Was Woodstock really a place of peace and love? No. Peter Townsend, a member of the band "The Who" which played during Woodstock, said, "What was going on off the stage was just beyond comprehension—stretchers and dead bodies, and people throwing up, and people having [drug] trips…I thought the whole of America had gone mad."[1]

Tempers flared; people were assaulted; a concession stand was almost ripped apart; roads were clogged for a twenty-mile radius. Nudity, sex, and drug dealing were going on everywhere. One young man was crushed in his sleeping bag by a backhoe. And when the uncontrollable crowd went on their way, they left behind acres of trash.

What was supposed to be a monument to free love and brotherhood was actually a hedonistic mess resulting in total chaos. Selfishness and a disregard for others reigned. The "Summer of Love" had turned into a time of disaster and disappointment.

> GOD'S LOVE IS THE *WHY* OF CREATION, WHEREAS HIS POWER IS THE *HOW*.

Love is a universal need of all humanity. Everyone wants to be loved. But what is love? Tragically, our world understands very little about true love. We must turn to our Mighty Creator and Perfect Judge to understand what love is all about.

In Part I, we glimpsed God's abilities through His power and majesty as Creator. In Part II, God's integrity as Perfect Judge shines brightly. But these facets of God's character do not mean much if we do not understand His love, mercy, and faithfulness—revealed to us in His role as gracious Savior. God's love is not just words on a page, but was demonstrated in the deepest kind of sacrifice—Christ's death on the cross. In this section, we will conclude our discussion of God's attributes by seeing God as the gracious Savior who died for us.

GOD IS THE SOURCE OF ALL LOVE

In New Testament times, there were three primary words for love: *eros* (sensual love); *phileo* (brotherly love); and *agape* (unconditional, supernatural love). Our world speaks mainly of *eros* or *phileo* love, but God's love is *agape,* the purest, deepest kind of love.

Love is the supreme expression of God's personhood and flows out of His goodness. It affects all His other attributes. The Bible does not say, "God is holiness" or "God is power," but "God is love."[2] God's heart overflows with His supernatural and unconditional love for us. The psalmist proclaims, "The LORD is good. His unfailing love continues forever."[3]

People are sometimes willing to violate standards of honesty, righteousness, and morality to please others, but God never compromises His standards. His love is pure and holy; it does not suppress or negate any of His other attributes.

Many years ago I spoke on God's unconditional love at a missions conference for the famous Park Street Church in Boston. A missionary with whom I had attended seminary twenty years earlier approached me afterward. "I would never preach a sermon like that," he scolded. "I leave talking about God's love to the theological liberals. My message emphasizes faith."

This man had lost sight of one of God's greatest qualities. Paul writes: "We know how dearly God loves us, because He has given us the Holy Spirit to fill our hearts with His love."[4]

God's love is the only reason we exist. It is the *why* of creation, whereas His power is the *how.* Love demands an object; therefore we are created as the object of God's love. Love flows from Him as a pure river of grace and mercy without detracting in any way from His holiness and righteousness. Everywhere we look we see evidence of God's loving concern for our well-being. Love is our doorway to knowing God intimately.

God's love is expressed to all people, not just those who love Him. He loved us first before we loved Him—even when we were unlovable. That is hard for us to accept at times. Yet all people benefit from His loving care: "He has shown kindness by giving you rain from heaven and crops in their seasons; He provides you with plenty of food and fills your hearts with joy."[5] When the sun rises, its warm rays are an expression of God's love; when the rains come, they demonstrate God's love to all.

GOD'S LOVE IS BEYOND EXPLANATION

Dwight L. Moody, a famous pastor and evangelist at the turn of the 20th century, tells of an experience shortly after building Moody Church. The congregation wanted to emphasize the love of God so they put "God is love" over the pulpit in lights. Every night they lit the sign so passersby could see them through the windows. Moody reports:

> A man walking past there one night glanced in through the door and saw the text. He was a poor prodigal, and he kept going. And as he walked away, he said to himself, "God is love? No. God is not love. God does not love me. He does not love me, for I am a poor, miserable sinner. If God were love, He would love me. God is not love." Yet there the text was, burning down into his soul. He went on a little further, turned around and came back, and went into the meeting. He didn't hear what the sermon was, but the text got into his heart, and that is what we want.
>
> It is of very little account what men say if only God's Word gets into the heart. And he stayed after the meeting was over, and I found him there weeping like a child. But as I unfolded the Scripture and told him how God had loved him from his earliest childhood all along, the light of the gospel broke into his mind, and he went away rejoicing.[6]

Why would God stoop to love such unworthy people as we are? Our mortal minds cannot comprehend its vastness or its consistency. We will never be able to answer why, but we can believe it is true, causing us to love, appreciate, worship, and praise Him all the more in return.

GOD'S LOVE IS FREE

One night, I was speaking to several hundred men gathered in a skid row mission. To illustrate to these men the love and grace of God, I pulled a $10 bill from my pocket and said, "The first person who comes to take this from my hand can have it as a free gift." Out of the hundreds of people seated before me, not a single person moved.

Finally, a middle-aged man, shabbily dressed like the rest, stood timidly to his feet and asked, "Do you really mean it?"

I said, "Sure, come and get it; it is yours."

He almost ran to grasp it, then he thanked me. The rest of the crowd began mumbling, as if to say, "Why didn't I have the faith to go and accept the gift?"

This gave me a marvelous opportunity to emphasize that we do not earn God's love. God's love is a gift to all who will receive it by faith; He offers it to us freely. Nothing we do will make God love us any more; nothing we do will make Him love us any less. He loves us because He is gracious, not because of who we are, but because of who He is.

Usually, in our world, the rich, beautiful, talented, and intelligent receive the most attention and "love." But our social situation has no bearing on God's love for us. When Jesus entered Jericho, He had to pass by that greedy tax collector, Zacchaeus, who was shunned by everyone in town. Zacchaeus's spiritual hunger was so great that he climbed into a tree to see Jesus. When Jesus passed under the tree, He looked up and said, "Zacchaeus, come down immediately. I must stay at your house today."[7]

Zacchaeus did not need a second invitation. Scrambling out of the tree, he quickly welcomed Jesus into his home.

God's love reaches out to the most socially despised and brings them within the circle of His love. As in the case of Zacchaeus and the prodigal described by D. L. Moody, God's love frees a person from sin and despair—no matter who that person is.

GOD'S LOVE IS UNCHANGING AND EVERLASTING

Some of the most devastating words a child can hear from his parents are: "I won't love you if you do that." The hurt of conditional love is also contained in the words of the teenage boy who says to a girl, "If you won't have sex with me, you don't love me." She yields to his embraces in a desperate attempt to hold someone who loves her, but when he gets what he wants, he leaves her. That same hurt reverberates like the echo in a canyon when after many years of marriage one partner says, "I don't love you anymore because…"

God's sacrifice in planning for our salvation was set in motion in eternity past: "He chose us in Him before the creation of the world to be holy and blameless in His sight. In love He predestined us to be adopted as His sons through Jesus Christ."[8] There was never a moment when God did not purpose in His love to make the ultimate sacrifice for us. He planned to leave heaven's glory, beauty, and peace and take on the body of a man. You and I, who are not even worthy to call His name, are so loved that we were always on His mind!

Just before His betrayal, Jesus enjoyed the Passover meal with His disciples. They were about to experience incredible trauma when they saw their Master led away by soldiers, put on trial, and crucified. The Book of John explains Jesus' intentions during that Last Supper: "Jesus knew that the time had come for Him to leave this world and go to the Father. Having loved His own who were in the world, He now showed them the full extent of His love."[9]

> YOU AND I…
>
> ARE SO LOVED
>
> THAT WE WERE
>
> ALWAYS ON
>
> HIS MIND!

First Jesus had a meal of fellowship, then He washed the disciples' feet. As the Lord washed Peter's feet, Peter proclaimed, "I will lay down my life for you."

Jesus responded, "Will you really lay down your life for Me? I tell you the truth, before the rooster crows, you will disown Me three times!"[10]

That is exactly what Peter did. During Christ's darkest hours, Peter turned his back on his Lord.[11] Did Jesus reject Peter because of his betrayal? As the soldiers bound and dragged Jesus through the crowd, Jesus caught Peter's eye. His look seemed to say, "Peter, I know you feel badly for what you have done. Please know that I still love you."

When we receive Jesus as our Savior and Lord, God envelops and infuses us with His everlasting love.[12] We enter into a special eternal relationship with Him. John recognized this and exclaimed:

"How great is the love the Father has lavished on us, that we should be called children of God!"[13] This love will be with us for eternity.

GOD BLESSES US BECAUSE HE LOVES US

Recently in Milwaukee, Wisconsin, a homeowner was approached by a man who wanted to borrow his barbecue grill. Being good-hearted, he let the man take it. When the borrower returned it several days later, he offered the grill owner four tickets to a Milwaukee Brewers baseball game. The owner was delighted, and even though the Brewers lost the game that day, he and his family had a good time. When they returned home, they discovered that thieves had cleaned out their house of all furniture and appliances while they were gone. What had appeared like a magnanimous gift of tickets turned out to be a trick to get the family to leave so their house could be burglarized.

Sometimes, we find ourselves wondering when God's goodness to us will end and we will find the "bottom line." But we do not need to be suspicious about the good things God offers us. He will never misuse our love for Him.

Nothing we do will take away His love for us. Paul writes, "I am convinced that nothing can ever separate us from His love. Death can't, and life can't. The angels can't, and the demons can't. Our fears for today, our worries about tomorrow, and even the powers of hell can't keep God's love away. Whether we are high above the sky or in the deepest ocean, nothing in all creation will ever be able to separate us from the love of God that is revealed in Christ Jesus our Lord."[14] We need never fear that His blessings are a disguise for other intentions. All God's actions toward us flow out of His pure love for us.

GOD'S LOVE INVOLVES HIS BEST FOR US

When iron ore is dug out of a mountain, it is worth only a few dollars per ton. But when that same ore is placed in a Bessemer furnace and put under tremendous heat and pressure, it is changed into a high grade of surgical steel.

God uses adversity in our lives, not to destroy us, but to build our faith and to refine us into the kind of people He wants us to be. He cannot use self-centered weaklings. During those difficult times, God assures us that He will work for our good.[15] Only He knows the future and how things will turn out. Most of the time we selfishly ask for things that we want, but they are not necessarily the things that are good for us. I am so glad that God has not always answered my prayers and given me what I wanted. I am sure I would have made situations worse. I am going to trust God, His wisdom, and His plan for my life through my adversity.

Because He loves us, God has prepared an incredible future for us. First He gives us an abundant life on earth. This is not a temporary provision, nor is it available only when we feel holy enough to accept it.[16] In addition, God gives us a heavenly future with Christ.[17] That is the hope of the one loved by God!

The words of this grand old hymn express God's love so clearly:

> O the deep, deep love of Jesus,
> Vast, unmeasured, boundless, free!
> Rolling as a mighty ocean
> In its fullness over me;
> Underneath me, all around me,
> Is the current of Thy love;
> Leading onward, leading homeward,
> To my glorious rest above.[18]

We worship our loving God, not as a religious exercise or ritual, but with a sincere response to the love He has already shown for us! Where else will we find the love and acceptance we so desperately need? Certainly not in some unbiblical "Love-In" or an immoral relationship. Such love can come only from the tender heart of God.

Every day, praise Him for His unconditional, perfect love. Praise Him when you wake up in the morning, thank Him as you work, and tell Him how much you love Him before you go to sleep. Respond to His limitless, ever-present love to you by expressing your heart of love to Him.

LIFE APPLICATION

EXALT YOUR GOD—Dedicate yourself in worship to our loving God through the words of the hymn, *May the Mind of Christ, My Savior:*

> May the mind of Christ my Savior, live in me from day
>   to day,
> By His love and power controlling all I do and say.
> May the Word of God dwell richly in my heart from
>   hour to hour,
> So that all may see I triumph only through His power.
> May the love of Jesus fill me, as the waters fill the sea;
> Him exalting, self-abasing—This is victory.
> May His beauty rest upon me as I seek the lost to win,
> And may they forget the channel, seeing only Him.

Praise Him for the many ways He has displayed His love in your life.

REFLECT HIS IMAGE—To help you understand love, read 1 Corinthians 13 repeatedly in as many translations as are available to you. Let the words and message sink into your mind and soul. Insert your name in place of the word "love." By faith, ask God to develop these qualities in you.

SHARE HIS MAJESTY—Is there someone in your life who needs to know how much God loves him? Perhaps a parent, spouse, or friend has not shown a healthy love to them. First John 4:18 says, "Perfect love expels all fear." Tell that person that there is someone who loves perfectly and unselfishly—our loving Creator. Look for ways to demonstrate God's love to that person.

CHAPTER 21

GOD HELPS US SPREAD HIS LOVE

Our heavenly Father loves us, His children, in innumerable ways. Occasionally, we are able to witness a human love that is a reflection, small though it may be, of God's sacrificial and unconditional love for us.

On a cold Christmas Eve in 1952, when Korea was in the throes of civil war, one young woman struggled along a village street, obviously soon to deliver a child. She pleaded with passersby, "Help me! Please. My baby." No one paid any attention to her.

A middle-aged couple walked by. The wife pushed away the young mother and sneered, "Where's the father? Where's your American man now?" The couple laughed and went on.

The young woman almost doubled up from a contraction as she watched them go. "Please…," she begged.

She had heard of a missionary who lived in a neighboring village who might help her. Hurriedly, she began walking to that village. If only he would help her baby. Shivering and in pain, she struggled over the frozen countryside. But the night was so cold. Snow began to fall. Realizing that her time was near to deliver her baby, she took shelter under a bridge. There, alone, her baby was born on Christmas Eve.

Worried about her newborn son, she took off her own clothes, wrapped them around the baby, and held him close in the warm circle of her arms.

The next day, the missionary braved the new snow to deliver Christmas packages. The sun sparkled over the countryside. As he walked along, he heard the cry of a baby. He followed the sound to a bridge. Under it, he found a young mother frozen to death, still clutching her crying newborn son. The missionary tenderly lifted the baby out of her arms.

When the baby was ten years old, his now adoptive father told him the story of his mother's death on Christmas Eve. The young boy cried, realizing the sacrifice his mother had made for him.

The next morning, the missionary rose early to find the young boy's bed empty. Seeing a fresh set of small footprints in the snow outside, he bundled up warmly in a winter coat and followed the trail. It led back to the bridge where the young mother had died.

As the missionary approached the bridge, he stopped, stunned. Kneeling in the snow was his son, naked and shivering uncontrollably. His clothes lay beside him in a small pile. Moving closer, he heard the boy say through chattering teeth: "Mother, were you this cold for me?"

That story reminds me of another mother and Son who sacrificed so much. One winter night, Jesus left his home, His glory, and the warmth of heaven to be born in a stable to an unwelcome world. Just before He was born, Mary, His mother, was not welcome in any of the cozy inns in Bethlehem. Instead, she delivered her baby in the darkness of a cold stable. The Creator of the Universe, the Perfect Judge who could destroy the world with a single word, was willing to endure this inauspicious beginning for you and me. That is unconditional love!

We who have experienced God's unconditional love are commanded to share that love with others. But how does God express His supernatural love through us? John writes, "We know how much God loves us, and we have put our trust in Him. God is love, and all who live in love live in God, and God lives in them."[1]

The secret is letting God use us as His instruments to love others. We begin that process by loving God and serving Him wholeheartedly.

GOD WANTS US TO LOVE HIM WHOLEHEARTEDLY

Jesus declared, "'You must love the Lord your God with all your heart, all your soul, and all your mind.' This is the first and greatest commandment."[2] God, in His sovereignty, has created us so we find our greatest joy and fulfillment in loving Him.

One day when I was preparing a message, my young son Zac suddenly appeared with his stack of books and sat silently beside me. I was deeply moved to think that there were dozens of places in our home where he could have gone to read. I broke the silence: "Zac, I want you to know how much it means to me that you have come to sit with me."

My heart melted to hear my son say, "Dad, that's the reason I've come. I just want to be with you."

In the same way, the great heart of God longs for fellowship with us. With incredible blessings in hand, He waits for us to open our eyes and ears and reach out in faith to receive them. Oh, how He desires to walk and talk with us as He did with Adam and Eve in the Garden of Eden. I encourage you to pour out your heart to Him; tell Him of your hurts, fears, and hopes. Read His letters of love found in the Bible. Then come into His presence through praise and worship. As you linger in His presence, His Spirit will commune with your spirit to refresh your body, soul, mind, and emotions.

GOD WANTS US TO LOVE OUR NEIGHBORS

As our intimate relationship with God deepens, we become more like His Son, Jesus Christ. As a result, we are able to love others unconditionally as God loves us. John writes, "Dear friends, since God loved us that much, we surely ought to love each other."[3] God wants us to express His supernatural, *agape* love to others. We become examples of God's love to the world as we love our neighbors through the enabling of His Holy Spirit.

I am reminded of the story of the Navajo Indian woman who had been cured of a serious ailment by a missionary doctor. She was greatly impressed by the love he manifested. "If Jesus is anything like the doctor," she said, "I can trust Him forever."

That woman did not need anyone to explain God's love to her. She saw it in action through the doctor. God wants His people to be living examples of His love to others.

God Wants Us to Love Ourselves

One of the great preachers and Bible teachers of our time, Charles Stanley, delivered a message at one of our staff training sessions in which he revealed that he had grown up not knowing the love of a father. He had come to faith in Christ, gone to seminary, and built a large church. One day when he was feeling burned out and at the end of his rope, he invited some trusted men to join him for a time of reflection on his life. For several hours he told them his story, how unloved he had felt as a child, how even as an adult he was not experiencing the love of God.

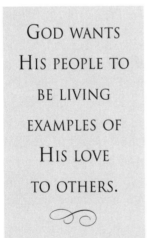

GOD WANTS HIS PEOPLE TO BE LIVING EXAMPLES OF HIS LOVE TO OTHERS.

Finally, one of the men asked him to rest his head on his folded arms on the table. "Imagine God putting His arms around you while you focus on the statement, 'God loves me.'"

As Stanley did so, tears began to flow. He felt overwhelmed by the love of his heavenly Father for the first time in his life. What had been an intellectual exercise of faith in the love of God had become very personal.

Jesus implied that we are to love ourselves when He said, "Love your neighbor as much as you love yourself."[4] You do not need to be brighter, thinner, prettier, or richer in God's eyes. These are the world's standards, not God's. He loves you and accepts you as you are. You have no reason to dislike yourself when your Creator demonstrated unconditional love by forgiving you and dying for you. You are complete; you have unfathomable value and dignity as a child of God!

GOD WANTS US TO LOVE OUR ENEMIES

Jesus taught His disciples, "Love your enemies and pray for those who persecute you."[5] That is difficult, if not impossible, without the ministry of the Holy Spirit in our lives.

One man who demonstrated God's love for his enemies is Richard Wurmbrand, a Romanian pastor who was imprisoned and tortured for his faith. He lost both parents, several sisters, a brother, and children during the Nazi Holocaust. During those terrible days, he was introduced to a Romanian soldier who boasted how he had killed Jews—even those who held little children in their arms.

This man did not realize that Wurmbrand was a Jew. Since Wurmbrand is a good German name and he was a Christian pastor, the soldier assumed that Richard was not Jewish. During the soldier's boasts of cruelty against Jews, Wurmbrand did not say a word. Instead, he invited the man to his home.

The soldier accepted the invitation. When they arrived, Wurmbrand explained that his wife was sick in bed. After conversing until late at night, the Romanian pastor said, "Sir, I have to tell you something. But promise me that you will listen to me ten minutes quietly. After ten minutes, you can say whatever you like." The soldier readily agreed.

Richard Wurmbrand then said, "In the other room, my wife is sleeping. She is Jewish, and I am Jewish too. Her family, which is also my family, perished in one of the big Nazi concentration camps. You boasted that you have killed in the same concentration camp where our family was sent. So you presumably are the very murderer of my family.

"Now I propose to you an experiment. We will go into the other room and will tell my wife who you are. I can assure you my wife will not say one word of reproach, will not look angrily at you, and will smile at you as at every guest. She will consider you an honored guest. Although she is sick, she will go and prepare for you coffee and some cookies. You will be received just like everybody else. If my wife, who is only human, can do this, if she can love you like this, knowing what you have done and can forgive you, then how much more will Jesus, who is love?"[6]

The tall German soldier tore at his jacket, crying, "What have I done, what have I done? I am guilty of so much blood." This man who had never heard a prayer before knelt with the pastor and asked God for forgiveness.

Then the two men came into the room where Mrs. Wurmbrand lay. She had heard nothing about what had happened in the next room, but when her husband woke her, she did exactly as he described she would. When she heard that the soldier had repented of his sins, she fell around his neck. They both wept. Pastor Wurmbrand writes of the scene, "It was a scene of love like in heaven. That is what Jesus can do. He is love."[7]

When Christians begin to love God, they will love their enemies. The world today, as in the first century, will marvel when they see our loving attitudes and actions, "How those Christians love one another."[8]

GOD'S LOVE IMPELS US TO TELL OTHERS

Have you ever been around a grandmother who has just returned from visiting her grandchildren? She is so in love with those grandchildren that she cannot stop talking about them. You had better be prepared to look at a stack of pictures.

Have you ever been around a new Christian who is so in love with Jesus that he cannot stop talking about our Savior? So what happens over time? All too often, like the church of Ephesus recorded in the Book of Revelation, many believers lose their first love and stop talking about the God who loved us so much that He gave His Son to die in their place on the cross.

The contrast between a new Christian and a "veteran" Christian is illustrated by the story of the young man who rushed back to his apartment one night after a Billy Graham meeting. He and his roommate had lived and worked together for several years. "I must tell you something," he said to his friend. "Tonight I invited

Christ to be my Savior, and He has changed my life!"

His friend smiled and said, "Wonderful! I have been a Christian for several years, all the time hoping that you would receive Christ as your Savior."

Surprised, the new Christian said, "Ever since I've known you, I have been trying to live up to your standards, but have failed miserably. Why didn't you tell me how I could know Christ?"

Paul writes, "Christ's love compels us, because we are convinced that one died for all, and therefore all died. And He died for all, that those who live should no longer live for themselves but for Him who died for them and was raised again."[9] When we genuinely realize how much God has sacrificed for us, our love for Him will stay warm and fruitful. We will not be able to keep the Good News to ourselves. God's love *is* the Good News we share with those who have no idea what it means to be loved by Christ.

Let us continually, day to day and moment to moment, drink deeply from the wellsprings of God's love. And after you are refreshed with that living water, pour some out onto dry, thirsty people around you. I assure you that seeing others respond to God's love and forgiveness will be one of the most joyful experiences you will ever have.

LOVING BY FAITH

My prayer for you is the same as Paul prayed for the believers in Ephesus: "May your roots go down deep into the soil of God's marvelous love. And may you have the power to understand, as all God's people should, how wide, how long, how high, and how deep His love really is."[10]

You may confess, "I don't have that kind of love to share with anyone." To experience and share God's supernatural love, claim it by faith.[11]

We have the potential to love anyone God puts in our path. One of the greatest lessons I have learned in my Christian life is "how to love by faith."[12] We may think we have lost our love for our spouse, for example. Yet when we *by faith* invite God's unconditional love for an "unlovable" spouse to flow through us, we will discover a rekindled love that is alive and well. That is true as well for an "unlovable" boss, associate, or employee. Nothing breaks up the hardened ground of unforgiveness and bitterness like sincere acts and words of love.

Sometimes you and I must take the first step of restoration, by faith in love. A positive response from others may not always be immediate, but keep on loving and reaching out. There is no power on earth stronger than supernatural love.

An attorney came to Arrowhead Springs one day to complain that he just could not get along with one of his partners. They hated each other, he reported. So I suggested he tell his partner that he loved him and ask him for forgiveness for not loving him.

> NOTHING BREAKS UP THE HARDENED GROUND OF UNFORGIVENESS LIKE LOVE.

"I could *never* do that," he protested. But after I explained the concept of how to love by faith, he agreed to approach his partner. He went into the office early the next morning and said to his partner: "Some time ago I became a Christian and my critical attitude toward you has changed. I've come to ask you to forgive me and to tell you that I love you."

His partner practically fell out of his chair because he was so amazed at the dramatically changed attitude of the man before him. He asked, "How can I have what you have?" The attorney led his partner to faith in Christ, and they became good friends. A few days later they came to tell me of the miracle of their reconciliation and of God's supernatural love.

Begin right now to love by faith. Make a list of everyone you do not like or have a hard time loving or those who have hurt you. Perhaps your list will include your boss, a coworker, your spouse, your children, a parent, a fellow believer, or a neighbor. Now ask the Holy Spirit to fill you with love for that person and claim by faith Christ's great love for them. Then the next time you meet them, by faith draw upon God's limitless, inexhaustible, overwhelming love for them. Through the enabling of the Holy Spirit, demonstrate your love by your actions.

Love, however, is incomplete alone; it requires action. Supporting God's great love is another of His attributes: His infinite mercy. In the next chapter, we will find out how His mercy complements His love to bring us a hope for the future and a security in His presence.

LIFE APPLICATION

WRITE IT ON YOUR HEART—Commit the following statement and verses to memory. Then as you encounter situations during this week where you need to remember that God loves you, claim these promises by faith.

- Because God is love, He is unconditionally committed to my well-being.

- 1 John 4:16—"We know how much God loves us, and we have put our trust in Him. God is love, and all who live in love live in God, and God lives in them."

- Romans 8:39—"Nothing in all creation will ever be able to separate us from the love of God that is revealed in Christ Jesus our Lord."

COUNT ON GOD—God gives a wonderful promise in Romans 8. As you read Romans 8:38,39, consider the struggles and worries in your life. Trust your compassionate God to lovingly sustain you no matter what your circumstance.

OBEY GOD—First John 4:10,11 says, "This is real love. It is not that we loved God, but that He loved us and sent His Son as a sacrifice to take away our sins. Dear friends, since God loved us that much, we surely ought to love each other." Is there someone in your life that you have difficulty loving? Do not wait until you "feel" like loving him. Love is much more than a feeling, and often we must first love them by faith. Begin by praying for that person. Then, actively reach out to them in a display of kindness. You will be surprised how quickly the "feeling" of love may follow. Obey God and determine to love even the "unlovable" today.

CHAPTER 22.

GOD

IS

MERCIFUL

❧

H eadlines in recent years have exclaimed: "Horrifying Earthquake Hits Japan," "Hurricane Mitch Is Most Devastating Storm on Record," "North Texas Hit By Severe Drought; Farmers Reeling."

Why are these things happening to good people? Of course, no one can read the mind of God to find out why He allows certain disasters to occur. However, these headlines also remind us of just how gracious God is to us. For the most part, the natural world around us functions according to an orderly plan. We realize that a fraction of change in our environment could destroy all life on Earth. If the distance between the Earth and sun was changed even slightly, our atmosphere would be too cold or too hot to sustain life. Without sufficient atmosphere around the Earth, harmful rays from outer space would kill us. But God sustains this planet on which we live in a marvelous fashion so that we enjoy night and day, summer and winter, rainy seasons and dry.

Jesus stated in the Sermon on the Mount, "[God] gives His sunlight to both the evil and the good, and He sends rain on the just and on the unjust, too."[1] God provides the necessities of life for every human born on this planet. Many times we take His mercy for granted—until we experience a devastating blizzard with the mercury plummeting, or when summer temperatures soar into the 100s for days on end. Then we complain about how bad things are.

Unfortunately, we rarely thank God for the thousands of days of beautiful sunshine. How often do we stop to be thankful that, year after year, the flowers bloom and our grocery store shelves are stocked with food grown in the farmers' fields? When was the last time you felt gratitude for your enjoyment of food, friendships, music, art, and so many other things?

When we think of these blessings, our thoughts eventually end up at the doorstep of mercy. God's mercy is an attribute that leads Him to show compassionate concern for His people and tenderhearted treatment of the needy.[2] Our merciful God always seeks the welfare, both temporal (life on earth) and eternal (life in heaven forever), of His children and those who have not yet accepted His love and forgiveness. Although many people show mercy to others, God is the grand master of mercy. His very nature desires to relieve us of the self-imposed misery and distress we experience because of our sin. Let me give you an allegory of a merciful judge that dramatically illustrates how amazing God's mercy is.

THE MERCIFUL JUDGE

The wretched, shackled prisoner trembled with fear as he stood before the imposing bench of the toughest, fairest judge in the district. "You have been found guilty," the judge solemnly announced. Courtroom observers held their breath, waiting for what they were sure was to come.

Without a doubt the man was guilty. The evidence was clear. The judge had no choice but to pronounce a death sentence. There were no appeals for the horrendous crime, no stays of execution allowed.

Suddenly to everyone's shock, the judge did something unprecedented in legal history. He said to the prisoner, "Justice must be served. You are guilty. You are totally unlovable. Nevertheless, I love you, in spite of yourself. And because of my love for you, I have decided to take your place. I will take your punishment for you. I will die in your place. You are a free man. You can go now." The judge's gavel pounded. The courtroom was silent.

After a stunned moment, courtroom guards unlocked the prisoner's handcuffs and legs irons, removed the judge's robe, and snapped the irons on his wrists and ankles. As the judge was led away to death row, the shocked prisoner numbly walked out of the courtroom door to freedom, tears of gratitude streaming down his cheeks.

This, of course, is an allegory about God's mercy. God is the judge. Since He is perfectly just, all His actions must serve the universal law of justice. We are like the prisoner. We all deserve the death sentence, because we are all guilty of numerous sins: "All have sinned and fall short of the glory of God."[3] In His fairness, God must judge our sin with the harshest punishment: "The wages of sin is death."[4] He cannot allow us to inhabit His perfect heaven, that place without a spot of uncleanness, a thought of wrongdoing, or a charge of guilt.

In the supreme act of mercy, God displayed divine favor and forbearance to us guilty offenders. He took our punishment upon Himself. That is what Jesus Christ did for us at Calvary: "The gift of God is eternal life in Christ Jesus our Lord."[5] By His sacrifice, all who put their trust in Him are declared "not guilty" and freed! That was true mercy and grace.

OUR GRACIOUS SAVIOR

The fact is that when we sin, we will never be excused from the penalty. As we saw earlier, because of God's holiness, sin must always be punished. All our claims that we were tricked into sin or that we did not know our action was sin gets us nowhere with God.

If that sounds cruel and unfair, here is the good news! Jesus provided a dramatic reprieve from our sentence and punishment. Jesus was beaten, tortured, and hung on a cross to die in our place to satisfy God's demand for justice. The Merciful Judge became Our Gracious Savior!

Peter explains, "[Jesus] bore our sins in His body on the tree, so that we might die to sins and live for righteousness; by His wounds you have been healed."[6] When Jesus came, His blood was spilled so we could experience God's mercy. Jesus' sacrifice is the ultimate expression of God's mercy.

Jesus Christ's sacrifice on the cross satisfied God's just nature. God, the divine Judge, showed mercy and clemency for us guilty sinners. It is the mercy of God that sees man weighed down by sin and therefore in a sorry and pitiful condition, needing divine help. At the cross, God's attributes of *both* justice and mercy found complete fulfillment—simultaneously! Is that not amazing?

GOD'S MERCY EXTENDS BEYOND OUR NEW BIRTH

God's mercy does not end with the forgiveness of our sins. As His children, He provides us an abundant life that is much more than we deserve or could ever expect. In His mercy, He provides what we need to begin growing in His Spirit. His mercy also gives us peace. He shows us compassion as we walk with Him day by day. And His mercy also means that He will discipline us as a father disciplines his child. Let us look at each of these aspects of God's mercy.

> AT THE CROSS, BOTH GOD'S JUSTICE AND MERCY FOUND COMPLETE FULFILLMENT.

First, God does not forgive our sins, then just send us our own way. He has a plan for our lives that will bring us to maturity in His grace.

Scott was a teenage gang member who lived in an eastern U.S. city. At 14 years old, he killed another gang member in a street fight. He was convicted and sent to a juvenile prison. While there, he attended a Bible study led by a Christian from the region. Based on the Scripture passages he was shown, Scott recognized that God's mercy extended even to him. Though feeling terribly unworthy, he received Christ as His Savior.

While in the juvenile prison, he met regularly for Bible study to grow in his new faith. He was still in his teens when he was released, but he did not want to go back to his inner city environment. Acting with the mercy of God, the Bible study leader took Scott into the home he and his wife had established as a discipling center for young men who showed genuine commitment to Jesus Christ while in prison.

Scott spent two years in the halfway house. He made such progress—completing his high school degree and growing as a Christian young man—that he was accepted as a student at a well-known Christian college. As a student, he began sharing the love and mercy of God with other young men incarcerated in the state juvenile detention centers. He wants to minister to inner city youth who are without hope because they do not know Christ.

Ephesians 2:4 describes God as being rich in mercy. Have you experienced this in your walk with God? He has an unlimited abundance of mercy, which originates in His being. He gives His abundance of mercy to us all the days of our lives—and for eternity.

God's Mercy Brings Us Peace

Some years ago, I was invited to speak to the inmates of one of the most infamous high-security prisons in America: the Federal Penitentiary in Atlanta, Georgia. When I arrived at the penitentiary's assembly room, several of the inmates rushed over to me, embraced me, and called me "brother." They told me they had heard my messages on tape, and had been introduced to Christ or discipled by my books. Before I spoke, several stood and gave testimony of how they had been forgiven by God through faith in Christ's death on the cross and His resurrection. One man spoke of how he had murdered five people. Another man confessed to killing three. Others had committed similar crimes. They told of how they came to the prison full of hate and fear—and then they met Jesus and were transformed.

Tears streamed down my face as I listened to these testimonies of God's forgiveness, mercy, and love. Again and again different prisoners said, "I'm glad I'm here. If I had not been sent to prison, I would not know Christ, and I would probably be dead because of my life of crime."

These prisoners—these men behind bars—had experienced the wonder of God's eternal pardon from their sins. They had received peace of heart and mind. They were experiencing purpose and meaning for their lives, even in their prison cells.

God's mercy enables us to break free from the habits of sin that have bound us. As a result, we can have peace, joy, fulfillment, and purpose. We will find the true meaning for living—serving God. We will find the true joy in life—serving others. We will find true peace and fulfillment—living in God's presence and will moment by moment.

GOD'S MERCY MEANS HE HAS COMPASSION FOR US

What astounds me as an imperfect human being is that God genuinely feels pity and compassion for us during our trials and difficulties. We have the assurance that "the LORD comforts His people and will have compassion on His afflicted ones."[7] Our loving Father does not just feel our pain, He wants to relieve our pain. He will if we will trust and obey Him.

The Gospels are filled with examples of how Jesus was moved with compassion to help those who were sick, suffering, and in need. The woman who had been ill with bleeding for many years was healed when she touched His garment. Jesus reached out His hands and healed the blind man, Bartimaeus, and the ten lepers. And the woman caught in adultery? He spoke compassionately to her and forgave her, saying, "Neither do I [condemn you]. Go and sin no more."[8] We can be sure that our merciful God is beside us through every trial we face and every pain we endure, and will help us live for His glory in every situation.

GOD'S MERCY IS EVIDENT IN HIS DISCIPLINE

If you are a parent, you know that your feelings of compassion and mercy toward your child will often be tested. At times you will have to exercise discipline. A child does not know he is loved unless his parents set up behavior boundaries and then enforce them in love and fairness.

When Vonette and I disciplined our sons, Zac and Brad, we did so in love. When one of our sons disobeyed us, we would first explain why we were punishing him, then we would follow through with the appropriate discipline. When it was all over, we would hug our son and emphasize that we disciplined him because we loved him.

One day Zac came home from kindergarten with a puzzled look on his face. With a serious tone of voice, he announced, "I don't think many of the children at school have parents who love them like you love me."

Mystified, Vonette asked, "Why do you say that, honey?"

"Because they are so disobedient," he said confidently. Zac had figured out that lovingkindness includes discipline.

The loved child understands when someone cares enough to take the time to correct wrong behavior. That is the way God is with us. When we become part of His family through our spiritual birth, He corrects and rebukes us for the things we do wrong.[9] As we listen to His Spirit and obey His Word, we become fulfilled, joyful members of His family.

GOD DISPLAYS HIS MERCY THROUGH US

The most exciting aspect of God's mercy is that we can be His example of mercy here on earth. Let me tell you a story about a beloved friend, a godly man whom I highly respect and admire.

Many years ago in Korea, Dr. Joon Gon Kim and his family were enjoying an evening together. Suddenly, an angry band of Communist guerrillas invaded their village, killing everyone in their path. In their trail of blood, the guerrillas left behind the dead bodies of Dr. Kim's wife and father. Dr. Kim was beaten and left for dead. In the cool rain of the night, he revived and fled for safety with his young daughter to the mountains. They were the sole survivors.

Can you imagine how we would feel if this happened to us? Since Dr. Kim is a man of God, he knew from Scripture that he must love his enemies and pray for those who persecute him. The Spirit of God impressed upon Dr. Kim to return to the village, seek out the Communist chief who led the guerrilla attack, and tell him that he loved him. Then he was to tell that man about God's love in Christ. Dr. Kim obeyed the impression God had given him. When he met the Communist chief, the man was dumbfounded because he had believed that the guerrillas had killed Dr. Kim. He knelt in prayer with Dr. Kim and committed his life to Christ. Within a short time, more Communists came to Christ, and Dr. Kim helped build a church for these and other Communist converts.

In 1958, Dr. Kim accepted the position as director of Korean Campus Crusade for Christ, our first international ministry. He is a living demonstration of God's mercy.[10]

As I walk in the Spirit and grow in appreciation for the mercy of God to me, I find that mercy overflows from my life into the lives of others. If I plant the seeds of God's mercy in the hearts and minds of others, they produce a harvest of love for God and repentance of sin.

GOD'S MERCY HAS AN END

Although God's mercy toward His own people extends throughout eternity, His mercy toward the unrepentant sinner does not last forever.

Before Alexander the Great would lay siege to a city, he would set up a light giving notice to those who lived within the city that if they came to him while that light was still burning, he would spare their lives. But once the light was out—no mercy was to be expected.

In very much the same way, God sets up light after light and waits year after year for sinners to come to Him so that they also may have eternal life. He does not want anyone to perish, so He is giving more time for everyone to repent.[11]

But be aware that a time is coming when there will be no more mercy. God does not want us to be destroyed by our sinfulness, so He offers us mercy, but we must be willing to accept it before we run out of time. Those who feel they can wait until later to receive God's offer of mercy can never be sure that they will have the time or opportunity to receive His mercy.

The time is so urgent to call people to repentance. We do not know who has a tomorrow, or whose hearts are soft toward God. Right now is the time to present them with God's message of mercy, to show them the mercy that God has liberally given us. As we approach a new millennium, we are reminded that our Lord Jesus may return at any moment. While we ourselves must be ready, we must warn those who have not heard of His gracious mercy or who have not heeded God's call.

In light of His mercy to us, our hearts should be filled with gratitude, praise, and worship. We should reach beyond our Christian circles of comfort and extend God's mercy to those who hate or ignore us. Author David Morris writes, "When Jesus came to earth, He changed seats with us and took on all our sin, rejection, and shame so we could see ourselves from His perspective."[12] We should never lose the awe and appreciation of what God has done for us. We once wore filthy garments stained by sin and corruption; now we are clothed in spotless robes of righteousness—all because of the mercy of God! That perspective will change the way we worship, reverence, and serve our God. We will see differently the need of the people to whom He is sending us.

> WE SHOULD NEVER LOSE THE AWE AND APPRECIATION OF WHAT GOD HAS DONE FOR US.

LIFE APPLICATION

EXALT YOUR GOD—Meditate on the following verses and praise God for the specific ways He has demonstrated mercy in your life.

To you, O LORD, I lift up my soul; in You I trust, O my God…No one whose hope is in You will ever be put to shame…Show me Your ways, O LORD, teach me Your paths; guide me in Your truth and teach me, for You are God my Savior, and my hope is in You all day long. Remember, O LORD, Your great mercy and love, for they are from of old. Remember not the sins of my youth and my rebellious ways; according to Your love remember me, for You are good, O LORD (Psalm 25:1–7, NIV).

God is so rich in mercy, and He loved us so very much, that even while we were dead because of our sins, He gave us life when He raised Christ from the dead (Ephesians 2:4).

Where is another God like You, who pardons the sins of …His people? You cannot stay angry with Your people forever, because You delight in showing mercy (Micah 7:18).

REFLECT HIS IMAGE—The Word of God states in Micah 6:8, "O people, the LORD has already told you what is good, and this is what He requires: to do what is right, to love mercy, and to walk humbly with your God." Do you love mercy? Are you quick to forgive? Spend some time with your compassionate God and ask Him to mold you into His image to become a lover of mercy.

SHARE HIS MAJESTY—Do you have a friend who needs to hear about God's mercy? If he does not know Jesus, share with him Appendix A, "How to Know God Personally." If he is a believer, remind him that his heavenly Father is "full of compassion and mercy" (James 5:11, NIV).

CHAPTER 23

GOD EXPECTS US TO EXTEND MERCY

Think of God's offer of mercy as a banquet to which you are invited. The table is filled with the most luscious foods: spicy appetizers, gourmet entrées steaming on heated plates, a vast array of juicy fruits, iced deserts, and cool, sweet drinks. The table is so large that it has enough room for more than the few who have come. But strangely enough, outside the door to the banquet hall stands a crowd who will not enter. They cry out, "I'm so hungry, so hungry!" You can almost hear their starved stomachs rumbling from lack of food. Yet for some reason, they will not step through the door and help themselves to the free banquet provided for them. A. W. Tozer gives this analogy when he writes:

> We may plead for mercy for a lifetime in unbelief, and at the end of our days be still no more than sadly hopeful that we shall somewhere, sometime, receive it. This is to starve to death just outside the banquet hall in which we have been warmly invited. Or we may, if we will, lay hold on the mercy of God by faith, not allow skepticism and unbelief to keep us from the feast of delicious foods prepared for us.[1]

God extended His mercy to us even before we were born, and before we acknowledged our need for His forgiveness. Without our Lord's sacrifice on the cross, we could not have a relationship with God. Now, because of Christ's willingness to die in our place, we can have a deep intimacy with the God who loves us unconditionally.

THE MERCIFUL EXTEND MERCY

One day Peter asked Jesus how many times he had to forgive someone. Peter thought that forgiving seven times was pretty good. "No!" Jesus replied, "seventy times seven!"[2] Then Jesus gave an illustration showing how God looks on our responsibility to forgive:

One day, a king was going over his accounts, settling old debts. He saw that one of his servants owed him millions of dollars. The king ordered the servant brought before him. When he arrived, the king demanded that the servant pay every penny. But the amount was beyond the servant's ability to pay. The king ordered the man and his family sold into slavery to pay the debt. The servant fell before the king and pleaded for mercy. The king felt pity and forgave him this tremendous debt.

That is such a wonderful picture of God's mercy. We are like the servant who could not pay the debt. But God, in His mercy, took pity on us and erased our sin debt completely.

But what did this servant do? He found a fellow servant who owed him a few thousand dollars and demanded payment. Just imagine. He came from the throne room where he had been extended so much mercy and grabbed his friend by the throat and demanded payment! The friend begged for mercy. But the servant would not forgive him and had him thrown into prison.

When the other servants saw the injustice, they went to the king and reported what had happened. The king was angry! He called in the servant and demanded to know why the man had acted so harshly toward his friend when he himself had been forgiven so much. Then the king commanded the servant be thrown into prison until he had paid every penny.

God gave His only Son to die in our place. That is mercy beyond comprehension, beyond description. How, then, can we ever refuse to give mercy to others when we have received so much mercy ourselves? What others may have done to you does not compare with what God has forgiven you. That is why God expects us to have mercy on others. To the degree that we show mercy to the poor, the wretched, and the guilty, we are like God. The lesson is clear: the merciful shall obtain mercy. And who among us is not a candidate for more of God's mercy?

OUR NEED FOR MERCY HELPS US SERVE OTHERS

Just like the unforgiving servant, sometimes the hardest place to extend mercy is the area where God has given us the most mercy —our area of weakness.

Ed DeWeese came home one afternoon to find that thieves had gone through his home. The TV, stereo equipment, and jewelry were missing—about $3,000 worth. He called his wife, Beth, at work and she rushed home. The police arrived and took a report. Because the DeWeeses had just moved in, they had not taken out homeowner's insurance. After the policemen left, they prayed, "Lord, we have no insurance and cannot afford to replace these things. Please return them to us."

That is when Ed's situation really hit him. He was an ex-offender. He had gone to jail for embezzlement—sophisticated burglary. He said to Beth, "We must first forgive."

After the thief had been arrested and released on bond, Ed asked a police officer to take him to the offender's home. When Ed met the man who had robbed him, he said, "I'm the man you ripped off. But brother, I forgive you in the name of Jesus."

Ed continued to visit the thief and gave a Bible to his little brother who had assisted in the crime. Soon, the robber told the police where the stolen things were hidden, and the officers recovered the DeWeeses's belongings. When the young man pleaded guilty to burglary, Ed testified in his behalf. He then helped the young man find a job. And Ed says, "Best of all, he and his brother did receive Christ as Savior."[3]

Our past failures can make us more sensitive to those who need mercy in the very areas in which we once needed mercy. We can minister to others in a more meaningful way because we understand and have experienced the reality of God's mercy in our area of weakness.

MERCY MEANS LETTING GO OF OLD HURTS

Corrie ten Boom encountered a situation in which her willingness to forgive was challenged. During those horrible days in 1944 in the Ravensbruck concentration camp, grim guards in blue uniforms and caps bearing the Nazi swastika stood in a line with leather crops swinging from their belts. The emaciated women dressed in prison garb worked long hours every day under the watchful eye of these guards. Corrie's sister, Betsie, died in Ravensbruck, a victim of the tortuous conditions.

In 1947, after the war, Corrie spoke to a group of Germans in a sparsely furnished Munich church basement. Her mission was to help those who were ravaged by the war. During her talk, she said, "I have a home in Holland for victims of the war. Those who have been able to forgive their former enemies have been able to rebuild their lives, no matter what the physical scars. Those, however, who have nursed their bitterness remain invalids. We, as Christians, have every reason to forgive each other, for our God richly lavishes His mercy on us—if we only ask Him."

> NO SIN IS TOO BIG TO BE THROWN INTO HIS OCEAN OF FORGIVENESS.

When she finished her talk, she was approached by a balding, heavyset man in a gray overcoat, a brown felt hat clutched between his nervous hands. Horror filled her as she realized he had been one of those guards who had abused Betsie in the camp. His name was Joseph.

Joseph thrust out his hand. "A fine message, Fraulein! How good it is to know that, as you say, all our sins are at the bottom of the sea!"

Dumbfounded, Corrie did not take his hand.

He went on, "You mentioned Ravensbruck in your talk. I was a guard there. But since that time, I have become a Christian. I know that God has forgiven me for the cruel things I did there, but I would like to hear it from your lips as well. Fraulein, will you forgive me?"

Corrie remembered how he had pushed Betsie with the butt of his gun. Corrie looked down at his outstretched hand. She whispered to herself, "Jesus, help me." Her hand slowly moved toward his. Their hands touched and she finally vigorously shook his hand. With tears in her eyes, she said, "I forgive you, brother …with all my heart."

God loves us no matter what we have done. He forgives us when we ask Him. No sin is too big to be thrown into His ocean of forgiveness. Since God richly lavishes His mercy on us, we must show mercy to one another. And that means letting go of all those old hurts caused by others.

EXTENDING MERCY HAS A COST

Often the most difficult place to show mercy is in close relationships—our family and friends. A middle-aged man sat in the pastor's office, nervously wiping perspiration from his brow with the back of his hand. "There is absolutely no way I can tell this to my wife," he said. "She would be devastated. She would never forgive me. I just cannot tell her. But I want forgiveness. I need relief from all this guilt."

In this family's case, the wife's career had soared with success, while the husband's work had plateaued. She traveled on extended business trips, gaining all kinds of recognition and earning a big salary. Meanwhile, the husband was at home keeping the family fed and attending to household chores. In a weak moment when loneliness drove his attention elsewhere, his wife's best friend began to meet his sexual and emotional needs. He was caught in an ugly trap of betrayal, with seemingly no way out.

After counseling with the pastor, the husband went home and confessed his sin to his wife. He told her exactly what had happened and why. He admitted he was very wrong and assured her that his adulterous relationship with her friend was over. Much to his surprise, she forgave him, and they started all over again. This act of mercy came at no small cost to this rejected wife, but it led to the restoration of the relationship they once had.

God will reward us when we show mercy. One of mercy's rewards is the intimacy we enjoy in our human relationships. Another reward is the intimacy we experience in our relationship with our Lord. Since mercy is of the highest priority to God, when we are merciful, we become instruments of blessing and enjoy communication with God.[4]

God's Mercy Helps Us in Our Failures

If you ask Steve about God's mercy, he can tell you that it is bottomless. He worked hard in his local church, raising four children with a wife he loved dearly. Yet he was not walking in God's Spirit. He began to have a problem—greed. Little by little, he began taking money from his job. In time, his $100,000 embezzlement was discovered, and he was taken to court. Still, Steve was not truly repentant. He did not realize his great need for God's mercy and help.

Because this was his first offense, the judge was lenient. Steve received a work-program sentence in which he had to spend his weekends doing community service. He was assigned to the sheriff's department. At first he did simple jobs like washing police cruisers, but soon police officials began trusting him with greater responsibilities. Eventually, they put him in charge of handling sales of items such as pepper spray. Over the next year, Steve began embezzling money from the sheriff's department until he had taken more than $20,000!

As you might guess, he was caught once again. But this time, the court did not have mercy on him, and he was sentenced to several years in prison. Because of a paperwork mix-up, he was sent to the state penitentiary for violent criminals. Suddenly, Steve's world collapsed. His wife divorced him and he was not able to see his children. Sitting in that prison cell surrounded by men for whom violence was a way of life, he decided to commit suicide. His birthday was coming up, and he felt as if his life was over.

His three daughters sent him a birthday letter in which they said, "Dad, all we ever wanted was you. We didn't want the money." Their words pierced Steve to his very soul. At that moment, he threw himself upon God's mercy—including his greed and his pride.

When Steve was paroled, he began rebuilding his life. At first, he felt so unworthy that he did not think he could ever serve God again. But little by little, God began to restore him and heal his hurt. Three years after his release, Steve felt God nudging him to work in the singles' ministry in his church. He approached the singles' pastor, his conviction papers in hand. "I want to be honest with you, Pastor Ron. I am a convicted felon. But if you could find any place for me to serve God, that's what I want to do."

After learning about Steve's past failures, Ron smiled and said, "Of course, we have a place for you to serve. We just won't put you in charge of any finances."

Since then, Steve has humbly served God in evangelism and church leadership ministry. In His mercy, God restored Steve gently and lovingly. He will do the same for you when you come before Him in humility. God wants us to be bold in asking Him for mercy when we need it.[5] If we are in distress, guilt-ridden, persecuted, lonely, facing disaster, experiencing the contempt of others, struggling with our weakness, or undergoing some other difficulty, God wants us to come humbly to Him in prayer seeking His help.

Remember, people all around you need to be pointed to the mercy of God. Their hearts ache for that unconditional love and complete forgiveness. As ambassadors of Christ, we know the comfort of God's mercy and can show others how to receive this unlimited gift.

GOD'S MERCY DOES NOT ELIMINATE ALL CONSEQUENCES

Isn't it wonderful to celebrate the mercy God has given us? At the same time, God will not remove all the consequences of our actions just because He is merciful. In Steve's case, his sin of embez-zlement still cost him his marriage. The pain for his children was real. If he could go back and do it all over again, he would rather rely on God's strength to keep him from sin and not on God's mercy to rescue him from his wrongdoing.

When David and Bathsheba committed adultery, God forgave David after he confessed his sin. Nathan the prophet says about David's forgiveness, "The LORD has forgiven you, and you won't die for this sin. But you have given the enemies of the LORD great opportunity to despise and blaspheme Him, so your child will die."[6] But David was also restored. Later, God allowed David and Bathsheba to have another child. That child became the wisest man who ever lived: King Solomon.

God does not forgive halfway. He cleared the sin-debt against David. But God, in His wisdom, knows that if we never suffer consequences for our actions, we will not learn our lesson com-pletely. What would unbelievers think if believers got away with all kinds of misbehavior with no consequences? What would the world say about us? That we serve God because He makes every-thing easy for us? Instead, our consequences can be a way to glor-ify God.

EXTENDING MERCY IS NOT BEING TOLERANT

People today, even many Christians, are more concerned about a need for *tolerance* than a need for *mercy*. There is a great differ-ence! Josh McDowell, a fellow Crusade staff member and founder of the "Right from Wrong" campaign, says that tolerance and Christian love cannot coexist. Similarly, tolerance and mercy can-not coexist. The Word of God exhorts Christians to speak the truth in love.[7] Mercy rooted in love demands that a person be told if he is doing something self-destructive or harmful to others.

The problem we encounter in separating mercy and tolerance is that we live in an age where the majority of our society does not accept the idea of absolute truth. The Biblical concept of sin has been replaced by a demand for tolerance of any activity. Consequently, tolerance has replaced mercy, especially in government, schools, colleges, industry, and the media. Tolerance is demanded for almost every bizarre and perverted belief and behavior.

When tolerance reigns and absolutes are eliminated, when diversity becomes the catch-all phrase for accepting even gross sinful behavior, then people feel no need for the mercy of God. Instead, many rationalize their behavior with excuses like these:

"Even if I am unfaithful to my wife, I'm sure God will understand. After all, He knows I have needs that are not being met."

"Remember, this is my first time with drugs. I am basically a good man who looks after my wife and kids, and I know God will recognize that."

What has happened? We have tried to reduce God to our size, to our standards, and to what we feel He ought to be like. This makes us feel comfortable. Too often we want *Him* to respond like *we* would respond to sin and injustice. We want *Him* to accept *us* on our standards of behavior. Since we are tolerant and non-judgmental with other's sins, we want everyone including God to be tolerant with ours. In this way, we do not have to change our ways or feel guilty about them. "Live and let live" is the world's philosophy, but it is not God's.

God set the example. He extends mercy and maintains His standards perfectly. He made the dearest sacrifice for our forgiveness; yet He judges and disciplines people for their sin. He loves unconditionally; yet He completely understands our weaknesses and failings. That is what mercy is all about. It is not sweeping bad things under the rug (like tolerance) and looking only at the good side. Mercy sees the whole picture, maintains right from wrong, and loves with the whole heart.

Can you do that? None of us can without the help of the Holy Spirit. Through Him, we can extend strong mercy without compromising with an attitude of unbiblical tolerance toward sin. Tolerance toward wrong behavior is not love; mercy is the loving response. Let us then follow Christ's example as we receive mercy from God and in return extend mercy to all we meet.

LIFE APPLICATION

WRITE IT ON YOUR HEART—Memorize the following statement and verses. Then as you encounter situations during this week where you need God's mercy, claim these promises by faith.

- Because God is merciful, He forgives me of my sins when I sincerely confess them.
- Daniel 9:9—"The Lord our God is merciful and forgiving, even though we have rebelled against Him" (NIV).
- Hebrews 4:16—"Let us come boldly to the throne of our gracious God. There we will receive His mercy, and we will find grace to help us when we need it."

COUNT ON GOD—Are you, or is someone close to you, in desperate need of God's mercy? No matter what you have done—large or small—God's mercy is sufficient. Go to Him and repent. Confess your sin, turn from it, and open your heart to His love and forgiveness. Your God of mercy will heal and restore you.

OBEY GOD—Are you harboring resentment against someone? Did someone wrong you and now you are having difficulty forgiving him? Read over the parable of the ungrateful servant in your Bible (Matthew 18). God has forgiven every sin you ever committed and any sin you will commit in the future. God has bountifully bestowed mercy on you. How ungrateful not to forgive someone who has wronged you! Obey God and go to that person today. Forgive him and experience the joy of showing mercy.

CHAPTER 24

GOD

Is

FAITHFUL

One day in Armenia in 1988, Samuel and Danielle sent their young son, Armand, off to school. Samuel squatted before his son and looked him in the eye. "Have a good day at school, and remember, no matter what, I'll always be there for you." He hugged his young son, and the boy ran off to school.

Hours later, a powerful earthquake rocked the area. Buildings crumbled; electrical power went out everywhere; people panicked. In the midst of the pandemonium, Samuel and Danielle tried to discover what happened to their son. As the day wore on, the radio announced that casualty estimates were in the thousands. People were trapped under beams and rubble in flattened buildings—even schools were destroyed.

Kissing his wife, Samuel grabbed his coat and headed for the school yard. When he reached the area, what he saw brought tears to his eyes. Armand's school was a pile of debris. Other grief-stricken parents stood nearby, weeping.

Samuel found the place where Armand's classroom used to be and began pulling a broken beam off the pile of rubble. He picked up a rock and put it to the side, then another, and another.

One of the parents looking on asked, "What are you doing?"

"Digging for my son," Samuel answered.

The man exclaimed, "You're just going to make things worse! This building is unstable," and tried to pull Samuel away from his work.

Samuel just asked, "Are you going to help me?"

The man's wife shook her head sadly, "They're dead. It's no use."

Samuel set his jaw and continued digging. As time wore on, one by one, the other parents left. Concerned, a firefighter tried to pull Samuel away from the rubble. "What are you doing?" he asked.

"Digging for my son," was the reply.

"Fires are breaking out. You're in danger. We'll take care of it."

"Will you help me?" Samuel asked without stopping his work.

The firefighter instead hurried off to a more pressing emergency, leaving Samuel still digging.

All through the night and into the next day, Samuel continued digging, his hole growing larger. Parents placed flowers and pictures of their children on the ruins. Soon, a row of photos of young, happy faces smiled up from the rubble. But Samuel just squared his shoulders and snatched up a beam. Wedging it under a stubborn boulder, he tried to pry it out of the way. Finally, the boulder gave.

A faint "Help!" came from under the rubble. Samuel stopped his work and listened. He could hear nothing. He kept digging.

The faint voice came again. "Papa?"

Samuel recognized the voice! "Armand!" He began to dig furiously. Finally, he could see his young son. "Come out, son!" he said with relief.

"No," Armand said. "Let the other kids out first, 'cause I know you'll get me."

Child after child emerged until, finally, a sputtering Armand appeared. Samuel took him in his arms.

"I told the other kids not to worry," Armand said confidently. "I told them that if you were alive, you'd save me and when you saved me, they'd be saved. You promised you'd always be there for me."

Fourteen children were saved that day because one father was faithful.[1]

How much more faithful is our heavenly Father! Whether trapped by fallen debris in an earthquake or trapped by life's hardships and struggles, we are never cut off from His love for us. As Jeremiah writes, "Because of the LORD'S great love we are not consumed, for His compassions never fail. They are new every morning; great is Your faithfulness."[2]

THE ANCIENT PATRIARCHS TRUSTED GOD'S FAITHFULNESS

We commonly speak of *faithfulness* as loyal, conscientious, or true in affection or allegiance. But as you look deeper at this word, you see the root word in faithfulness is "faith." Spiritually, the word means being full of faith. Hebrews 11 defines what God means by faith: "It is the confident assurance that what we hope for is going to happen. It is the evidence of things we cannot yet see."[3] If you read this entire chapter in Hebrews, you will see a thread running through it: "By faith." Hebrews lists great deeds of faith by the ancient patriarchs.

Hebrews 11:7 mentions Noah, who "built an ark to save his family from the flood. He obeyed God, who warned him about something that had never happened before." Abraham is sometimes called the "father of the faith." Hebrews says, "It was by faith that Sarah together with Abraham was able to have a child, even though they were too old and Sarah was barren. Abraham believed that God would keep his promise."[4] Abraham believed that God would keep His commitment to provide an heir because *he considered God faithful.* In time, God did send a son, Isaac, to Abraham and Sarah. Isaac became the physical link to the Messiah, Jesus Christ.

The most serious challenge to Abraham's trust came when God asked him to sacrifice his own son. Strengthened by his experience with God's faithfulness to His promises, Abraham bound Isaac and placed him on an altar, lifting the knife to sacrifice his son to God. Abraham believed that when God said that He would provide a physical line through Isaac, God would fulfill that promise—even if it meant raising Isaac from the dead. That is when the faithful God provided the ram in the thicket as a substitute for Isaac.[5]

Isaac blessed Jacob because he believed that God would be faithful to the promise He made to Abraham that his offspring would be as numerous as the stars in the sky or the sand on the seashore. The parents of Moses hid him for three months after he was born because they were not afraid of the edict of the Pharaoh. They knew God had a special purpose for their son.

In the experience of the patriarchs, God did not exist in a vacuum. He was working in their behalf at each step of life's journey. Their faith flowered into heroic deeds because they trusted in an absolutely faithful God. Their God was faithful down to the smallest detail.

God's Faithfulness to Us

All of us understand a little bit of how an automobile engine functions. Pistons, fan belts, water pumps, and thousands of moving parts all whirl around within a small space, making power for us to drive our car. Each piece in the motor has a different part to play in helping the engine function as it should. If one piece gets even a fraction of an inch out of line, the engine malfunctions. At the same time, oil and coolant circulate to keep the engine running smoothly. The parts all work together harmoniously as part of the whole engine.

That is the way God's attributes function too. If you took away love, God's character would not be complete. God's love works with all other attributes, like His justice, to produce the right kind of results. We can compare God's faithfulness to the oil in the engine that keeps the internal parts running smoothly. God's faithfulness means that each attribute in His character is working at full capacity at all times. When does God's love fail? Never, because He is faithful. When is God less than holy? Never, because His character is pure and He is always faithful to who He is and what He says. Therefore, you can count on Him to keep His promises and carry out His purposes.

In fact, God's faithfulness is at the core of God's nature. He is always all-knowing, all-powerful, ever-present, holy, righteous, merciful, and loving because He is faithful to His own character. He never changes any of His attributes to accommodate someone else's wishes. Paul drew on that knowledge when he wrote to the Thessalonians that they could depend on God because "the one who calls you is faithful and He will do it."[6] The psalmist writes, "Your faithfulness continues through all generations; you established the earth, and it endures."[7]

So when you get up in the morning and the sun is shining, thank God for His faithfulness. When you look outside and find it raining, thank God for His faithfulness in watering the earth and all the plants on it. If as evening approaches lightning flashes and a thunderstorm roars, thank God for His faithfulness in producing valuable nitrogen to renew the plants and trees. Truly, God's faithfulness is new every morning and refreshes us every night.

> TRULY, GOD'S FAITHFULNESS IS NEW EVERY MORNING AND REFRESHES US EVERY NIGHT.

One experience I recall about God's faithfulness began in the early 1970s. God impressed upon me that Campus Crusade for Christ should start a university to train hundreds of thousands of Christian leaders. Specifically, I understood God to say *go purchase 5,000 acres for this school and endowment residencies.* Due to legal and zoning complications, the dream never came to reality. From a human perspective, the setback did not make sense to me, but I continued to trust God. Now, more than 25 years later, God is helping us to start the International Leadership University with extensive worldwide outreach and impact. God has been so faithful to Campus Crusade for Christ and to me.

GOD'S FAITHFULNESS IS NOT CHANGED BY MAN'S RESPONSE

We tend to put conditions on our relationships. "If you look good,

I will love you." "If you have lots of money, you can be part of my inner circle." "If you do this for me, I'll do that for you."

God's faithfulness, however, is unconditional. We can sometimes see that quality reflected in the godly examples of faithfulness among His people. Let me give you an example.

Dr. Robertson McQuilkin was the well-loved president of the highly respected Columbia International University. When his wife began to show symptoms of Alzheimer's disease, Dr. McQuilkin resigned his distinguished position to care for her. Hearing of someone who is faithful to another, like Dr. McQuilkin, lifts our spirits because this kind of sacrifice is so rare. We realize that actions like these are not normal to our human nature, but that they must come from a higher source.

God's faithfulness is so much a part of who He is that He cannot become unfaithful to anyone—whether to grateful believers or to skeptics who doubt the reality of God—despite the cost. Paul assures us, "If we are faithless, He will remain faithful, for He cannot disown Himself."[8]

God also is faithful to us when we feel we have no faith left in us. Paul writes: "What if some did not have faith? Will their lack of faith nullify God's faithfulness? Not at all! Let God be true, and every man a liar."[9] God's faithfulness is not affected by anyone's lack of faith.

GOD KEEPS HIS PROMISES

It follows then, that in His faithfulness, God *always* keeps His covenants, or promises—without fail. The psalmist declares: "He remembers His covenant forever, the word He commanded, for a thousand generations."[10] Paul writes, "No matter how many promises God has made, they are 'Yes' in Christ. And so through Him the 'Amen' [so be it] is spoken by us to the glory of God."[11]

That is why we can completely trust God's Word. The writer to the Hebrews reminds us: "Let us hold unswervingly to the hope we profess, for He who promised is faithful."[12]

One way I have seen God's faithfulness over the years is that His Word produces fruit in the lives of those who love Him. As reporter Clarence W. Hall followed American troops through Okinawa in 1945, he and his Jeep driver came upon a small town that stood out as a beautiful example of a Christian community. He reported, "The old men proudly showed us their spotless homes, their terraced fields, and their prized sugar mills." The newsman saw no jails and no drunkenness, and divorce was unknown in the town.

Why was this village so unusual? An American missionary had come thirty years earlier and led two elderly townspeople to Christ and left them with a Japanese Bible. These new believers studied the Bible and started leading their fellow villagers to the Lord Jesus.

The reporter's Jeep driver was equally amazed at the difference: "So this is what comes out of only a Bible and a couple of old guys who wanted to live like Jesus." God's faithfulness to His Word had resulted in the transformation of the whole village.

I have found God faithful to His Word on tithing and sacrificial giving. When God's Word tells me "God loves a cheerful giver,"[13] I believe it. When I read, "God is able to make all grace abound to you, so that in all things at all times, having all that you need, you will abound in every good work,"[14] I believe it—and act on it. I constantly check to make sure that our tithes are paid up-to-date. I would rather live on bread and water to save money than to get behind in paying our tithes. I also feel we should give offerings above our tithes in a spirit of gratitude, compassion, and concern. Believers who give tithes, offerings, and alms to the poor and needy have few if any financial problems. In all my years of ministry, God has always provided everything I have needed in order to do what He wanted me to do.

God never forgets a promise He has made. God is perfectly capable of standing behind His Word. God is ready and able to deliver all He has promised. But we must claim His generous promises!

EXERCISING OUR FAITH

I recently boarded a plane in Europe bound for the United States. A man I had never seen before, whose name I did not even know, boarded the same plane, entered the captain's cabin and seated himself at the controls. A short time later, the aircraft began to move, and soon—by some means that I do not understand—it left the ground. Hours later we touched down in Orlando.

Not once during our flight did it occur to me to question the man at the controls. I never even thought to ask for his pilot's license or some other identification to prove he was capable of flying that plane. I never asked him to explain to me the physical laws by which he could keep such a heavy object in the air. I have flown millions of miles to most parts of the world. On each of those flights, I have placed my faith in such a stranger, believing he was capable of taking me safely to my destination.

Every day in hundreds of similar situations, believers and nonbelievers alike exercise faith without even thinking twice. If we have such unquestioning faith in fellow human beings—who are not only fallible, but also deliberately sinful and even unfaithful at times—how much more should we put all our faith in God, whose character and capabilities for faithfulness are beyond question?

God is reliable. He is trustworthy. He cannot be otherwise. His faithfulness ensures that every attribute we have studied so far is available to us. He wants us to reflect His faithfulness on earth. He is the example; we are His ambassadors to the world. Yet even though we understand this fact, in our humanity, we must grow in our Christian experience. That means exercising our faith in Him daily to build our trust in God as the Faithful One. Each time He proves Himself faithful in our life, our trust will become stronger.

What can you trust God for today that you were unable to trust Him for yesterday? What circumstances do you struggle with that you can begin turning over to Him? Exercising faith is just like exercising a muscle. The more you use it, the stronger it becomes. If you have difficulty trusting God, take baby steps of faith. Then lengthen these steps in the days to come.

In the next chapter, we will discover additional ways we can become more faithful as God is faithful.

LIFE APPLICATION

EXALT YOUR GOD—Worship our faithful Creator by singing the wonderful hymn, *Great Is Thy Faithfulness.*

> Great is Thy faithfulness, O God my Father,
> There is no shadow of turning with Thee;
> Thou changest not, Thy compassions, they fail not;
> As Thou hast been Thou forever wilt be.

> Great is Thy faithfulness! Great is Thy faithfulness!
> Morning by morning new mercies I see;
> All I have needed Thy hand hath provided;
> Great is Thy faithfulness, Lord, unto me!

Praise Him for the ways He has been faithful to you personally.

REFLECT HIS IMAGE—Search your heart by answering the following questions:

- Do people consider you someone they can count on?
- When you say you will do something, do you always come through?

Go to God with your answers to these questions, and ask Him to help you become a faithful person.

SHARE HIS MAJESTY—What insights have you gained about God's faithfulness from this chapter? Share them with a friend or family member and encourage them to draw even closer to their faithful Father.

CHAPTER 25

GOD ENABLES US TO BE FAITHFUL

nfaithfulness has become a hallmark of contemporary society. Too often, husbands and wives are unfaithful in keeping their marriage vows. Parents are frequently unfaithful in their commitment to the well-being of their children. Children tend to disobey their parents. Employees do not always serve their employers as they should, and some employers take advantage of those who work for them.

God is the only one we can completely trust because He has the integrity and flawless character that enables Him to be absolutely faithful to His Word and commitments. No one else can fulfill all promises as He does.

The Bible is filled with praises for the faithfulness of God. David writes, "Your unfailing love, O LORD, is as vast as the heavens; Your faithfulness reaches beyond the clouds."[1] Psalm 89:8 declares, "O LORD God Almighty! Where is there anyone as mighty as you, LORD? Faithfulness is your very character."

But merely understanding God's faithfulness is only part of our responsibility as Christians. God's faithfulness is the essential foundation to building faithfulness in our lives. Let me give you an analogy that will help explain this principle.

The sun is the most important body in our sky. From it we get warmth, light, and beauty. If the sun would ever burn out, we could not survive. The moon is also a familiar sight in our sky. It has its own beauty, but it does not provide us with heat or light. All the light that comes from the moon is actually a reflection from the sun.

Almost every year, you could travel to some place in the United States to see a lunar eclipse. It usually lasts an hour or two. It is caused when the Earth moves between the moon and the sun, and the Earth's shadow falls upon the moon. Because the moon generates no light of its own, when the sun's light does not strike the surface of the moon, the moon is dark. We cannot see it.

We are like the moon. In our own strength, we cannot be faithful. At best, we are inconsistent, wavering, and selfish. Even when people who do not know God personally act in a faithful manner, it is only because they are created in God's image. They are reflecting God's quality of faithfulness. But it is only believers, walking in the power of the Holy Spirit, who can become truly faithful to God, their families, and themselves. Whenever we allow any sinful act of disobedience to break our fellowship with God, we no longer reflect His faithfulness. Our lives become like that darkened moon.

God wants us to have a better understanding of His faithfulness, which will result in more intimate fellowship with Him. We know that "God, who has called you into fellowship with His Son Jesus Christ our Lord, is faithful."[2] Daily, the faithfulness of God should cause us to love Him more, study His Word, share the message of salvation with others, and pray without ceasing. Such responses draw us ever deeper into our fellowship with the Savior. As we spend more time with Him, our lives begin to reflect more of His faithfulness in how we love others and in the mercy we are able to give.

OUR FAITHFUL GOD HAS PLANNED
A LIFE OF JOY FOR US

God's faithfulness enables us to live a life of joy and fruitfulness.

Years ago, a friend told me the story of Sally, a woman whose life is a vivid illustration of the bittersweet way many Christians live.

When Sally's husband, Jeb, died years before, as far as she knew, he left only enough life insurance to pay off the mortgage. Now she was almost penniless. The house was deteriorating around her. Her car had been junked long ago when she could not keep up with the repair and insurance bills. When the electric bill got too high to pay, she made do with a camping stove and candlelight. She lived this way for years: destitute, lonely, and defeated.

One day an old acquaintance remembered her childhood friend and decided to visit. Miriam was heartbroken when she saw Sally's living conditions. She decided to stay a few days to encourage her friend. As she helped straighten up the house, Miriam made a startling discovery. Tucked away in the file drawer of Jeb's old roll-top desk was a folder labeled "For Sally." Inside, Miriam found a bank savings book and a key.

Sally discovered that the key fit a safety deposit box at the bank. Her eyes widened as she lifted the metal lid. Inside were several bundles of cash totaling $32,000, a pile of stock certificates, and three folders of rare coins. In all, Sally was worth more than $883,000! She had been living in misery and despair when more money than she would ever need had been available to her all along.

Although God has promised us all the strength and help we will ever need, many of us try to "go it alone." We seem unaware of the boundless resources God has provided in the person of the Holy Spirit and His faithfulness to bring about everything He promised to do. As a result, we live like Sally—unfulfilled, fruitless, and spiritually malnourished. Frantically hurrying about in our self-imposed spiritual poverty, we never cash the checks of joy, peace, and abundance that are in our hands. No wonder we think at times that God has abandoned us.

God has not moved away from us; we have just not taken advantage of the miraculous life He has planned for us. Our faithful God has reserved for us a life of abundance and joy; we have the key of the Spirit-filled life to give us access to all that God has provided for us.

I urge you to rely on our faithful God for every part of your life—emotional, financial, and spiritual. He is faithful to give us whatever we need to enjoy every moment here on earth.

GOD IS FAITHFUL DURING TRYING CIRCUMSTANCES

We all experience hard times in our lives. These struggles with sickness, danger, financial problems, grief, or depression happen to each of us at times. But these only prompt us to cling ever tighter to God—not to turn away from Him, blaming Him for causing or allowing all our troubles. He does not promise to prevent problems from coming into our lives, but He does promise to go through them with us. Suffering and death are as much a part of living as eating and breathing, and we can rely on God to use these situations to build character and faith in our lives.

God will never fail us! Moses exhorted the people of Israel, "Understand, therefore, that the LORD your God is indeed God. He is the faithful God who keeps His covenant for a thousand generations and constantly loves those who love Him and obey His commands."[3] The more we understand this, the less room we have in our hearts for worry.

> GOD'S FAITHFULNESS IS A GREAT ENCOURAGEMENT WHEN WE FACE TEMPTATION.

I have found that as I rely on God's faithfulness and the promises in His Word, He has proved more than able to walk with me through every situation. Truly, He's been faithful to me!

In Pakistan during a time of great political upheaval, Vonette and I finished a series of meetings in Latbre and rushed to the train station. Although we did not know it, an angry crowd of thousands was marching on the station to destroy the train with cocktail bombs. The director of the railway line rushed us to our compartments and told us not to open our doors under any circumstances.

As I put on my pajamas for the night, a peace filled my heart. From my studies of God's Word, I knew the Lord was with Vonette and me and our party. I was confident God would protect us. It was not until we arrived in Karachi some 28 hours later that I discovered how guardian angels had indeed watched over us. The train before us had been burned when rioting students had lain on the track and refused to move. The train ran over them and, in retaliation, the mob burned the train and killed the officials.

Our train was next to arrive. The angry mob was prepared to do the same to us, but God miraculously went before us, and we arrived safely in Karachi to discover that martial law had been declared and all was peaceful. It was during this incredible, memorable train ride that I revised my book, *Come Help Change the World.*

Today even more than ever, I rely on God to faithfully respond to my prayers when I pray in accordance with His Word and will. David writes of this assurance, "O LORD, hear my prayer, listen to my cry for mercy; in Your faithfulness and righteousness come to my relief."[4] God does not promise to make life easy for us. But He promises to be with us in all our trying circumstances, protecting us from anything that is not in the center of His will. He will be there by our side as we walk through all the difficulties and trials that come our way.

GOD FAITHFULLY PROTECTS US FROM TEMPTATION

Paul wrote to the church in Corinth, "Remember that the temptations that come into your life are no different from what others experience. And God is faithful. He will keep the temptation from becoming so strong that you can't stand up against it. When you are tempted, He will show you a way out so that you will not give in to it."[5]

God's faithfulness is a great encouragement when we face temptation. He knows exactly the limits of what we can bear. He promises that He will not allow us to get into situations where we are overpowered by temptation.

Whenever we give in to sin, it is not because we cannot say

"no." Rather, it is because our focus is on the attractiveness of the temptation, instead of on God's faithfulness to deliver us from that situation. Scripture declares, "The Lord is faithful; He will make you strong and guard you from the evil one."[6] God limits Satan and his demons from tempting us beyond our ability to resist. If we trust and obey God, He always gives us a way out of any predicament without having to yield to sin.

Often, we are more afraid of offending individuals with their own worldly agenda than we are of offending our holy, righteous, loving God. The results can be catastrophic. But never forget—God is as loving and faithful as He is just. Every day try to live before Him in a spirit of reverential awe as a child who knows that God loves and cares for him.

> GOD GAVE US EVERYTHING WE NEED FOR OUR LIFE OF WORSHIP AND WITNESS.

GOD FORGIVES US WHEN WE ARE UNFAITHFUL

When we first trusted in Christ to forgive our sin, He did so. Not one person who has called on God in faith has been refused. He has always been—and always will be—faithful to the sinner who comes to Jesus in faith.

The Holy Spirit inspired John to write, "If we confess our sins to Him, He is faithful and just to forgive us and to cleanse us from every wrong."[7] Since John was writing to believers, we have assurance that God has also forgiven all the sins we commit after our spiritual birth as well as the ones we had piled against our account before we received Christ as our Savior. No matter when we are unfaithful to God, He will be faithful to forgive when we ask. But on our part, we must be sincere in our repentance and not abuse God's grace.

Because we are still in these bodies of flesh, we have a tendency to sin and, ultimately, to be unfaithful. Our unfaithfulness may be motivated by fear or desire. At other times, our fleshly weakness competes with our desire to do God's will. No matter the cause, how encouraging it is to remember God's promise to be faithful to us even when we fail Him!

GOD FAITHFULLY GIVES US GIFTS TO SERVE HIM

God's faithfulness continues beyond the act of giving us new life in Christ and help in times of need. Paul writes to the Corinthians:

> Therefore you do not lack any spiritual gift as you eagerly wait for our Lord Jesus Christ to be revealed. He will keep you strong to the end, so that you will be blameless on the day of our Lord Jesus Christ. God, who has called you into fellowship with His Son Jesus Christ our Lord, is faithful.[8]

Our faithful God called us into fellowship with His Son—and in that act He also committed Himself to our future. That starts with giving us everything we need for our life of worship and witness, for we "do not lack any spiritual gift." Our faithful God never gives us an assignment for which He has not prepared us and enabled us.

God leads us into work experiences and training when we are available to Him. While in his teens, a young man committed himself to serving the Lord wherever God wanted to use him. In his late teens, he began teaching a preteen Bible study class on Sunday morning and as a mission outreach Sunday afternoon. Some years later, he taught high schoolers in one church and early teens in another church. While serving the Lord in the bookstore at Moody Bible Institute, he interacted with neighborhood African-American children who came into the store. Thus he was not surprised when he was called to write Sunday school curriculum for inner city teenagers. Later he was given an opportunity to write Bible studies for preteen boys for a national magazine. The Lord prepared him for these assignments over two decades—both by giving him a gift for writing and by providing life experiences that matured him in his service for God.

God is also faithful to give us less tangible gifts when we experience suffering, such as the pain of a child turning away from the Lord, a friend rejecting us, or the death of a loved one. In these life experiences, God gives us strength, wisdom, and peace to enable us to reflect His faithfulness through the situation.

In his letters to the early Christians, Peter wrote at length about the benefit of suffering. He concludes: "So then, those who suffer according to God's will should commit themselves to their faithful Creator and continue to do good."[9] Peter recognized that it is easy to turn inward and become bitter during times of inner pain and suffering. That is why he urges us to turn upward to our faithful Creator and commit ourselves to Him and find the purpose He has for us in these situations.[10]

Paul reminds us in 1 Corinthians 1:8 that "He will keep you strong to the end, so that you will be blameless on the day of our Lord Jesus Christ" (NIV). That is the glorious promise of God to all who follow Him. He will keep us faithful to the end, so that we will be with Him in eternity.

NO BETTER WAY TO LIVE

As we have seen, it is God's plan for us to become holy and advance His kingdom, and He is faithful to bring this to pass. He will leave nothing undone to bring us to a point of maturity in our Christian growth and faith. Paul declared to the Philippians, "I am sure that God, who began the good work within you, will continue His work until it is finally finished on that day when Christ Jesus comes back again."[11]

In what area of your life is fear of failure beginning to plague you? Which of your relationships is in danger and you wonder who cares? What task do you face that you feel you cannot do? You can make it through anything—for our faithful God is there for you even when you do not feel like a hero of the faith. He is working in your life right now, even though you may not see Him at work or feel His presence. Let His faithfulness in the past fuel your faith and the power of His Holy Spirit fill your soul. Then you, too, can be a hero of the faith in whatever situation you face.

Once He has filled your heart with the joy of His faithfulness to you, He will strengthen you with His power. Then you will reflect His faithful nature to others. They will see the love of God shine through you as you relate to others. Your friends and relatives will notice the consistency of your standards in all areas of your life, opening up many opportunities to help others understand the depth of God's faithfulness. As God meets your needs, lifts you up during trying circumstances, and gives you gifts to serve Him beyond your expectations, you will be a reflection of His holy nature and never-failing love and joy.

I cannot imagine a better way to live. If we can just be more and more faithful as God is faithful, we truly will change our corner of the world for Him!

As we consider all the attributes we have studied, it leads us to a characteristic of God's nature that assures us that God will always act in the way the Bible describes. This quality enables us to come to God in an intimate way with complete confidence. This attribute is that God never changes. In our last two chapters on our Gracious Savior, we will see how God's unchanging nature brings us comfort and security.

LIFE APPLICATION

WRITE IT ON YOUR HEART—Commit the following statement and verses to memory. Then as you encounter situations during this week where you need to remember that God is faithful, claim these promises.

- Because God is faithful, I can trust Him to always keep His promises.

- 1 Peter 4:19—"If you are suffering according to God's will, keep on doing what is right, and trust yourself to the God who made you, for He will never fail you."

- 2 Timothy 2:13—"If we are unfaithful, He remains faithful, for He cannot deny Himself."

COUNT ON GOD—The Bible states, "Without wavering, let us hold tightly to the hope we say we have, for God can be trusted to keep His promise" (Hebrews 10:23). People, institutions, and even churches may fail us, but our faithful God can always be trusted. Is there a specific problem or situation that you have a hard time placing in His capable hands? Give it to Him right now. He will strengthen you and help you through any difficulty.

OBEY GOD—Are you faithful to God? Do you love Him more than anything else? Jesus says in John 14:23, "If anyone loves me, he will obey My teaching" (NIV). We demonstrate our faithfulness by our obedience. In what areas of your life are you in disobedience to God's Word? Ask God to reveal these areas to you. Start today obeying the little things you know to do. Your faithful Lord will help you obey the big things when they come along later.

CHAPTER 26.

GOD
NEVER
CHANGES

About 4,500 years ago, Pharaoh Khafre carved the Sphinx from limestone bedrock. Since then, this 66-foot statue of a man's head with a lion's body has stood in the Egyptian desert. For thousands of years, it has remained unchanged.

Or has it? Actually, this monument has undergone many changes. Khafre never finished the statue in his lifetime. For about a thousand years, it was abandoned to the Egyptian sands. In 1400 B.C., Thutmose IV uncovered the statue and painted it blue, yellow, and red and erected a statue of his father in front of the Sphinx's chest. Then another great pharaoh, Ramses II, extensively reworked the Sphinx in 1279 B.C. After that, the Egyptian sands once again began filling up around the gigantic face and body. Wind began to erode what the Pharaohs had done.

As early as the 15th century A.D., an Arab historian wrote that the Sphinx's face was disfigured. In 1818, a Genoese sea captain cleared away the debris from the statue's chest and uncovered an ancient chapel in front of it. He also discovered fragments of the Sphinx's stone beard, which are now in the British Museum. In the early 1900s, a French engineer cleared the Sphinx down to its

271

base and shored up the weathered headdress with stone. During the 1980s, large slabs were added to try to stop the erosion. Still, in 1988, part of the right shoulder fell off.

The Sphinx is eroding even faster today. During the last decade, repairs are once again being made to the ancient statue. The large slabs added in the 1980s are being replaced by more natural-looking stone. Many plans for helping save the Sphinx from greater deterioration are being suggested.[1]

The real fact of life on earth is change. Since the fall of Adam when sin was introduced, change has been a part of human life. The moment we are born, we begin to age. We grow, develop, and deteriorate. No matter what modern science does to slow down this process, it continues on without stopping. Our great monuments like the Sphinx are not really a testimony to our power to create something unchanging, but merely to our best efforts to delay the deterioration and ravages of time.

Our only hope in this life lies in one fact: God never changes. He is the constant that we can count on while everything else around us deteriorates.

THE UNCHANGING NATURE OF GOD

One fascinating fact about many of the religions of the world is the unpredictable character of their gods. New Agers believe that everything is god and god is everything. The source of authority or "truth," they say, is what you experience. Shirley MacLaine, proponent of New Age religion, says, "My own out-of-body experience…served to validate the answers to many questions—the surest knowledge being derived from experience."[2] In other words, you may believe one thing to be true today, but then an experience tomorrow will change that truth. And what you believe to be true will not be true for me. For New Agers, truth changes.

But we learned that God's truth never changes. It is the same today as it has always been.

Buddhists believe that salvation is in karma. Kenneth Latourette, a leading church historian, explains this Buddhist belief: "Karma may be described as the sum of an individual's thoughts and actions in all his previous incarnations. In each incarnation, he modifies his karma for either good or bad…The ultimate aim is not only to improve one's karma, but to do more, namely, to escape from the endless series of changes, the appalling eternal succession of births and rebirths. This would be salvation."[3]

How different this is from God's simple, unchanging plan of salvation! With God's plan, we know where we stand, what we must do, and the result—an eternal, unalterable place in the family of God.

Animists and idol worshippers have developed their understanding of how their gods work from accumulated folklore. Their gods are so capricious that they must constantly be appeased with sacrifices and a variety of rituals so they will not change the rules of the game. But we can read God's rules in His never-changing Word.

The God of the Bible is the only unchanging Supreme Being. He has never altered one bit of His character or His purpose. That is what I love about our wonderful and marvelous God. I have known Him personally since 1944, and today He is just the same in His holiness and love, His grace and mercy as He was when I first turned my life over to Him. Theologians call this consistency and dependability God's *immutability.*

When I get up in the morning to pray, His response will not be different from when I pray to Him at bedtime. When I confront a difficult situation, I have calmness of heart because I know His unchanging Holy Spirit is present to guide me.

The Bible presents the God we worship as One who is the same from eternity to eternity. The writer of the Book of Hebrews compares the immutability of God to His changing creation: "They will perish, but You remain; they will all wear out like a garment. You will roll them up like a robe; like a garment they will be changed. But You remain the same, and Your years will never end."[4] He never changes in His essential being, never varies how He reacts to sinful man, to man's repentance, or to man's worship. Sin and unbelief always displease Him; obedience and faith always warm His heart.

God's Name Indicates His Unchangeable Nature

In the beginning of this book, we discovered God's most holy name, I AM. Through this name, God introduced the concept that He is unchangeable. He identifies Himself with that incredible statement: "I AM WHO I AM. This is what you are to say to the Israelites: 'I AM has sent me to you.'"[5] The use of the present tense in I AM means that the God who met Adam and Eve in the Garden of Eden was the same God who met Abraham and Sarah and gave them a son—and He is the same God who acts on our behalf today.

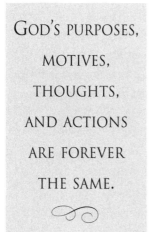

GOD'S PURPOSES, MOTIVES, THOUGHTS, AND ACTIONS ARE FOREVER THE SAME.

God's unchanging nature applies to all of His attributes as well. We are exceedingly glad that His love, grace, and mercy are unchanging. We appreciate the fact that His holiness cannot change. Emotions or circumstances do not affect God. He "does not change like shifting shadows."[6]

The fact that we can depend on God's immutability is tremendously reassuring for us today. We must admit that at times we violate one of God's unchanging attributes, such as His holiness. But we know that when we repent, His unchanging grace brings us forgiveness and favor.[7] We can proclaim God's message of love and forgiveness without fear that God will change the rules the next day.

God Does Not Grow or Develop

When you look at a newborn baby, you realize the tremendous amount of growing and learning that little person has to do. He cannot talk, walk, or reason. His body does not have the ability to sing, scratch his back, or throw a ball. His mind cannot tell you what he is feeling or remember what a tree feels like. He must go through all the stages of maturity—toddlerhood, childhood, puberty, adulthood, middle age, old age. In each stage, he will learn many new things.

God has never had to grow or change or develop. Although Jesus did grow in His physical body, He has always known everything and been able to do everything. He laid aside His divine majesty and assumed human nature in the form of a servant.[8]

Therefore, God has never had to learn anything—He has always been omniscient. God has never had to develop talents or skills —He has always been able to do everything. He has never needed to mature—He has always been perfect in all of His attributes.

God is also not moody, like we are. When I come before Him in prayer, I do not have to worry that He has just heard prayers of someone who really made Him angry and will take His anger out on me. He does not get tired, and He is not too busy to listen to my concerns. As the faithful Father, He is always there when we need Him. He is not more loving one day because He feels good and more judgmental the next because He wakes up on the wrong side of the bed. Because God's attributes always exist in fullness and in cooperation with each other, God's purposes, motives, thoughts, and actions are forever the same.

GOD'S WORD NEVER CHANGES

If God's character does not change, then it follows that His Word does not change either. If His purposes do not change, then the instructions He gives to us do not change.

Isaiah 40:6–8 records that "people are like the grass that dies away. Their beauty fades as quickly as the beauty of flowers in a field. The grass withers, and the flowers fade beneath the breath of the LORD. And so it is with people. The grass withers, and the flowers fade, but the word of our God stands forever."

Let us take a look at how true that is. The first verse in the Bible, Genesis 1:1, reads: "In the beginning God…" In Revelation 22:13, the last book of the Bible, Jesus says, "I am the Alpha and Omega, the First and the Last, the Beginning and the End."

Salvation has never changed in God's Word. When God referred to Abraham, He said, "Abram believed the LORD, and the LORD declared him righteous because of his faith."[9] In the New

Testament centuries later, Romans 3:27,28 says, "Can we boast, then, that we have done anything to be accepted by God? No, because our acquittal is not based on our good deeds. It is based on our faith. So we are made right with God through faith and not by obeying the law."

The principles throughout the Old and New Testaments are the same. God deals with each of us in the same way, with the same love and graciousness.

IMMUTABILITY INCLUDES VARIETY

A common, misinformed picture of heaven today is of saints floating around on clouds playing harps—for eternity. Nothing disturbs their little bit of heaven, as they presumably stay right where they are—forever! Is that your picture of heaven? Does the fact that God never changes bore you?

When we speak of God's immutability, we are not speaking of a lack of variety. They are two separate things. Look at God's creation. An elephant and a mosquito both have four legs and an appendage on the front of their faces. But who would describe an elephant and a mosquito as alike? How about a mouse and a whale? They both have tails, pointed noses, and sleek bodies. But, oh, the differences!

Immutability and creativity are not the same either. Although God never changes, He is all-creative. Just think about how many different personalities He has created throughout the world. No person is just like another. How about the many different kinds of plants He has made—from a pear cactus flower to an orchid; from a giant redwood to a delicate bluebell; from moss to seaweed. There is no end to God's creativity.

What does not change are the principles and the character that underlie the variety and creativity. God's plans for us are always to conform us to the image of His Son. He changes the way He works out His plan to fit our personalities, our circumstances, and our needs.

Sometimes, however, the unchanging nature of God's work is plain to see. Do you remember the story of Paul and Silas in prison for proclaiming God's message? Their preaching and that of other Christians produced phenomenal growth during the days of the early Church. It also produced persecution for the sake of Christ, which is why Paul and Silas were in prison. While they were praying and singing hymns at midnight, a great earthquake shook the prison's foundations. All the doors flew open and the chains fell off every prisoner.

In those days, if a Roman jailer lost his prisoners, the law required a sentence of death. The Roman jailer awoke, assumed all the prisoners had run away, and was going to commit suicide. Paul shouted, "Don't do it. We're all here!" The jailer, when he saw that the prisoners had not escaped, fell on his knees before Paul and Silas and asked how he could be saved.

Paul and Silas shared the Word of God with him, and he and his entire household believed in our Lord. The next day, the city officials released Paul and Silas.

Centuries later, the pattern repeated. In the 1930s, missionaries planted the Word of God in the southwestern mountains of Ethiopia. When World War II erupted and the missionaries were forced to leave, they left a church of only 48 believers. But in five years of foreign occupation in their land, the Ethiopian church grew to 10,000!

Raymond Davis, who worked in the interior of Ethiopia, tells of a miraculous story of God's work among the Wallamo people. The Christians had been horribly persecuted for proclaiming God's message, but their congregation had grown to more than a thousand. The government forced them to tear down their precious church building, which they had built with such sacrifice of labor and materials.

Later, they dared to rebuild their church building. Consequently, several of the church leaders, including a man named Toro, were taken to the marketplace, stripped, and beaten. Then they were thrown into jail where their jailers taunted them for believing in God. Davis writes:

> Some time later, a group of the believers in prison were praying together when a terrible rain and thunderstorm came

up. Toro says he doesn't remember the lightning ever being fiercer or the thunder claps louder. While they were praying and singing, the wind blew with such terrific force that the entire iron roof of the prison was torn completely off. The torrents of rain pouring down onto the exposed mud walls made them crumble and melt. The prisoners were free!

Many of the non-Christian prisoners fled. The terrified jailers, convinced that the storm was the direct intervention of God on behalf of the Christian prisoners, came to Toro pleading that he pray to God to withhold His anger and fury —and they would be released. The jailers kept their word.[10]

Of course, not every person imprisoned for his faith is freed by an act of God, but these two incidents show that God is still at work as He was in the lives of the first-century believers. He never changes! You can count on Him!

> WE NEED GOD'S PERSPECTIVE ON THE EVENTS OF LIFE—HE SEES IT IN WAYS WE DO NOT.

PRAISING GOD FOR HIS UNCHANGING NATURE

When you fly from Chicago to Los Angeles on some airlines you will fly over one section of the Grand Canyon. If you happen to fly over it during the late afternoon sun, the canyon's shadows help you see the incredible depth and breadth of it. But the fact remains—you are seeing only a small segment of it, for it runs well over a thousand miles. Now imagine yourself circling the Earth in the Mir space station and you come over the Grand Canyon. How much of it will you see now? All of it in one glance.

When we look at life on Earth, we see only a minute sliver of it, one minuscule slice of eternity. But God sees all of eternity at once, the end from the beginning. That is why we need God's perspective on the events of life—He sees it in ways we do not. As a result He can take corrective action to keep us from wandering off course or hurting ourselves as we march through life's parade of circumstances and events.

What a great God we have! We can trust Him not to turn against us, for His love is unchanging. We can trust Him for life after death, for He is eternal. That is why the writer of Hebrews could say: "Jesus Christ is the same yesterday, today, and forever."[11]

That is the God we worship and adore—and serve unconditionally. It is the God we proclaim to the entire world without ceasing, for He is worthy not only of our worship but also our obedience to His Great Commission to go and to love.

St. John Chrysostom, a third-century church leader, wrote of His Lord and Savior:

> It is fitting and right to sing of you, to praise you, to thank you, to adore you in all places of your dominion. For you are the ineffable God, inconceivable, invisible, incomprehensible, existing forever and yet ever the same, you and your only-begotten Son and your Holy Spirit. You brought us into being out of nothingness, and when we had fallen, you raised us up again. You have not ceased doing everything to lead us to heaven and to bestow upon us your future and your only-begotten Son and your Holy Spirit. You do this for all the benefits of which we know, for those of which we are ignorant, and for those that are manifest to us and those that lie concealed.[12]

I urge you to take time to enjoy the wonder of God's attributes. As you learn more facts about His greatness, thank Him, glorify Him, and praise Him for all He means to you. Let the Holy Spirit fill your mind with His love and grace, and touch your deepest feelings with His comfort and gentleness. The more you worship and meditate on His attributes, the more you will become like Him. Worship Him through giving, serving, praising, singing, and giving thanks. That is the sure road to developing an intimate relationship with God!

LIFE APPLICATION

❧

EXALT YOUR GOD—Worship God with the powerful words of the hymn *Immortal, Invisible.*

> Immortal, invisible, God only wise,
> In light inaccessible, hid from our eyes.
> Most blessed, most glorious, the Ancient of Days,
> Almighty, victorious, Thy great name we praise.
>
> To all, life Thou givest—to both great and small;
> In all life Thou livest, the true life of all;
> We blossom and flourish as leaves on the tree,
> And wither and perish—but naught changeth Thee.

REFLECT HIS IMAGE—By nature, we, as humans, change. We grow older, taller, thinner, or fatter, and our emotions fluctuate. But we can reflect God's unchanging nature by being people who are consistent—in our relationships and in our love for God. Examine your heart and ask God to make you a person who perseveres no matter what, a person who, as Jesus said, "stands firm to the end" (Matthew 10:22, NIV).

SHARE HIS MAJESTY—Jesus stated in Matthew 24:35, "Heaven and earth will disappear, but my words will remain forever." The Bible has encouraged and challenged individuals for thousands of years, and still speaks to us today. With whom can you share God's unchanging word? Choose a verse that has spoken to you and use it to encourage someone today.

CHAPTER 27

GOD GIVES US REST IN HIM

~~~~~~~~

D o you ever wish time would stand still? Has your neighborhood changed, or a loved one grown distant or passed away? Have dear friends moved away?

One of the hardest changes for a parent is when children grow up, move away, and become independent. I remember the day that Vonette and I helped our older son, Zac, settle into his dorm room at Life Bible College in Los Angeles. Later we helped our younger son, Brad, pack his car to leave home and drive across the country to Washington, D.C. to work for Senator William Armstrong from Colorado.

Before each of our sons left home, we got down on our knees together to thank God for him and pray for his safety. When we rose, we embraced and expressed our love. Of course, as parents, we always had a few last-minute instructions. My eyes misted as I silently thanked God for each of my boys.

As Brad drove away toward Washington, D.C., Vonette and I waved valiantly. I forced a smile and stemmed my tears. *My little boy isn't little anymore*, I thought as his car disappeared around a bend. *He's on his own now.*

281

I treasure the heartwarming memories of Zac and Brad when they were young and in our home. Vonette and I will always love our sons, and look forward to spending time with them whenever possible. Today we still miss them as much as when they left home. As many of you know, the "empty nest" syndrome that comes when your last child leaves home is very real.

But our boys are independent adults now. They do not need us like they did when they were young. Of course, I would not wish for them to come back because they have lives, families, and ministries of their own. Some of the memories of separations are erased with our delight in visiting with our grandchildren. Yet we will never forget the emotionally difficult change we experienced when each of our sons left home.

Today, we live in a time of hyper-change. Fashions and trends change weekly; people relocate frequently; technological advances quickly make the past obsolete. A way of life that was once familiar and comfortable to us rapidly fades away. This change produces a great deal of stress. As we search for stability, we wonder if there is any permanence anymore. Is there some anchor that will hold us so we will not be swept away by the waves of change washing over society?

There are several reasons we are drawn into the undercurrents of change. For one, sin and our fallen nature promote a process of decay and deterioration. Things get progressively worse when left to themselves. You can understand that if you have ever had to maintain an old house. The water heater needs replacing; the screen door comes off its hinges; the roof leaks.

Another reason we change is because we experience pressure from others or from our circumstances. We change well-laid plans because of illness or because a family member is in crisis and needs help. An airline goes on strike so our flight is canceled. All kinds of events make us modify what we want to do.

A third reason is because of boredom. We do not want every day to be exactly the same as the last. A little spice and variety make life more enjoyable.

Also, technological achievements and other kinds of improvements stimulate change. Computers have dramatically altered the way we do things. Seldom do we mail a package of important papers. Now we can e-mail a file or fax the pages immediately. Everyone expects instant turnaround time.

But the influences that cause change in our lives have no effect on God. Let us look at several benefits we enjoy because God never changes.

God's Unchanging Nature Provides Stability

A story is told of a shipwrecked sailor who clung to a rock in great danger until the tide went down. Later a friend asked him, "Didn't you shake with fear when you were hanging on the rock?"

He simply replied, "Yes, but the rock didn't."

Life and its uncertainties may shake us, but God—who is the Rock of Ages—does not move. If we cling to Him, His strength sustains us.

Since God never changes,[1] God's character is constant. Unlike us, He does not compromise or change His values. He cannot be manipulated or persuaded to go against His word. He does not have a Dr. Jekyl and Mr. Hyde personality where He will comfort us one moment and snap at us the next.

God's Unchanging Purpose Gives Us Eternal Significance

Psalm 33 states, "The LORD's plans stand firm forever; His intentions can never be shaken."[2] God's plan existed at the beginning of creation and remains the same today. It unfolds in phases and stages, which may give us the impression of change, but His original design has always been consistent. God's purposes for us are fulfilled within the framework of time and history.

The nation of Israel is the clearest example of this truth. The Lord declared to the people of Israel, "Everything I plan will come to pass, for I do whatever I wish…I have said I would do it, and I will."[3] From the day God placed Adam and Eve in the Garden of Eden, God's hand has been leading and guiding His people.

And we are part of His plan! We share His purpose. Paul wrote to the believers in Ephesus, "For we are God's masterpiece. He has created us anew in Christ Jesus, so that we can do the good things He planned for us long ago."[4] We no longer need to feel as if we are unimportant in the cosmos. As God's people, we are His loved ones whom He has planned from the beginning to bless and to live with forever!

GOD'S UNCHANGEABLE WAYS ASSURE US OF UNWAVERING GUIDANCE

In the early 1960s, President Kennedy challenged NASA to send a man to the moon. The man in charge of that seemingly impossible assignment was a marvelous Christian and a dear friend. He told me that they had nothing to build on except the unchanging laws of God's creation. Imagine the frustration had God's laws of science, physics, and creation not been dependable. That is where the scientists started, and sure enough—the impossible mission happened on schedule!

Just as the natural laws of the universe never change, God's principles for life never change. David writes, "As for God, His way is perfect. All the LORD'S promises prove true."[5] Following His guidelines, given in Scripture, will produce fruitful lives. Not only that, He assures us that His Holy Spirit living inside us will complete what God has begun in our lives. As I look back over the events of my life, I can clearly see how God has guided me in ways that produced what He intended even when it was impossible for me to accomplish. All He required was my availability and willingness to do what He asked of me.

For example, in 1945, as a new Christian I had a dream to produce a film about the life of our Lord. I was hoping to finance the film with the profits from my business. I was long on zeal, but short on practical knowledge.

At that time, our ministry did not have the funds to produce such an ambitious project. Yet for more than 33 years, our board of directors, the staff, and I discussed the need for a film on the life of Christ which could be used as an evangelistic tool. We reviewed more than thirty films, but most of them were not scripturally accurate. We even seriously considered buying the rights to one of these films and reworking it to make it biblically accurate. But we were never able to raise the huge amount of money for the production costs. Yet I still believed that God wanted me to complete this project.

Then in 1976, I met John Heyman, a movie producer who had produced more than thirty feature-length films. I introduced John to Paul Eshelman, our U.S. Field Ministry director who later headed the *JESUS* film project. A few months later, Bunker and Carolyn Hunt, long-time friends and generous supporters of the ministry, agreed to provide financing for the film. God began to fulfill the dream that He had placed in my heart over three prior decades.

Accuracy and authenticity were crucial as a team of researchers painstakingly produced a 318-page document giving the biblical, theological, historical, and archeological background of every scene as presented by the Gospel of Luke. During the filming in Israel, John Heyman demanded excellence. For example, he once stopped the cameras when he noticed a ripple-soled tennis shoe print in the dust. But excellence was what we needed to produce a film that could touch the world.

> WE ARE HIS LOVED ONES WHOM HE HAS PLANNED FROM THE BEGINNING TO BLESS.

We prayed that the *JESUS* film would become a mighty evangelistic instrument to introduce millions to God. When the filming and production were completed, *JESUS* opened in America in the fall of 1979 in Warner Brothers theaters. By the end of the commercial run a year later, more than four million people had seen the film. From the beginning, however, we planned that *JESUS* would go beyond American shores. We developed a strategy to bring the film to urban centers, rural areas, islands, mountaintop villages, and countries where electricity is a rarity.

To date, more than two thousand *JESUS* film teams have been sent to remote villages and great metropolitan areas. You can imagine the excitement when a team begins to set up its equipment in places where people have never had the opportunity to view a movie, particularly in their own language.

As of April 1, 1999, *more than 2 billion people in almost 500 languages in 225 countries have viewed JESUS.* Hundreds of millions have responded with salvation decisions. God has used our thousands of staff and volunteers, almost 1,000 mission organizations, and tens of thousands of local churches of many denominations to introduce people to Jesus through this film.

God demonstrated His unchanging faithfulness when He began to work in me through a vision to fulfill His purposes.[6] Then 33 years later He brought together the resources and personnel to make the dream come true. I am sure you can point to many instances in your life where God's guidance, true to the unchanging principles of His Word, made a huge difference in your life and ministry and the lives of others. We can depend on His guidance every day of our lives if we continue to trust and obey Him.

GOD'S UNCHANGING WORD EQUIPS US WITH TIMELESS TRUTH

God does not change what He says based on opinion polls or focus groups. His words and commands are timeless. They are valid throughout all eternity. They apply to every culture, race, and nationality.

That is why the Bible has remained relevant throughout the ages and to all civilizations. What God says is always pertinent. It never becomes obsolete. His timeless truth is the surest foundation for anything we attempt.

Almost to a man, the founding fathers of our nation sought to serve and glorify Jesus Christ with their lives. One study found that of 15,000 writings by the founding fathers included in newspaper articles, pamphlets, books, monographs, and other documents, 94 percent of all quotes either directly or indirectly cited the Bible.[7] Fifty-two of the 55 framers of the Constitution were avowed biblical Christians. They were inspired by God to dedicate this new republic for His honor and glory. Even the curriculum of the institutions of higher learning used the Bible as a textbook. The efforts of our founding fathers produced miraculous results. The United States Constitution is currently the oldest operating document of any government in the world. Every other nation on earth has instituted a new form of government since our founding documents were written. The U.S. Constitution is unlike any other political instrument because the liberties it guarantees are greater than the liberties granted to the citizens of any other nation. And all this resulted in God's unchanging principles, which provided the timeless truths for our governing documents.

Abraham Lincoln, our 16th President and the man who guided our country through a civil war, stated, "I believe the Bible is the best gift God has given to man. All the good Savior gave to the world was communicated through this Book."[8]

Former President Ronald Reagan, a devout believer from his youth, declared on numerous occasions that if only the American people would "live closer to the Commandments and the Golden Rule," the problems we face would be solved.[9] As you know, the Ten Commandments and the Golden Rule are basic principles from God's Word. Tragically, we are now reaping the consequences of a society that has abandoned biblical truths. Yet as we each base our lives on His Word, we will see the joy and blessing that come from living according to God's unchanging truths.

God's Unchanging Commitment Guarantees Us Everlasting Security

Recently, I stood at the grave sites of two dear friends, and as I reflected on their lives, I realized that the most important moment we can experience is our death. When we breathe our last earthly air and take our first breath of the celestial, we transition into the presence of God! This life on earth is but a prelude to eternity. My friends had no fear of crossing over, for they knew the reality of God's unwavering faithfulness to them.

Hebrews states, "God also bound Himself with an oath, so that those who received the promise could be perfectly sure that He would never change His mind."[10] We who have given ourselves to God through the death and resurrection of Jesus Christ have received eternal life. God is committed to our redemption, our Christian walk, and our eternal destiny. God's unchanging nature assures us that we will indeed live with Him forever as He promised. God's commitment is as strong as He is constant. No one and nothing can violate His promise: "[The Holy Spirit's] presence within us is God's guarantee that He really will give us all that He promised."[11] We can bank our entire future on His unchanging character. What a sure anchor for our faith!

> GOD ALTERS
> HIS TEMPORARY
> PURPOSES IN
> RESPONSE TO
> OUR FAITH
> AND ACTIONS.

Perhaps you are thinking: *If God never changes, what is the purpose of prayer and other communication with God?* I want to caution you about using God's immutability as an excuse not to pray or to ask Him to intervene in your daily life. Although He will never change His plans, Scriptures abound that show how God alters His temporary purposes in response to our faith and actions. For example, He reverses His judgment because of sincere repentance of sinners.[12] At other times, He responds to the needs of human beings or the fervent prayer of the righteous.[13] This is one of the mysteries of God's nature. We know that God never changes, and yet He relates to us and gives us our free will. When we pray and ask Him to intervene in our lives, He does so—when it is in line with His will. He works through us as we walk and talk with Him. So I encourage you to take comfort in the fact that God never changes; but realize that when we seek His face in repentance, we can expect Him to respond to our prayers and deal with our sin.

Now that we have discovered many facets of God's character, how will our knowledge affect our lives? Intimacy with God requires changes on our part. It also means that we will give God the praise and adoration He deserves. This is where our study of

God's attributes will really bring blessings to our lives, including lasting joy, peace, fruitfulness, and confidence. In the conclusion to this book, you will find helpful suggestions on how you can cultivate a healthy fear of God and become transformed by His majesty.

LIFE APPLICATION

⟳

WRITE IT ON YOUR HEART—Commit the following statement and verses to memory. Then as you encounter situations during this week where you need to remember that God never changes, claim these promises by faith.

- Because God never changes, my future is secure and eternal.
- James 1:17—"Whatever is good and perfect comes to us from God above, who created all heaven's lights. Unlike them, He never changes or casts shifting shadows."
- Hebrews 13:8—"Jesus Christ is the same yesterday, today, and forever."

COUNT ON GOD—Paul writes in Philippians 1:6, "I am sure that God, who began the good work within you, will continue His work until it is finally finished on that day when Christ Jesus comes back again." Because God never changes, He will never change His mind, go back on His word, or leave unfinished what He has started. Every day He is molding you, maturing you, and preparing you to spend eternity with Him—and He will complete what he has begun. What promise can you claim for an area of your life where you know God is helping you change? Use your Bible concordance to find a promise and claim it for your situation.

OBEY GOD—God's standards do not vacillate based on the latest fads or opinion poll. Society's perception of right and wrong may be different from what it was just a generation ago, but this does not alter the truth. Take God's commands seriously in an area where His Word contradicts society's beliefs. Ask God to help you confirm your stance in this issue.

PART IV.

CONCLUSION

"Oh, that they would always have hearts like this, that they might fear Me and obey all My commands! If they did, they and their descendants would prosper forever."

DEUTERONOMY 5:29

CHAPTER 28

CULTIVATING A HEALTHY FEAR OF GOD

I grew up on my parents' ranch in Oklahoma where my father had a reputation of being one of the best ranchers in the county. Nobody could ride horses like he could. He taught my four brothers and me how to ride wild broncos. Although I learned how to feel comfortable and secure around those big horses, my father raised me to always have a healthy respect for them. I knew that if I was not careful around those powerful wild horses from Montana, I could easily be hurt or even killed if I did something foolish.

As boys growing up on a ranch, we often swam in the lakes and rivers in our county. Once, when I was about 6 or 7 years old, I ventured out into a lake far away from my brothers and friends. Suddenly, my energy gave out and I started to sink. As I went down for the third time, my older brother and one of his friends pulled me out of the water and helped me get my breath. I could have easily drowned that afternoon. Since then, I have had a respect for swimming alone in deep water.

When I was a teenager, my father and uncle taught me how to drive an automobile. I remember the thrill I experienced as I sat behind that steering wheel, stepped on the accelerator, and felt the surge of power thrust me down the country road. Once again, my parents instilled in me a healthy respect, this time for the automobile. I could have been injured or even killed if I acted foolishly behind the steering wheel of that car.

We naturally fear and respect things that have great power or that can alter our lives in the fraction of a second. We treat these things much differently than we do the ordinary objects or people in our lives.

What about God? He is the sovereign Creator and Ruler of our universe. We have glimpsed His power, holiness, and justice. How much respect should we have for Him?

In His Word, God commands us to fear Him. When the Lord was giving the children of Israel the Ten Commandments, He spoke to them from the heart of the fire on Mount Sinai. The people were greatly frightened because they understood they were in the presence of their awesome Creator God. He commanded them to fear Him.[1]

This is only one of many places throughout the Bible where God's people are instructed to fear God. But what does fearing God really mean?

When I approached one of those wild broncos, I did so with caution. I made sure the horse knew where I was and what I was going to do. When swimming in deep water, I carefully follow safe swimming rules. As I drive a car, I observe traffic laws, including speed limits. I do not recklessly hurtle down a freeway at 100 mph, because I realize that my reaction time and inability to control the car at those speeds could cause a horrible accident.

These illustrations are demonstrations of the respect and fear I have for things more powerful than I am. That is part of what it means to fear God.

WHAT DOES IT MEAN TO FEAR GOD?

God is not some hateful warlord who desires to do us harm. He is not reckless or foolish in the use of His great power and limitless abilities, so we will never become random victims of His lack of control. He is not a spooky, hideous creature who hides in the darkness to scare us when we least expect it. These are some of the reasons we normally fear someone. But that is not the kind of fear God is talking about. The psalmist records, "The LORD delights in those who fear Him, who put their hope in His unfailing love."[2] When the Scriptures tell us to fear God, it means we are to have awe, reverence, and respect for our magnificent God.

The following explanation, from *Hard Sayings of the Bible*, helps us to understand the phrase "fear the Lord":

> The term for *fear* can describe everything from dread, or being terrified, to standing in awe or having reverence. When used of the Lord, it applies to both aspects of the term, a shrinking back in recognition of the difference or holiness of God and the drawing close in awe and worship. It is an attitude of both reluctance and adoration that results in a willingness to do what God says. The fear of the Lord, then, is absolutely necessary if we are even to begin on the right foot in learning, living, or worshiping.[3]

WHY SHOULD WE FEAR GOD?

The relationship between little children and their parents may help us grasp this kind of fear. As a child, I had a loving relationship with my parents and was very close to them. Yet I was very aware that my parents were much bigger and stronger than I was. I knew that if I contradicted their rules I was powerless against them, because my parents had great authority over me. They could give or take away privileges. They expected me to behave within predefined boundaries or face the consequences.

God wants us to approach Him in the same way—with an attitude of humility, submissiveness, and a sense of respect. I believe this is one of the reasons God calls Himself our heavenly Father and us His children. We all cringe when we see tiny children sassing their parents or ignoring their requests. It is against the order of things to see children act that way. How can we behave that way toward God? We must treat Him with the greatest respect as our ultimate authority and guide.

The Word of God states, "The fear of the LORD is the beginning of wisdom, and knowledge of the Holy One is understanding."[4] Here are three reasons why we should fear God.

God Is Infinitely Superior to Us

The ancient scribes who performed the laborious task of copying the Holy Scriptures had a practice that illustrated their respect for God. When they were about to write the name of the Lord, they stopped their work and performed ceremonial washing. Then, with their clothes and body clean, they would take up a new writing utensil and carefully pen God's holy name.

What a contrast their example is to how many people treat God today. God's name has become a swear word, and even those of us who claim to serve Him often speak His name flippantly and without respect. Now that you understand more about God's character, you also understand why this is such an affront to God.

God's abilities eclipse anything we could ever think or do. He is infinitely great, and we are so small. When we stand on a beach and gaze out on the ocean, its vastness overwhelms us. Those waves can easily overpower a swimmer with their undercurrents. They can destroy houses and anything else in their path. Yet God is infinitely more powerful than all the waves in all the earth's oceans —even the super-currents generated by hurricanes and typhoons. The contrast between God's omnipotence and our impotence is beyond our ability to even imagine.

God is also infinitely perfect, and we are so imperfect. He is without any fault, without any blemish, and without any deficiency. In contrast, we have innumerable shortcomings. Compare the sight of the entire countryside covered with the purity of newly fallen snow to the slush of a tiny, dirty mud puddle. The difference between God's perfection and our imperfection is infinitely greater.

Yet with all His power and perfection, God is supremely committed to His people who are so fickle in their commitment to Him. When we consider the depth of His love for us—the magnitude of the sacrifice He has made for us, the plans and desires

He has for our eternal future—and compare that with our natural self-centered tendencies, the contrast is beyond our understanding.

Dear friend, I urge you to take a few moments to consider the immeasurable gulf between you and God. With all you now know of His superiority, does it not make you tremble at your own insignificance? At the same time, when you think of how much He loves us, tiny microscopic mites on planet Earth, does it not cause great respect for Him to well up in your heart? Keep this attitude of humble submission and respect close to you throughout your days as you serve Him.

God Has Supreme Authority Over Us

Most tyrants and dictators have been recluses who had no personal relationship with the people of their countries. God's authority over us, however, is revealed in His personal relationship to us. As we have seen, His authority comes from His three primary roles: Creator, Judge, and Savior. Let me briefly recap these areas.

As our Creator, God personally designed us and gave us life. As our Maker, He is totally justified in doing whatever He wishes with us, for He knows what is best for us.

How can we shake our fists at our Designer? How can we presume to know ourselves and run our lives better than He can? It is not possible. We are completely dependent on His omniscience and omnipresence for every moment of our being.

As Perfect Judge, God determines our eternal future. He has the authority to condemn us to eternal damnation or allow us to live in His glorious presence forever and ever, depending on our response to Him.

If we lived under the dictatorship of a supreme human ruler, we would have a clearer understanding of what it means to submit to someone greater than we are. When a dictator proclaims a law, everyone must obey without excuse or argument. If the dictator is benevolent, people prosper; if he is harsh, the people suffer. We have a God who is more than benevolent, He is perfectly just and loving. How much more should we submit to Him out of respect for His authority!

As our Redeemer, God freed us from slavery. We have been purchased with a price, and now belong to Him. First Corinthians 6:19,20 reminds us, "You do not belong to yourself, for God bought you with a high price." He bought us with His blood and now He has total authority over us in a beautiful love relationship.

We would deeply respect a friend who gave his most prized possession for our welfare. Think of someone who would sell an irreplaceable piece of jewelry that had been handed down for generations to pay a debt you incurred and could not repay. How would you feel about this person? Jesus paid our sin-debt with His blood! How much more deeply should we love and respect Him!

God Blesses Those Who Reverence Him

Clearly, God is worthy of our reverence and awe simply because of who He is. When we fear Him, the Bible promises bountiful rewards: "The love of the LORD remains forever with those who fear him" (Psalm 103:17); "Fear of the LORD gives life, security, and protection from harm" (Proverbs 19:23); "Those who fear the LORD are secure; He will be a place of refuge for their children" (Proverbs 14:26); "He will be the sure foundation for your times, a rich store of salvation and wisdom and knowledge; the fear of the LORD is the key to this treasure" (Isaiah 33:6, NIV).

God does not want us to be cowering slaves; we are His beloved children. On the other hand, it is wrong to treat our all-powerful, infinite Maker as though He were our casual friend or the "Man Upstairs." Even the Son of God revered His heavenly Father. Jesus said, "I do nothing on My own, but speak what the Father taught Me...For I always do those things that are pleasing to Him."[5] God's magnificence demands respect; His position demands honor; His holiness demands praise.

DO YOU HAVE A HEALTHY FEAR OF GOD?

Years ago, many Christians were known as God-fearing people. What has happened to our Christian culture for us to lose that distinction?

Over time we developed a distorted view of who God is and

lost our sense of reverence, respect, and fear of Him. Instead of seeing God as our sovereign Ruler, He is more commonly viewed as our "buddy" or "pal." Instead of recognizing Him as our awesome Creator and holy Judge, we relegate Him to the position of a peer. We have become too casual with God, even in our places of worship. In the past we referred to such places as holy sanctuaries, houses of prayer, or altars where the glory of God came down upon His people. Today, we have lost even the sense of the presence of the holy, awesome God among us when we come together to praise, worship, and learn about Him.

Fearing God arises out of a conscious commitment to give God the honor He deserves. This attitude must be cultivated in our daily lives. To do so, ask yourself the following questions:

"Do I have a reverential awe of God?" Certainly, your heart soars when you gaze up at the massive ceiling of a cathedral, at the stars on a clear night, or when you stand at the foot of a snowcapped mountain. How much more should we be overcome by a sense of wonder when considering God who created over 100 billion galaxies by merely speaking them into existence!

> WE HAVE BECOME TOO CASUAL WITH GOD, EVEN IN OUR PLACES OF WORSHIP.

Let the thought of our magnificent Creator move you to worship Him in the magnitude of who He is and how far He surpasses anything we could ever begin to imagine with our puny, finite minds. Make it a practice to take time out of each day to meditate on God's glory and to praise Him. Use your favorite worship music or commune with God in the beauty of nature. Look through the Life Applications in this book to find verses that can help you praise and worship God. Or note Scripture passages that mean a lot to you as you read your Bible, then meditate on them later.

"Do I desire to please God more than people?" If you do not, then you lower God to a human level. The world values appearance,

wealth, and position. God values a heart that is right with Him. To whose voice are you listening? If what others think is more important to you than what God thinks, what does that say about the authority and importance He has in your life?

To give God preeminence in your life, spend more time with Him. That may be as simple as talking to Him during your daily routine. Thank Him for the small blessings He gives you. For each decision, big or small, ask Him what He would have you do. Desire to please Him even in the small details of your life. As you do, your intimacy with God will grow and you will allow God to have first place in your life.

"Do I have a hatred for sin and evil?" God detests sin. The Bible says, "Don't be impressed with your own wisdom. Instead, fear the LORD and turn your back on evil. Then you will gain renewed health and vitality."[6]

What is your attitude about wickedness, sin, and evil? Do you find yourself tolerating it? Do you view it as not being so bad— especially the sin you commit?

God expects us to oppose those things that He opposes. A good rule to follow is to love what God loves and hate what God hates. Evaluate your life to see what you might be harboring that God detests. Perhaps it is a superior attitude toward people who are different. Or maybe you have a love for something, such as money, a car, or your position, that is greater than your love for God. Each of us has areas that give us trouble. Ask God to help you see the sin in your life for what it is and to help you break the patterns of evil-doing. This is a life-long process. But God will be faithful to deliver you from all sin.

Most of all, spend time in God's Word reading how Joseph, Moses, David, Daniel, Mary, Paul, and others exhibited a healthy fear of God. Remember His promise, "As high as the heavens are above the earth, so great is His love for those who fear Him."[7]

Once we begin cultivating a healthy fear of God, we will see amazing changes in our lives. God will begin doing things that we never dreamed possible. In our concluding chapter, we will discover how intimacy with God will transform our very lives!

CHAPTER 29

TRANSFORMED BY HIS MAJESTY

What difference are these new insights about God making in your life? God encourages us not just to listen to the Word but to follow through and do what it says.[1] Otherwise, we are like the ship's officers on the *Titanic,* who were warned by a nearby ship that icebergs had been sighted, but did nothing with the information. Because they did not act on this knowledge, the great ship struck an iceberg and sank, sending thousands to a watery grave. Truly, knowledge without action is worthless.

We are accountable to God for what we know. We must be careful to fully apply the truth He has given us and allow it to transform our lives. Only then will we experience God's best in our lives and become all God intended us to be.

The truth about God will transform your life. Paul explains the process of transformation:

> I plead with you to give your bodies to God. Let them be a living and holy sacrifice—the kind He will accept. When you think of what He has done for you, is this too much to

ask? Don't copy the behavior and customs of this world, but let God transform you into a new person by changing the way you think. Then you will know what God wants you to do, and you will know how good and pleasing and perfect His will really is."[2]

How foolish for any of us to get in the way of God as He lovingly works out His will in our lives. This chapter presents six ways to open up your heart to God and apply the truths you have learned about His majestic character to your life. You may have already begun applying them as you worked through the Life Application at the end of each chapter. The following sections will provide a more complete look at God's attributes to enable us to transform our lives.

1. Write It On Your Heart

What we hear and what we read can easily be forgotten unless we make an effort to remember. Spend time meditating on and memorizing Scripture passages that give insight into who God is and how He wants to be involved with you. Vonette and I regularly meditate on these thirteen statements related to each of the attributes presented in this book:

- Because God is a personal Spirit, I will seek intimate fellowship with Him.
- Because God is all-powerful, He can help me with anything.
- Because God is ever-present, He is always with me.
- Because God knows everything, I will go to Him with all my questions and concerns.
- Because God is sovereign, I will joyfully submit to His will.
- Because God is holy, I will devote myself to Him in purity, worship, and service.
- Because God is absolute truth, I will believe what He says and live accordingly.
- Because God is righteous, I will live by His standards.
- Because God is just, He will always treat me fairly.

- Because God is love, He is unconditionally committed to my well-being.
- Because God is merciful, He forgives me of my sins when I sincerely confess them.
- Because God is faithful, I will trust Him to always keep His promises.
- Because God never changes, my future is secure and eternal.

We had those statements printed on a laminated card that fits inside a shirt pocket or purse. We carry the cards with us wherever we go. Throughout the day as we have an opportunity, we pull out those cards and meditate on how wonderful God is.

Many times when I awaken in the middle of the night, I ponder those principles and praise God for His glorious attributes. Vonette and I often pray about these principles as we take walks together. These statements remind us of how God is at work in our current circumstances. In fact, I offered my grandchildren small awards for memorizing them. I know nothing that will help them more than a basic understanding of who God is and how they should relate to Him. You may wish to do the same with your children and grandchildren. (For more information on the *GOD: Discover the Benefits of His Attributes* card, see the end of this book).

In addition to memorizing these statements, I encourage you to select meaningful Scripture passages from previous chapters and commit them to memory. Nothing will transform your thinking more than memorizing the Word of God.

2. Exalt Your God

Make worshipping God for who He is and the great things He has done a regular part of your devotional time and your Sunday routine. Here are several ways to do this:

- Consider His marvelous attributes one at a time, thanking and praising Him for His magnificent qualities.
- Select hymns and praise songs that focus on God's attributes and honor Him by singing them to Him as an offering of wor-

ship. Some people enjoy singing the words of Scripture, making up their own tunes as they go.

- Study the many names of God in the Bible and praise Him for each one. Each name reveals a different role God exhibits among His people and reflects His glorious nature. For names of our marvelous Lord, see Appendix C.

3. Trust in God

Trusting someone means we are willing to commit our concerns to that person. What we entrust may be a secret, a struggle, some valuable asset, or even our family. Certainly by now you must realize that there is no one more trustworthy than God.

> OUR LOVING FATHER WANTS US TO ACT IN A WAY THAT IS CONSISTENT WITH WHO WE ARE.

People often fail us because they are unable to do what they said they would do. This is never the case with God. Sometimes people make promises they never intend to keep. But our God is completely honest in keeping all His promises. Perhaps a person has failed you because he or she was too busy, or only half-heartedly promised to do something. You can be assured that God is always willing to help. Someone has aptly written, "When you don't understand, when you can't see His hand, you can trust His heart." Because of His perfect attributes, you can always trust God.

Are you in a difficult situation right now? Keep your eyes focused on Him and His magnificent character qualities instead of becoming preoccupied with your circumstances. Always remember that God is bigger than any problem you may have.

The storms of life are constantly changing, but God remains the same. He is consistent and reliable. He is our anchor. Do not permit yourself to become distracted. Whatever your problems, whatever your circumstances, keep your eyes on Jesus instead of your problems. The more you grow in your relationship with

God, the easier it will be to trust Him with everything.

4. Obey God

With every command from God there is an expressed or implied promise to enable us to do what He commands us to do. God gives us commands to protect us from harm and to provide for our well-being. Every command that God gives us is consistent with His nature and a reflection of who God is. His laws are not intended to keep us from finding happiness or having a good time in life. Quite the contrary. His laws are the guardrails that keep us on the road to a happy, fulfilled, and satisfied life for all eternity.

If you are a typical Christian, your biggest problem is not that you do not know God's commands, but that, for whatever reasons, you are selectively obeying them. Surrender your will completely and irrevocably to God. Do not allow your prideful, worldly desires to create a rebellious spirit toward God. Humble yourself before Him and depend on the Holy Spirit to help you obey God completely.

5. Reflect His Image

When I think of reflecting God's image, I turn to 2 Corinthians 3:18, which says that God wants us to "be mirrors that brightly reflect the glory of the Lord. And as the Spirit of the Lord works within us, we become more and more like Him and reflect His glory even more."

God is certainly concerned with what we do, but He is even more concerned with what we are becoming. He is in the process of making us more and more like His Son. The more clearly we understand what our Triune God is like, the clearer picture we have of Jesus Christ and the character qualities God is in the process of instilling in us.

Since we are children of God, our loving Father wants us to act in a way that is consistent with who we are. As members of His royal family, when we serve Him, our actions are consistent with His glorious calling and commission on our lives.

6. Share His Majesty

Are you excited about the new things you have learned about God's magnificent nature? Do His greatness, holiness, and gracious love captivate you? Which truths have been the most life-changing to you? Now ask yourself: How can I possibly keep quiet about my new experiences with God?

Certainly you would tell others about a great book you just read, an entertaining movie you saw, or a fabulous restaurant, museum, or concert you enjoyed. How much more eager should you be to introduce people to this wonderful God who lives inside you! Look for opportunities to tell others about God's majestic qualities. Focus your thoughts on God and remain alert to what He is doing in the world around you. Do not be afraid or intimidated into silence, but speak freely to anyone who will listen about your understanding of God and what He is doing.

If someone does not know this wonderful God personally, use your conversation as a springboard to tell them how they can have a relationship with Him. Simply share with them Appendix A, "How to Know God Personally."

As you tell fellow believers what you have learned of God's attributes, they will rejoice with you. You will encourage them in their walk of faith.

AN ENCOUNTER WITH MAJESTY

It is my prayer that these insights into the magnificent character of our awesome God will become the sparks for igniting revival in your life. As His power, holiness, justice, mercy, and love become more real to you, your life will be changed forever.

The transformation of the disciples from weak, frightened followers to bold, authoritative proclaimers of the gospel was due to a promise Jesus made to reveal Himself to each one of them.[3] He also promised to give them supernatural power to preach the gospel and live overcoming lives through the gift of the Holy Spirit.[4] God wants to do the same for us today! He desires to have a close, warm, confidential, and continuing relationship with each of us—to which no human relationship can compare.

What if your life radiated the very nature of God to all around you? If you allowed God to live out His love, mercy, faithfulness, and righteousness through you, imagine what a difference it would make in your family, church, neighborhood, and work place. And what if others in your church were also impacted in this way? Just think how your church could change and what effect would this have on your community and the world at large!

There is only one word that can describe the result—revival. Revival always begins with a renewed view—a right biblical view —of God. But revival starts at the heart of the matter—our sin, disobedience, and pride.[5] Then it spreads as we hunger for God and begin to worship Him with clean hands and pure hearts.[6] This leads to renewed minds and spiritual eyes to see the awesome character and nature of our great God. The more time you spend with God, the more you will get to know His magnificent attributes and the more you will reflect the radiance of God's presence to those around you.

Will you invite God to begin a transforming work in you?

THE RADIANCE OF GOD'S PRESENCE

One of the most dramatic changes I have ever heard in a person's life happened just a few miles from Campus Crusade for Christ's headquarters in Orlando, Florida. It is the story of Jesse Blocker. Jesse had his first taste of alcohol at the age of eight. By age fourteen, he was an alcoholic. By age thirty-six, he was a hopeless drunk and drug user living on the streets. But God had another plan for Jesse's life.

One night after getting drunk at the ABC Lounge, he passed out on the railroad tracks. Several days later he awoke in the hospital with both legs missing and one arm mangled courtesy of a passing freight train. The believers at Pine Castle United Methodist Church heard about Jesse's tragic accident and began to pray for this desperate man. The church is in view of the lounge and the scene of the accident. Hospital visits availed little as Jesse let everyone know unmistakeningly about his views of God and his vow never to darken the doors of a church again. He resented these "pretty" people with their fine clothes, cars, and neat little children.

After his release from the hospital, Jesse went back to drinking. Why not? He felt his life was over—no legs, no home, no future, and no hope. He would often sit in his wheelchair at the corner of the Pine Castle UMC property holding a sign saying he would "work for food," conning anyone who came by. This pitiful sight of a man with matted long hair, disheveled clothes, and a dirty face and hands moved many churchgoers to give him a few bucks. Before most of them got home from church, Jesse had wheeled himself down to the lounge to buy just enough liquor to drown his pain one more time. Satan had Jesse bound and imprisoned in a hell on earth not too far from a fiery eternity.

One Sunday night, the Holy Spirit moved in a special way at Pine Castle. The altar was crowded with men and women crying out to God for forgiveness and revival. After several hours, one of the prayer warriors, Delores Kagi, slipped out to take a friend home. As they left the church they saw Jesse sitting at the street corner, drunk as usual with his sign collapsed over his lap. She felt led to talk to him, but instead, decided to take her friend home first. She reasoned with herself that if Jesse was still there when she returned, she would bring him into the church.

When she returned, Delores approached Jesse asking what she could do for him. He asked for a bowl of soup. She brought him the soup and stayed with him until he finished eating. Afterwards the dazed alcoholic offered no resistance when Delores wheeled him into the church and up to the altar. Those still praying at the altar gathered around Jesse and his wheelchair. After intense prayer for his salvation and deliverance, they gave Jesse a Bible and left that night with faith that God would answer their prayers for him. But Jesse continued to drink.

His family considered him not only a threat to himself, but also to others. So they petitioned a judge to order Jesse to a treatment center. The judge agreed and sent a U.S. Marshall to pick up Jesse and take him to a detoxification center for help. Because the processing took so long for those ahead of him in the line,

Jesse quietly slipped out of the building unnoticed. With a few dollars in his pocket, he headed for a liquor store, a decision that launched a thirty-day drinking binge.

Jesse became suicidal. Several days later, he and a friend were drinking on the pier at Lake Conway. Jesse tried to commit suicide by rolling himself off the pier. As he was sinking to the bottom of the lake, he said he saw the gates of hell open and felt the heat of the lake of fire. He cried out to God and said, "Dear Lord God, in the name of Jesus..." The next thing he remembered was his drinking buddy pulling him out of the murky water and struggling to get him up on the dock. Dripping wet and smelling of alcohol, he raced his wheelchair to the Pine Castle church with those scenes of hell searing his mind. The Wednesday night service was in progress as he rolled into the sanctuary and up to the altar. The church people gathered around praying and laying their hands on him as he wept his way to repentance and forgiveness.

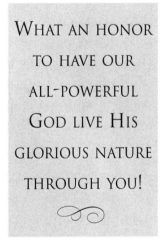

WHAT AN HONOR TO HAVE OUR ALL-POWERFUL GOD LIVE HIS GLORIOUS NATURE THROUGH YOU!

The next morning a U.S. Marshall again picked up Jesse taking him to the Orange County Jail. While Jesse sat in his cell, God allowed him to review his entire life and relive those times of desperation when he cried out to God with all his heart. He saw that God had been there for him all those times. God began to soften Jesse's hardened heart, making it pliable like clay on a potter's wheel. There our loving Savior with His tender hands began to mold and reshape the broken life of Jesse Blocker.

God loved Jesse so much that He arranged for Leon, an inmate and new believer, to be Jesse's cell mate. Leon began to disciple Jesse, helping him read the Gospel of John three times. The precious Word of God came alive as the Holy Spirit opened Jesse's understanding. He saw for the first time that he, Jesse Blocker, could come to know and trust the God who is all powerful, holy, and righteous, yet loving and merciful.

As Jesse progressed through nine months of detoxification, God placed a passion in his heart to reach the homeless, the alcoholic, and the addict with the good news of Jesus Christ.

Jesse began to go to his old friends on the streets and bring them back to his one-room duplex to sober up and to come to Christ. The neighbors began complaining about the drunks hanging around their homes, yet crack houses, prostitutes, and fortunetellers lived all around him. Jesse and his band of converts faced eviction.

Once again the prayer warriors at Pine Castle began to call out to God—this time with Jesse—for a place to bring the lost off the streets where they could get the help they needed. God miraculously provided a house, then another and another, until today there are five homes for men, one for women, and one for couples. The ministry also supports a children's home in a depressed neighborhood.

Jesse became the President of the Foundation for Life whose sole concern is to reach the homeless for Christ, disciple them in the Word of God during a six-month course, and see these men and women restored as godly people working again in the community. More than 300 men and women have gone through the program. What a thrill to see several rows at Pine Castle UMC filled nearly every Sunday morning and evening with men and women who were former street people. And you will always find Jesse sitting in his wheelchair at the end of a row. Recently, the church raised funds to send a busload of "Jesse's men" to a Promise Keeper's event. But the transformation does not stop with spiritual needs. The Foundation for Life helps its graduates find jobs, apartments, rented houses, furniture and appliances, medical treatment, food, and clothing. Daily you can find Jesse and praying believers of Pine Castle UMC combing the streets, woods, and prisons of Orlando sharing hope with the hopeless, deliverance with those in bondage, and provisions for the needy.

Just as the living Christ dramatically transformed Jesse's life, you, too, can find the help to change. Like Jesse, your life can then reflect God's glory shining the light of His great attributes to your world. What a privilege to have our infinite, all-powerful God live His glorious nature through you! Your life will dramatically change, and others will be drawn to our awesome God as they glimpse His glory radiating through your life.

Commit yourself right now to allowing God to transform you by His majesty!

HELPS FOR SPIRITUAL GROWTH

"Everything that was written in the past was written to teach us, so that through endurance and the encouragement of the Scriptures we might have hope."

ROMANS 15:4

APPENDIX A

HOW TO KNOW GOD PERSONALLY

Just as there are physical laws that govern the physical universe, so are there spiritual laws that govern your relationship with God.

LAW 1: *God loves you and offers a wonderful plan for your life.*

God's Love
"God so loved the world that He gave His one and only Son, that whoever believes in Him shall not perish but have eternal life" (John 3:16, NIV).

God's Plan
[Christ speaking] "I came that they might have life, and might have it abundantly" [that it might be full and meaningful] (John 10:10).

Why is it that most people are not experiencing the abundant life? Because…

LAW 2: *Man is sinful and separated from God. Therefore, he cannot know and experience God's love and plan for his life.*

Man Is Sinful
"All have sinned and fall short of the glory of God" (Romans 3:23).

Man was created to have fellowship with God; but, because of his own stubborn self-will, he chose to go his own independent way and fellowship with God was broken. This self-will, characterized by an attitude of active rebellion or passive indifference, is an evidence of what the Bible calls sin.

Man Is Separated

"The wages of sin is death" [spiritual separation from God] (Romans 6:23).

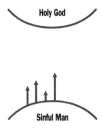

This diagram illustrates that God is holy and man is sinful. A great gulf separates the two. The arrows illustrate that man is continually trying to reach God and the abundant life through his own efforts, such as a good life, philosophy, or religion—but he inevitably fails.

The third law explains the only way to bridge this gulf...

LAW 3: *Jesus Christ is God's **only** provision for man's sin. Through Him you can know and experience God's love and plan for your life.*

He Died In Our Place

"God demonstrates His own love toward us, in that while we were yet sinners, Christ died for us" (Romans 5:8).

He Is the Only Way to God

"Jesus said to him, 'I am the way, and the truth, and the life; no one comes to the Father but through Me'" (John 14:6).

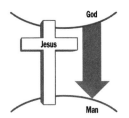

This diagram illustrates that God has bridged the gulf that separates us from Him by sending His Son, Jesus Christ, to die on the cross in our place to pay the penalty for our sins.

It is not enough just to know these three laws...

LAW 4: *We must individually **receive** Jesus Christ as Savior and Lord; then we can know and experience God's love and plan for our lives.*

We Must Receive Christ

"As many as received Him, to them He gave the right to become children of God, even to those who believe in His name" (John 1:12).

We Receive Christ Through Faith

"By grace you have been saved through faith; and that not of yourselves, it is the gift of God; not as a result of works that no one should boast" (Ephesians 2:8,9).

When We Receive Christ, We Experience a New Birth

(Read John 3:1–8.)

We Receive Christ Through Personal Invitation

[Christ speaking] "Behold, I stand at the door and knock; if any one hears My voice and opens the door, I will come in to him" (Revelation 3:20).

Receiving Christ involves turning to God from self (repentance) and trusting Christ to come into our lives to forgive our sins and to make us what He wants us to be. Just to agree intellectually that Jesus Christ is the Son of God and that He died on the cross for our sins is not enough. Nor is it enough to have an emotional experience. We receive Jesus Christ by faith, as an act of the will.

These two circles represent two kinds of lives:

Self-Directed Life
S – Self is on the throne
† – Christ is outside the life
● – Interests are directed by self, often resulting in discord and frustration

Christ-Directed Life
† – Christ is in the life and on the throne
S – Self is yielding to Christ
● – Interests are directed by Christ, resulting in harmony with God's plan

Which circle best represents your life?
Which circle would you like to have represent your life?

The following explains how you can receive Christ:

You Can Receive Christ Right Now by Faith Through Prayer
(Prayer is talking with God)

God knows your heart and is not so concerned with your words as He is with the attitude of your heart. The following is a suggested prayer:

> *Lord Jesus, I need You. Thank You for dying on the cross for my sins. I open the door of my life and receive You as my Savior and Lord. Thank You for forgiving my sins and giving me eternal life. Take control of the throne of my life. Make me the kind of person You want me to be.*

Does this prayer express the desire of your heart? If it does, I invite you to pray this prayer right now, and Christ will come into your life, as He promised.

How to Know That Christ Is in Your Life

Did you receive Christ into your life? According to His promise in Revelation 3:20, where is Christ right now in relation to you? Christ said that He would come into your life. Would He mislead you? On what authority do you know that God has answered your prayer? (The trustworthiness of God Himself and His Word.)

The Bible Promises Eternal Life to All Who Receive Christ

"God has given us eternal life, and this life is in His Son. He who has the Son has the life; he who does not have the Son of God does not have the life" (1 John 5:11–13).

Thank God often that Christ is in your life and that He will never leave you (Hebrews 13:5). You can know on the basis of His promise that Christ lives in you and that you have eternal life from the very moment you invite Him in. He will not deceive you.

An important reminder…

Do Not Depend on Feelings

The promise of God's Word, the Bible—not our feelings—is our authority. The Christian lives by faith (trust) in the trustworthiness of God Himself and His Word. This train diagram illustrates the relationship among fact (God and His Word), faith (our trust in God and His Word), and feeling (the result of our faith and obedience). (Read John 14:21.)

The train will run with or without the caboose. However, it would be useless to attempt to pull the train by the caboose. In the same way, as Christians we do not depend on feelings or emotions, but we place our faith (trust) in the trustworthiness of God and the promises of His Word.

Now That You Have Received Christ

The moment you received Christ by faith, as an act of the will, many things happened, including the following:

- Christ came into your life (Revelation 3:20; Colossians 1:27).
- Your sins were forgiven (Colossians 1:14).
- You became a child of God (John 1:12).
- You received eternal life (John 5:24).
- You began the great adventure for which God created you (John 10:10).

Can you think of anything more wonderful that could happen to you than receiving Christ? Would you like to thank God in prayer right now for what He has done for you? By thanking God, you demonstrate your faith.

To enjoy your new life to the fullest...

Suggestions for Christian Growth

Spiritual growth results from trusting Jesus Christ. A life of faith will enable you to trust God increasingly with every detail of your life, and to practice the following:

G *Go* to God in prayer daily (John 15:7).

R *Read* God's Word daily (Acts 17:11); begin with the Gospel of John.

O *Obey* God moment by moment (John 14:21).

W *Witness* for Christ by your life and words (Matthew 4:19; John 15:8).

T *Trust* God for every detail of your life (1 Peter 5:7).

H *Holy Spirit*—allow Him to control and empower your daily life and witness (Galatians 5:16,17; Acts 1:8; Ephesians 5:18).

Fellowship in a Good Church

God's Word instructs us not to forsake "the assembling of ourselves together" (Hebrews 10:25). If you do not belong to a church, do not wait to be invited. Take the initiative; call the pastor of a nearby church where Christ is honored and His Word is preached. Start this week, and make plans to attend regularly.

APPENDIX B

HOW TO BE FILLED WITH THE HOLY SPIRIT

Every day can be an exciting adventure for the Christian who knows the reality of being filled with the Holy Spirit and who lives constantly, moment by moment, under His gracious direction.

The Bible tells us that there are three kinds of people:

1. **Natural Man:** One who has not received Christ.

   "A natural man does not accept the things of the Spirit of God; for they are foolishness to him, and he cannot understand them, because they are spiritually appraised" (1 Corinthians 2:14, NASB).

   Self-Directed Life
   S – Self is on the throne
   † – Christ is outside the life
   ● – Interests are directed by self, often resulting in discord and frustration

2. **Spiritual Man:** One who is directed and empowered by the Holy Spirit.

   "He who is spiritual appraises all things" (1 Corinthians 2:15, NASB).

   Christ-Directed Life
   S – Christ is in the life and on the throne
   † – Self is yielding to Christ
   ● – Interests are directed by Christ, resulting in harmony with God's plan

3. **Carnal Man:** One who has received Christ, but who lives in defeat because he trusts in his own efforts to live the Christian life.

"I, brethren, could not speak to you as to spiritual people but as to carnal, as to babes in Christ. I fed you with milk and not with solid food; for until now you were not able to receive it, and even now you are still not able;

Self-Directed Life
S – Self is on the throne
† – Christ dethroned and not allowed to direct the life
● – Interests are directed by self, often resulting in discord and frustration

for you are still carnal. For when there are envy, strife, and divisions among you, are you not carnal and behaving like mere men?" (1 Corinthians 3:1–3).

The following are four principles for living the Spirit-filled life:

1 God has provided for us an abundant and fruitful Christian life.

"Jesus said, 'I have come that they may have life, and that they may have it more abundantly'" (John 10:10, NKJ).

"The fruit of the Spirit is love, joy, peace, patience, kindness, goodness, faithfulness, gentleness, self-control; against such things there is no law" (Galatians 5:22,23).

Read John 15:5 and Acts 1:8.

The following are some personal traits of the spiritual man that result from trusting God:

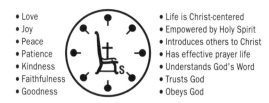

- Love
- Joy
- Peace
- Patience
- Kindness
- Faithfulness
- Goodness

- Life is Christ-centered
- Empowered by Holy Spirit
- Introduces others to Christ
- Has effective prayer life
- Understands God's Word
- Trusts God
- Obeys God

The degree to which these traits are manifested in the life depends on the extent to which the Christian trusts the Lord with every detail of his life, and on his maturity in Christ. One who is only beginning to understand the ministry of the Holy Spirit should not be discouraged if he is not as fruitful as more mature Christians who have known and experienced this truth for a longer period.

Why is it that most Christians are not experiencing the abundant life?

2 Carnal Christians cannot experience the abundant and fruitful Christian life.

The carnal man trusts in his own efforts to live the Christian life:

- He is either uninformed about, or has forgotten, God's love, forgiveness, and power (Romans 5:8–10; Hebrews 10:1–25; 1 John 1; 2:1–3; 2 Peter 1:9).
- He has an up-and-down spiritual experience.
- He wants to do what is right, but cannot.
- He fails to draw on the power of the Holy Spirit to live the Christian life (1 Corinthians 3:1–3; Romans 7:15–24; 8:7; Galatians 5:16–18).

Some or all of the following traits may characterize the carnal man—the Christian who does not fully trust God:

- Legalistic attitude
- Impure thoughts
- Jealousy
- Guilt
- Worry
- Discouragement
- Critical spirit
- Frustration

- Aimlessness
- Fear
- Ignorance of his spiritual heritage
- Unbelief
- Disobedience
- Loss of love for God and for others
- Poor prayer life
- No desire for Bible study

(The individual who professes to be a Christian but who continues to practice sin should realize that he may not be a Christian at all, according to 1 John 2:3; 3:6–9; and Ephesians 5:5.)

The third truth gives us the only solution to this problem...

3 Jesus promised the abundant and fruitful life as the result of being filled (directed and empowered) by the Holy Spirit.

The Spirit-filled life is the Christ-directed life by which Christ lives His life in and through us in the power of the Holy Spirit (John 15).

- One becomes a Christian through the ministry of the Holy Spirit (John 3:1–8.) From the moment of spiritual birth, the Christian is indwelt by the Holy Spirit at all times (John 1:12; Colossians 2:9,10; John 14:16,17).

  All Christians are indwelt by the Holy Spirit, but not all Christians are filled (directed, controlled, and empowered) by the Holy Spirit on an ongoing basis.

- The Holy Spirit is the source of the overflowing life (John 7:37–39).

- In His last command before His ascension, Christ promised the power of the Holy Spirit to enable us to be witnesses for Him (Acts 1:1–9).

How, then, can one be filled with the Holy Spirit?

4 We are filled (directed and empowered) by the Holy Spirit by faith; then we can experience the abundant and fruitful life that Christ promised to each Christian.

You can appropriate the filling of the Holy Spirit right now if you:

- Sincerely desire to be directed and empowered by the Holy Spirit (Matthew 5:6; John 7:37–39).

- Confess your sins. By faith, thank God that He has forgiven all of your sins—past, present, and future—because Christ died for you (Colossians 2:13–15).

- Present every area of your life to God (Romans 12:1,2).

- By faith claim the fullness of the Holy Spirit, according to:

  His command: Be filled with the Spirit. "Do not get drunk on wine, which leads to debauchery. Instead, be filled with the Spirit" (Ephesians 5:18).

  His promise: He will always answer when we pray according to His will. "This is the confidence we have in approaching God: that if we ask anything according to his will, he hears us. And if we know that He hears us—whatever we ask—we know that we have what we asked of Him" (1 John 5:14,15).

How to Pray in Faith to be Filled With the Holy Spirit

We are filled with the Holy Spirit by faith alone. However, true prayer is one way of expressing your faith. The following is a suggested prayer:

> Dear Father, I need You. I acknowledge that I have been directing my own life and that, as a result, I have sinned against You. I thank You that You have forgiven my sins through Christ's death on the cross for me. I now invite Christ to again take His place on the throne of my life. Fill me with the Holy Spirit as You commanded me to be filled, and as You promised in Your Word that You would do if I asked in faith. I pray this in the name of Jesus. As an expression of my faith, I now thank You for directing my life and for filling me with the Holy Spirit.

Does this prayer express the desire of your heart? If so, bow in prayer and trust God to fill you with the Holy Spirit right now.

APPENDIX C

NAMES OF GOD

God is called by many names in the Bible. These names hold an important key to understanding the doctrine of God and His revelation to His people. The truth of God's character is focused in His names. His names express various aspects of His nature, character, and never-changing relationship to His people. Following are some of His names and their meanings.

Adonai – Lord or Master, denoting ownership. (Psalm 39:7; 54:4; 71:5; 73:28; 86:5; 86:12; 86:15; 140:7; Isaiah 6:8; Ezekiel 18:25; Luke 6:46.)

El – A generic term for God or deity. (Psalm 22; Mark 15:34.)

Elohim – The strong, faithful One; the only true God. (Genesis 1:26.)

El-Berith – The God of the Covenant. (Judges 8:33; 9:46.)

El-Elyon – The Exalted One and all others are below Him; the Most High God. (Numbers 24:16; 2 Samuel 22:14; Psalm 18:13; Isaiah 14:12–15; Daniel 7:27.)

El-Olam – Eternal, perpetual, everlasting; the Everlasting God. (Genesis 9:16; 17:8; 21:33; Exodus 40:15; Deuteronomy 33:27; Proverbs 10:25; 45:17; Jeremiah 20:11; 31:3; Daniel 4:3; Habakkuk 3:6; John 3:16; 2 Thessalonians 1:8,9; Hebrews 5:9.)

El-Roi – To see, to perceive, understand, and know; the God who sees. (Psalm 139:1,2,7; John 5:19.)

El-Shaddai – Most powerful in strength; the Almighty God. (Genesis 17:1,2; Exodus 6:3; Job 40:2.)

Immanuel – God with us. (Matthew 1:23; Galatians 4:4,5.)

Jehovah – I AM, or self-existence; translated as Yahweh or LORD. (Exodus 3:14,15; John 4:25,26; 8:12, 8:28; 10:9,11,36; 15:1; James 1:17; Hebrews 13:8.)

Jehovah-Jireh – To have regard for the one seen, to see to his every need with provision and care; the Lord our Provider. (Genesis 22:8,14; Hebrews 22:17–19.)

Jehovah-Mekaddesh – To purify, cleanse, and sanctify unto God; the Lord who sanctifies. (Exodus 13:2; Leviticus 19:2; 20:7,8; 25:10; 1 Samuel 2:2; Psalm 103:1; Proverbs 9:10; Isaiah 6:3; John 17:17; Romans 12:1; 1 Peter 1:15,16.)

Jehovah-Nissi – A banner set up on a high place in case of invasion, assembling the people for victory; the Lord our Banner. (Exodus 14:13; 17:15,16; Deuteronomy 20:3,4; Isaiah 13:2–4,11; John 3:14; 16:33; 1 Corinthians 15:57; Ephesians 2:8,9; 6:10–12.)

Jehovah-Rohi – To tend as one cares for sheep; the Lord our Shepherd. (Isaiah 40:10,11; Ezekiel 34:11–16; Psalm 23:1,4; 139:2; John 10:11; Hebrews 13:20; 1 Peter 2:25.)

Jehovah-Rophe – Jehovah who heals; God our healer. (Numbers 12:13; Psalm 103:2,3; Jeremiah 3:22; 30:17,26; Malachi 4:2; Matthew 4:23; 11:4,5; Luke 4:18; John 5:36; Revelation 22:17.)

Jehovah-Sabaoth – An army or warriors who stand and fight against an enemy; the Lord, the captain of our salvation. (1 Samuel 1:3; Jeremiah 11:20; Zechariah 4:6.)

Jehovah-Shalom – Peace; the Lord our Peace. (Numbers 6:24–26; Judges 6:13,23,24; Isaiah 9:6; 26:2–4,12; Matthew 11:28,29; John 14:27; 16:33; Romans 5:1; 15:33; Philippians 4:5–7; Colossians 1:20.)

Jehovah-Shammah – There, in that place, therein; the Lord is there. (Exodus 33:14–16; Psalm 132:8,13,14; Isaiah 63:9; Ezekiel 43:1–7; 48:35; Matthew 28:20; John 1:14; 14:2,3; 1 Corinthians 3:16; 6:17; 2 Corinthians 6:16; Ephesians 2:19–22.)

Jehovah-Tsidkenu – Righteousness, rightness; the Lord our righteousness. (Deuteronomy 32:4; Psalm 89:14; 129:4; Jeremiah 23:5,6; 33:6–26; Daniel 9:7,8; Acts 3:14; Romans 3:20; 5:16–19; 6:11–13,18; 1 Corinthians 1:30; 2 Corinthians 5:21.)

Sources:

Nathan Stone, *Names of God* (Chicago: Moody Bible Institute, 1944).

Trent C. Butler, General Editor, *Holman Bible Dictionary* (Nashville: Holman Bible Publishers, 1991), 1004–1006.

Areon Potter, *From Darkness to Light: Demonic Oppression & the Christian* (Arvada, CO: Adonai Resources, 1994), 222–262.

END NOTES

Chapter 1

1 A. W. Tozer, *The Knowledge of the Holy* (San Francisco: HarperSanFrancisco, 1961).

2 "Karl Marx," *The New Encyclopedia Britannica*, vol. 23 (Chicago: Encyclopedia Britannica, Inc., 1978).

3 James M. Kittleson, "The Breakthrough," *Christian History*, Issue 34, 15.

Chapter 2

1 John 4:24.
2 Isaiah 41:8.
3 Exodus 33:8–11, TLB.
4 Genesis 5:24; 6:9.
5 John 15:15.
6 Numbers 23:19; Genesis 16:13; 1 Kings 8:30.
7 John 17.
8 John 10:30; Colossians 2:9.
9 Colossians 1:18.
10 Romans 8:34.
11 Romans 8:11; John 16:13.
12 John 16:8; 1 Corinthians 2:10.
13 Genesis 1:1.
14 Colossians 1:16.
15 Psalm 104:30.
16 Luke 1:35.
17 Matthew 3:16,17.
18 Acts 2:32.
19 John 10:18.
20 Romans 1:4.
21 1 Peter 1:2.
22 Hebrews 9:14.
23 John 14:15–23.

Chapter 3

1 J. B. Phillips, *Your God Is Too Small* (New York: MacMillan Publishing, 1953).

2 Exodus 3:14, NIV.
3 Psalm 145:1–7, TLB.
4 1 Timothy 1:17, KJV.
5 Revelation 1:17,18, NIV.
6 *Our Daily Bread*, June 11, 1995 (Grand Rapids, MI: RBC Ministries).
7 Isaiah 40:12,13, NASB.
8 Colossians 1:17; Hebrews 1:3.
9 John 16:13.
10 Psalm 63:1.

Chapter 4

1 Psalm 19:1–4, NIV.
2 Pam Beasant, *1000 Facts About Space* (New York: Kingfisher Books, 1992), 10,11.
3 Isaiah 40:26
4 Psalm 33:6,9; Job 38:4.
5 Romans 1:20.
6 1 Chronicles 29:12, NIV.
7 Ephesians 1:19.
8 Isaiah 40:15.
9 Daniel 4:35, NIV.
10 John 16:11, NIV.
11 Matthew 8:28–32, NIV.
10 Isaiah 46:10.
11 Job 42:2, NIV.
14 Psalm 33:6–9.
15 Tony Evans, *Our God Is Awesome* (Chicago: Moody Press, 1994), 162.
16 Hebrews 1:3.
17 1 Chronicles 29:10,11,13.

Chapter 5

1 Isaiah 40:28,29, TLB.
2 Isaiah 40:30,31, TLB.
3 Isaiah 14:26.
4 Romans 13:1,2.

5   Psalm 66:5,7.

6   Ephesians 1:19,20.

7   Philippians 4:13, NIV.

8   Colossians 1:11, NIV.

9   Galatians 5:16.

10 2 Peter 1:3.

11 Romans 6:1–8; Ephesians 5:18.

12 1 John 5:14,15, NIV.

13 2 Corinthians 12:9.

14 Colossians 1:28,29.

15 Acts 1:8.

16 Ephesians 3:20.

17 David Jeremiah, *Knowing the God You Worship*, audio cassettes (San Diego: Turning Point, 1994).

Chapter 6

1   Jeremiah 23:23,24, NIV.

2   John 3:8.

3   1 Kings 8:27.

4   A. W. Tozer, *The Knowledge of the Holy* (San Francisco: HarperSanFrancisco, 1961), 75,76.

5   Bill Hybels, *The God You're Looking For* (Nashville: Thomas Nelson Publishers, 1997), 24.

6   Website of the U. S. Department of Energy, www.ornl.gov/hgmis/faq/faqs1.html.

7   2 Corinthians 4:6, NIV.

8   Ephesians 5:12,13.

9   Psalm 34:18.

10 In Matthew 28:18–20, Christ gave the Great Commission where He commands His followers to take His message of love and forgiveness to the entire world.

11 John 1:14,18.

12 John 14:16,17, NIV.

13 1 Corinthians 3:16,17, NIV.

14 John 14:17, NIV.

15 Brother Lawrence, *The Practice of the Presence of God* (Pittsburgh: Whitaker House, 1982), 17.

16 Lawrence, 19.

Chapter 7

1   Psalm 139:8–10, NIV.

2   Isaiah 65:24.

3   Psalm 22:1,2.

4   Psalm 22:9,23,24.

5   Corrie ten Boom with John and Elizabeth Sherrill, *The Hiding Place* (Washington Depot, CT: 1971), 197.

6   Matthew 28:20.

7   Judy Nelson, "Golden Opportunities," *Worldwide Challenge*, January/February 1999, 41.

8   Matthew 6:4, NIV.

9   Luke 6:35, NIV.

10 Hebrews 4:13.

11 Brother Lawrence, *The Practice of the Presence of God* (Pittsburgh: Whitaker House, 1982), 38.

12 Ibid., 59.

13 Psalm 32:8, NIV.

14 Isaiah 41:10, NIV.

15 Jim Cymbala, *Fresh Wind, Fresh Fire* (Grand Rapids, MI: Zondervan Publishing House, 1997), 56.

16 David Jeremiah, *Knowing the God You Worship*, audio cassettes, (San Diego: Turning Point, 1994).

17 1 Corinthians 10:13.

18 Psalm 34:18.

19 1 Peter 5:7, NIV.

20 John 15:15.

21 Hebrews 13:5, NIV.

22 Romans 8:38,39.

Chapter 8

1   "Albert Einstein," *Compton's Encyclopedia Online* v. 3.0 (The Learning Company, Inc., 1998).

2   Isaiah 40:13,14, NIV.

3   Romans 11:33.

4   "Computers," *Compton's Encyclopedia Online* v. 3.0 (The Learning Company, Inc., 1998).

5   Ibid.

6   Stephen Charnock, *The Existence and*

Attributes of God, Vol. 1 (Grand Rapids, MI: Baker Books, reprinted 1996), 409.

7 Matthew 11:27.

8 Cited by Marcus Chown in "Let There Be Light," *New Scientist* (vol. 157, February 7, 1998), 30. As quoted in Henry M. Morris, "The Stardust Trail," *Back to Genesis* (no. 121, January 1999), a.

9 Isaiah 46:9,10.

10 Isaiah 43:25,NIV.

11 1 John 1:9.

12 Psalm 33:13–15.

13 Luke 22:31,32, NIV.

14 Deuteronomy 30:3; Isaiah 11:11,12; Jeremiah 23:3,4; Zephaniah 3:20.

15 Psalm 139:1–6.

Chapter 9

1 Matthew 10:30.

2 Isaiah 49:15,16, NIV.

3 Psalm 103:14, NIV.

4 Psalm 37:23.

5 Psalm 103:14.

6 Jeremiah 17:9,10.

7 David Jeremiah, *Knowing the God You Worship*, audio cassettes (San Diego: Turning Point, 1994).

8 Sherwood Eddy, *Pathfinders of the World Missionary Crusade* (New York: Abingdon-Cokesbury, 1945), 125. As quoted in Ruth A. Tucker, *From Jerusalem to Irian Jaya* (Grand Rapids, MI: Zondervan Publishing House, 1983), 239.

9 Acts 2:23.

10 Ephesians 1:4, NIV.

11 James 1:5,6.

12 Hosea 4:6.

13 Proverbs 3:5,6.

14 1 Corinthians 10:13, NIV.

Chapter 10

1 Charles Allen and Sharada Dwivedi, *Lives of the Indian Princes* (New York: Crown Publishers, Inc., 1984), 18.

2 Ibid., 211.

3 Anne Edwards, *Royal Sisters* (New York: William Morrow and Company, Inc., 1990), 257.

4 Psalm 24:8–10, NKJ.

5 Revelation 19:1,6,16.

6 Revelation 4:2–11.

7 Daniel 2:21.

8 Jeremiah 18:6.

9 Romans 9:20, NIV.

10 Stephen Charnock, *The Existence and Attributes of God* (Grand Rapids, MI: Baker Books, reprinted 1996) vol. 2, 366.

11 Job 37:6,10–13.

12 Dick Edic, "Miraculous Memory," *Keep In Touch,* Winter 1999, Campus Crusade for Christ Alumni Relations.

13 Psalm 75:7, NIV.

14 2 Kings 24:1–4.

15 Isaiah 45:13.

16 Ephesians 1:5.

17 Ephesians 1:4.

18 Acts 1:8.

19 Romans 14:17; John 18:36.

20 Matthew 6:19–21,24–34.

21 Hebrews 4:15,16.

22 Luke 23:34.

23 A. W. Tozer, *The Attributes of God* (Camp Hill, PA: Christian Publications, 1997), 181.

Chapter 11

1 Isaiah 46:10, NIV.

2 Proverbs 19:21, NIV.

3 James 4:13–16, NIV.

4 Romans 5:12–21.

5 Genesis 3:16–19.

6 Charles Stanley, "Where Our Needs Are Met," audio cassette, (Atlanta, GA: InTouch Ministries).

7 Romans 8:28.

8 1 Peter 5:7.

9   Ephesians 1:9,10.

10 Revelation 21:26–22:5.

Chapter 12

1   Quoted in Max Boot, *Out of Order* (New York: Basic Books, 1998), 176.

2   David Jeffery, "Yellowstone: The Great Fires of 1988," *National Geographic*, February 1989, 265.

3   A. W. Tozer, *The Pursuit of God* (Camp Hill, PA: Christian Publications, 1993), 37.

4   Exodus 15:11.

5   *Nelson Study Bible*, (Nashville, TN: Thomas Nelson Publishers, 1997), 2120.

6   Isaiah 6:1–4.

7   Isaiah 6:5.

8   Stephen Charnock, *The Existence and Attributes of God* (Grand Rapids, MI: Baker Books, reprinted 1996), vol. 2, 112.

9   Louis Berkof, *Systematic Theology* (Grand Rapids, MI: Wm. B. Eerdmans Publishing Co., 1941), 73.

10 Romans 7:12.

11 Jude 4, NIV.

12 Jude 5, NIV.

13 Jude 6, NIV.

14 Matthew 7:12.

15 Joshua 24:19.

16 Proverbs 9:10.

17 Beth Moore, *A Woman's Heart: God's Dwelling Place* (Nashville, TN: Lifeway Press, 1995), 161.

18 Psalm 96:9, NIV.

19 Isaiah 6:7.

Chapter 13

1   Romans 8:1–4.

2   Psalm 2:11.

3   Proverbs 9:10, NIV.

4   Psalm 5:4.

5   Hebrews 10:10,14,18–20.

6   Isaiah 59:1,2.

7   1 Timothy 6:16.

8   1 John 1:5,7.

9   John 8:12.

10 1 Peter 1:15.

11 Romans 12:1,2.

12 Exodus 20:3–5.

13 1 Peter 1:16.

14 Ephesians 5:25–27.

Chapter 14

1   Josh McDowell, *The Myths of Sex Education* (San Bernardino, CA: Here's Life Publishers, 1990), 58.

2   McDowell, 59.

3   George Grant, *Grand Illusions: The Legacy of Planned Parenthood* (Brentwood, TN: Wolgemuth & Hyatt Publishers, Inc., 1988), 30. As quoted in Josh McDowell, *The Myths of Sex Education*, 60.

4   Robert C. Noble, "There Is No Safe Sex," *Newsweek*, April 1, 1991, 9.

5   Lorraine Day, M.D., website "Are You Safe From AIDS? You May Be In for a Big Surprise" (www.drday.com/doctors.htm).

6   *Barna Report, 1997: American Witness* (Dallas, TX: Word Publishing, 1997).

7   George Barna, *What America Believes* (Ventura, CA: Regal Books, 1991), 84–85.

8   Leviticus 18:22; 20:13; Romans 1:24–28; 1 Corinthians 6:9,10; 1 Timothy 1:8–10.

9   Charles Colson, "Neale Donald Walsch: The Words…" *The Wall Street Journal*, July 9, 1997, A12.

10 Exodus 20:14.

11 Numbers 23:19, NIV.

12 Exodus 19:18.

13 Exodus 34:1.

14 John 17:17, NIV.

15 2 Timothy 3:16.

16 John 14:6.

17 John 14:16,17, NIV.

18 John 4:24.

Chapter 15

1 "Interviews from Death Row: Reporter Kathy Chiero's developing relationship with Karla," *CBN Interviews Online*, January 30, 1998, 1.

2 "New Life on Death Row: The Karla Faye Tucker Story," *CBN Interviews Online*, 1,2.

3 1 John 4:5, NIV.

4 Proverbs 12:19.

5 Psalm 119:151,152, NIV.

6 2 Timothy 3:16.

7 Hebrews 10:23, NIV.

8 John 14:3.

9 John 14:12.

10 John 14:27.

11 John 8:44.

12 John 8:12.

13 Hebrews 13:5.

14 Matthew 6:33, NIV.

15 Philippians 4:19, NIV.

16 Matthew 16:25,26.

17 1 Corinthians 6:18.

18 Hebrews 13:4.

19 Exodus 20:14.

20 Luke 12:2.

21 Galatians 6:7, NIV.

22 Ephesians 4:31, NIV.

23 Romans 12:17,19, NIV.

24 Luke 6:27.

25 Jeremiah 17:10, NIV.

26 John 8:31,32.

27 John 10:28.

28 Titus 1:2, NIV.

29 Hebrews 6:16–18.

30 Lisa Master, "Houston, We Have a Problem," *Worldwide Challenge*, July/August 1997, 24.

31 Matthew 16:24,25.

32 1 Corinthians 13:5.

33 Romans 8:15, NIV.

34 Jeremiah 29:11.

35 Ephesians 5:18.

36 1 John 5:14,15.

Chapter 16

1 Millard J. Erickson, *Concise Dictionary of Christian Theology* (Grand Rapids, MI: Baker Book House, 1986), 75.

2 Ibid., 144.

3 Psalm 145:17, NIV.

4 Psalm 71:19, NIV.

5 Psalm 97:2.

6 Jeremiah 9:24, NIV.

7 Robert J. Wagman, *The Supreme Court: A Citizen's Guide* (New York: Pharos Books, 1993), 169–171.

8 Psalm 119:137, NIV.

9 Isaiah 64:5,6.

10 Romans 4:23,24, NIV.

11 1 Thessalonians 5:23,24.

Chapter 17

1 Psalm 116:5, NIV.

2 Romans 3:22–25.

3 Ephesians 4:22–24.

4 Matthew 6:33, NIV.

5 Psalm 5:12, NIV.

6 Henry T. Blackaby and Claude V. King, *Experiencing God* (Nashville, TN: Broadman and Holman Publishers, 1994), 167.

7 Proverbs 14:34.

8 November 11, 1620. William Bradford, *The History of Plymouth Plantation 1608–1650* (Boston, MA: Massachusetts Historical Society, 1856).

9 Quoted in *The New American*, December 12, 1986, 10.

10 Henry Halley, *Halley's Bible Handbook* (Grand Rapids, MI: Zondervan, 1965), 18.

11 October 11, 1798, in his address as President to the Military. Charles Francis Adams, ed., *The Works of John Adams–Second President of the United States* (Boston: Little, Brown, & Co., 1854), 9:229.

12 1828, in the preface to his *American Dictionary of the English Language* (San

Francisco: Foundation for American Christian Education, reprinted 1967), 12.

13 September 5, 1864, addressing the Committee of Colored People from Baltimore, *Washington Chronicle.* Quoted in Stephen Abbott Northrop, D.D., *A Cloud of Witnesses* (Portland, OR: American Heritage Ministries, 1987), 285.

14 October 12, 1816, *The Correspondence and Public Papers of John Jay*, Henry P. Johnston, ed., (New York: Burt Franklin, 1970), 4:393.

15 February 29, 1892, Justice Josiah Brewer, *Church of the Holy Trinity v. United States*, 143 US 457-458, 465-471, 36L ed 226.

16 For more information on how you can get involved in the fasting and prayer movement to be an advocate for righteousness in your area, call (800) 888-FAST (3278). If you want to read more about exciting testimonies like the one about Houston, read my book *The Transforming Power of Fasting and Prayer.* Order by calling *NewLife* Publications at (800) 235-7255.

Chapter 18

1 David Protess and Rob Warden, *A Promise of Justice* (New York: Hyperion, 1998), 222.

2 Jeremiah 17:10, NIV.

3 Robert J. Wagman, *The Supreme Court: A Citizen's Guide* (New York: Pharos Books, 1993), 7,11,12,16,17.

4 Deuteronomy 32:4.

5 *Wycliffe Bible Encyclopedia* (Chicago: Moody Press) 1975, 1:981.

6 Genesis 18:25, NIV.

7 James 4:12, NIV.

8 Quoted in Max Boot, *Out of Order* (New York: Basic Books, 1998), ix.

9 Psalm 7:11, NIV.

10 Psalm 90:8,9,11.

11 1 John 1:9.

12 Ephesians 5:18.

13 1 John 5:14,15.

14 Ecclesiastes 12:14, NIV.

15 Jeremiah 12:1.

16 Galatians 6:7, NIV.

17 Deuteronomy 32:35, NIV.

18 Romans 2:5–8, NIV.

19 Revelation 20:11–15, NIV.

Chapter 19

1 Deuteronomy 32:4, NASB.

2 Judy Nelson, "The Persecuted Church," *Worldwide Challenge*, September/October 1997, 36.

3 Raleigh Washington, "I Would Not Agree to It Because It Was Not True," *Worldwide Challenge*, March/April 1992, 24.

4 Isaiah 5:1–10.

5 Luke 18:3, NIV.

6 Luke 18:5, NIV.

7 Luke 18:7,8, NIV.

8 Robert J. Wagman, *The Supreme Court: A Citizen's Guide* (New York: Pharos Books, 1993), 41.

9 March 30, 1863. James D. Richardson, *A Compilation of the Messages and Papers of the Presidents*, 1789–1897 (Published by Authority of Congress, 1899), 6:164.

10 Merril D. Patterson, ed., *Jefferson Writings* (New York: Literary Classics of the United States, Inc., 1984), 289, from Jefferson's *Notes on the State of Virginia, Query XVIII*, 1781.

11 2 Corinthians 5:10.

12 Matthew 12:36,37.

13 Colossians 3:23,24.

14 Matthew 25:21.

15 Daniel 12:3, NIV.

16 Hebrews 6:10, NIV.

17 Colossians 3:23,24, NIV.

Chapter 20

1   "1969 Woodstock Festival & Concert" (www.woodstock69.com).
2   1 John 4:8.
3   Psalm 100:5.
4   Romans 5:5.
5   Acts 14:17, NIV.
6   Dwight L. Moody, "The Love of God," *Classic Sermons on the Attributes of God*, compiled by Warren W. Wiersbe (Peabody, MA: Hendrickson Publishers), 1989, 12.
7   Luke 19:5, NIV.
8   Ephesians 1:4,5, NIV.
9   John 13:1, NIV.
10 John 13:37,38, NIV.
11 Luke 22:32.
12 Jeremiah 31:3, NIV.
13 1 John 3:1, NIV.
14 Romans 8:38,39.
15 Romans 8:28.
16 Romans 5:1,2.
17 John 14:2,3.
18 Words by Samuel Trevor Francis, 1834–1925, *O the Deep, Deep Love of Jesus*.

Chapter 21

1   1 John 4:16.
2   Matthew 22:37,38.
3   1 John 4:11.
4   Matthew 22:39, TLB.
5   Matthew 5:44, NIV.
6   Richard Wurmbrand, "Love Conquers Everything," *The Voice of the Martyrs*, March 1999, 10.
7   Ibid.
8   John 13:35.
9   2 Corinthians 5:14,15, NIV.
10 Ephesians 3:17,18.
11 Hebrews 11:6.
12 To read more about loving by faith, order my booklet *How to Love by Faith* by calling *NewLife* Publications at (800) 235-7255.

Chapter 22

1   Matthew 5:45.
2   Millard J. Erickson, *Concise Dictionary of Christian Theology* (Grand Rapids, MI: Baker Book House, 1986), 67.
3   Romans 3:23, NIV.
4   Romans 6:23, NIV.
5   Romans 6:23, NIV.
6   1 Peter 2:24, NIV.
7   Isaiah 49:13, NIV.
8   John 8:1–11.
9   Hebrews 12:6,7.
10 Micah 6:8.
11 2 Peter 3:9.
12 David Morris, *A Lifestyle of Worship* (Ventura, CA: Renew Books, 1998), 201.

Chapter 23

1   A. W. Tozer, *The Knowledge of the Holy* (San Francisco: HarperSanFrancisco, 1961), 92.
2   Matthew 18:22.
3   Adapted from Ed DeWeese, "The Right Man to Rob," *Worldwide Challenge*, January/February 1995, 5.
4   Luke 6:35,36.
5   Hebrews 4:16.
6   2 Samuel 12:13,14.
7   Ephesians 4:15.

Chapter 24

1   Jack Canfield (ed.), Mark Victor Hansen, *Chicken Soup for the Soul: 101 Stories to Open the Heart and Rekindle the Spirit* (Health Communications, 1995), 273,274.
2   Lamentations 3:22,23, NIV.
3   Hebrews 11:1.
4   Hebrews 11:11.
5   Genesis 22:13.
6   1 Thessalonians 5:24, NIV.
7   Psalm 119:90.
8   2 Timothy 2:13, NIV.
9   Romans 3:3, NIV.

10 Psalm 105:8, NIV.
11 Corinthians 1:20, NIV.
12 Hebrews 10:23, NIV.
13 2 Corinthians 9:7, NIV.
14 2 Corinthians 9:8, NIV.

Chapter 25

1 Psalm 36:5.
2 1 Corinthians 1:9, NIV.
3 Deuteronomy 7:9.
4 Psalm 143:1, NIV.
5 1 Corinthians 10:13.
6 2 Thessalonians 3:3.
7 1 John 1:9.
8 1 Corinthians 1:7,9, NIV.
9 1 Peter 4:19, NIV.
10 Romans 5:3.
11 Philippians 1:6.

Chapter 26

1 Mark Lehner, "Computer Rebuilds the Ancient Sphinx," *National Geographic*, April 1991, 32–39.
2 Shirley MacLaine, *Dancing in the Light*, 35. As quoted in Josh McDowell and Don Stewart, *Deceivers: What Cults Believe, How They Lure Their Followers* (Nashville: Thomas Nelson Publishers, 1992), 236.
3 Kenneth S. Latourette, *Introducing Buddhism* (New York: Friendship Press, 1956), 4. As quoted in Russell P. Spittler, *Cults and Isms* (Grand Rapids, MI: Baker Book House, 1962), 96.
4 Hebrews 1:11,12, NIV.
5 Exodus 3:14, NIV.
6 James 1:17, NIV.
7 1 John 1:9.
8 Philippians 2:7,8.
9 Genesis 15:6.
10 Raymond Davis, *Fire on the Mountains* (Grand Rapids, MI: Zondervan Publishing House, 1975), 135,136.
11 Hebrews 13:8.
12 "Adoring the Ineffable: Prayers from the Liturgy of St. John Chrysostom," *Christian History*, vol. XIII, No. 4, 38.

Chapter 27

1 James 1:17.
2 Psalm 33:11.
3 Isaiah 46:10,11.
4 Ephesians 2:10.
5 Psalm 18:30.
6 Philippians 2:13.
7 John Eidsmoe, *Christianity and the Constitution*, (Grand Rapids, MI: Baker Book House, 1987), 51,53.
8 Abraham Lincoln, September 5, 1864, in an address to the Committee of Colored People from Baltimore.
9 Ronald Reagan, Gales Quotations CD-ROM (Detroit, MI: Gale Research Inc., 1995).
10 Hebrews 6:17.
11 Ephesians 1:14, TLB.
12 Jonah 3:4–10.
13 Numbers 14:1–20; 2 Kings 20:1–6; Luke 18:1–8.

Chapter 28

1 Exodus 19:17,18; 20:18–20.
2 Psalm 147:11, NIV.
3 Walter C. Kaiser, Jr., et al, *Hard Sayings of the Bible* (Downers Grove, IL: Intervarsity Press, 1996), 284.
4 Proverbs 9:10, NIV.
5 John 8:28,29.
6 Proverbs 3:7,8.
7 Psalm 103:11, NIV.

Chapter 29

1 James 1:22.
2 Romans 12:1,2.
3 John 14:21, Acts 4:13.
4 John 14:15–18; Acts 1:4,5,8.
5 2 Chronicles 7:14.
6 Psalm 24:3–6.

GOD: Discover His Character
Bill Bright

"Everything about our lives is determined and influenced by our view of God," writes Bill Bright.

In his thorough but easy-to-grasp new book, *GOD: Discover His Character*, the founder and president of Campus Crusade for Christ—a man whose ministry has impacted millions of lives worldwide—shares the fruit of his personal, lifelong study of God. These wonderful truths are certain to energize your life and walk with God, just as they have his. Through these pages Dr. Bright will equip you with a biblical vision of God. So when you're confused, you can experience His truth. When you're frightened, you can know His peace. When you're sad, you can live in His joy.

Hardcover / 336p / ISBN 1-56399-121-7 / $19.99

GOD: Discover His Character Video Series
Bill Bright

In these 13 sessions, complete on three videos, Dr. Bill Bright will equip you with a biblical vision of God. Each session will fit in a one-hour format, allowing for discussion and personal application. Dr. Bright's clear teaching is illustrated by fascinating dramas and vignettes that bring home the truth of God's attributes in everyday life. This video series, with the accompanying video guide, is ideal for youth, college, and adult Sunday school classes or study groups.

Our Great Creator (Vol. I)

Dr. Bright explores God as all-powerful, ever-present, all-knowing, and sovereign—and how those attributes can give you hope and courage in life.

Video / 120 minutes / ISBN 1-56399-122-5 / $19.99

Our Perfect Judge (Vol. II)

God, your perfect Judge, is holy, true, righteous, and just, and Dr. Bright explains how those characteristics help you to live a righteous life.

Video / 120 minutes / ISBN 1-56399-123-3 / $19.99

Our Gracious Savior (Vol. III)

Dr. Bright introduces you to the God who is loving, merciful, faithful, and unchangeable, and shows how you can experience those awesome attributes every day.

Video / 120 minutes / ISBN 1-53699-124-1 / $19.99

GOD: Discover the Benefits of His Attributes
Bill Bright

God deeply desires that you know Him better. Now there is a full-color, laminated card that can help energize your life and walk with God as you get to know His character. The handy 3" × 5" size is perfect to carry in your pocket or purse, or for sharing with friends.

Card (Package of 10) / ISBN 1-56399-130-6 / $3.99

GOD: 13 Steps to Discovering His Attributes
Bill Bright

In this handy guide, the founder and president of Campus Crusade for Christ International shares the fruit of his personal, lifelong study of God. These wonderful truths regarding God's character are certain to energize your life and walk with God, just as they have his. Keep this condensed booklet in your pocket or purse to read during quiet moments, and experience God's truth and encouragement wherever you go.

Booklet / 32p / ISBN 1-56399-126-8 / $.99

RESPONSE FORM

☐ I have received Jesus Christ as my Savior and Lord as a result of reading this book.

☐ As a new Christian I want to know Christ better and experience the abundant Christian life.

☐ I want to be one of the two million people who will join Dr. Bright in forty days of prayer and fasting for revival for America, the world, and the fulfillment of the Great Commission.

☐ Please send me *free* information on staff and ministry opportunities with Campus Crusade for Christ International.

☐ Please send me *free* information about the other books, booklets, audio cassettes, and videos by Bill and Vonette Bright.

NAME (please print)

ADDRESS

CITY   STATE   ZIP

COUNTRY   E-MAIL

Please check the appropriate box(es), clip, and mail this form to:

Dr. Bill Bright
Campus Crusade for Christ
P.O. Box 620877
Orlando, FL 32862-0877 U.S.A.

You may also fax your response to (407) 826-2149, or send E-mail to newlifepubs@ccci.org. Visit our website at www.newlifepubs.com, www.discovergod.org, and www.rsm.org.

This and other fine products from *NewLife* Publications are available from your favorite bookseller or by calling **(800) 235-7255** (within U.S.) or **(407) 826-2145** (outside U.S.).